T0245942

© 2024 Andrew Waters

Maps by Tracy Dungan © Westholme Publishing

All rights reserved under International and Pan-American Copyright Conventions. No part of this book may be reproduced in any form or by any electronic or mechanical means, including information storage and retrieval systems, without permission in writing from the publisher, except by a reviewer who may quote brief passages in a review.

Westholme Publishing, LLC
904 Edgewood Road
Yardley, Pennsylvania 19067
Visit our Web site at www.westholmepublishing.com

ISBN: 978-1-59416-431-6

Also available as an eBook.

Printed in the United States of America.

For Eli, gifted historian and beloved son

CONTENTS

Illustrations

MAPS

HALFTONES

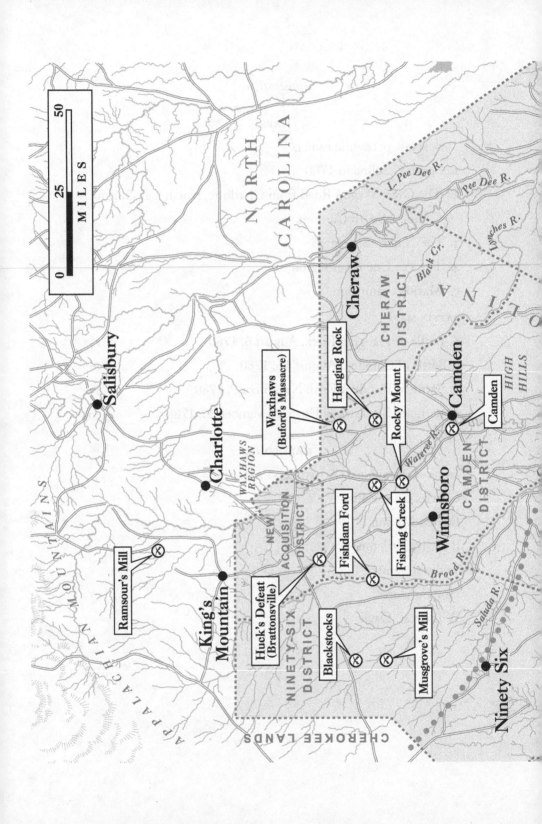

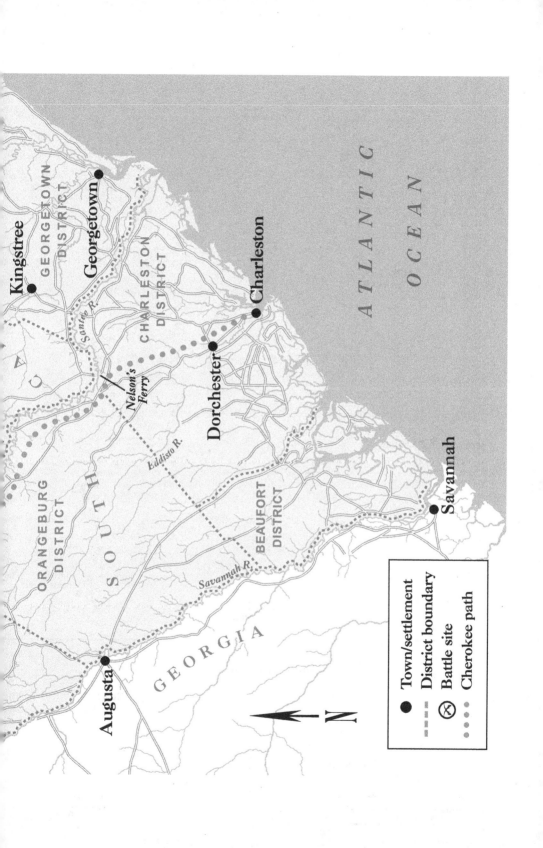

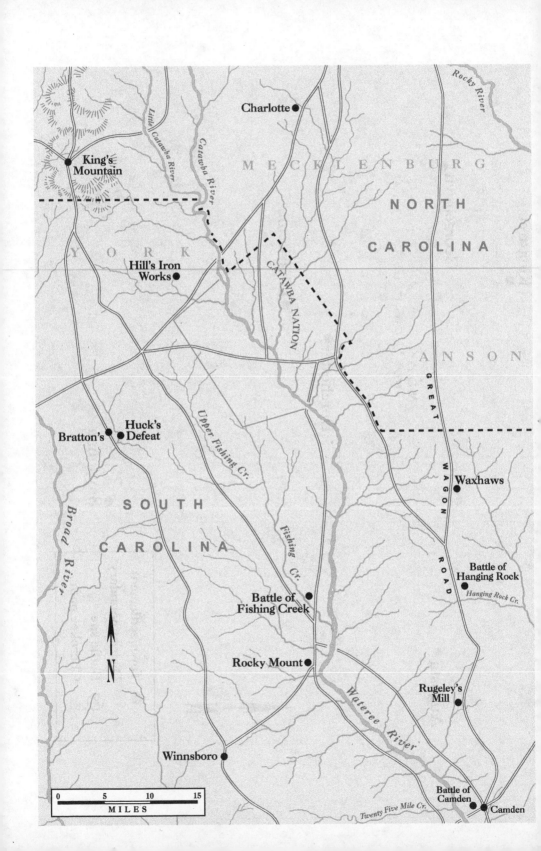

Charlotte

King's
Mountain

Little Catawba River

Catawba River

MECKLENBURG

NORTH

CAROLINA

Rocky River

YORK

Hill's Iron
Works

CATAWBA NATION

ANSON

GREAT

Bratton's

Huck's
Defeat

Upper Fishing Cr.

WAGON

Waxhaws

SOUTH

CAROLINA

Broad River

Fishing Cr.

ROAD

Battle of
Hanging Rock

Hanging Rock Cr.

Battle of
Fishing Creek

N

Rocky Mount

Rugeley's
Mill

Wateree River

Winnsboro

Battle of
Camden

Camden

Twenty Five Mile Cr.

0   5   10   15
MILES

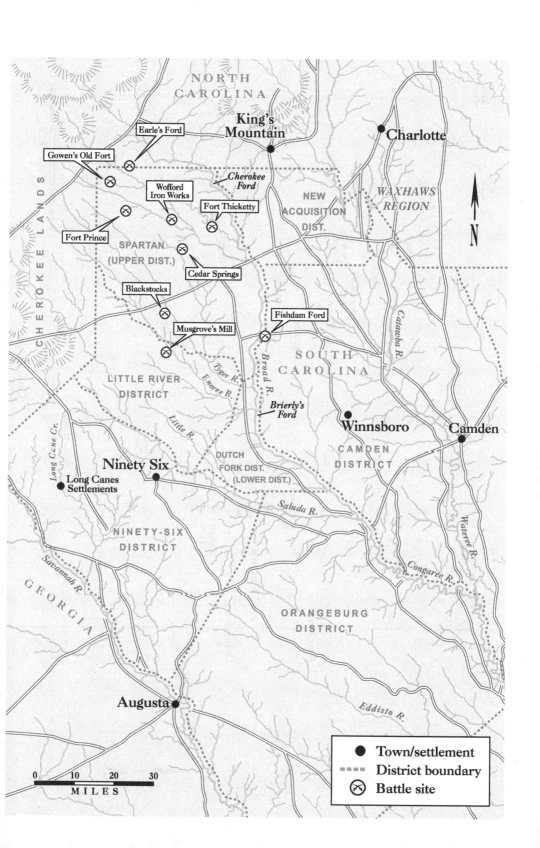

NORTH
CAROLINA

King's
Mountain

Charlotte

Earle's Ford

Gowen's Old Fort

Cherokee
Ford

NEW
ACQUISITION
DIST.

WAXHAWS
REGION

N

Wofford
Iron Works

Fort Thicketty

Fort Prince

SPARTAN
(UPPER DIST.)

Cedar Springs

Blackstocks

Fishdam Ford

Musgrove's Mill

SOUTH
CAROLINA

Tiger R.

Broad R.

Enoree R.

LITTLE RIVER
DISTRICT

Brierly's
Ford

Little R.

Winnsboro

Camden

CAMDEN
DISTRICT

Long Cane Cr.

Ninety Six

DUTCH
FORK DIST.
(LOWER DIST.)

Long Canes
Settlements

Catawba R.

Wateree R.

NINETY-SIX
DISTRICT

Saluda R.

Savannah R.

GEORGIA

ORANGEBURG
DISTRICT

Congaree R.

Augusta

Eddisto R.

CHEROKEE   LANDS

●	Town/settlement
----	District boundary
⊗	Battle site

0   10   20   30
MILES

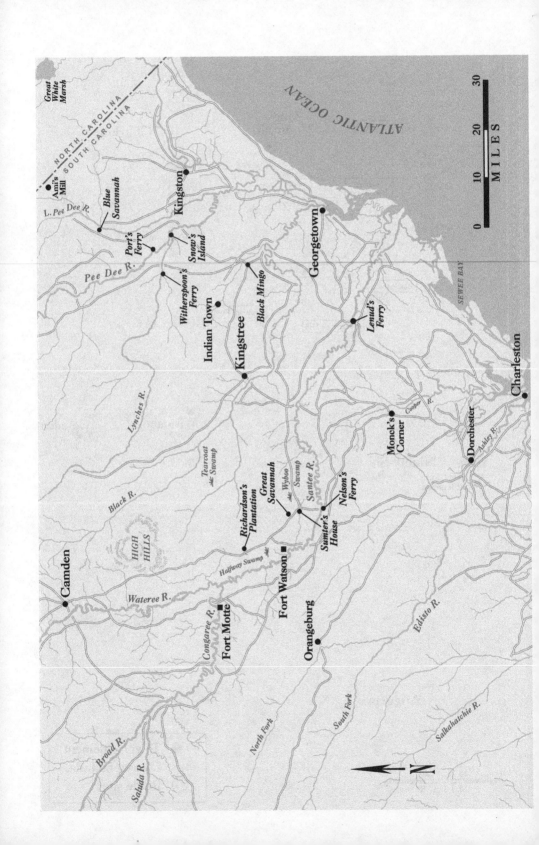

malaria, the curse of the British army in the South, leaving others to lead his legion. Americans may little remember the profane Christian Huck or the barbarous James Wemyss (pronounced "Weems"), but, I argue, their stories contribute heavily to the modern-day perception of Banastre Tarleton. Indeed, I would argue, the amalgamation of Tarleton types became the prototype for all the haughty, sneering British officers that afterward occurred in American pop culture.

The great irony is that Bloody Ban never met the Swamp Fox on the field of battle, although the two are inexorably linked in the story of South Carolina's Backcountry War. But that is not to say that one did not influence the other, and vice versa, so that is the account I present here.

In this book I give you the rise of Marion, Sumter, and Tarleton, but others also played important roles in the Backcountry War, and several times during this narrative, I leave our central players to focus on these secondary ones.

Chief among them is Charles Cornwallis, a man I believe could have won the American Revolution, or at least dictated a more successful resolution for England, had he only pushed on into North Carolina following his victory at Camden. In his own words, Cornwallis will tell you that his men were too battle-worn and weary to pursue and finish the Continentals after Camden, but with hindsight we can see the ghosts of great opportunities lost for Cornwallis and his army in Camden's wake, confirming Napoleon's maxim that the strength of an army is its mass times its rapidity.

This book might have been called, *The Rise of Francis Marion, Thomas Sumter, and Banastre Tarleton through the Perspective of Charles Cornwallis*, for I rely heavily on Cornwallis's correspondence in my research and writing. However, that title doesn't capture the inherent drama of the story. Nevertheless, Cornwallis's perspective is central here, and we can sense the prim British lord becoming more and more undone as the Swamp Fox and the Gamecock disrupt his plans repeatedly.

Other secondary characters also abound. For several chapters the great American cavalry officer William R. Davie plays a central role, as does the American general Horatio Gates, whose shattered reputation following his defeat at Camden I make some effort to resurrect. On the British side, we can see and appreciate the steady leadership of Cornwallis subordinate Francis Lord Rawdon, as capable an officer as the British had in the war, despite his young age, as well as the contribution of the aforementioned Huck and Wemyss, among others.

More significantly for me as a writer and historian, I try to explain the background for the Backcountry War, describing the years of ethnic and class tensions roiling South Carolina in the years leading up to 1780. I think this background is absolutely necessary to understand the context for the Backcountry War and our central protagonists' role in it.

I won't belabor these preliminary musings any longer, except to say that the fascinations of the nine-year-old Andrew endure, and I wrote this book for him as much as I did for you. If the following narrative lacks the romanticisms of *The Swamp Fox of the Revolution*, or attempts to discredit Marion, Sumner, or Tarleton to some degree, it is nevertheless drawn from the same fascinations that young boy found in these characters that remain with me today. It is a story of our American experience that deserves to endure, and I have written my own version. I hope you enjoy it.

NO
ORDINARY
WAR

T HE MAN WE KNOW AS Charles Cornwallis was no ordinary British
soldier. Even in an era when the British army officer corps was largely
comprised of noblemen and gentry thanks to a system that put the cost of
a commission beyond the means of ordinary citizens, Cornwallis was
among the army's aristocratic elite. Lord Cornwallis, as he would have been
addressed in proper British nomenclature, was the firstborn male heir of
the first Earl Cornwallis, also a Charles, and became the second Earl Cornwallis when his father died in 1762.

The rank came with peculiar status, if not much wealth, for the Cornwallis family was land rich but cash poor. Nevertheless, upon his father's
death, Cornwallis not only became an earl, a rank only below duke and
marquess in the British nobility system, but also a permanent member of

the House of Lords and a Peer of the Realm, a select group of noblemen that numbered just over two hundred, the cream of British society. And in addition to the many honorific titles that came to him through birth and inheritance, Cornwallis had by the time of the American Revolution added several more to his resume, including vice treasurer of Ireland and constable of the Tower of London, thanks in part to a close, personal relationship with King George III.[1]

But as a soldier, even a man as aristocratic as Charles Cornwallis had his superiors, among them King George, of course, but also Frederick, Lord North, the British prime minister, and Lord George Germain, North's secretary of state for the colonies, with primary responsibility for running the American war. And then there was Sir Henry Clinton, born to a lesser aristocratic realm than Cornwallis, though still commanding officer of all British forces in America, and thus Cornwallis's boss, at least as far as military protocol was concerned.

And no one, not even someone as privileged and aristocratic as Lord Cornwallis, enjoys giving his bosses bad news, although since taking command of British forces in the American South, following the surrender of Charleston on May 12, 1780, and Clinton's return to New York City the following month, Cornwallis had been forced to deliver more than his fair share of it. The British invasion of the South had always depended on the theory the region contained a large, silent majority of loyal British subjects requiring only the arrival of the British army to rise against their rebel oppressors and reclaim their colonies for the Crown. Now known broadly as the "Southern Strategy," this theory had by August 1780, after a miserable summer spent by Cornwallis and his British soldiers in an ineffectual effort to quell South Carolina's rebel insurrection, largely proven false. For the purposes of this book, we shall call that rebel insurrection pertaining to the South Carolina countryside in 1780 the "Backcountry War," based on a popular term of the time referring to South Carolina's interior regions.

And this was no ordinary war. Indeed, with the exception of a successful encounter by the young British cavalry commander Banastre Tarleton against remnants of the Continental army at the Waxhaws on May 29, 1780, British control of South Carolina had diminished throughout the course of the summer, and Cornwallis's letters to his superiors during this time contained mostly bad news, though like any subordinate, he did his best to frame it in affirmative light. Following a brief period of calm following the Waxhaws and the surrender of Charleston, rebel forces had quickly reorganized, stringing together a series of successful raids and skirmishes at places like Hanging Rock, Brattonsville, and just over the North Carolina border at Ramseur's Mill. Meanwhile, the Continental army, decimated at Charleston, was now reorganizing in North Carolina under the leadership of Horatio Gates, the general who had commanded the American forces' greatest victory at Saratoga in September and October 1777. "I fear the enemy will make incursions into the country and shake the confidence, and consequently the fidelity, of our friends," reads one particularly dire missive from Cornwallis to Clinton. "I see no safety for this province but in moving forward as soon as possible."[2]

The "forward" he referred to was a push into North Carolina, and if all went well, also Virginia. A key tenet of the Southern Strategy was this sweeping invasion northward, forcing George Washington's Continental forces into a decisive conflict or the Continental Congress into a negotiated peace. But first the Backcountry War would have to be won, or at least the interior region of South Carolina brought under firm control. We can imagine Cornwallis's particular delight then as he wrote Germain on August 21, 1780: "My Lord, it is with great pleasure that I communicate to your Lordship an account of a compleat victory obtained on the 16th instant by His Majesty's troops under my command over the rebel southern army commanded by General Gates."[3]

The "compleat victory" he referred to was the Battle of Camden, fought on August 18, 1780. In it, Gates's American forces were decimated in a classic British army attack, disciplined and overwhelming. Cornwallis's force of 2,239, mostly British regulars, crushed Gates's mixed army of approximately three or four thousand, the majority untrained southern militia. In Cornwallis's battle report, he claimed between eight and nine hundred Americans were killed, and about eight hundred taken prisoner, many of them wounded. His own losses he reported at 324 British killed and wounded.[4]

The numbers do tell a compelling part of the story. The American losses were significant, but it was the militia war Cornwallis was losing, and Patriot militia then seemed as inexhaustible to the British soldiers as the stars in the sky. Meanwhile, Cornwallis's losses comprised roughly 15 percent of his fighting strength, delaying any opportunity to immediately invade North Carolina following the battle. But the victory's true measure was its propaganda effect, not necessarily the body count. The despair of a Patriot countryside devastated by news of the defeat could have only been compounded when it learned Gates had disgracefully fled from the battlefield, leaving his men to die and suffer, while he sprinted 180 miles to North

Carolina's temporary capital in Hillsborough on the Continental army's fastest horse.

Even more delicious for Cornwallis was news that Tarleton had defeated and dispersed the accursed Thomas Sumter the following day at a place called Fishing Creek, on the west side of the Wateree/Catawba River.[5] Sumter had been a particular thorn in Cornwallis's side, leading the successful attack on the forward base at Hanging Rock less than two weeks before, on August 6, 1780, in a victory solidifying his status as leader of South Carolina's rebel forces, though he wasn't yet called the "Gamecock," the popular nickname by which he is widely known today. On August 15, the day before the Battle of Camden, Sumter's forces had seized all the passes on the west side of the Wateree River, along with over forty wagons of crucial British supplies, eliminating any hopes of resupply or a British retreat to the west. "I had now my option to make, either retire or attack the enemy, for the position at Camden was a bad one to be attacked in, and by General Sumter's advancing down the Wateree my supplies must have failed me in a few days," Cornwallis admitted to Germain.[6]

Attack he did, and with Gates decimated, Sumter was on the run. Eager to eliminate this scourge, Cornwallis "detached Lt. Colonel Tarleton with the Legion cavalry and infantry," with orders to attack Sumter wherever Tarleton could find him. Feeling secure at an old camp on Fishing Creek, Sumter halted his troops for a midday rest on the nineteenth, while he disrobed and climbed under a wagon to sleep. Astonishingly, Sumter posted only a light guard, though he knew Tarleton pursued him. Taking Sumter's camp unawares, "Lt. Colonel Tarleton executed this service with his usual activity and military address, totally destroying or dispersing" Sumter's whole detachment of seven hundred men, "killing 150 on the spot and taking two brass cannon and 300 prisoners and 44 waggons," Cornwallis informed Germain.[7] Sumter himself fled the melee, arriving at the American camp in Charlotte the following day without a single follower, perhaps still in his bedclothes.[8]

With the Americans in disarray, Cornwallis now had good reason to be optimistic about his North Carolina invasion plans. "It at present appears to me that I should endeavor to get as soon as possible to Hillsborough and there assemble, and try to arrange, the friends who are inclined to arm in our favour," he explained to Clinton in a letter written August 23, two days after he had written Germain.[9]

True, the letter written to Germain would have to travel across the Atlantic, but there were personal reasons for the order of Cornwallis's corre-

PART ONE

STARS COME TUMBLING DOWN

ONE

SWIFT, VIGILANT, and BOLD

T HEY HAD BEEN MARCHING for almost two months, these Virginia
Continentals under command of Col. Abraham Buford, and by now
weariness and starvation seemed their fate. Their ordeal began on March
29, 1780, when they departed from Petersburg, Virginia, headed toward
Charleston, South Carolina, to reinforce the city's defenses against imminent British attack. In early May they arrived on the outskirts of Charleston
only to find the city already surrounded by the British and impossible to
reinforce. On May 12, 1780, Charleston was surrendered, and Buford and
his Continentals were now ordered to retreat toward Hillsborough, North
Carolina, to unite with other Continental reinforcements headed south.
So, they turned around, in the direction from which they had come, in what
must have seemed a long, pointless loop of drudgery and deprivation, as
soldiers must necessarily endure.[1]

On May 29, 1780, however, as they marched the muddy wagon road north toward Hillsborough, in a region of the Carolina frontier south of modern-day Charlotte known as the Waxhaws, named after a local Native American tribe, they encountered a different form of misery—fear, appearing as the specter of green-coated dragoons, or horse soldiers, pursuing them on the road from Charleston. And on their lips, they gave this fear a name: *Tarleton*.

It was a name they knew well, for Buford's men had encountered Lt. Col. Banastre Tarleton before. On May 6, at a place called Lenud's Ferry on the Santee River, forty miles north of Charleston, they had watched from the other side of the river as Tarleton and his dragoons had charged and scattered Continental cavalry under Col. Anthony White. Some of White's men escaped by swimming the Santee River. And a few of those escaped Continental cavalry soldiers were now among Buford's troops.[2]

Some of White's cavalry probably had been at Biggin's Bridge on April 14, when Tarleton's dragoons surprised and routed Continentals and American militia under Continental general Isaac Huger. And if Buford's men did not know of Tarleton from the tales of these survivors, they'd probably heard rumors of his exploits from earlier in the war, how he had captured the great American general Charles Lee in December 1776 in New Jersey then narrowly missed capturing their fellow Virginian, cavalry commander Henry Lee, in January 1778 (though unlike Charles Lee, to whom he was not related, "Light-Horse Harry" narrowly escaped). Some may have heard rumors that following Biggin's Bridge, dragoons from Tarleton's "Legion," a Provincial, or Loyalist, unit including both mounted dragoons and regular infantry, had attempted to ravish several ladies at the home of a nearby "Whig," a term used to describe supporters of the American cause.[3]

By the afternoon of May 29, this fear would have gripped them for hours. In his account of the action, Buford reported he had been aware of Tarleton's pursuit since nine o'clock that morning. At around one o'clock that afternoon, he had received a messenger from Tarleton with terms of surrender.[4] The terms offered were not unreasonable, the same received by Continental general Benjamin Lincoln at Charleston two weeks before: unconditional surrender, but parole for the officers. In his memoir, Tarleton admitted the offer included a ruse: in it he declared he was pursuing with a force of seven hundred, not the 270 with which he actually rode, and that "Earl Cornwallis" was "likewise within a short march with nine British battalions."[5] In reality, Cornwallis was following Tarleton from Charleston with approximately two thousand men, but he was still over a hundred miles away.

Dr. Robert Brownfield was with Buford's regiment and many years later gave a written account of the actions that day to historian William Dobein James. In Brownfield's memory, Buford called a council of officers after receiving Tarleton's demand for surrender and presented them with three options: comply with the summons, abandon the baggage and flee to safety, fortify themselves and wait for Tarleton's attack.

"The first and second were decidedly rejected by the unanimous voice of the council," Brownfield recalled, "declaring it to be incompatible with their honor as soldiers." The third also was rejected, based on the grounds that Buford's soldiers could offer little effectual resistance to Tarleton's overwhelming force, especially if Cornwallis was nearby with reinforcements. So Buford rejected all of these options, and instead resumed his march north.[6] "Colonel Buford, after detaining the flag for some time, without halting his march, returned a defiance (to the demand for surrender)," Tarleton recalled in his memoir.[7] In Buford's own account, he claimed to have rejected Tarleton's surrender terms immediately, sending Tarleton's messenger away before consulting with his officers, who unanimously supported his decision to keep marching.[8]

Given Tarleton's reputation for swift and violent attack, and the carnage Buford himself had witnessed at Lenud's, the choice seems almost inconceivable, perhaps influenced by weariness and the mental fog that afflicts humans under extreme duress that can be particularly dangerous in times of war. Buford later admitted his horses and men were sapped by the long march, and the conditions of the road, made dreadful by the early summer heat, heavy rains, and the heavy wagons with which he was traveling, only increased his vulnerability to attack.

Buford did send ahead out of harm's way South Carolina governor John Rutledge, traveling to exile in North Carolina after Charleston's surrender. Otherwise, he made no disposition for battle, other than posting a small guard in his rear, and instead kept on his march until around three o'clock in the afternoon, when Tarleton and his men appeared behind him on the road, the specter come to life in green jackets, horseflesh, and sharpened steel.[9]

THE DEMON DRAGOON WHO APPEARED TO Buford and his men in the Waxhaws heat probably bore only a faint resemblance to the famous portrait of Banastre Tarleton by Joshua Reynolds hanging in London's National Portrait Gallery. Painted between January and April 1782, shortly after Tarleton's return from America, the portrait is irresistibly romantic, presenting Tarleton surrounded by war clouds, dressed in the green waist-length jacket of the British Legion. While a faceless subordinate attempts to calm a pair of seething horses, Tarleton presents his left leg forward, wrapped in tight riding breeches, as if preparing to draw his saber and enter the battle's storm. A plumed helmet is cocked above red hair and the almost feminine features of a youthful face, for when Tarleton sat for Reynolds's portrait he was still only twenty-seven years old. The historian John Buchanan reports the pose was inspired by a fourth-century BC statue of Hermes recently imported to England that had received a sensational response.[10]

Yet according to the few eyewitness accounts that have survived, Banastre Tarleton was a stocky man, though not without a physical charisma, powerfully built but with features far less delicate than the ones depicted by Reynolds. One observer who saw him in Philadelphia in 1777 described him as "rather below middle size, stout, strong, and heavily made, large muscular legs, and an uncommonly active person. His complexion dark, and his eye small, dark, and piercing." Tarleton biographer Anthony J. Scotti suggests Reynolds's portrait "emphasizes the boyish aspects of the countenance at the expense of its intensity."[11]

Tarleton was born on August 21, 1754, in Liverpool, where his family had grown rich trading slaves. His father, John, owned a large shipping interest and investments in West Indies' plantations. With his wife, Jane, John Tarleton had seven children, of which Banastre was the second-born son and therefore had little chance to inherit the bulk of the family fortune. Not much is known of Tarleton's childhood, aside from the supposition that it was one of relative privilege. Tarleton's biographer Robert D. Bass describes him as "intelligent and uncommonly strong and active. Most of his time was spent on the cricket field. He was not a good student, but he was well grounded in Latin. He was fond of acting and speaking, and so his father marked him for the law."[12]

He was entered into University College at Oxford, where law was a specialty, and where Tarleton became friends with Francis, Lord Rawdon, soon to be a colleague in the British army. Otherwise, Tarleton's Oxford days were undistinguished. According to Bass, he devoted most of his time there to the playing fields, where he was a "leading figure in riding, boxing, tennis, and cricket."

When his father died in 1773, Tarleton took his £5,000 pound inheritance to London, where he continued his legal studies at Middle College but remained an indifferent student. His Oxford tutor, William Scott, would later write, "He continued his studies for some time, but not with the assiduity which is necessary for success in such an arduous and sedentary course of life." It was the theater, and especially the gambling tables, that commanded young Banastre's "assiduities," and perhaps not surprisingly, his inheritance quickly disappeared. Of this period, Maria Elizabeth Robinson, the daughter of Tarleton's long-time paramour, the famous actress Mary Robinson, would write, "With a volatile disposition and a lively genius, he was soon drawn by gay companions into a vortex of fashionable amusements, and by the eager pursuit of them, exhausted his finances. In this situation he turned his thoughts to the military line."[13]

And so, young Banastre entered the British army on July 24, 1775. The commission, as cornet, was the lowest officer grade in a British cavalry regiment and probably purchased for him by his mother.[14] He was twenty-one years old and war was brewing in the American colonies. Eager for action, Tarleton volunteered for an expedition to America under the command of Charles, Lord Cornwallis, departing late that year. Cornwallis's command was part of a joint British expedition under overall command of British general Henry Clinton that would meet off the coast of North Carolina's Cape Fear later that spring. On June 4, 1776, this combined armada arrived at Charleston, South Carolina.

Though one of the busiest and most prosperous ports in the New World, Charleston's harbor was difficult to navigate, and on its northern shore, was now defended by a fort on Sullivan's Island, its earthen walls lined with logs of the spongy palmetto tree, or *Sabal palmetto*, native to the South Carolina coast. Commanding Charleston's defenses was Charles Lee, a former British officer who now found himself a general in the meager Continental army. Both irascible and eccentric, Lee wanted "Fort Sullivan" abandoned after observing its indifferent construction, but he was opposed by South Carolina governor John Rutledge, who had a greater faith in its utility and its chief architect, a low-country planter named William Moultrie who was now a general of South Carolina troops.

Recognizing the importance of Fort Sullivan, later renamed "Fort Moultrie" in honor of its commander and supervising architect, Clinton planned to assault it from the north, after receiving intelligence that his soldiers could ford a narrow channel to Sullivan's Island from adjacent Long Island. Meanwhile, the British navy would bombard Fort Sullivan from the south. The plan failed disastrously, however, when Clinton's amphibious force found the channel from Long Island too deep to ford, and British cannonballs bounced ineffectively off Fort Sullivan's spongy palmetto walls.

Banastre Tarleton's first action in America had been a disastrous one, though no fault of his own. Finding Charleston's defenses impenetrable, at least for the time being, the British fleet retreated in disgrace to New York, where Tarleton and the rest of the British troops under Cornwallis were disembarked on Staten Island in preparation for the assault on New York. This would prove a more successful operation, with Long and Manhattan Islands, along with most of New Jersey, captured by the British during the fall and winter of 1776. Now serving with the 16th Dragoons, Tarleton is known to have fought at the Battle of White Plains in October 1776 and in the successful captures of Fort Washington and Fort Lee on November 16 and 18.[15]

Early on the morning of December 13, Tarleton was on patrol with the 16th when they received intelligence that Charles Lee was quartered nearby. Following his successful defense at Charleston, Lee had also returned to the northern theater, where his eccentric behavior soon earned George Washington's chagrin. Perhaps best remembered for his utter devotion to his dogs, most famously his Pomeranian "Spado," Lee is "traditionally remembered as a troublemaker," writes historian John Shy.[16] Following the defeat at New York, Washington continually ordered Lee to cross the Hudson River with his brigade of 5,400 to help defend New Jersey, while Lee contemplated operations of his own on the east side of the river. Finally acquiescing, Lee left his army at Vealtown, New Jersey, on December 12 to spend the night three miles away at White's Tavern in Basking Ridge, where he was accompanied only by a small guard.

Arriving at White's Tavern the next morning, Tarleton was ordered to lead the attack on the tavern with five men. "I went on at full Speed," Tarleton reported, finding only two sentries at the tavern door. "I push'd at them making all the Noise I cou'd. The Sentrys were struck with a Panic, dropped their arms and fled." Though "fired upon in front, flank & rear," Tarleton commenced an attack on the house while the rest of the British cavalry approached. "I fir'd twice thro the Door of the House and then address'd myself to this Effect: that 'I knew Genl. Lee was in the House, and if he would surrender himself, he and his Attendants shoud be safe.'" Though some of his guards attempted to escape, and were cut down, Lee surrendered, remaining a British prisoner until he was finally exchanged in April 1778.[17] For his heroics, Tarleton received a brevet, or "provincial," promotion to captain. Perhaps more importantly, the young officer's name was now known to British army superiors and subordinates alike. "This is a most miraculous Event," Tarleton wrote to his mother, recognizing the moment's significance, "it appears like a Dream."[18]

Tarleton was still with the 16th Dragoons for the Philadelphia campaign, fighting at Brandywine on September 11, 1777, and undoubtedly on prominent display when the British army marched into Philadelphia on September 26. In Philadelphia, Tarleton and the rest of the British army soon settled into a boisterous and pleasant winter quarters. Always an enthusiastic thespian during his college days, Tarleton joined a theater company organized under Captain John André, who would later be captured as a spy and executed in Benedict Arnold's conspiracy to betray West Point. According to Tarleton's biographer Robert D. Bass, André's plays delighted overflowing audiences that winter and spring with productions of Shakespeare's *Henry IV, Part 1,* along with lesser-known fare such as *The Constant Couple* and *Duke and No Duke.*

On May 18, 1778, Tarleton appeared as a villainous knight in the "Mischianza," an elaborate farewell party organized by André for General William Howe, the British commander in America who had been recalled to England for his lack of initiative. Appearing on a black charger adorned in black and orange for a mock medieval tournament that was part of the festivities, Tarleton bore a standard whose motto was "Swift, Vigilant, and Bold," though "Lascivious" might also apply, for Bass reports that Tarleton enjoyed several Tory mistresses during his Philadelphia quarters, with one London magazine reporting he "was fairly caught in bed" with the mistress of a fellow British officer.[19]

But life in Philadelphia was not all pleasure and sexual intrigue. That January, British cavalry commander William Erskine had learned Continental captain Henry Lee was quartered in the Spread Eagle Tavern about six miles from the Continental headquarters at Valley Forge. Though only twenty-one, Henry Lee had quickly emerged as one of the Continental army's most talented cavalry officers, earning the admiration of his fellow Virginian, George Washington, though today he is perhaps best remembered as the father of Confederate general Robert E. Lee.

Tarleton was among a brigade of two hundred dragoons assembled for a surprise attack on Lee, arriving at Spread Eagle Tavern at daybreak on January 20. Lee was alerted at the last minute and successfully barricaded the tavern's doors, then began firing on the British from its windows with his small force of eight men. Tarleton was selected for a small squad assigned to drive off Lee's horses. "The dragoons charged," writes Bass. "With Tarleton at their head they bore down upon the Spread Eagle as a year before they had borne down upon White's Tavern at Basking Ridge."[20] But

Henry Lee would not surrender as readily as Charles Lee had the year before. Five of the charging British dragoons were cut down by gunfire from inside the house before the attack was called off. In the charge, Tarleton's helmet was blasted from his head and three buckshot passed through his jacket, though he emerged unscathed.

The skirmish at Spread Eagle Tavern only increased the reputation of both young cavalry officers. That April, Lee was named major-commandant of a new corps that would eventually become known as Lee's Legion and would emerge as one of the elite Continental units of the war.[21] On January 8, 1778, Tarleton had been elected captain in the newly created 79th Regiment of Foot (or infantry), raised from within the City of Liverpool. And on June 13, 1778, still basking in the notoriety of his skirmish with Lee, Tarleton received his second captaincy, this time in the 1st Regiment of Dragoon Guards, his original unit.[22] Noteworthy was that, in an age when most British officers had to purchase their promotions, at least in the lower ranks, Tarleton's were awarded for merit, which was relatively unusual for the time.

While Tarleton's career thrived, the occupation of Philadelphia faltered, and on June 18, the British army completed its evacuation, now under overall command of Henry Clinton, the same British general who had led the unsuccessful attack on Charleston two years before. Returning overland to New York, Clinton took with him fifteen thousand British soldiers as well as several thousand Philadelphia Loyalists who feared Whig, or Patriot, persecution if left behind. Memories of the British defeat at Saratoga the previous fall were still fresh, and with the announcement of the United States' new strategic alliance with France, signed March 13, British strategy had shifted, prompting the evacuation.

Instead, the British would return to their more defensible position at New York, but in close pursuit was George Washington, eager for retribution after the disastrous fall campaign at Brandywine the previous fall, his army now restored and drilled into discipline during the long winter quarters at Valley Forge. The Continental army attacked the retreating British at Monmouth Courthouse on June 28, 1778. As usual, Tarleton was in the thick of the action, leading a cavalry charge with the 16th Dragoons in the early stages of the battle, which ended in a bloody draw after an all-day fight.[23]

With France's entry into the war threatening other British colonies, Clinton was ordered to send a large portion of his American forces to protect British interests in Florida and the West Indies, making him rely more heavily on Loyalist units. In Philadelphia, Clinton had combined several of these Loyalist, or "Provincial," companies into a *legion*, an eighteenth-century term for a military unit the size of a regiment but consisting of both infantry and cavalry—or infantry, cavalry, and artillery—all under one command. Unlike a regular army cavalry or infantry unit, trained and equipped for conventional battlefield tactics, a legion was designed for scouting, reconnaissance, and irregular operations. In command of this new regiment, named the "British Legion," he placed Lord William Shaw Cathcart.

Around this same time, Clinton formed another Provincial corps made primarily of Irish immigrants under the command of Francis, Lord Rawdon, Tarleton's old Oxford University chum, who was now himself a member of the young officer corps stationed in Philadelphia. "These two corps afterwards filled fast," reports Clinton, "and being employed on active service the rest of the war, had frequent opportunities of signalizing themselves."[24]

As second-in-command for the British Legion, Cathcart selected Banastre Tarleton, still three weeks shy of his twenty-fourth birthday. "Without wealth, without title, without political friends, but on valor alone, in four years he had risen from obscurity to envied rank," writes Bass, with a bit of poetic license.[25] On August 1, 1778, Tarleton was promoted to lieutenant colonel of the British Legion. Though this was also a "provincial" rank, and by regular army commission he was still a captain, the promotion was nevertheless significant for such a young officer. And it is by this rank that he is primarily remembered today for his role in the American Revolution.[26]

Back in New York for the rest of 1778 and 1779, the British Legion was employed in scouting and patrols, while the focus of the American Revolution shifted to other theaters in Rhode Island and Georgia. Operating in conjunction that fall with the Queen's Rangers, another Provincial regiment, Tarleton engaged in several raids and attacks while posted at Kingsbridge, guarding the northern approaches to Manhattan Island from what is today the Bronx and Westchester County. That August, Tarleton led a charge against a party of Stockbridge Indians in an action described in the memoir of John Graves Simcoe, commander of the Queen's Rangers: "That active officer [Tarleton] had a narrow escape; in striking at one of the fugitives, he lost his balance and fell from his horse; luckily, the Indian had no bayonet, and his musket had been discharged." On September 16, 1778, Simcoe and Tarleton were in action again, this time against an American colonel named "Gist," who with his light corps "made frequent patroles."

Though Gist discovered the British attack shortly before it commenced, "Lt. Col. Tarleton fell in with a patrole of cavalry," and dispersed the Americans.[27]

"Thus Tarleton passed the autumn weeks in constant activity," writes Bass, "riding, patrolling, and skirmishing."[28] If these minor affairs lacked the glory of his earlier escapades against Charles and Henry Lee, Tarleton was adding to his reputation as a bold cavalry commander whose favorite tactic was the decisive, brazen charge, using the thunder of galloping horses and the flash of swords to terrify and scatter the enemy. That winter of 1778–1779, during a mostly inactive winter quarters on Long Island, Cathcart received a temporary assignment as the British army's quartermaster general, leaving Tarleton as the Legion's de facto commander.[29]

By May of 1779, Tarleton was at Kingsbridge again, preparing for a British expedition through Westchester and Dutchess Counties. By now Westchester County and the Hudson Highlands around Peekskill was a no-man's land "infested by roving bands" of both Tories and Patriots, "all pretending to redress wrongs and punish political offences; but all prone in the exercise of their high functions, to sack hen-roosts, drive off cattle, and lay farm houses under contribution," wrote Washington Irving.[30]

To maintain morale, both sides instituted a series of raids and surprise attacks that spring, with little significant effect. However, in late June, the British intercepted a letter indicating a Continental dragoon regiment under the command of Elisha Sheldon was encamped at the village of Pound Ridge, New York, near Bedford in Westchester County, and that another Continental dragoon regiment under Stephen Moylan was ordered to join him there.

Eager to catch the Continental regiments unaware, Clinton ordered Tarleton to move against Pound Ridge, in what would be his first independent command. Approaching Pound Ridge from the northern road out of Bedford with a force he reported as two hundred men, Tarleton came on the town around four o'clock in the morning on July 2. What might've been a complete surprise was ruined when Tarleton's guide overshot a turn in the road, alerting Sheldon. Assuming Tarleton was Moylan, Sheldon sent Major Tallmadge and a few troopers toward the unidentified unit, where they soon encountered Tarleton's advance guard and raced back to warn the Continental camp.

Tarleton reacted in typical fashion, ordering his men to immediately attack. Thankfully for the Continentals, Tallmadge's warning gave some of them time to mount their horses, though they were soon overwhelmed by the fury of the British charge, and Sheldon ordered a retreat, with Tarleton in close pursuit.

Some Continental light horsemen continued to flee down the road and some dispersed through the countryside, either on horseback or foot. Some stopped to fight, and others stopped to surrender. Most, reports historian John Milton Hutchins, "just rode their horses as fast as they could." Though the action was not the complete surprise of which Tarleton had hoped, his first independent command was considered a success. In reporting the action, Sheldon concluded, "The enemy pursued hard on our rear for more than two miles, in the course of which a scattering fire was kept up between their advance and our rear and a Constant charge with the sword."[31]

There was a dark side to Tarleton's victory at Pound Ridge, however, portending brutality to come. Following the battle, Tarleton's discipline lapsed, and his soldiers were allowed to loot the surrounding houses and abuse noncombatants, including at least two women who tried to stop British soldiers from robbing their homes. As the looting continued, the local militia formed, peppering the British with gunfire. In response, Tarleton ordered the burning of several homes and the local Presbyterian meeting house before leaving the village.

Tarleton reported twenty-seven American casualties in the action, which Hutchins estimates as a gross misrepresentation, with actual American casualties probably only eight to twelve. Eager for good news, Clinton ignored Tarleton's exaggerations and any concerns about British looting, forwarding Tarleton's report on the action to London, where it was published in the *London Gazette*. Hutchins argues the action reinforced some of the troubling traits the British Legion would exhibit more prominently in the southern campaigns:

Tactically speaking, Tarleton learned that it often was no disadvantage to fly to the attack even when the enemy was alerted. This was a risky lesson. . . . In addition, Tarleton learned it was no detriment, at least as far as his superiors and the British press were concerned, to destroy churches and burn houses down over the heads of women and children.[32]

For Tarleton, repercussions for actions such as these were far away. In the present, he remained a rising star of the British army, even as their American occupation faltered. As summer turned to fall, the British army continued their endless campaigning around New York City, achieving no great advantage. In October, John Graves Simcoe was wounded and taken prisoner in a skirmish in Brunswick, New Jersey. With Simcoe captured, the dragoons of his Queen's Rangers were added to Tarleton's command. In recognition of Tarleton's enhanced status, Clinton named him "commandant" of the British Legion, an honorary title that nevertheless enhanced Tarleton's prestige at an opportune time. For British strategy was shifting yet again, and by December 1779, Banastre Tarleton and his British Legion were preparing for a journey south.

TWO

A SHY
BITCH'S
REVENGE

A FTER A STORMY SIX WEEKS AT SEA, General Charles Cornwallis
and a British invasion force under the overall command of Henry
Clinton arrived off Tybee, Georgia, in the first week of February 1780.[1]
Cornwallis had been this way before. In his first expedition to the American
colonies in 1776, while accompanied by the freshly commissioned Banastre
Tarleton, Cornwallis's command of 2,500 troops had joined at sea off Cape
Fear, North Carolina, with a similarly numbered force under Clinton in
the campaign that led to the ill-fated attack on Charleston, South Carolina,
later that June at the Battle of Sullivan's Island.

Now four years later, Cornwallis found himself in similar circumstances,
again under the command of Henry Clinton, again sailing toward an attack
on the vital port of Charleston. Cornwallis was still in his prime, forty-one

years old, with an aristocratic air suitable to his status as a British lord and
peer of the realm. This noble bearing was accentuated by a quizzical countenance resulting from a childhood eye injury on the hockey fields of Eton.
True, he projected the cool confidence of the *homme de guerre*, the Enlightenment ideal of the "man of war," yet underneath the martial sheen was a
compassion that endeared him to his troops even as it sometimes exposed
to opponents his weaknesses. And this compassion was now coupled with
the enduring melancholy of grief, for he was still mourning the death of
his beloved wife, Jemima, the previous year.

Despite Cornwallis's status as Clinton's second-in-command, he had
every reason to believe that whatever fate awaited Clinton at Charleston
would soon enough belong to him. In a pique over lack of reinforcements,
Clinton had submitted his resignation the previous fall by overseas post to
Lord North, England's prime minister, and George Germain, the colonial
minister responsible for conducting the American war. Once ashore, where
correspondence from London could again find them, both Cornwallis and
Clinton fully expected to receive word that Clinton's resignation had been
accepted and Cornwallis named his successor.

In truth, the two men were eager to be rid of one another, for their relationship had deteriorated during the course of the war. Their feud can be
dated to the Battle of White Plains in 1776, when during a moment of
frustration, Clinton made a disparaging remark about British commander-
in-chief William Howe in the presence of Cornwallis, who subsequently
repeated it to Howe. A petty betrayal, it was all Clinton required to harbor
one of his many long-standing grudges. In 1779, Clinton believed Cornwallis betrayed him again, when Cornwallis returned from his extended
leave of absence in England without promise of the reinforcements Clinton
had sent him there to obtain. Instead, Cornwallis had spent the leave tending to Jemima, then mourning her death, leaving little evidence he seriously
attempted to execute Clinton's orders.

Since then, their relationship had only grown more acrimonious, with
factions forming openly around both men in and around the British army's
New York City headquarters during the fall of 1779. And the long, stormy
ocean voyage south had only intensified their feud. So, this vast, mysterious
American South seem to promise Cornwallis a promotion, if nothing else,
his first independent command, and the chance to be rid of a rival. With
him for this mission he had gathered some of his most loyal and talented
subordinates, including the young officers Cornwallis tended to favor like
Francis, Lord Rawdon, and the spirited cavalry officer Banastre Tarleton.

The task in front of him no doubt would be a challenging one. Like Clinton, Cornwallis believed the British war effort in America was undermanned and underresourced, and he doubted reports of Loyalist support in the southern colonies. Yet he trusted in his men and the might and organization of the British army, and in some sense, no doubt, believed in his own ability to fight his way through the challenges to come.

EVEN IF ENGLAND BOASTED THE MOST POWERFUL and administratively complex army in the world in 1775, it still faced a manpower problem. That year, the British army included approximately forty-five thousand to thirty-eight thousand infantry and seven thousand cavalry. But these troops were spread out over a global empire, with England herself requiring a home guard of fifteen thousand and troublesome Ireland requiring an occupation force of another twelve thousand. In America that year, as trouble erupted around Boston, were slightly less than nine thousand British troops, none of them cavalry, and with rebellion brewing, Lord North and King George quickly realized they needed more soldiers in the American colonies.

By the following year's attack on New York, the British army numbered thirty-two thousand in its camp on Staten Island, the greatest expeditionary force Great Britain up to that point had ever sent from its shores, though the number included eight thousand mercenaries from the German provinces of Hessen-Kassel, Hessen-Hanau, and Brunswick (collectively, the "Hessians").[2] Over the course of the American conflict, the British would hire over thirty-six thousand Hessians, who helped solve the manpower problem but created other ones—from the start, the Hessians proved difficult to control, and their cost was adding to England's already escalating war-time debt.[3]

With expenses and logistical issues mounting, England was eager to believe reports that a vast population of Loyalist supporters in the American colonies only awaited British military support to rise against their Whig oppressors. Fueling this rumor, in particular, were three royal governors in the South: Josiah Martin in North Carolina; John Murray, Earl of Dunmore, in Virginia; and Lord William Campbell in South Carolina. In the summer of 1775, Martin sent a plan for subjugating the southern colonies to Lord Dartmouth, Germain's predecessor as the colonial secretary of state. Martin claimed he could "reduce to order and obedience every colony southward of Pennsylvania," if only Dartmouth would send to North Carolina some artillery, ten thousand muskets, ammunition, and a generous "supply of money."

Similarly, Dunmore wrote with his own assurances that with the assistance of only a few hundred British regulars, he could "reduce, without the smallest doubt the whole of this southern Continent to a perfect state of obedience." And from South Carolina, Campbell bragged, "three regiments, a proper detachment of artillery, with a couple good frigates . . . would do the whole business here."[4]

But these arguments were always based on suspect assumptions. One was that the Whig militias of the American South could be easily subdued by England's professional army. Another was that the southern majority was still loyal to the Crown but misrepresented by a vocal minority of Whig bullies. "Of all foundations whereon to build the conduct of a campaign this is the loosest, the most treacherous, the fullest of peril and delusion," complains British historian John Fortescue.[5]

Nevertheless, Dartmouth was eventually swayed by the "sanguine" reports of his southern governors, among others, though he never made much effort to confirm their assertions. Eventually, he authorized an expedition to North Carolina, along with a war chest of several thousand pounds sterling to finance the recruitment of Loyalist troops, before passing the whole scheme off to Germain, who shortly thereafter took his place. This was the plan for separate commands under Clinton and Cornwallis to join at sea before assisting the southern governors with their plots in the spring of 1776.

Eventually, this combined expedition would find defeat and disaster at Charleston in June 1776. However, while he awaited Cornwallis to join him on the high seas, Clinton first called on Dunmore in Virginia, only to find "the Governor of Virginia . . . had no government but ship."[6] Persecuted and pursued by Virginia's Patriot legislators, led by Patrick Henry, and Patriot militia under the legislature's command, Dunmore had been forced to flee Virginia's capital in Williamsburg to exile aboard a British warship in the York River.

Realizing Dunmore's promises for Virginia were rubbish, Clinton traveled next to North Carolina's Cape Fear region, where Martin had assured him a force of six thousand Loyalist was eagerly awaiting his arrival. Many of those promised were immigrant Highland Scots, who had established an enclave around the Cape Fiver River settlement at Cross Creek, just outside of modern-day Fayetteville. These were highlanders who had remained loyal to the British government during "The Forty-five," the Scots uprising led by Charles Edward Stuart, part of a failed effort to regain the British throne for his Catholic father, James Francis Edward Stuart. As reward for their loyalty, these highlanders had received land bounties along the Cape Fear, where they lived in isolation and maintained their loyalty to the English Crown.[7]

But the great army of Highland Scots that Martin had promised was nowhere to be found. Instead, after his arrival at Cape Fear, Clinton discovered a force of not more than 1,400 Loyalists had already been defeated by 1,900 Whig militia at the Battle of Moore's Creek on February 27, 1776. Since then, Martin also had fled North Carolina to exile aboard a British naval ship. And now arriving off Cape Fear in a British frigate of his own was Campbell, forced to admit that the Loyalist support in South Carolina was far from the strength he had earlier promised the British ministry, as his current circumstance demonstrated.[8]

What to do next? Eager to find some success for this calamitous expedition, Clinton chose to cautiously accept reports he could subdue Charleston's insufficient coastal defenses with relative ease. After he was finally joined by Cornwallis's reinforcements in May, he set sail for South Carolina, arriving off Charleston Harbor on June 1.[9] Here, too, he was misinformed, and his attack on June 28, 1776, was an abject failure. "'Tis clear to me that there does not exist in any one [province] in America a number of friends of government sufficient to defend themselves when the troops are withdrawn," Clinton complained that spring. "The idea is chimerical, false, and if the measure is adopted . . . all the friends of the government will be sacrificed *en détail*."[10] Defeated and humiliated, Clinton rushed from his defeat at Charleston back to New York City, where he had been ordered to return in time for a fall campaign.

Here, then, were sown the seeds of Clinton's skepticism about America's Loyalist support, a doubt that lingered. Yet despite his reservations, and those of other British field officers as the war progressed, Germain and North never abandoned this idea for a "southern strategy." The British ministry realized that assurances of a second front, reliable or not, were necessary to overcome the British public's increasing concerns about the American war.

And so, the idea of a southern strategy resurfaced after France joined the American side in 1778. England now found itself engaged in a global war extending far beyond America to its other colonies, especially its lucrative West Indies plantations, not to mention the very real prospect of an invasion on its home shores. Since the Treaty of Paris in 1763, ending the Seven Years' War, France's navy had improved substantially, and when combined with the very real threat of Spain joining the French side (which it did in 1779), England was now faced with an existential threat on the high seas. "After 1777 Britain rarely had complete mastery of the western Atlantic, and even in European waters she faced frequent threats from the French and Spanish fleets," writes historian John Pancake.[11]

From Boston to New York to Philadelphia and Providence, Rhode Island, even including the ill-fated southern expedition of 1776, England's war strategy had relied heavily on its naval superiority along America's Atlantic coast, not only to move troops and bombard American cities, but also to supply and provision its troops. Now with France joining the American side, no longer could England enjoy unfettered control of these waters, and moving forward, all strategic planning required obsessive speculation over the positions and possible destinations of the French fleet.

This shift in naval strategy was accompanied by the shift in army command from Sir William Howe to Henry Clinton. Serving as the American commander in chief since April 1776, replacing the ineffectual Thomas Gage, Howe scored impressive victories in New York later that fall. But he was soon frustrating London with his lethargic campaigns. With adequate resources and political backing to finish off the American insurrection, at least in those early years, when Washington's Continental army was little more than a collection of amateurs, Howe had followed victory at New York with embarrassing defeats at Trenton and Princeton later that winter.

If grumbles about 1776's missed opportunities were not enough to sink Howe's command, his mismanagement of the 1777 campaign was. Determined to capture Philadelphia, he changed plans constantly, baffling Germain and North, then chose to approach the city by an arduous six-week naval voyage up the Chesapeake Bay that eliminated any opportunity of supporting British general John Burgoyne's invasion of the Hudson River valley to the north, as Burgoyne had expected him to do. And though Howe was not directly responsible for Burgoyne's defeat by Horatio Gates at Saratoga that September and October, his delays and mismanagement contributed to it.

He did capture Philadelphia with little difficulty, winning an important victory at Brandywine, but it achieved little strategically. Washington and the Continental army escaped to fight another day, emerging as a more professional army after the preceding winter at Valley Forge. And if Howe's officers and soldiers appreciated his aloof, genial style, North and Germain did not. Sensing the political winds shifting against him, Howe offered his resignation on October 22, 1777, complaining that his recommendations for large-scale operations in America were consistently ignored, and infeasibly insisting he needed at least ten thousand more troops to win the war.

Some write that he resigned fearing the repercussions of Saratoga. Not true, though those repercussions certainly influenced his status in London, and so on February 4, 1778, North accepted Howe's resignation.[12]

Command now fell to Clinton, Howe's most experienced subordinate. In many ways, he was also the most gifted. After his disasters in the south, Clinton had distinguished himself in the Battle of Long Island on August 27, 1776, emerging as England's best military strategist in America during the early years of the war. But Clinton was peevish and difficult to get along with, always seeing betrayal or deception in others. In a comparison between Clinton and Howe, Clinton's biographer William B. Willcox describes Howe as "easygoing and friendly," Clinton as shy. "One took the world as he found it and was usually undemanding of himself or those about him; the other was quick to assume that any colleague was incompetent. Neither man was deceitful or malevolent; but Howe never expected the others to be, and Clinton constantly did."[13]

Indeed, Clinton even once referred to himself as a "shy bitch,"[14] and he was driven by the urge to quarrel. "In all his squabbles he held true to form. He would not meet conciliatory advances, let alone make them," notes Willcox. "Forces were at work in him of which he was utterly unconscious, and they affected every aspect of his life, from military plans to friendships. The evidence is overwhelming that he was in neurotic conflict, and that it varied greatly in intensity." Of such conflict's sources, Willcox suggests some family dynamic. His father, George Clinton, was a British admiral who served as royal governor in Newfoundland and New York, where Clinton spent his youth before joining the British army in 1751. "Clinton as an adult had a particularly intense craving for authority of his own, because at some deep level he was still trying to free himself from that of his parents," writes Willcox.[15] Perhaps this colonial upbringing also made him feel the perennial stranger among the rigid hierarchies and class pretensions of the British army.

Whatever its reasons, Clinton's personality disorders crippled his popularity within the British army, both its enlisted and its officers, though given his status, he naturally had his share of sycophants. And despite his gifts as a strategist, these psychological conflicts seemed always to hinder their execution. "Clinton had a sound and at times brilliant military mind, but he often failed in execution," notes Pancake. "It may well be that he was fearful that failure would ruin his reputation . . . as though his craving for heroic enterprise was overcome by a subconscious guilt that he was not deserving of such authority."[16]

Given these shortcomings, Clinton was always a misfit as commander in chief. But for Germain and North, he represented the "least worst" option, especially after Lord Jeffrey Amherst, successful conductor of Canadian operations during the French and Indian War, turned down the command. Cornwallis was perhaps the preferred candidate, for he was close to King George and a confidant of Germain, but at that time he was on yet another leave in England and unavailable for the post.

The timing of Clinton's appointment only fueled his paranoias, for accompanying it in the spring of 1778 were orders that he dispatch eight thousand men from his American force to Florida and the Caribbean—five thousand to St. Lucia and three thousand to Florida—with smaller detachments ordered to reinforce British colonies in Nova Scotia and Newfoundland. At the time of the American Revolution, West Indies staples such as sugar and rum accounted for £4,500,000 in England's annual imports, more than twice the value of imports from the mainland colonies. These assets had to be protected from the threat of French attack, so Clinton was ordered to evacuate Philadelphia, consolidate his forces once more around New York City, and dispatch a large proportion of his troops to England's other colonial outposts once finished with the fall campaign.[17]

Clinton was probably correct in presuming this new troop disposition doomed his command to failure even before it started. And these suspicions were only confirmed when the British ministry sent a peace delegation to America under the leadership of Frederick Howard, the Earl of Carlisle, later that spring. This "Carlisle Commission" was authorized to make any concession necessary to the Continental Congress to end the conflict, save one: it could not offer the American's their independence. Thus, it also was doomed, for sensing a strategic shift with their victory at Saratoga, and with a powerful new ally in France on its side, America would settle for nothing less.

That Clinton dutifully abandoned Philadelphia just as the Carlisle Commission arrived there only emphasized its absurd position. "We all look grave, and perhaps we think we look wise," observed Lord Carlisle. "I fear nobody will think so when we return. . . . I don't see what we have to do here."[18] Further undermining their position was the Continental army's furious rearguard attack on the retreating British at Monmouth Courthouse on June 28. Though Clinton performed well in the battle, the only one he ever led as commander in chief, its actions revealed a striking change in the American army. Out of the grim winter at Valley Forge, and thanks to the freshly instilled discipline of a new drill master, the Prussian officer Baron

Friedrich von Steuben, the Continentals fought at Monmouth with a stern resolve and grim determination never faced by Howe, yet another bad omen for Clinton's new command.

Things in London were turning bleak. As debt mounted so did political opposition to the American conflict. The navy was challenged on the seas, threatening the West Indies, if not England herself, and Ireland, as usual, was in turmoil. But King George refused to capitulate on the issue of American independence, leaving North and Germain in a "lose-lose" situation that threatened their political careers. Meanwhile, refugee Loyalists in London and the Americas resurrected the old myths that a silent majority of America's Loyalists would rise against their Patriot oppressors if only supported by the British army.

One of these storytellers was Joseph Galloway, a former member of the Continental Congress, who had served as the principal Loyalist civil administrator in Philadelphia until its evacuation by the British in 1778. Now exiled in London, Galloway published several pamphlets detailing the untapped potential of American Loyalists. Upon their return to London, members of the Carlisle Commission also spoke favorably of dormant but vast Loyalist support based only on a few anecdotal discussions during their American expedition. Meanwhile, the three southern governors—Campbell, Martin, and Dunmore—continued to insist Loyalist support in the American South was particularly strong, though all three were now exiled in London. "The fact that all three of these royal officials had been run forcibly out of their gubernatorial mandates by vastly superior Whig armies seemed to be of no consequence to their thinking," writes historian David K. Wilson.[19]

Never mind the experience of Clinton in 1776, when similar promises of Loyalist support in the South proved false, nor lackluster Loyalist support in the North throughout the course of the war. "Germain was not yet cured of reliance on the loyal section of the American population, and the King was tempted by the thought of retaining the southern provinces," observes Fortescue.[20] And so, the "Southern Strategy" reemerged: the north could be left alone to wither on the vine in isolation, while a southern invasion would give England control of America's most valuable exports—tobacco, rice, indigo, and lumber, among others—bolstering British control of Florida and the West Indies. And once the South was subdued, England could sweep north toward the Chesapeake, either driving Washington and his Continentals into a decisive conflict there or forcing them into some negotiated peace.[21]

Ever the clear-eyed strategist, Clinton doubted such absurdities. Early in the 1778 campaign, he first requested his recall to England, eager to avoid blame for the British ministry's wishful thinking.[22] But that request had been denied, and while Clinton settled sullenly into his New York headquarters, he received a pleasant surprise. In command of the three thousand troops he had been forced to send to Florida, Clinton had placed Lt. Col. Archibald Campbell, the enterprising commander of the 2nd Battalion of the 71st Regiment of Foot, a Scots highlander unit also known as Fraser's Highlanders. And at Germain's suggestion, Clinton's orders to Campbell directed him to attempt an attack on the Georgia capital and port at Savannah on his way to St. Augustine.

With modest expectations for this expedition, Clinton was elated when Campbell captured Savannah with relative ease on December 29, 1778, suffering only three killed and ten wounded, compared to about eighty-three American casualties and 453 taken prisoner.[23] Although a subsequent attempt by Campbell to capture Augusta, Georgia, failed, the British now had a firm foothold in the American South.

"This acquisition [of Savannah] was a great detriment to the enemy and of the utmost importance to us, as it deprived the rebels of one of their principal sources of remittance to Europe and formed an excellent barrier to East Florida, while it furnished at the same time a near situation of the King's troops to assemble at in any future enterprise against the Carolinas," Clinton recalled. "It also supplied a safe opportunity of making the so much desired experiment to prove how far the restoration of the civil government might operate in calling back the disaffected colonists to the affections and sovereignty of their parent state."[24]

During the spring of 1779, Germain continued to press Clinton for a full-scale southern invasion, and after an ineffectual campaign against Washington around the Hudson River that summer, Clinton's doubts about a southern strategy now began to waver, though in typically temperamental fashion. "Indeed, having in a manner pledged myself to administration for making the attempt, I could not now go from it without justly exposing myself to censure."[25] He now began to plot a second attempt on Charleston, which would be preliminary to a full-scale invasion of the Carolinas, Georgia, and if things went well, the Chesapeake.

Never mind that Savannah's capture had done little to reveal the promised wellspring of Loyalist fervor. Because, once initiated, Clinton never intended to complete the strategy he now embraced. For the failures of 1779 only increased his psychological isolation. That July, Cornwallis returned from his extended leave of absence in England without promise of the reinforcements Clinton had sent him there to obtain. Clinton believed himself forsaken by the British ministry beyond the point his honor could endure. If the cabinet and King George would not give him the troops he needed, how could they expect him to win the war? Following Cornwallis's return, Clinton again offered his resignation both to King George and to Germain.

Clinton seemed to sense the criticisms of his officers and soldiers as much as he heard them. Confiding freely in British officer Charles Stuart, who left an account of the conversation in a letter, Clinton "stated how particularly cruel it was to be served so ill by subordinate Officers.... He told me with tears in his eyes that he was quite an altered man—that business oppressed him, that he felt quite incapable of his station." Believing that he was hated, "nay, detested in this Army," he told Stuart, he was eager to resign.[26] And such complaints were not pure delusions. From an account of May 1779, Hessian officer Johann Ewald recalled visiting the post of Simcoe's Rangers on Long Island and "found that all the officers of this corps were speaking very badly about General Clinton."[27]

This time, both Clinton and Cornwallis fully expected Clinton's resignation to be accepted, and Cornwallis to be named Clinton's successor. But correspondence traveled slowly in the late eighteenth century, and while they waited for Germain's response, there was an invasion of South Carolina to conduct, and so it had made sense for Cornwallis to accompany Clinton when the southern expedition set sail from Sandy Hook, New Jersey, on December 26, 1779.[28] Both men assumed that, once ashore, they would soon enough receive word that Clinton's resignation had been accepted, and Cornwallis would be promoted to overall command of British army forces in the American war. Clinton, the logic went, could leave Cornwallis in charge in South Carolina, and he could return to London finally free from the burdens of command.

ARRIVING OFF TYBEE WITH AN INVASION FORCE of 8,708 men,[29] this second attempt to capture Charleston would be by land, not another risky attack by sea. The British arrival, however, was anticipated, and inside the city were over 5,000 American defenders, approximately 2,500 militia, and 2,650 Continental soldiers, under the command of Continental general Benjamin Lincoln.[30]

After an amphibious landing far south of Fort Moultrie (the renamed Fort Sullivan) and Charleston's other coastal defenses on February 11 and

12, Clinton himself supervised construction of siege lines outside the city. Meanwhile, Cornwallis commanded operations in the surrounding countryside, his primary assignment to stop reinforcement and supplies from entering the city.

With Cornwallis was the still only twenty-five-year-old Banastre Tarleton, who after his spectacular rise through the British ranks, would be charged with command of British mounted forces in the southern expedition. Throughout the entire course of the American Revolution, the British army only ever employed two regular cavalry regiments in the conflict, the 16th and 17th Light Dragoons. Instead, it relied heavily on Provincial regiments like Tarleton's Legion for its mounted troops.[31] And during the siege of Charleston, mounted units were imperative for securing the swamps and vast plantations on the city's outskirts, where Cornwallis leaned heavily on Tarleton and his Legion dragoons.

On April 14, 1780, Tarleton was in command of a detachment of dragoons and mounted infantry sent to capture Biggins Bridge (or Biggins Creek Bridge in some accounts), an important gateway through the Charleston neck connecting the peninsular city to the rest of mainland South Carolina. Biggins Bridge was located just outside the crossroads settlement of Monck's Corner, thirty-two miles north of Charleston. Defending the bridge was Continental general Isaac Huger (pronounced *You-gee*), along with Continental cavalry under Lt. Col. William Washington, a distant cousin of George Washington. Employing his favorite tactic, Tarleton ordered a blitzkrieg-style charge on Huger's position, executed "with the greatest promptitude and success."[32] The Americans were routed. Fifteen Americans were killed, eighteen wounded, and sixty-three captured, including the wounded. The remainder, along with Huger and Washington, "fled on foot to the swamps . . . where being concealed by the darkness, they effected their escape," but leaving behind four hundred horses and fifty wagons loaded with "arms, clothing, and ammunition."[33]

But in the aftermath of the victory, Tarleton's discipline again faltered. As his dragoons spread out to reconnoiter the countryside, some attempted to ravish several women at the house of Sir John Collington, a notable Whig living in the vicinity. Loyalist surgeon Uzal Johnson later attended the women:

They (the women) had been shockingly abused by a Plundering Villain, Lady Colliton badly cut in the Hand by a Broad Sword, and bruised very much, after I dressed her wounds, I went with an officer and twelve men, to the Plantation a mile from Camp to Protect Miss Fasseaux who this Villain had likewise abused in a similar manner, here I found a most accomplished amiable Lady in the greatest distress imaginable.[34]

The offending Legion soldiers were arrested, and later tried and whipped, but the incident cast further suspicion on Tarleton's disciplinary rigor, at least among some of his fellow British officers.[35]

On May 6, Tarleton was patrolling the outskirts of Charleston when he received news that Continental cavalry under Lt. Col. Anthony White were nearby. White's cavalry was part of the Virginia Continental troops sent south by George Washington to reinforce Charleston that included Buford's 350 infantry. Now finding Charleston surrounded and impossible to reinforce, White was harassing British patrols, joined by the remnants of William Washington's cavalry regiment after its disgrace at Biggin's Bridge. Earlier that day, White had captured eighteen of Tarleton's light infantry soldiers at the plantation of Colonel Elias Ball then moved toward Lenud's Ferry on the Santee, where he planned to cross with his prisoners and rejoin Buford's infantry, awaiting him on the other side.

Eager to regain his men, the hard-charging Tarleton sprang into action, pushing his dragoons in pursuit, overcoming White's patrol around three o'clock, just as they were reaching Lenud's. Without hesitation, Tarleton ordered an attack, catching the Americans off guard. "The [Continental] corps being completely surprised, resistance and slaughter soon ceased," Tarleton recounted. "Five officers and thirty-six men were killed and wounded; seven officers and sixty dragoons were taken prisoners; and the whole party of the light infantry were rescued, as the boat was pushing off to convey them to the opposite shore."[36] Once again, William Washington was forced to swim for his escape, this time accompanied by White. Both made it across, but some of the Americans who followed them into the river drowned. Once again, Tarleton observed that swift and decisive attack could dumbfound the poorly disciplined Americans.

The final elements of the Continental Cavalry now decimated, White and Washington retreated into eastern North Carolina to refit and recruit, leaving a few mounted troops with Buford to guard the infantry's retreat to Hillsborough. Tarleton reported the loss of two men and four horses in the action.[37]

Meanwhile, Clinton finished his siege works, completing his stranglehold on Charleston. On May 6, British and Hessian sappers drained the canal protecting the American defenses on the Charleston Neck, and Clinton demanded Lincoln's unconditional surrender. When negotiations faltered, Clinton ordered a devastating two-day cannonade on the city beginning May 9. "It appeared as if the stars were tumbling down," recalled Continental general William Moultrie of that night. "The fire was incessant almost the whole night, cannonballs whizzing, and shells hissing, continually among us, ammunition chests and temporary magazines blowing up, and wounded men groaning along the lines. It was a dreadful night."[38]

By May 12, the city had endured enough, and Lincoln formally surrendered. Captured inside Charleston were 5,618 men, including 2,571 Continental soldiers, almost the entirety of its "Southern Department," the rest were militia and armed citizens. "This was the largest bag of American prisoners during the Revolution," notes historian Mark M. Boatner, "and was not exceeded in American military history until the surrender of 10,700 Union troops to Stonewall Jackson at Harpers Ferry in 1862."[39] In the days and weeks that followed, British and Provincial troops spread out through South Carolina, establishing a series of garrisons and outposts to control the countryside.

WITH THE DEFEAT OF CHARLESTON AND THE occupation of South Carolina, England now controlled a vast swath of the American South. Florida and all of the North American territory east of the Mississippi had been ceded to England in 1763 as part of the Treaty of Paris between England, France, and Spain that ended the Seven Years War, also popularly known as the French and Indian War. And thanks to the capture of Savannah in 1778, and establishment of the British outpost in Augusta, Georgia also was now under British control, despite pockets of Patriot resistance.

All that was left now was to organize the residents of South Carolina into Loyalist militia, to guard the state while the British army completed their sweep north, into North Carolina and Virginia, a daring bid to force George Washington into a final conflict somewhere in the vicinity of the Chesapeake Bay. But Clinton had no intentions of executing this strategy himself, though he would not be returning to England, as he had hoped and planned. On March 19, Clinton had finally received Germain's long-awaited reply to his submitted resignation. In a letter dated November 4, Germain wrote, "Though the King has great confidence in His Lordship's abilities, His Majesty is too well satisfied with your conduct to wish to see the command of his forces in any other hands."[40] In the subtext of this letter were the machinations of England's politics. Neither Germain nor British prime minister Frederick North were necessarily Clinton fans, for his discontented nature grated even on them, an ocean away, but they considered the timing of the request inopportune. "What would happen to the country in these critical times if a commander resigned because his force was inadequate for what he hoped to do?" ponders Clinton's biographer, William B. Willcox, as explanation for the resignation's refusal.[41]

The news strained Clinton and Cornwallis's relationship to the breaking point. From this point forward, Cornwallis refused to be consulted on any of Clinton's plans for the Charleston siege, content to manage his own operations in the surrounding countryside. For the rest of the campaign, observes Willcox, Clinton "had no second in command. He did not seek the Earl's [Cornwallis's] advice, even formally, and did his best to prevent anyone else from seeking it."[42]

Cornwallis's insubordination casts him disparagingly here, portending disastrous insubordination to come. The eighteenth-century *homme de guerre* was bound by honor to his troops and his king, but in the factional and class-conscious ranks of the British army officer corps, honor was a complex thing. "The eighteenth century witnessed considerable tension between the formal rules of military discipline, recently enhanced by the increased state power, and this culture of honor," observes historian Armstrong Starkey. "The latter led to individual acts of disobedience that would be inconceivable to the modern military professional but were perfectly compatible with the chivalric traditions of earlier ages."[43] True, Clinton was Cornwallis's superior officer in military terms, but as a Lord and peer of the realm who enjoyed a close relationship with King George, one might even call it a friendship, Earl Cornwallis was not necessarily bound by the normal rules of military disciplines, nor could Clinton dispose of him like any common subordinate.

But the shy bitch would have his revenge. His reprisal against Charleston now complete, Clinton made plans to return to British army headquarters in New York City, where he still hoped to launch a summer campaign against Washington in the Hudson Highlands,[44] and where his critics always accused him of finding too much comfort, prominently in the form of his married mistress, Mary Baddeley.[45]

In charge of the South Carolina expedition Clinton would place his talented subordinate and troublesome rival, Charles Cornwallis. As difficult and petulant as Clinton could be, he was no fool, and this move solved two problems at once. First, he would give Cornwallis command of his own theater, acknowledging Cornwallis's status while creating geographic and psychological distance between them. More importantly, he could distance himself from the execution of North and Germain's "Southern Strategy," hanging its efficacy on the reputation of the man who betrayed him at Charleston.

For Cornwallis, the results were bittersweet. No, he would not earn overall command of the American theater, not yet or not ever, but he would finally be shed of Clinton's direct oversight, and the man regarded as England's best fighting general would finally be able to take the battle to the American rebels on his own terms. If this fate awaited him in the vast, inscrutable interiors of the American South, at least it would be a fighting one.

THREE

TARLETON'S QUARTERS

WHILE HENRY CLINTON prepared his return to New York, Cornwallis departed the Charleston vicinity on May 18, his destination the South Carolina interior town of Camden on the Wateree River. From there, he would establish a series of outposts across the South Carolina interior to pacify the countryside and recruit Loyalist militia. Accompanying him were 2,500 men, including the 23rd and 33rd British regiments, the Volunteers of Ireland, a Provincial unit commanded by Francis, Lord Rawdon, and of course, Tarleton's British Legion.[1]

At this point in Cornwallis's career, he was more the actor than the director, more brawler than corner coach, and had gained a reputation as England's best combat general in the American war. Even as a schoolboy at Eton, a prestigious training ground for England's elite, where the curriculum "served as a way of maintaining class distinctions," it was the playing fields where he excelled, not the classroom.[2]

Cornwallis was born December 31, 1738, to a prominent, aristocratic family. His father was the first earl Cornwallis and his mother was the daughter of Lord Townshend, a prominent member of the British cabinet, and the niece of Robert Walpole, generally regarded as Great Britain's first prime minister. The family estate was Culford, about sixty miles northeast of London in Suffolk. Early on described by his father as a "very military" young man, Cornwallis was given an army commission purchased for him by his family in the 1st, or Grenadier, Guards when he was eighteen. However, he was not entirely through with his formal education, for a year later, in 1757 he attended a military academy in Turin, Italy, where the curriculum included mathematics and fortification as well as ballroom dancing and diplomacy.

This training distinguished Cornwallis from most of his fellow officers. Though the British army was a "visible . . . symbol of imperial splendor and power," write Cornwallis biographers Franklin and Mary Wickwire, its "officers did not necessarily know their trade," at least not in the sense of formal military training or education.[3] Still, thanks to the near endless cycle of warfare on the European continent, it could fight, and Cornwallis learned to be an army officer on the battlefields of Minden, Kirch Donkern, Wilhemstadt, and Lutterburg during the Seven Years' War.

Promoted to lieutenant colonel of the 12th Foot in 1761, he was by 1766 the colonel of his own regiment, the 33rd. By then, however, his interests had turned to domestic and political matters. Though biographer Hugh F. Rankin notes that "he was neither particularly active nor original in politics,"[4] he attracted powerful patrons, including George III. In 1768, he married Jemima Jones, a frail, witty woman whose family lacked the social status of Cornwallis's. Thus, the marriage failed to alleviate Cornwallis's financial burdens, though it was a successful love match, producing two children, and Cornwallis proved a devoted family man. The Wickwires speculate it was this devotion to family, as well as king and country, that attracted him to George, who shared similar values. "Probably George III liked Cornwallis for his domestic virtues," they write.[5] Whatever the reason, the relationship served Cornwallis well. In 1769, he was named vice treasurer of Ireland. In 1770, he was named a privy councillor, and in 1771, a constable of the Tower of London. Though primarily ceremonial roles, these positions enhanced both Cornwallis's social status and his pocketbook—one source from 1823 indicates the vice treasurer of Ireland position came with an annual stipend of seven to eight thousand pounds, "for which nothing was done."[6] Similar connections played a role in his promotion to major general on September 29, 1775, and lieutenant general on January 1, 1776.

As a commander, Cornwallis cultivated an affiliation with his officers and troops typical of the gallant *homme de guerre*, or man of war, described by the French officer de Tressan as the "rigorous minister of the vengeance of kings," who could "distinguish between the necessary evil and the unnecessary" and "that amid the cruel spectacle and chaos of war, pity should always have easy access to his heart." The military historian Armstrong Starkey argues the *homme de guerre* "was the essence of a military culture that combined obedience to the sovereign with a concern for status and self respect." The concept also justified the aristocratic character of the British officer corps. "Aristocrats remained the natural leaders of society and of men in time of war," Starkey explains of the ideal. "Honor insured that officers would act bravely and set an example for their men. Honor provided that officers would act as the guardians of the traditional values and institutions of society."[7]

As the *homme de guerre*, Cornwallis volunteered to serve in America, despite his wife's objections. "His example will give credit & spirit to our proceedings against America," praised Lord North.[8] He traveled there in 1776 to join Henry Clinton in the southern expedition that resulted in the Battle of Sullivan's Island, then sailed north to join the main army in New York. In the battle of Long Island, he commanded the reserve, exposing himself to enemy fire in support of Henry Clinton's flanking movement through Jamaica Pass on August 27. Three months later he led the mission across the Hudson River to capture Fort Lee on the Jersey shore.

His first mistake followed on January 2, 1777, when he allowed Washington's troops to escape Trenton for a successful surprise attack on Princeton, but he redeemed himself with distinction at Brandywine and Germantown. "In the first eighteen months in America, the earl had distinguished himself in subordinate roles and proved he was an able and colorful field commander," writes Rankin.[9]

His optimism for the American conflict dimmed, however, after a trip home in December 1777, where he found Jemima's health declining. He returned to America in time to participate in the evacuation of Philadelphia, then brilliantly commanded the rearguard action at Monmouth on June 28, 1778, that disrupted the American attack. Ensconced comfortably in New York, however, Cornwallis soon grew bored with what was essentially garrison duty and requested another leave to England to attend to Jemima in November 1778. Clinton agreed on the condition he would lobby King George and North for desperately needed reinforcements.

Jemima died in February 1779 with Cornwallis by her side, probably a victim of hepatitis. In the depths of her illness, Cornwallis had resigned his commission, vowing to stay by Jemima's side, and putting little effort into his mission to garner reinforcements, but with her death, he decided to recommit himself to service in America. When he returned to New York in July 1779 without a commitment for more troops, Clinton perceived it as Cornwallis's participation in one of the innumerable conspiracies imagined against him, setting off the decline of their personal relationship.

At least the South promised action, though it also demanded new levels of administrative acumen, to which he was then not well suited. "Cornwallis in practice was a better battlefield commander than a planner of grand strategy," observes Rankin. "Administrative duties bored him."[10] But as of May 27, 1780, with Clinton still in Charleston, those weaknesses had not yet been revealed. On that day, Cornwallis and his expedition of 2,500 men arrived at Nelson's Ferry, a strategic Santee River crossing approximately halfway between Charleston and Camden, where he received news South Carolina governor John Rutledge was escaping into North Carolina under the escort of Continental Lt. Col. Abraham Buford and 350 Continental infantry, along with a small detachment of Continental cavalry. Also with Buford at that time were seven hundred North Carolina militia under the command of General Richard Caswell, but Caswell separated from Buford as they departed Camden, turning northeast toward the Pee Dee basin, while Buford, Rutledge, and the Continentals continued north on the main road toward Salisbury, North Carolina.[11]

Though Buford had a sixty-mile head start, Cornwallis was eager to capture Rutledge, who had long been a thorn in the British side. A brilliant lawyer and prominent Charlestonian, Rutledge had served in the Continental Congress (1774–1775) and as president of the South Carolina General Assembly (1776–1778) before being elected South Carolina's first Whig governor in January 1779. When the South Carolina Assembly adjourned in March 1780 as Clinton and Cornwallis's second expedition approached Charleston, Rutledge had been awarded with what were essentially dictatorial powers over the state, and even after evacuating the city, he had remained in the nearby countryside, attempting to rally local militia while he maintained correspondence with his subordinates and military commanders still inside.[12]

Rutledge would go on to play a prominent role in the war, accompanying Nathanael Greene during Greene's 1781 campaign, but for now he was on the run, and Cornwallis realized his capture would send a powerful message to the people of South Carolina that their state was now firmly returned to British control. But Cornwallis's brigade was marching too slowly to catch Buford and Rutledge on the run, so he ordered Tarleton to pursue with a detachment of forty regular British cavalry from the 17th British Dragoons, 130 from the British Legion dragoons, and one hundred of the British Legion infantry, also mounted, though some doubling up, two to a horse.[13] "Lieutenant-Colonel Tarleton, on this occasion, was desired to consult his own judgement, as to the distance of the pursuit, or the mode of attack," Tarleton recounted in his memoir.[14]

Tarleton drove his men hard, losing several horses in the pursuit, "in consequence of the rapidity of the march, and the heat of the climate." Along the way, however, he sent small squadrons or patrols to search the countryside for noted Whig leaders, burning their homes and property if the fugitive could not be found.[15] The following evening, May 28, Tarleton reached Camden, where he learned Buford and Rutledge had stopped at the plantation of Henry Rugeley, twelve miles north. Here, Tarleton decided to ignore Caswell and the retreating North Carolina militia who had turned to the east, to focus his pursuit on Rutledge and Buford. Tarleton stayed in Camden only briefly, leaving town at two o'clock the next morning, May 29.

Henry Rugeley was a merchant and businessman with connections on the important trade route between Camden and Charleston. On the main road north of Camden leading into North Carolina, he and his brother had built a small industrial village featuring a sawmill, gristmill, two bolting mills, a waterwheel, a tanyard, a store, and several slave dwellings, along with an "elegant" dwelling Rugeley named "Clermont."[16] Though he would soon profess his allegiance to the Loyalist cause, Rugeley was politically shrewd enough to offer Rutledge his hospitality for the night. Learning of Tarleton's pursuit, Rugeley awoke his guests around midnight, advising them of Tarleton's approach, persuading them to escape posthaste.[17]

Tarleton arrived at Rugeley's by daylight, learning Buford was only twenty miles away. In the account from his memoir, Tarleton reports that from Rugeley's he sent a messenger forward with a summons, its contents a deliberate ruse, designed to either trick Buford into surrender or delay his retreat. In it was the false declaration that he was pursuing with a force of seven hundred, not the 270 he had with him, and that "Earl Cornwallis is likewise within a short march with nine British battalions." He ordered Buford's unconditional surrender; the same terms Lincoln had accepted from Clinton at Charleston.[18]

Buford received Tarleton's flag around one o'clock in the afternoon. Of the deliberations he conducted with his officers over Tarleton's threats and terms, we have already recounted. The history here is obscured by conflicting accounts, but undeniable is that he marched on, refusing to take any defensive measures at all aside from leaving a small, inadequate guard in his rear. Earlier Buford had received news that a corps of four hundred American infantry, cavalry, and artillery was approaching Camden from the north under command of a Lt. Col. Potterfield, and he may have hoped that he could rendezvous with Potterfield before Tarleton overtook him. Citing evidence from the account of British captain Charles Cochrane, Tarleton's second in command, historian James Piecuch suggests Buford believed Tarleton rode with "only a few light Horse," who could pose no match for his 350 Continentals.[19]

It was a terrible assumption. "Buford's refusal to give Tarleton's message serious consideration, or to pause and assess the condition of his own men, doomed his troops, and did so unnecessarily," surmises Piecuch.[20] Driving his men with relentless abandon, Tarleton finally came on Buford's rear in the Waxhaws, a vast settlement in the region between Camden and Charlotte. He had ridden 154 miles in fifty-four hours, though the journey was not without its casualties: Tarleton reports that by this time "many of the British cavalry and mounted infantry were totally worn out, and dropped successively into the rear." Also left behind in the chase was a field artillery piece and the exhausted horses towing it. Nevertheless, and true to form, the bellicose Tarleton "determined as soon as possible to attack, there being no other expedient to stop" the Continental's progress.[21]

Tarleton's vedettes, or advanced guards, quickly overtook Buford's rear guard, a meager squad of a sergeant and four dragoons commanded by a Lt. Pearson. By all accounts, Pearson's rear guard was overwhelmed "under the eyes of the two commanders," who "respectively prepared their troops for action."[22]

Buford still refused to establish defensive measures. "Instead of throwing his wagons into a line across his front as a barricade peculiarly advantageous in opposing a cavalry attack, he drew his men up in open ground," observes historian Christopher Ward. In fact, Buford had sent ahead his wagons and artillery, perhaps under the guard of about one hundred of his infantry, further suggesting he underestimated Tarleton's strength.[23] Instead, he arrayed his men in a standard infantry line on the east side of the road in what was described by Tarleton as an "open wood," placing his handful of cavalry troopers, perhaps along with a few of his infantry, in a meager reserve behind the main line.[24]

Tarleton meanwhile formed his exhausted men atop a small hill opposite Buford's center. "Though not in a suitable condition for action," Tarleton admits, he "determined as soon as possible to attack." On his east flank, he placed his infantry and some dismounted dragoons under Captain Charles Cochrane, his second in command, to support his cavalry charge, while Captains Corbet and Kinlock were directed to charge the American center with the British 17th Dragoons supported by some Legion dragoons. Tarleton, "with thirty chosen horse and some infantry" would assault the American's western flank. The stragglers coming up in the rear "with their tired horses" and the three-pounder cannon "were ordered to form something like a reserve, opposite the enemy's center, upon a small eminence that commanded the road."[25]

An account from John Marshall, the fourth chief justice of the Supreme Court, who also wrote a four volume biography of George Washington, claims that once formed for battle, the two sides continued to negotiate terms of surrender. Marshall was a Buford associate who allegedly received his account from Buford himself. "While the flags were passing, Tarleton continued to make his dispositions for the assault," Marshall wrote, but "the instant the truce terminated, his cavalry made a furious charge on the Americans, who, having received no orders, seem to have been uncertain whether to defend themselves or not."[26]

Henry Bowyer, Buford's adjutant general, provides a similar account. He recalled that just as "the sound of Tarlton's bugles was heard," a British officer "was perceived riding forward," proposing to Buford, "the same terms of surrender as those granted to the Garrison of Charleston," though those terms were rejected by Buford, "without hesitation, who "did not believe that a force as strong could have reached the neighbourhood through which he was marching."[27]

In Bowyer's account, it was at this point that Buford and his officers considered defensive measures. Buford's account to the Virginia General Assembly, written just a few days after the battle, however, indicates this was the discussion that took place around one o'clock in the afternoon earlier that day, before Tarleton's force had appeared in his rear. Nevertheless, both accounts report Buford doubted the number of Tarleton's troops. "One officer . . . proposed that the wagons should be brought together and a barrier to the enemy formed, behind which the detachment should be posted. But it was suggested that such a plan would probably further the view of the British commander, who might have sent forward only a small body of soldiers to amuse and detain Beaufort till a force adequate to his destruction could be brought up," wrote Bowyer. If true, this account suggests Buford sent forward his wagons and their infantry escort only after Tarleton had appeared in his rear, not earlier in the day.[28]

Tarleton is vague on the timing of this attempt to negotiate a surrender, but his memoir suggests it was earlier in the day, as his own weary troops straggled forward in the heat and exhaustion, not after the two sides had formed for battle, supporting Buford's account. Tarleton wrote that, finding himself "not far distant from the enemy," he "determined as soon as possible to attack," a timeline that could be one of several hours or several minutes. Nevertheless, by around 3:30 in the afternoon, the negotiations were over. "The disposition being completed without any fire from the enemy, though within three hundred yards of their front, the cavalry advanced to the charge," wrote Tarleton. His dragoons raced toward the American line, "with the horrid yells of infuriated demons." Tarleton recounted that as the British cavalry approached the Americans, he "was surprised to hear their officers command them to retain their fire till the British cavalry was nearer. This forbearance in not firing before the dragoons were within ten yards of the object of their attack, prevented their falling into confusion on the charge, and likewise deprived the Americans of the farther use of their ammunition."[29]

The success of the eighteenth-century cavalry charge depended on shock and velocity. If the foot soldier wasn't terrorized by the thunderous sound of the cavalry approach, he was soon overwhelmed by the sheer mass of horse and rider, and the existential threat of slashing sword. Defense, therefore, depended on laying down a sheet of musket fire at a reasonable distance, thirty to fifty yards, disrupting the charge before panic swept through the ranks. A volley fired at ten yards, as Tarleton reported, could not impede the momentum of the cavalry charge, no matter how effective, and left the likely terrified American infantry no time to reload or prepare mentally for the cavalry in their midst. Writing in his own memoir, Continental general William Moultrie agreed Buford's fatal mistake "was his ordering his men not to fire upon the enemy (who were chiefly cavalry) 'til they came within ten yards of him." Moultrie was by now a prisoner in Charleston, and presumably would have heard of the action through the gossip of his British guards.[30]

In his memoir, Tarleton depicted the battle as a total drubbing, the American's almost instantly routed and flustered by the British charge. The American battalion "was totally broken," he recalled, though Tarleton himself was briefly trapped under a fallen horse and did not reach the American position until the "slaughter was commenced. . . . Thus in a few minutes" the affair ended. To the incredible success of the British attack, Tarleton attributes the mistakes committed by Buford: "If he had halted the waggons as soon as he found the British troops pressing his rear, and formed them into some kind of redoubt . . . in all probability he would not have been attacked, or by such a disposition might have foiled the attempt."[31]

American accounts suggest a more resolute resistance. Dr. Robert Brownfield was traveling with Buford and left an account written over two decades after the battle. Several elements of Brownfield's account are contradicted by others, and so his recollections must be regarded critically. Nevertheless, Brownfield reported the British dragoons were "received with firmness, and completely checked, until the cavalry were gaining the rear."[32] In his report to the Virginia General Assembly, Buford reported his "men and officer's behav'd with the greatest coolness & Bravery," and that after his main line was broken, his troops reformed and rallied in the rear. After the fighting commenced, Buford claimed to have sent an officer with a flag of surrender to Tarleton, which was "refused in a very rude manner." This account is supported by Bowyer, who wrote that he was the soldier ordered forward with a flag of surrender, with instructions to accept Tarleton's original terms of surrender. "The Adjutant remonstrated by saying, that as the firing still continued, the execution of the order would be impracticable." But Buford insisted, and Bowyer claims to have ridden forward "with a handkerchief displayed on the point of his sword," indicating the American flag of surrender. However, when Bowyer got "close to the British commander" to deliver his message, "a ball at that moment striking the forehead of Tarleton's horse, he plunged, and both fell to the ground, the horse being uppermost," ruining the surrender attempt. Brownfield also recounted a surrender attempt during the battle, although in his recollection it was a young officer named Ensign Cruit who was cruelly "cut down" as he advanced with surrender flag.[33]

Piecuch suggests if a formal American surrender attempt was made, it was never received by Tarleton or his senior officers in the confusion of battle. Likely, individual Americans or small groups attempted to surrender after Tarleton's British had routed their lines, while some fought on. Buford claimed that around this point in the battle he was surrounded and forced to flee the field, though as he was making his escape, many of his men "were killd after they had lain down their arms."[34] Brownfield recalled that after Cruit was "cut down," some of the Americans "viewing this as an earnest of what to expect," resumed their fighting in an attempt "to sell their lives as dearly as possible."[35]

Clearly, there was much confusion and disorder, with terrible results for the Americans. The British were quickly within the American lines, attacking with sword from horseback, or shortly afterward, with a British bayonet. To the nature of this attack, we can ascribe many characteristics of the casualties described later by Americans such as Samuel Gilmore, who in his pension application recalled receiving "twenty-two wounds from the enemy, most of which were with the broad sword, several of them so split my fractured head that there was five pieces of my skull bone taken out before I was Cured . . . I was taken and kept as prisoner at the place where the battle was fought for three weeks without ever having a surgeon." Similarly, Sgt. John Thompson reported "several dreadful and horrible wounds in his head, face & body . . . fell and became a prisoner with a great many others with five sever & dangerous wounds."

In these American accounts the horror goes on and on. "Hewn down by a horseman receiving three cuts (one very deep) in the head," reads the pension application of John Ballard. "Afterward one of the infantry pierces his side with the bayonet in consequence of which he was left for dead on the ground." Similarly, Jonathan Burnside reported he was "wounded in the left arm and was stabed in the right side and cut in the face by a sword," then "strippd of his clothes and left for dead upon the field of battle." And John Thompson recounted "several dreadful & horrible wounds in his head, face & body."[36]

Brownfield's account contains two particularly gruesome depictions of Americans wounded in the battle: Lt. Pearson, the officer who commanded Buford's rear guard and was struck down even before the battle started and Captain John Stokes, a native of Pittsylvania County, Virginia. "Pearson was inhumanely mangled on the face as he lay on his back," Brownfield wrote. "His nose and lip were bisected obliquely; several of his teeth were broken out of his jaw, and the under completely divided on each side. These wounds were inflicted after he had fallen, with several others on his head, shoulders, and arms." Remarkably, Pearson apparently survived, though he lay for five weeks, with "Job-like" patience, "without uttering a single groan."[37]

Stokes received twenty-three wounds, according to Brownfield. Assailed by two dragoons early in the encounter, the dragoon on his right, "by one stroke, cut off his right hand." Now attempting to cover his head from the attack, his left arm was "hacked in eight or ten places from the wrist to the shoulder. His head was then laid open almost the whole length of the crown to the eye brows. After he fell he received several cuts on his face and shoulders."[38]

But was this a brutal war crime or simply the toll of eighteenth-century warfare? Fought during the transition between modern ballistic technology and what military historian Armstrong Starkey calls the ancien regime, the American Revolution was a conflict where officers from both sides preferred the attack of bayonet and sword to the armed firefights of modern military conflict. It was the rifle, not the sword or bayonet, deemed "intrinsically inhumane," writes Starkey, because rifles permitted killing from afar, especially dangerous for the eighteenth-century officer, who was often its target. "This sort of innovation won no more favor among the eighteenth-century officer corps than did the cross-bow among medieval knights," writes Starkey. In contrast, the brutal hand-to-hand combat of sword and bayonet was considered standard, even preferred, practice. "Bayonets violated no military conventions and their use was consistent with the conservative attitude of many officers. . . . Thus one may conclude that the preference for bayonets and swords in combat was not a question of honor, but of effectiveness."[39]

However, even if there was no organized American attempt to surrender at the Waxhaws, it does appear the British pushed their brutalities a step beyond the day's common (yet vague and unwritten) "code of honor." But does this constitute a massacre? Modern-day historians disagree. "There was a confused, brief battle, in which the American line was quickly broken. . . . In this confusion, with officers unable to exert control, some Legion troops in all likelihood killed Americans who attempted to surrender," argues Piecuch.[40] Historian Anthony J. Scotti even suggests it was the Americans who violated the "code of honor," not the British. "Under the rules of eighteenth-century warfare, an enemy force called upon to surrender which fails to do so forfeits its right to quarter in any upcoming combat," he writes.[41]

In his systematic review of 134 pension accounts from Waxhaws survivors, historian C. Leon Harris admits only two use the word "massacre" to describe the day's atrocities. "On the other hand, it is difficult to read so many accounts of suffering without the word 'massacre' coming to mind." Harris conducted a statistical analysis on the injuries described in the pension accounts, his hypothesis that injuries to arms and hands indicate the wounded were unarmed "because people instinctively parry blows with muskets, or other solid objects in preference to arms and hands." Comparing the Waxhaws accounts to pension accounts from four other battles—Cowpens, Guilford Courthouse, Camden, and Eutaw Springs—Harris found significant probability the carnage at the Waxhaws "was not the usual outcome of battles between cavalry and infantry, and that more than half of the wounded Americans were unarmed and incapable of resisting."[42]

Almost 250 years later, we may never know what truly happened at the Waxhaws, though clearly the debate continues. Tarleton himself admitted a "a vindictive asperity not easily restrained" in accounting for the high rate of American casualties. To this he attributes his men's concern for his own safety when his horse was shot from under him, leading to a false report the British "had lost their commanding officer."[43] British officer Charles Stedman, who was not at the Waxhaws but serving with Cornwallis during the time, wrote, "execution done in this action was severe. . . . The king's troops were entitled to great commendation for their activity and ardour on this occasion, but the virtue of humanity was totally forgot."[44]

Tarleton reported the American losses at "one hundred officers and men killed on the spot" and "above two hundred prisoners."[45] This count roughly corresponds to that of historian Christopher Ward, who adds that 150 of the American prisoners were so badly wounded they could not be immediately moved, and the remaining fifty prisoners who were capable of being transported to Camden were also "mostly wounded." Of the Americans, only the soldiers Buford had sent ahead with his wagons prior to the battle escaped, along with Buford himself and a few other mounted Americans who abandoned their men in the midst of battle. Tarleton reported British losses at five killed and fourteen wounded.[46]

But the reality mattered little, for the most important effect of the Battle of the Waxhaws was not the American defeat. It wasn't the number killed or wounded, or even the truth about American attempts to surrender. The most important effect was the psychological impact on the surrounding countryside. "This barbarous massacre gave a more sanguinary turn to the war," reports historian David Ramsay. "Tarleton's quarters became proverbial and in subsequent battles a spirit of revenge gave a keener edge to military resentments."[47] Ramsay was a prominent Charleston physician and member of the South Carolina legislature. After the war, he served as a South Carolina delegate to the Continental Congress. His two volume history, published in 1785 and 1789, was the first account of the American Revolution written and published by an American, making it influential in subsequent written accounts of the nineteenth and twentieth centuries.[48]

However, finding primary accounts to support Ramsay's claims about the proverbial nature of the term "Tarleton's quarters" proves difficult, although clearly news and rumors about Buford's defeat spread quickly through the surrounding countryside and beyond. Writing to his brother from Fredericksburg, Virginia, on June 20, Continental colonel Otho Holland Williams admitted there was yet no official account of Buford's defeat, "so that the circumstances we are told of relative to the Action may not be correct. But that the Troops were effectually routed is most certain."[49] Secondary accounts from the Battle of Kings Mountain indicate American sharpshooters cried out "Buford, Buford. Give them Tarleton's Quarters," and American soldiers at the Battle of Cowpens supposedly taunted their British prisoners with cries of "Tarleton's Quarter."[50]

Piecuch has unearthed a newspaper account dated July 18, 1780, from the *Maryland Journal, and Baltimore Advertiser* reporting that "Colonel Buford ordered his men to ground their arms . . . but instead of meeting with that reception which the feelings of humanity dictates . . . no quarters were given."[51] The memoirs of American militia commanders Richard Winn and William R. Davie indicate rumors of the battle spread quickly through the region, and though Brownfield wrote his account decades later, we might presume the hyperbole of his description was similar to those heard by Winn and Davie: "Tarleton and his cruel myrmidions was in the midst of them [Buford's troops], when commenced a scene of indiscriminate carnage never surpassed by the ruthless atrocities of the most barbarous savages. The demand for quarters, seldom refused to a vanquished foe, was at once found to be in vain—not a man was spared," Brownfield wrote.[52] After the battle, many of the wounded were eventually transported to the nearby Waxhaw Meeting House, a local church where they were eventually observed by North Carolina militia soldier Joseph Graham, who noted, "perhaps a more complicated scene of misery, in proportion to their numbers, was not exhibited in the whole war."[53]

Historian Holger Hoock, among others, observes Americans were eager to publicize such atrocities as part of a broader effort to exaggerate British violence. "British massacres became highly effective assets in the Patriots' moral war: they helped them win the battle for the support of the American population while shaming Britain in the eyes of the world."[54] Thus, Ramsay's statement about the "proverbial" use of "Tarleton's quarters" as a propaganda weapon rings true, even if the details are a bit sketchy.

Same goes for "Bloody" Tarleton, or more familiarly, "Bloody Ban," a nickname that has long since attached itself to Banastre Tarleton. Though England's aristocratic class considered use of the word "bloody" obscene or profane, it was a popular term for "abominable" during the eighteenth century and common in the vernacular of England's lower classes. Tarleton biographer Anthony J. Scotti admits it is likely, even probable, that "Bloody"

Tarleton was a popular nickname for Tarleton at the time, though he finds it unusual there is no contemporary written account, either American or British, using the name. Here, as with "Tarleton's Quarters," we must rely on the preponderance of secondary accounts to suggest common usage during the Backcountry War. But whatever name they used, the people of the South Carolina backcountry were savagely introduced to Banastre Tarleton at the Waxhaws, and with him came the threat of brutal death and destruction. It was a reputation Tarleton would both use to his advantage and have used successfully against him in the fighting to come.

FOUR

OLD SCORES

N O SINGLE THEORY explains the allegiances of South Carolinians between Whig and Loyalist, or Patriot and Tory, during the American
Revolution, though some have tried. One assumption ascribes the choice
to ethnic divisions. Certainly, many of South Carolina's most ardent Whigs
were the Scots-Irish settlers of the state's interior, while smaller German,
Dutch, Scots, and Irish populations tended to remain loyal to England.
Another theory ascribes these allegiances primarily to length of residency,
with recent immigrants taking the Loyalist side and more established settlers the Whig, while a third promotes a "Leading Man" hypothesis, suggesting most settlers simply adopted the allegiances of their local militia or
political chieftain.

All three theories contain some truth. But to better understand these
complicated loyalties, we must look deeper at South Carolina's patterns of
immigration and socioeconomic development over the preceding decades,

and its legacy of class and religious conflict. In his sweeping historical account of the state, *South Carolina: A History*, historian Walter Edgar describes South Carolina's early migration routes. Her first settlers were mostly English, recruited by the lords proprietors, eight English aristocrats who were granted the rights of 850,000 square miles in the New World (the original grant stretching north from modern-day Daytona Beach, Florida, to North Carolina's northern border with Virginia, then west from the Atlantic coast all the way to the Pacific). Charles Town, or modern-day Charleston, was settled in 1670 by these English but was soon filled with immigrants from many ethnic and cultural backgrounds, including a large population of French, Scots, Irish, German, Welsh, Dutch, and African slaves.

By the 1730s, these non-English low-country settlers mostly had been assimilated into Anglican society, with much of the white population grown comfortable, if not rich, on vast lowland plantations of rice, indigo, and cotton. Of course, working these plantations were slaves imported from Africa and the West Indies. By the beginning of the American Revolution, Africans and their descendants comprised roughly 60 percent of the colony's 175,000 population.[1]

As the Charleston region grew, so did a lucrative trade with the Native Americans in the colony's interior. In 1729, the £160,000 of agricultural produce and naval stores Charleston merchants exported to Britain included seventy-five thousand deer skins, the bulk of which were acquired from the Cherokee and Creek. Mostly, these skins and other Native American trade goods traveled down the "Cherokee Path," an early trade route connecting Charleston to the Cherokee "lower towns" in what is now Oconee and Pickens Counties in the far northwestern corner of South Carolina.

In 1730, surveyor George Hunter was commissioned to survey this Cherokee Path. At a fork on a level site, estimating the location as ninety-six miles from the Cherokee lower town of Keowee, Hunter placed the label "96" on his map. Soon, "Ninety Six" became a popular camping spot, then eventually the most prominent trading post on South Carolina's western frontier.[2]

While the Cherokee Path brought settlers and traders from Charleston into the region of South Carolina west of the Broad River, settlement in the north and central part of the colony was fed primarily by the "Great Wagon Road," the settler highway running from Harrisburg, Pennsylvania, south through the Appalachian Mountains and into the Carolina Piedmont. Branches of the Wagon Road eventually ran west into East Ten-

nessee, Kentucky, and Georgia, but at its southern terminus was the South
Carolina town of Camden (first called Fredericksburg, then Pine Tree Hill
until the name was changed to Camden in 1768 to honor Charles Pratt,
the Earl of Camden) in the Catawba River valley.[3]

For much of the eighteenth century, Scots-Irish immigrants and their
descendants comprised the bulk of traffic on the Great Wagon Road. These
were not the Highland Scots or Irish Celts of kilt-wearing fame, but rather
Protestant dissidents of the Scottish Lowlands, persecuted by the English
for their religious beliefs and recruited or forcibly settled in the Ulster
province of Northern Ireland, where they often endured deprivation, hostility, and misery. Not surprisingly, many soon fled to the New World. From
1715 until 1775, a quarter million Scots-Irish emigrated from Ulster to
America, many landing in Philadelphia, where their bellicose character and
religious separatism often clashed with that region's Quaker society. So, for
many Scots-Irish, it was to the West or the South they migrated, seeking
land and perhaps, above all, freedom from the political and religious persecution of the previous centuries.[4]

In the South Carolina interior they found ample supplies of both, for
the colony's royal administration concerned itself mainly with Charleston's
commerce and trade, tending little to either governance or the eternal soul
of its frontier settlers. Indicative of this disregard was the term "backcountry," used generically by Charleston's planter and merchant class for any
part of the colony exceeding fifty miles from its coast. "In the low country
parish of St. George Dorchester was a crossroad called Parish End," writes
Edgar. "The name said it all, except that it might have been more appro-
priately called 'World's End.' The rest of the colony was dismissively referred to as the backcountry."[5]

At first, this disregard suited the Scots-Irish just fine, for they tended
to migrate and settle in family or religious clans, with little need for outside
society. For many, their Presbyterian or, occasionally, Baptist congregations
were all they required or wanted for social structure. And this Catawba
River valley of the central Carolinas offered land in abundance. Comprised
mostly of low-rolling Piedmont hills with plentiful rivers and streams, it
was ill-suited for large-scale, plantation-style production but more than adequate for the sustenance farming and grazing the indigent of Ulster knew
and craved.

Named for the nearby Waxhaws Indians, the Waxhaws was a vast region
on the Catawba's east bank where many of these Scots-Irish settlers established their farms. Its borders extended roughly north to south from just

below the outskirts of modern-day Charlotte to a point near Camden, encompassing much of present-day Mecklenburg, Union, and Anson Counties in North Carolina, along with portions of South Carolina's Chester and York Counties. But its geographic and social center was known as the Waxhaw Settlement, in the general area of today's Lancaster County, South Carolina.[6]

Others settled west of the Catawba in the region eventually known as the "New Acquisition District," the name deriving from a border dispute between North and South Carolina that was finally resolved by a 1772 survey officially designating the area as a part of South Carolina. Comprised of modern-day York County, South Carolina, along with portions of Chester, Cherokee, and Union Counties, the New Acquisition District was a fertile, abundant region supporting production of indigo, hemp, tobacco, wheat, and Indian corn. At the time of the 1772 survey, it boasted a relatively large population of five thousand settlers.[7]

In fact, nearly one-half of South Carolina's total population, and almost 80 percent of its white inhabitants, resided in the backcountry at the time of the American Revolution. To the west of the New Acquisition, across the Broad River, the Ninety Six District centered around the trading village of Ninety Six, which also continued to grow and prosper, creating tensions with the Cherokee, who still resided in the colony's northwestern corner. Although many of the Scots-Irish traveling down the Great Wagon Road eventually found their way to the Ninety Six District, other nationalities and religious groups also traveled up the Cherokee Path from Charleston to settle there, giving South Carolina's western regions a slightly more heterogenous flavor, at least regarding their political and religious loyalties, than its central and eastern ones. For instance, the Ninety Six District tended to host more Baptist congregations than either the Waxhaws or New Acquisition districts.

"By the 1750s, backcountry society was still not very community-minded," writes Edgar. "Sectarian and ethnic animosities, individualism, and a general lack of respect for social and civic institutions resulted in a society that was disorganized and unstable." With legal and real estate claims still administered in Charleston, land disputes were common, and with no authorized law enforcement, personal disputes were occasionally settled with "frontier-justice." But if there was one cause against which the backcountry settlers could unite, it was the Cherokee.[8]

Disturbed by the flood of Europeans settling on their traditional territory and agitated by French agents provocateur operating against the English in the French and Indian War, the Cherokee finally attacked white settlements on the Carolina and Virginia frontier in late 1759 and early 1760. In broader American history, these actions are typically encompassed within the scope of the French and Indian War. In South Carolina, Cherokees murdered twenty-four white traders in January 1760, then terrorized the Long Canes settlement in the Savannah River valley, massacring twenty-three settlers and driving away hundreds more, before launching an unsuccessful attack on Ninety Six itself.[9]

The First Cherokee War had begun (the name given in relation to future Cherokee conflicts later in the eighteenth century). Terrorized settlers established a series of blockhouses throughout the Ninety Six District as Cherokee raids continued in the Saluda River valley in modern-day Laurens, Newberry, and Saluda Counties.

South Carolina's royal administration had passed a militia act in 1747 requiring "white males between the ages of 16 and 60" to participate in up to six militia musters per year.[10] However, the First Cherokee War galvanized backcountry militia organization and administration into a formal structure that would survive into the American Revolution. In 1761, militia regiments from across South Carolina joined the Grant Expedition, a retaliatory mission against the Cherokee led by British Lieutenant Colonel James Grant. Gathering men and supplies as he marched up the Cherokee Path from Charleston, including future military leaders of the American Revolution such as Andrew Pickens, Francis Marion, and William Moultrie, Grant burned and raided the Cherokee "Middle Towns" in western North Carolina, forcing the Cherokees into a treaty by 1762.[11]

Peace with the Cherokee brought new waves of settlers into the South Carolina backcountry, including a criminal class drawn by the region's lack of formal law enforcement or judicial administration. By the latter half of the 1760s, many backcountry settlers had grown so frustrated with the royal administration's failure to provide basic legal protections that they organized into vigilante mobs eventually known as the "Regulators." Closely associated with the Scots-Irish Presbyterians, the Regulators were successful in subduing criminal activity, but their vigilante tactics frightened Charleston authorities. And in June 1768, the Regulators went a step too far, authorizing an extrajudicial legal code called the "Plan of Regulation" that included Christian fundamentalist moral standards. "The Regulators intervened in family life, disciplined wayward husbands, and enforced debt collection," writes Edgar. "With no one to challenge their authority, some Regulators took advantage of the opportunity to settle old scores. Punishments became cruel and unusual. Flogging to excess became a sadistic entertainment rather than a punishment for wrongdoing."[12]

With the Regulators organizing for the fall 1768 general assembly elections, Charleston's royal administration sent militia under the command of Col. John Schofield to suppress the vote and arrest Regulator leaders. After these "Schofieldites" began terrorizing homes in the Ninety Six District, approximately six or seven hundred Regulators formed a corps to march against them. They found these Schofieldites, or "Moderators," at their camp on the Saluda River, and the two equally matched sides squared off for armed battle. However, bloodshed was avoided when prominent backcountry politician and militia leader Richard Richardson arrived and negotiated a reluctant truce.[13]

Tensions between the Regulators and Moderators were finally reduced when King George III approved a South Carolina circuit act in 1769, permitting new courts to be established in the backcountry districts of Ninety Six, Camden, Cheraw, and Orangeburg, along with Georgetown and Beaufort on the coast. Though courthouses and jails would come slowly, a government system of law and order had finally come to the backcountry. But many in the backcountry long remembered the Regulator's overreach, often associated with Scots-Irish zealotry. "While there is no perfect correlation between Regulators and rebels, on the one hand, and moderators and loyalists on the other," observes historian Robert Stansbury Lambert, "the animosities generated between individual families and neighbors in the Regulator struggle very probably carried over into the civil war that raged through the backcountry during the Revolution."[14]

By the early 1770s, some backcountry settlers had accumulated considerable wealth, injecting new elements of class and economic conflict into old feuds over religion and boundary disputes. Although most of South Carolina's slave population worked the vast plantations of the low-country region, by the 1770s slave ownership was an increasingly important component of backcountry economics—a backcountry planter with nine to twelve hands could earn an annual income of £250 to £500 sterling (roughly $22,000 to $44,000 in today's dollars) planting indigo and hemp.

William Hill was born in 1741, probably in Ireland, and by 1768 obtained numerous land grants in what is now York County, South Carolina. A prominent leader of nearby Bethel Presbyterian Church, Hill was best known for the ironworks he owned on Allison Creek. Across the Broad River lived James Williams, who listed as assets in his 1780 will 3,600 acres and at least one mill in the Little River District, located between the Enoree and Saluda Rivers, where he also ran a prosperous mercantile business. Not surprising then that William Hill owned ninety slaves and James Williams's will listed ownership of thirty-three slaves, nor that many who aspired to the economic prosperity of a Hill or Williams saw slave ownership as a path toward it.[15]

In his sociological study of the Waxhaws region, historian Peter N. Moore suggests class distinctions between established settlers like Hill and Williams and more recent settlers fueled later political loyalties. By the 1770s, a second wave of Scots-Irish immigrants was pouring into the Waxhaws, arriving directly from Northern Ireland via Charleston, not down the Great Wagon Road. With few social ties to the established Scots-Irish population, these newcomers settled primarily in the far eastern portion of the Waxhaws, a region of poorer soils and few roads that was known as the "blackjack" area after a scrubby blackjack oak that thrived there. "Blackjack immigrants brought their poverty with them," writes Moore, "they immigrated with much smaller households than had the earlier Pennsylvania immigrants, giving them fewer headrights, less land, and fewer hands to help put their family farms on sound financial footing." And their brand of Presbyterianism tended to be less "evangelically inclined" than established Waxhaw congregations. Moore's research finds blackjack farmers were more likely to join the British, or remain neutral, than the established Scots-Irish population of the region. "In sum, the data from the Waxhaws point to a clear correlation between neighborhood length of residency and support for the Americans," he writes. "Blackjack residents made up a poorer, ethnically distinct, religiously 'dissenting' neighborhood whose growing population brought tensions to the community."[16]

However, the recently arrived were not necessarily the only backcountry settlers who remained loyal to the Crown. One of the most prominent backcountry leaders on either side of the conflict was Robert Cunningham, who remained a steadfast Loyalist throughout the war. Born probably in Ireland, Cunningham had migrated down the Great Wagon Road from Pennsylvania, settling with his three brothers in 1769 in the Little River District around modern-day Laurens, South Carolina. There he became a surveyor, justice of the peace, and militia captain, and "almost immediately he was looked on in his neighbourhood as a man of consequence," writes historian Ian Saberton. Though Cunningham opposed British taxation of the colonies "without their concurrence," he did not go so far "as to favor severing the constitutional ties between Britain and America, believing that it would lead to arbitrary, oppressive rule by the revolutionary party."[17]

Another prominent Loyalist in the Ninety Six District was Thomas Fletchall, who immigrated to South Carolina around 1760 and established a homestead on Fair Forest Creek in the Spartan District around modern-day Spartanburg, where he acquired 1,600 acres of land, operated a grist mill, and also served as a militia leader, magistrate, and coroner. Although older than Cunningham, Fletchall wielded considerable influence, later inducing many of the Fair Forest Creek settlement's Baptists to remain loyal to the Crown.[18]

Backcountry settlers relied on trade with Charleston for household necessities such as tea, lead, saltpeter (used both as a preservative for meat in its mineral state and as an ingredient in gunpowder), and more, but with little hard currency to acquire such items, most lived lives of yeoman farmers, producing for their own needs and living as self-sufficiently as possible. Little surprise then that when the low-country planters and their representatives in the Commons House of South Carolina's Assembly began to squabble with its royal administration over import laws and equitable representation, the backcountry mostly kept to itself.

Edgar depicts the conflict between South Carolina's Charleston gentry and her royal government as one of power, not trade policy. "The British government insisted that the governor and Royal Council had to agree to all expenditures and that the assembly could not appropriate money for any purpose outside South Carolina. It was a serious constitutional issue that threatened the hard-won prerogatives of the Commons House. Neither side would back down." Yet it is fair to say that trade and commerce became an important venue through which this power struggle was conducted. In 1769, a group of Charleston merchants signed an agreement of "Association and Non-importation," pledging to boycott most goods imported from England and refusing to trade with anyone not signing the agreement. Meanwhile, the Commons House effectively boycotted the English administration, refusing to endorse or support its mandates. "As a result, in 1771 royal government ground to a halt," writes Edgar. "Most South Carolinians simply ignored the British establishment and went about creating an alternative government."[19]

In 1773, these low-country dissidents formed the General Committee, an alternative government. At its meeting on July 6, 1774, the General Committee agreed to send five delegates to the Continental Congress meeting in Philadelphia, and later in 1774, it called for elections to South Carolina's First Provincial Congress, which convened in Charleston in January 1775. Out of 187 seats in the Provincial Congress, backcountry representatives were awarded only 55, despite representing 60 percent of South Carolina's white population. "The members of the low country elite were behaving toward the backcountry population with an imperiousness not unlike the manner in which British officialdom treated them," writes Edgar.[20]

BY THE SPRING OF 1775, WITH NEWS OF THE conflict at Lexington and Concord fought on April 19 sweeping through the colonies, South Carolina's Provincial Congress turned its attention to backcountry Loyalists like Cunningham and Fletchall. Earlier in the winter session, it had formed two infantry regiments to provide security for the Charleston region. In balloting for officers, Huguenot planter Francis Marion was elected a captain of the Second Regiment, and prominent low-country planter William Moultrie its colonel.

In June, the Provincial Congress formed a third regiment of mounted "Rangers." The Cherokees remained closely allied with the British and their agents, men such as Col. John Stuart, who had grown wealthy enough from his official contacts with the Cherokee to build a fine Charleston home on Tradd Street. Now the Provincial Congress was concerned these British agents would provoke the Cherokee into another attack on backcountry settlements. But a covert objective also was to keep backcountry Loyalists like Cunningham, Fletchall, and their followers in check, so officers for the ranger regiment were selected from backcountry districts. For its colonel, the Provincial Congress selected William Thomson, a highly respected militia leader from Amelia, in present-day Calhoun County. Running for one of its majors was Robert Cunningham, who lost the balloting to James Mayson. "Mayson got the Commission, which so exasperated the others that they immediately took the other side of the question," recalled Andrew Pickens decades later. Pickens believed if Cunningham had won the election, or been appointed colonel of the rangers, "we would not have had so violent an opposition to our cause."[21]

Meanwhile, on June 17, South Carolina's royal governor, William Campbell, arrived in Charleston Harbor to assume his new appointment. Campbell, we may recall, was one of those English sycophants who later in the war tried to persuade Dartmouth, North, and Germain of South Carolina's vast and ardent Loyalist population. He had served most recently as the royal governor of Nova Scotia and received the South Carolina appointment, in part, because of his marriage to Sarah Izard, the daughter of a prominent Charleston family. British officials hoped these connections would soothe animosities between South Carolina and the Crown. But the effort was too little too late, and after spending the summer squabbling with representatives of the Provincial Congress, Campbell fled Charleston on September 15, 1775, in a British warship, essentially surrendering the colony to its Whig administration.[22]

That summer, tensions ran high between those loyal to the Royal government and supporters of the Provincial Congress. At the beginning of its 1775 session, the Provincial Congress adopted new resolutions of "Association and Non-importation," which had been passed by the Continental Congress the previous October. Similar to earlier efforts to boycott English trade and goods, the "Continental Association" included provisions for enforcement by committee, who were authorized "attentively to observe the conduct of all persons touching the Association." These duties included administration of the "Association" pledge, essentially an oath of allegiance to the cause of American independence. The Continental Congress left individual colonies with considerable latitude on the formation of these committees, but many took on a sinister, Orwellian character, with citizens informing on one another, and those who refused the "Association" pledge subject to ostracism, abuse, and even exile. "The committees scrutinized and chastised those they suspected of violating Association rules," observes historian Holger Hoock. "In towns and counties across America, the committees fostered a dangerous climate that threatened psychological and physical violence."[23]

With its session drawing to a close in June 1775, South Carolina's Provincial Congress formed a Council of Safety to oversee security in the colony, including administration of the "Association" pledge. Essentially, this council acted as an executive committee while the Provincial Congress was not in session. Named president of this council was Henry Laurens, a prominent low-country planter, slave trader, and politician who would later serve as president of the Continental Congress. Also named to this council was William Henry Drayton, a firebrand Charleston lawyer who was an outspoken proponent of the Whig cause.

Elections to the next Provincial Congress were scheduled for August, so that summer the Council of Safety sent Mayson's Ranger company into the backcountry to keep Loyalist sentiment in check. Mayson was also ordered to seize a supply of gun powder stored in Augusta, ostensibly to protect it from Cherokee attack. But after securing the gunpowder, Mayson was arrested by Robert Cunningham, who accused him of stealing it from the royal government. During the confrontation, some of Mayson's regiment deserted to the Loyalist side. Meanwhile, every man of Thomas

Fletchall's Fair Forest militia regiment refused to sign the Association pledge at a muster in late July, undoubtedly influenced by Fletchall's opposition to it himself. "I am resolved, and do utterly refuse to take up arms against the king," Fletchall wrote to Laurens.[24]

Headstrong and ambitious, Drayton decided to address this backcountry turmoil himself, marching toward Ninety Six with a delegation including Richard Richardson to preach the principles of the Association while keeping an eye on the upcoming election. At the German settlements in Saxe Gotha, south of modern-day Columbia, South Carolina, Drayton was discouraged when not a single German settler attended his meeting. Though never a significant part of the South Carolina population, the state's German population primarily remained loyal to the Crown throughout the American Revolution, though most played no active role in the conflict.

Drayton's delegation then split into two. Richardson headed north, into the valley between the Broad and the Catawba, where most were eager to take the Association pledge. But Drayton had less luck at a meeting in Dutch Fork, between the Broad and Saluda Rivers, where both Robert Cunningham and Thomas "Burnfoot" Brown from nearby Augusta, Georgia, spoke against the Association and not a single man signed. Brown's unusual nickname came from an incident earlier that year, when he had refused the Association oath. In retaliation, a Whig mob tarred and feathered Brown's legs, after subduing him with a rifle blow to the head, then scalped him and burned his feet over a fire before carting him around town in humiliation.[25] Brown no doubt still bore the scars of his earlier torture when he showed up to ruin Drayton's meeting.

Meanwhile, Richardson crossed the Broad and visited the home of Thomas Fletchall on the evening of August 16. There, Brown and Cunningham also soon arrived. Though he received Richardson cordially, Fletchall complained that his resistance was the result of neglect and exploitation of South Carolina's "Gentlemen, as they are called," Charleston's planter and merchant class.

Again, refusing the Association pledge himself, Fletchall nevertheless agreed to muster the Upper Saluda militia to listen to its arguments. On August 23, Drayton appeared before them, but again Cunningham and Brown spoke in opposition, and again the crowd refused to sign the pledge. Discouraged by this violent reception, Drayton nevertheless found sympathetic audiences at his next three stops: at Lawson's Fork, in the Upper Spartan District just outside of modern-day Spartanburg; at Ninety Six; and at the nearby Long Canes settlement along the Savannah River, where he was received warmly by Andrew Pickens, a prominent leader of the Long Canes community.

Drayton now became convinced the key to subduing Loyalist sentiment in the backcountry was subduing its local leaders—most prominently Fletchall and Cunningham. Embodying the Patriot militia of Ninety Six, led by Gen. Andrew Williamson, and also Mayson's Ranger Regiment, he eventually organized a force of 1,200 men. Yet Fletchall, Brown, and Cunningham raised 2,200 Loyalist militia. The two sides seemed destined for armed conflict until their respective delegations negotiated the Treaty of Ninety Six, granting amnesty to "nonassociators," those who refused the Association pledge, as long as they remained neutral in any future conflict between England and South Carolina's Whigs. Fletchall, now maudlin and drunk, agreed to sign the treaty, but Cunningham refused and stormed away with sixty men.

Dated September 16, 1775, the Treaty of Ninety Six convinced many backcountry settlers to join the Whig side. But Cunningham remained opposed, rallying many of the backcountry's "King's Men" who shared his sentiment. Drayton now ordered his arrest, sending a small squad of militia soldiers to Cunningham's home, where he was caught unawares and quickly transported to a Charleston prison.[26]

Robert Cunningham's brother, Patrick, now mustered Loyalist elements of the Little River militia. And though they failed to rescue Robert, they remained embodied, patrolling up and down the Cherokee Path, eventually capturing a Patriot supply train intended as a peace offering for the Cherokees containing one thousand pounds of powder and two thousand pounds of lead. Meanwhile, Drayton was elected president of the Provincial Congress in early November 1775 and announced his intention to crush the King's Men between the Saluda and Broad Rivers. Returning to Ninety Six from the Provincial Congress, where he had been a delegate, Andrew Williamson called out the Whig members of the Ninety Six militia, who eventually set up a stockade just outside Ninety Six at a field on the property of Col. John Savage. On November 19, 1775, Williamson's Whig militia of approximately six hundred was attacked by Patrick Cunningham's Loyalist militia of 1,900. The shooting continued for three days, with only light casualties, until both sides agreed to a truce. Nevertheless, this Battle of Ninety Six is considered the first armed conflict of the American Revolution in South Carolina.[27]

With the backcountry still seething, and Drayton and his Whig allies in the Provincial Congress convinced there were more Loyalists in the backcountry than Whigs, Drayton ordered Richard Richardson to embody a militia expedition against Patrick Cunningham. With a force that eventually numbered five thousand, Richardson marched through the backcountry. Patrick Cunningham and his followers fled to a hiding place in the Great Cane Brake on the lower Reedy River, a luxuriant growth of river cane in what is now the southern portion of Greenville County. There, he was attacked on December 22 by Col. William Thomson's ranger regiment. The Loyalists were completely surprised, losing 6 wounded and killed, and 130 captured, although Patrick Cunningham got away.[28]

Following the Battle of the Great Cane Brake, Richardson disbanded his army. The weather brought snow, earning Richardson's expedition the name of The Great Snow Campaign, and although Patrick Cunningham remained at large, Richardson succeeded in capturing Thomas Fletchall, ten of his militia captains, and dozens of prominent backcountry Loyalists. Most significant, however, was the campaign's psychological impact. "The size of his corps, the greatest force ever seen in the back country, struck terror into the Loyalists," writes historian Robert D. Bass.[29] And Patrick Cunningham would be captured and imprisoned the following March, after the South Carolina government put a bounty on his head.[30]

Eventually, the Cunninghams, Fletchall, and other Loyalist prisoners would be released, but Whig persecutions against Loyalist supporters continued to disrupt the fabric of South Carolina society during the late 1770s. To further suppress Loyalist influence, the general assembly gerrymandered the Ninety Six District into Whig subdistricts, ensuring that both their elected and militia officials would be selected from Patriot supporters. And during the winter of 1777, the general assembly established an "oath of abjuration and allegiance," required by "all the late officers of the King of Britain" and all others suspected of "holding principles injurious to the rights of this State."

As with the Association oath endorsed by the Continental Congress two years earlier, this new oath was used to persecute Loyalist sympathizers, at the penalty of exile, confiscation of property, or worse. By spring, many of those who refused the oath, including natives and longtime residents, prepared to leave South Carolina. The following winter the general assembly passed an even more draconian oath requirement, An Assurance of Allegiance and Fidelity Act. According to this act, persons who failed to pledge allegiance to the Whig cause were ineligible to vote, hold office, serve on juries, acquire or convey property, use the courts, or practice their trades or professions.

William Creighton was a Charleston merchant who refused to take the oath. Exiled for this dissent, he was forced to sell a plantation and eighty slaves for £35,000 and sixteen thousand pounds of indigo before booking passage on a vessel bound for Bourdeaux, France, which was subsequently seized by British privateers. Though his assets were eventually restored, the indigo had lost a substantial portion of its market value, ruining him financially. Louisa Wells's Loyalist family was also exiled after refusing the oath. Three days after their departure on a chartered ship, Wells and her party were captured by the HMS *Rose* and escorted to New York, where their release was eventually determined by a British vice admiralty court, delaying their return to England by an excruciating three months. Lambert estimates perhaps as many as fifty low-country families eventually left South Carolina by spring 1778 because they refused to take the oath, most of them drawn from the region's Scottish community.[31]

Not all Loyalists simply packed up and left. Some formed their own partisan militia regiments or joined the regiments of others to fight for the Loyalist cause. After his torture and persecution by Whigs early in the conflict, Thomas "Burnfoot" Brown fled Augusta, Georgia, to Loyalist strongholds in East Florida, where he eventually raised his own Loyalist regiment called the King's Rangers. Lambert estimates as many as six hundred men from the backcountry of Georgia and the Carolinas reached East Florida by the end of 1778, with a substantial number of those South Carolinians. So many in fact, that British general Augustine Prévost formed the South Carolina Loyalists, a Provincial regiment comprised of South Carolina refugees.[32]

David Fanning was a member of the South Carolina Loyalist militia who fought at the Battle of Ninety Six in November 1775 and at the Battle of the Great Cane Brake that December. During the ensuing five years, Fanning either served with Loyalist partisans in Georgia and East Florida, or was in and out of jail in the Carolinas, persecuted by the Whigs for his Loyalist allegiances.[33]

Yet for every Loyalist who risked exile by refusing Whig pledges or joined partisan bands in the wilds of East Florida, there were thousands who simply acquiesced to Whig control, preferring silence to a political activism that could result in their ruin. "Presumably, the majority of Loyalists remained in their homes engaged in the routine pursuits of backcountry life, unwilling or unable to risk the exile from their families," agrees Lambert.[34]

One was Robert Cunningham, who returned to the life of a prominent backcountry citizen after his temporary imprisonment. Yet his status in the

Little River District remained undiminished, and in 1778, he was elected the district's senator in the South Carolina General Assembly election.

His opponent was James Williams, who by now had emerged as a leader of the local Whig militia. Tensions during the campaign ran high—in one campaign appearance, Williams was speaking before a group of people when he noticed Cunningham at his elbow. "You stand too near me," Williams reportedly complained. "I stand very well where I am," Cunningham retorted; fisticuffs ensued. According to one account, Williams's wife joined the fray, reportedly seizing Cunningham by his cue, the braid of hair at the back of his head. After Mrs. Williams was removed, the brawl continued "in Cunningham's favor."[35] Remarkably, Cunningham went on to win the election, despite Whig gerrymandering, but Williams nevertheless got the Senate seat because Cunningham refused the oath of allegiance necessary to assume office.

Indoctrinated by centuries of hyperbole and myth, today's America might easily believe the choice between Whig and Loyalist was clear. A tyrannical British king had imposed unjust sanctions—"Taxation without Representation"—and his dutiful American colonists had no other option but to seek their liberty. But certainly in South Carolina, as in other American colonies, history presents a more complicated story, with the abuses and discriminations of the Whigs, and their predecessors such as the Regulators, easily as excessive as that of a brutal and unsympathetic king. Allegiances during this period were complex, based not only on politics but also ethnic origin, class, prejudice, and local influence. And with the British occupation of South Carolina in 1780 eliminating the final shreds of civil society in the backcountry, these complexities would erupt into bloody civil war.

FIVE

A LION
ROUSED

I F MAY 1780 FOUND Charles Cornwallis preparing to take command of British army forces in the South, Thomas Sumter was enjoying the life of a country squire on his considerable South Carolina estate. In September 1778, Sumter had resigned his colonel's commission in the Continental army, returning full time to the roles of planter and politician while expanding his business and real estate ventures along the Santee River. By now he was forty-five, considered elderly for the time, and though he surely followed news of the British siege at Charleston, Sumter resisted calls to participate in the city's defenses that spring, perhaps indulging a sense of privilege already earned during years of service to the American cause and certainly nurturing one of stewardship to his small, fragile family.

Sumter's biographer Anne King Gregorie believes May 28, 1780, found Sumter residing at a summer home in the High Hills of the Santee, a geological anomaly of low-lying hills located north of the Santee River in what is modern-day Sumter County. For this was the day Banastre Tarleton and his Legion rode through the region in their furious pursuit of South Carolina governor-in-exile John Rutledge and Abraham Buford's Continentals. And as he passed through the Santee region, Tarleton sent small squads of dragoons searching for local Whig leaders.

According to tradition, Sumter left the house that day just before the arrival of British captain Charles Campbell, perhaps alerted to the approach of the Legion dragoons by his neighbors or slaves. But Sumter's paralytic wife, Mary, was still at the home, along with their only son, Tom Jr., age twelve. When Mary refused to reveal her husband's whereabouts, Campbell had his men pick her up in her chair and carry her to the yard, where she watched his men plunder her home.[1]

The use of fire had been adopted as a practical, if controversial, practice of certain British officers earlier in the war. Both Henry Clinton and Charles Cornwallis understood the negative implications of such practices, and in general, urged officers to avoid the wanton destruction and plundering of the countryside. But even they acknowledged its practice was useful, or perhaps unavoidable, in certain situations. And some British officers, convinced only "fire and sword" could bring the American countryside into submission, employed the tactic frequently, especially when far from the scrutiny of their senior commanders.[2]

Banastre Tarleton was among those who believed in the power of the torch, a conviction he shared with his junior officers. In some accounts, probably based on oral tradition, Sumter watched from the woods while the British looted his property, terrorized his family, and finally set his home ablaze. Outmanned, his own life in danger, there was little more he could do, except trust even the scourge of the British Provincial soldier would not harm a defenseless woman and child, if he witnessed the scene at all.

However, in the High Hills that day, the British Legion set fire to more than just a frontier home. Francis Marion biographer William James observed famously the Legion's raid on Sumter's property "roused the spirit of the lion," and Sumter biographer Robert D. Bass speculates Sumter was "inflamed against the invaders who had driven him from his family and home."[3] Ambition is not a notion conceived fully formed but evolves to the conditions in which it is tended. For a time, at least, it smolders. A lion roused, Sumter left the High Hills that same day, riding toward Salisbury, North Carolina, not to rally the people of a state, surely not intending to write his way onto the pages of history, but in pursuit only of that most common of human aspirations: revenge.

THE YOUNG THOMAS SUMTER WHO GREW UP on the banks of Preddy's Creek, near modern-day Charlottesville, Virginia, would have struggled to recognize himself as the forty-five-year-old country squire. And Sumter, the country squire, apparently had little interest in looking back on himself as the ragamuffin boy from Preddy's Creek.

Sumter was probably born there on August 14, 1734. According to family lore, his mother, Patience, was from a prosperous London family but eloped to America with a young husband from a lower social class, named either Thomas or William. Sumter's father may have established a mill at Preddy's Creek before his death, leaving Patience a widow with four children including young Thomas, a brother, and perhaps two sisters, though the records aren't clear. Patience took up midwifery to support her family. Sumter biographer Gregorie observes that, according to family accounts, Sumter "felt mortified at the idea of his low birth (his father being a miller, and his mother a mid-wife), and that he wished every thing connected with his early life to be forgotten."[4]

By the 1750s, young Thomas Sumter had been schooled in frontier life, working in the family farm and mill, though he had little formal education. Bass describes him as "slender, muscular, and wonderfully quick and powerful," though "only of medium height," with a passion for "gambling, cock-fighting, and horse racing."[5] Coupled with what seems to be a keen intellect and a natural charisma, these passions occasionally led Sumter to trouble, but like many an ambitious, rambunctious young man before and since, and with the French and Indian War brewing, he was soon enough drawn to military service.

Following the infamous "Braddock Expedition" of 1755, where George Washington, Horatio Gates, Daniel Morgan, and others were ambushed and defeated by a coalition of Native American and French forces in the wilderness near modern-day Pittsburgh, Pennsylvania, Sumter enlisted with the Virginia troops fighting for the British. In that service he served in several campaigns against the Native Americans and their French allies over the subsequent years. In 1761, Sumter joined an expedition to invade Cherokee territory under Col. Adam Stephen. But shortly after Stephen finished erecting Fort Robinson on the Holston River, at modern-day Kingsport, Tennessee, a Cherokee delegation arrived to bargain for peace.

As part of the peace treaty negotiated there on November 19, the Cherokee required an American officer be sent to their settlements to ensure their safety. Lt. Henry Timberlake volunteered for the assignment, and with him went his sergeant, Thomas Sumter. But first both Timberlake and Sumter loaded their canoe with trade goods, hoping to profit during their Cherokee sojourn. Sumter acquired his share of the goods with sixty pounds borrowed from Alexander McDonald. Accompanied by an interpreter named John McCormack, Sumter and Timberlake paddled away on the Holston River on November 28. Almost from the start, the journey was ill-fated—before reaching the Cherokee towns in late December, they were attacked by bears, endured starvation, lost most of their trade goods overboard, and almost drowned in the freezing river.

Yet they were greeted warmly by Cherokee chief Ostenaco and wintered in his village, Tomotley, on the Little Tennessee River south of modern-day Knoxville, where Sumter picked up some of the Cherokee language. That March, with Sumter and Timberlake's diplomatic mission drawing to a close, Ostenaco volunteered to escort the American's back to the Virginia settlements with a party of one hundred Cherokee warriors. By now, Virginia officials were eager to reestablish trade with the Cherokee after the cessation of the French and Indian War's hostilities. They greeted Ostenaco's delegation warmly and eventually conveyed them to Williamsburg, Virginia, where Virginia's lieutenant-governor Francis Fauquier, acting governor at the time, rolled out the proverbial red carpet in welcome.

During the feasting and negotiations that followed, Ostenaco encountered a portrait of King George III at William and Mary College. "Long have I wished to see the King my father," Ostenaco supposedly said. "This is his resemblance, and I am determined to see himself. I am near the sea. Never will I depart from it till I have obtained my desires."[6] Facing a diplomatic quandary, Fauquier managed to arrange a journey to England for Ostenaco, along with his fellow chiefs Conne Shote and Wooe Pigeon. Due to their relationship with the Cherokee, Timberlake and Sumter were recruited to travel with them to England as their attachés.

Sumter's journey to England would prove an eventful one. Dying on the voyage was the delegation's interpreter, William Shorey, leaving the role to Sumter and Timberlake with the smattering of Cherokee they had learned during their time with the tribe. The delegation arrived in England on June 16, 1762, and later that summer, Sumter struggled to interpret Ostenaco's heartfelt speech to the newly coronated King George III, then only twenty-four years old. Sumter "spoke softly, his eyes shifting from Cherokee to King and his ears catching every word of his Sovereign," interprets Bass. "As he stood before King George III, Sergeant Thomas Sumter was a long way from Preddy's Creek."[7]

As the visit progressed, Sumter and Timberlake bought sumptuous red uniforms, which they sported to pass themselves off as British officers while the delegation was squired around town for tours of Westminster Abbey, the Tower of London, and St. Paul's Cathedral. At a visit to Vauxhall Gardens, a crowd of ten thousand curious onlookers mobbed the Cherokee chiefs, and so many visitors called at their Suffolk Street quarters, eager for an audience, that servants eventually began charging admission.

The ship carrying the Cherokee delegation back to America was scheduled to be stationed on the southern coast, so British authorities sent them home via Charleston, instead of their embarkation port of Hampton Roads, Virginia, permitting Sumter to renegotiate the terms of his service contract. To accommodate the change, the adroit Sumter negotiated an extra commission of £150, with £100 due on arrival. The delegation arrived at Charleston on October 28, 1762, and impressed with Sumter's service, the Cherokees requested he accompany them on the journey back to their villages in what is now eastern Tennessee.

Sumter agreed and spent another winter among the Cherokee. While there, he learned that a French provocateur named Baron des Jonnes was agitating the Cherokee in the Overhill towns against the British. Sumter wanted to arrest him, but first he had to get permission from his Cherokee hosts. They agreed, but only if Sumter could subdue des Jonnes frontier-style, in unassisted, hand-to-hand combat. According to family tradition, Sumter whipped des Jonnes in a wrestling match and tied his subdued captive to his horse, then delivered him to British authorities.

Sumter then returned to Virginia, where in November 1763, he was placed in debtor's prison for the money he still owed Alexander McDonald for the trade goods he had acquired on credit two years before. Family lore said an old friend slipped the imprisoned Sumter a tomahawk and ten guineas, and with the use of "one or both," he escaped, fleeing to sanctuary back in South Carolina. By tradition, he spent some time in the Long Canes settlement on the Cherokee border, before opening a country store near Nelson's Ferry, an important Santee River crossing about sixty miles inland from Charleston along the main route into the northern portions of the colony.

How Sumter financed this new business venture is not entirely clear, although he seems to have been successful at negotiating an additional payment from South Carolina's royal administration, perhaps in return for escorting the Cherokee from Charleston back to their villages in eastern Tennessee. Though his source of capital remains a mystery, he chose his locale well, essentially on the border between South Carolina's low-country and the backcountry. "At the fork in front of his store converged most of the traffic between the capital and the frontier," writes Bass. "And a couple of miles behind it flowed the Santee, its surface dotted with canoes, rafts, and boats . . . around Sumter's store lived well-to-do hospitable folks, mostly Huguenot or Scotch-Irish, with large and fertile plantations. . . . Among these neighborly people Thomas Sumter was busy, selling, swapping, buying, and talking."[8]

By 1765, Sumter owned property and was affluent enough to mortgage three slaves, a pair of horses, and a new wagon to a neighbor for £1,000. In October 1766, he acquired two hundred acres on the south side of the Santee River adjacent to the estate of Charles Cantey, a prominent landowner in the region. And in 1767, the thirty-three-year-old Sumter married Cantey's daughter, Mary.

Perhaps as much as eleven years older than Sumter, Mary had been previously wed to another prosperous planter named William Jameson, inheriting a considerable portion of Jameson's £19,000 estate after his death in 1766, the rest going to Jameson's sister in Ireland. Though he was clearly astute enough to recognize its economic advantages, Sumter's marriage to Mary seems an affectionate one, and on August 30, 1768, in what was probably Mary's forty-fifth year, she bore him a son named Thomas Jr., who would be Sumter's only known descendent to survive into adulthood. A daughter named Mary, born in 1771, was said to have died when she was only eight months old.

Fueled by Mary's inheritance and his own industry, fired by ambition, Sumter now prospered. On the Great Savannah in St. Mark's Parish, north of the Santee River, Sumter built a fine new home, probably on the plantation Mary had inherited from Jameson. Nearby at Jack's Creek, along the road to Camden, he built a sawmill and gristmill, then a larger store to replace the first one, all the while furiously acquiring and trading real estate. Records researched by Gregorie show he obtained 2,400 acres by grant between 1770 and 1774. And in 1774, he advertised for sale a property of 13,300 acres in St. Mark's Parish, "which in a comparatively settled country is remarkable for a man who had not owned an acre ten years before."[9]

Sumter appears too busy and ambitious during this point in his life to be engaged much in South Carolina politics. Just a day's ride from Charleston on horseback, he could easily travel to the city to attend to his legal matters, making the complaints of the Regulators and those who believed the Charleston gentry ignored legal administration and law enforcement in the backcountry mostly irrelevant to his own circumstances. But later in life, he recalled that it was during his visits to Charleston that he "first saw and felt the effects of concerted and orderly associations of men in resisting and restraining usurped power, and unconstitutional abuses of power."[10]

Yet for the time being it was business and real estate that demanded Sumter's attention, not politics. In one real estate development enterprise, he recruited residents from his childhood home among the Virginia foothills to settle property he owned on the Santee. Of the initiative, an itinerant preacher in 1767 observed Sumter had "thirty families" settled near his plantation and store. But Sumter was too astute to ignore politics altogether, and by 1773, after the region around Nelson's Ferry had been incorporated into the Camden district by the latest round of judicial redistricting, he was appointed a justice of the peace, which was then an important regional position of legal authority.

By the election for South Carolina's First Provincial Congress in 1774, "Squire" Sumter was a man of status and means. Backed by his powerful relatives in the Cantey family, Sumter was elected to represent the Camden District east of the Wateree. Recall this was a dissident body, not authorized by South Carolina's royal administration, though nevertheless acting as the colony's de facto government. It was also the first South Carolina legislative assembly with representatives from the backcountry, which included Sumter's Santee settlement. During the first congressional session in January 1775, Sumter probably became acquainted with many who would go on to prominent roles in the American Revolution, including John Rutledge, William Moultrie, Richard Richardson, Andrew Williamson, and Francis Marion.

Conflict was in the air, and though the meager records of the First Provincial Congress don't recognize the voice of Thomas Sumter, he was certainly exposed to a hot debate between its Whig and Loyalist representatives, including administration of the resolutions of "Association and Non-importation" recently called for by the Continental Congress. It was during the second legislative session that summer that the Provincial Congress authorized the three regiments to protect Whig interests, two infantry regiments, and one regiment of "mounted rangers" primarily intended to patrol the backcountry, subduing both Cherokee and Loyalist. This "ranger" regiment was the same one for which Robert Cunningham lost the election to major, perhaps transforming him into the colony's staunchest Loyalist militia leader for the remainder of the war.

Instead, James Mayson was elected its major, serving under the overall command of Col. William Thomson. Like Robert Cunningham, Moses Kirkland was another prominent backcountry politician and planter from the Ninety Six District who lost the major's ballot. Kirkland was instead named a captain, but as with Cunningham, his loyalties were in flux. And when the ranger company was assigned to guard a supply of gun powder stored in Augusta, Georgia, during the summer of 1775, Kirkland was among those who conspired with Robert Cunningham to stage the shipment's capture, then defect to the Loyalist side.

Following this defection, Kirkland recommended Sumter as his own replacement to serve as captain in the ranger company. The nomination from a known Loyalist sympathizer briefly cast a pall of suspicion on Sumter's political allegiance. It was only after Andrew Williamson's Patriot militia of 600 was attacked by Patrick Cunningham's Loyalist militia of 1,900 at the Battle of Ninety Six on November 19, 1775, that concerns over Sumter's loyalties were finally discarded and his officer's commission in Thomson's Ranger Regiment was approved.[11]

Sumter joined the Rangers in time for the final stages of Richard Richardson's "Snow Campaign," participating in the arrest of Thomas Fletchall and, probably, in the Battle of the Cane Brakes on December 22, 1775, when Robert Cunningham's brother, Patrick, escaped into temporary exile. But with Fletchall captured and snowy weather setting in, Richardson disbanded the "Snow Campaign" shortly after the Battle of the Cane Brakes, and Sumter returned to his Santee estate after only a month's service with the Rangers. However, this brief service solidified Sumter's status as a trusted Whig officer. In February 1776, the Provincial Congress decided to raise two more state regiments, and Thomas Sumter was commissioned a lieutenant colonel in the second one.

Usually a talented recruiter and motivator of men, with some notable exceptions, Sumter immediately drew £3,000 from the South Carolina treasury and headed toward the Catawba Indian Nation near the Waxhaws to recruit for his new regiment. Unlike today's military, where recruitment is a specialized profession, eighteenth-century officers were primarily responsible for recruiting their own soldiers. The previous year, the Catawbas had sent a delegation to Charleston seeking an update on the emerging conflict with England. "They had been told different stories and they came down to know the truth," recounted William Moultrie.[12] Sumter recalled that during that visit the Catawba delegation had expressed an interest in joining the fight. Recalling their interest, Sumter successfully recruited during his trip several Catawba braves for his new South Carolina regiment, as well as others from the Camden and New Acquisition districts. Stephen McElhaney was a seventeen-year-old recruit from the Waxhaws who enlisted with Sumter on March 1, 1776, for a fifteen-month term and recalled quartering at Ten Mile Springs near Charleston with Sumter's regiment for the following two months.

Sumter's new commission corresponded with South Carolina's first serious threat of the war, the first British attack on Charleston. On May 31, 1776, the British fleet was sighted off Dewees Island, "and the next day, a wretched rainy day, it came to anchor fifty sail strong off the harbor bar," writes Gregorie.[13] During the subsequent British attack, Sumter's South Carolina regiment campaigned with Thomson's Rangers, engaging in a few skirmishes with British expeditionary detachments in the weeks leading up to the battle. During the battle itself, on June 28, 1776, Sumter and Thomson's regiments manned a redoubt at Bolton's Landing on Breach Inlet, opposite the main British amphibious assault on Long Island (now known as the Isle of Palms). In a memoir, Thomson recalled the enemy was so close his men might have shaken hands with them, if they were so disposed, although Bass writes that "Sumter and his riflemen watched enviously," from Bolton's Landing, while the main thrust of the battle occurred nearby at Fort Moultrie on Sullivan Island.[14]

With the British temporarily driven away from the South after their defeat at Charleston in the Battle of Sullivan's Island, South Carolina next turned its attention to the Cherokee, who were again threatening war on the western frontier. Accounts from the nineteenth and early twentieth century often report the Cherokee War of 1776, or what is also referred to as the Second Cherokee War, was the result of a coordinated British strategy to agitate the Cherokee against American settlers on the western frontier while they attacked from the coast. True, the British maintained an active network of Cherokee agents, including John Stuart, the British superintendent for Indian Affairs, who had been forced to take refuge in St. Augustine, Florida, after South Carolina's royal governor William Campbell fled Charleston in September 1775, along with his lieutenant Alexander Cameron, who had married into a prominent Cherokee family and lived many years among the Overhill settlements on the lower reaches of the Little Tennessee River in what is now eastern Tennessee.

However, modern scholarship finds little evidence to suggest Stuart and Cameron were active in agitating the Cherokee in 1776, and some evidence even suggests Cameron may have attempted to stop or at least delay the

Cherokee attacks. A more likely explanation is that the Cherokees were influenced by a delegation of northern tribes, including the Iroquois, Ottawa,
Shawnee, Delaware, that had visited them that spring. Agitated by increasing encroachment on their land, this tribal confederation wanted to take
advantage of the conflict between the Americans and British to defend
their territorial boundaries. Although some Cherokee resisted the northern
delegation's argument for war, others found it enticing, and beginning in
July 1776, a faction of Cherokee warriors began raiding American settlements up and down the western frontier in Georgia, Virginia, and the Carolinas.[15]

In South Carolina, Cherokees attacked settlements on the Tyger River
and the Long Canes District along the Savannah River. Rather than sow
further dissent between the Whigs and Loyalists, however, the Cherokee
War actually united South Carolina settlers from both sides against a common cause, at least temporarily. When Maj. Andrew Williamson called out
the militia of Ninety Six to retaliate against the Cherokee, Robert Cunningham, newly released after eight months in a Charleston jail, was but
one prominent Loyalist who attempted to join the expedition, although his
service was rejected by Williamson.

In two expeditions during August and September 1776, Williamson
and his militia, including Capt. Andrew Pickens, destroyed thirty-two
towns and villages in the Cherokee Lower and Valley settlements in eastern
Georgia and western North Carolina, defeated Cherokee war parties in five
battles, and scorched Cherokee fields, destroying crops, orchards, and livestock. Sumter and Thomson's regiments were ordered to assist Williamson
in early August. On August 12, Sumter drew £1,500 for recruiting expenses
and again traveled to the upper Catawba River valley to recruit again among
the Waxhaws, the New Acquisition District, and the Catawba Indian Nation. On September 12, he arrived in Williamson's camp with 270 men, in
time to participate in the latter part of Williamson's brutal campaign. Similar expeditions by North Carolina and Virginia militia decimated the upper
Cherokee towns, forcing the Cherokee into a peace treaty that ceded all of
their lands east and south of the Blue Ridge Mountains.[16]

Sumter's biographers do not describe his thoughts about participating
in such wanton destruction against the people with whom he had enjoyed
close associations, even friendships, almost twenty years before. The relationship between the Cherokee and the European settlers on the western
frontier in the seventeenth and eighteenth centuries is too complex for convenient analysis here, but Sumter's ambivalence about his ties to them seems

typical for the time, like others such as Andrew Pickens and the Patriot militia leader Elijah Clarke who were capable of both fellowship and almost inconceivable violence against their Cherokee neighbors.

It was while fighting the Cherokee that Sumter and his regiment were matriculated into the Continental army, when the South Carolina General Assembly voted to place its six regiments of state troops in the Continental establishment in September 1776.[17] With the change in status, Sumter was now a colonel of the Continental army, commanding the 6th Regiment of the South Carolina Continental Line. However, with the Cherokee defeated and the British temporarily chased back to New York, Sumter's new status coincided with a temporary cessation of hostilities in South Carolina. By November 1776, Sumter was back at his Santee River plantation, resuming the business and political roles of a prosperous planter. Although Sumter remained a colonel in the Continental army, his military duties were intermittent during the following two years. Sumter's 6th Regiment campaigned against Loyalists around Savannah, and in northern Florida in 1777 and 1778, and conducted garrison duty in Charleston for part of that time, but after the Cherokee campaign, they never fired their rifles in action during this period, despite marching hundreds of miles through difficult coastal terrain.

The activity took a toll on the now middle-aged Sumter, whose focus increasingly turned to family and business interests. He suffered a bout of malaria during this time. Mary's health had always been fragile, but during this period she became permanently disabled, probably the victim of a stroke. In September 1778, Sumter resigned his Continental army commission, resuming the life of a planter and politician, serving in the South Carolina General Assembly in 1779 and expanding his business and real estate ventures along the Santee River. When the British attacked Charleston again in May 1780, Sumter stayed home, keeping a watch on his property and fragile family. But it was a peace destined to be ruined by the torch of "Bloody Ban's" British Legion.[18]

SIX

IN THE
RIGHT

I N THE HEART OF CHARLESTON'S famed Historic District is an unassuming home at 104-106 Tradd Street. It sits just a few blocks away from "Rainbow Row" and Battery Park, with views overlooking Charleston Harbor to Fort Moultrie, far in the distance, where the British navy was dealt a stunning defeat in the summer of 1776. The home is privately owned and not opened for tours, and so the location is perhaps easy to overlook, although the National Register of Historic Places reports the house is "considered to be the finest example in the southern colonies of a three-story, Georgian, frame town home."[1] Though the home's double-deck porch on its west side and the octagonal frame wing on its northwest corner were added in the eighteenth century, today it looks much as it did when originally constructed in 1772—the fan-lighted entrance flanked by Corinthian columns, original dog-ear trim highlighting the first- and second-floor windows on the street façade.

It was built and originally owned by Col. John Stuart, then an important official in England's royal administration of her American colonies. In 1761, Stuart was named superintendent of Indian affairs for the Southern District of North America, England's chief Native American agent and administrator in the South. "The salary and perquisites of this position enabled Stuart to become a substantial indigo planter and slaveholder on Lady's Island near Beaufort and owner of a handsome house in Charleston," writes historian Robert Stansbury Lambert.[2]

But Stuart was forced to flee Charleston in 1775 during the prelude to the American Revolution, when those loyal to King George III and his royal agents were subject to increasingly strident persecutions and abuse, administered by the supporters of South Carolina's independence, then known as "Whigs," the term perhaps derived from a Scottish word for sour milk and dating back to the heated struggle to exclude James, Duke of York (and afterward James II), from succession to the British Crown. Originally, the word "connoted nonconformity and rebellion," a usage it retained proudly in the American Revolution.[3]

By 1780, the home was occupied by Capt. Alexander McQueen, an officer in the Continental army, and by traditional accounts it was here that McQueen invited his fellow Continental officer Francis Marion to a dinner party on or around March 19.

From a modern perspective, it was perhaps a curious time for a party. On February 10, 1780, a British armada had been sighted off the Charleston coast, and a month later, the city was furiously preparing for an attack by Sir Henry Clinton, the commanding officer of the British army in America. According to his orderly book, Lt. Col. Marion, commandant of South Carolina's Second Regiment of the Continental Line, probably spent the day with his troops at the "Hornworks," the three-tiered artillery works guarding Charleston's landward gate on King Street opposite British siegeworks.[4]

But in an age before television and the internet, in a society as robust as Charleston, then one of the most cosmopolitan places in all of North America, social gatherings were the de rigueur entertainment of the time, and siege or no siege, the societal gears ground on. Likely, Marion dreaded this social obligation. Still a bachelor now well into his forties, he by all accounts preferred the comforts and settled routines of his farm on the Santee River. Born into a close-knit family of French Huguenots, known for their humility and modest lifestyles, Marion was a misfit in the rigid social hierarchies of Charleston, which demanded the conventionalities of a raucous dinner party even in times of war.[5]

But after serving mostly in and around Charleston these last five years, Marion was by now a part of these hierarchies, whether he embraced them or not, and perhaps the invitation to McQueen's that night was one he could not refuse. Yet who among us has not longed to escape from such obligations once trapped there? And as McQueen locked the home's downstairs doors after dinner, and the night turned to the interminable round of booze-soaked toasts "to liberty" that were a custom of the time, his guests practically obliged to get rip-roaring drunk, the "abstemious" Marion looked for his.

According to tradition, one of those windows "flanked with dog-ear trim" still stood open. "Finding, at last, that there was no other way of escaping a debauch, but by leaping out of one of the windows of the dining room, which was on the second story, he bravely undertook it," write his biographers Peter Horry and M. L. Weems. "It cost him, however," and Marion broke one of his "badly formed" ankles in the fall to the ground below.[6]

Myths are curious things, their transformative power often dependent on their more arcane details, and in the crumpled body of Francis Marion, the oddball American officer, lying on the ground beside Tradd Street, we find the origin of the "Swamp Fox," the famed guerilla commander, star of books and screen, hero of the American Revolution. For if Marion had not broken his ankle in that fall, he undoubtedly would've been captured and taken prisoner of war with the other 2,500 Continental officers and soldiers when Charleston finally surrendered on May 12, 1780. Instead, he was carried out of town on a litter, probably sometime around April 12, when Continental general Benjamin Lincoln, commanding the American defenses in Charleston, ordered "all officers who were unfit for duty" to "quit the garrison and retire to the country."[7]

Presumably, the sober and dignified Marion was embarrassed by these circumstances. But like other Americans forced to flee British persecution, if not arrest, after Charleston's surrender, Marion would not be daunted. He escaped the city in disgrace, true, but in so doing he secured his place in history.

WHILE THOMAS SUMTER RACED OFF TO North Carolina in May of 1780, his fury enflamed by the British abuse of his family and home, Francis Marion was in hiding, still nursing his broken ankle.

Technically, Marion remained commandant of South Carolina's Second Regiment, although the distinction mattered little now, as the majority of his men had surrendered on May 12, 1780. Many of these enlisted prisoners would eventually die of disease and starvation while confined in the rank, filthy holds of prison ships anchored in Charleston Harbor—General William Moultrie, himself taken prisoner that day, noted that by the beginning of 1781, only about 1,400 of the 2,500 Continental prisoners at Charleston remained available for exchange.[8] Despite his disgrace and the capture of his regiment, Marion still held his lieutenant colonel commission, and he planned to rejoin the Continental army at their new headquarters in North Carolina as soon as his ankle was sufficiently healed.

Born during the winter of 1732, Marion was now forty-eight years old, three years older than Sumter, and following Charleston's surrender, he went into hiding among the farms and plantations of his French Huguenot relatives on the Santee River, not far from Thomas Sumter's own estate.[9]

The Huguenots were French Protestants, persecuted after the Edict of Nantes, which had guaranteed their religious rights, was revoked by Louis XIV in 1685. Over the next decade, as many as 400,000 Huguenots fled their home country, including a small colony of approximately 1,500 who arrived in South Carolina, where a smaller colony of Huguenots was already established. The early naturalist John Lawson wrote memorably of this Huguenot community in his famous travelogue *A New Voyage to Carolina*, one of the first written accounts of the Carolina interior, documenting his 1701 journey from Charleston to North Carolina's Pamlico Sound.

By the time Lawson arrived there, many of these Huguenots, including the grandparents of Francis Marion, had established a small settlement on the Santee River, in what was then the South Carolina frontier.[10] The Huguenots preferred simpler lifestyles than their English counterparts, living modestly in spartan homes even though many grew quite wealthy. Describing his brief visit with the Huguenot settlement on the Santee, "not above 36 Miles" from Charleston "by way of Land," Lawson wrote:

Many of the French follow a trade with the Indians, living very conveniently for that interest. Here are about seventy families seated on this river, who live as decently and happily as any planters in these southward parts of America. The French being a temperate, industrious people, some of them bringing very little effects, yet by their endeavours and mutual assistance among themselves . . . have outstript our English, who brought with them larger Fortunes, though (as it seems) less endeavour to manage their Talent to the best advantage. 'Tis admirable to see what Time and Industry will (with God's Blessing) effect.[11]

Lawson went on to describe the Huguenot community as "kind, lovable, affable people," though they wondered "about our undertaking such a voyage through a country inhabited by none but savages."[12] Lawson did not record any interaction with the grandparents of Francis Marion, though he did spend a night with a Mons. Eugee, probably an ancestor of future South Carolina general Isaac Huger, whose last name is pronounced the way it was phonetically spelled by Lawson (You-gee).

Despite a separatist nature, the Huguenots assimilated into South Carolina society over the course of the eighteenth century. By the time of Francis Marion's birth in 1732, his parents, Esther and Gabriel Marion, had moved to St. John's Parish and established a plantation called Goatfield near the small modern-day community of Cordesville, about thirty miles north of Charleston.[13]

Francis was the youngest of Esther and Gabriel's six children. "I have it from good authority, that this great soldier, at his birth was not larger than a New England Lobster," writes Marion's colleague and later biographer, Peter Horry, a "puny appearance" characterized by malformed knees and ankles that, Horry reports, Marion retained through much of his youth.[14]

Describing Marion at age forty-eight, William Dobein James, who also knew him personally, wrote: "He was rather below the middle stature of men, lean and swarthy. His body was well set, but his knees and ankles were badly formed. . . . He had a countenance remarkably steady; his nose was aquiline; his chin projecting; his forehead was large and high, and his eyes black and piercing."[15]

Apparently not much resemblance to Leslie Nielsen, the actor who played Marion memorably in an eight-episode *Walt Disney* miniseries that ran originally from 1959–1961, nor that of Mel Gibson, whose 2000 American Revolution saga, *The Patriot*, was loosely based on Marion's life. Luckily, perhaps, given James's unflattering description, no portrait of Marion taken from life is known to exist, leaving later artists with the artistic license to depict him as they please, with some taking a more romanticized approach than James's description would suggest.

When Marion was no more than six, his family moved to a plantation on Winyah Bay in Prince George Parish, near Georgetown, South Carolina. It was here that Marion spent the majority of his youth, perhaps receiving some rudimentary education. As a fifteen-year-old, Marion tried his hand at sea craft, shipping aboard a schooner bound for the West Indies, but the voyage ended in disaster—when the schooner was reportedly damaged by a whale and abandoned at sea, Marion and the rest of the small crew endured a torturous seven-day journey in a lifeboat back to land. This horrific experience appeared to cure the young Marion of his wanderlust, and he settled into a conventional life of planting and hunting. Biographer Hugh Rankin reports that when Marion's father died in 1750, it was Francis who assumed management of the family property, despite his status as the family's youngest son.[16]

Marion's militia service appears to have begun on January 31, 1756, when he and his brother, Gabriel, enlisted in the militia company of the Upper St. John Parish, though he saw little active service until 1761. That year, Marion was commissioned a lieutenant in the militia regiment of Capt. William Moultrie and marched to join the expedition of British lieutenant colonel James Grant against the Cherokees in the backcountry frontier in the First Cherokee War.

As described earlier, the brutalities of Grant's expedition included the burning of approximately fifteen Cherokee towns and the complete destruction of their crops. Grant later boasted he drove five thousand Cherokee into the mountains to starve.[17] Noteworthy here, however, was the obvious military leadership of Francis Marion. Although he had never before been under fire, Marion was chosen to lead a mission to clear a pass near the Cherokee town of Echoe where a previous detachment under the command of Lt. Col. Archibald Montgomerie had been ambushed. Sure enough, the Cherokee ambushed again, though Marion remained steady, pushing his men forward despite twenty-one casualties among his small unit of only thirty men, with the main body of Grant's force following close behind.

"Feed fights" was a term used to describe the white settler practice of destroying Native American crops at a point in the harvest season when it was too late to plant new ones, subjecting its victims to a winter of starvation. The historian Holger Hoock equates this practice with a form of genocide.[18] The Grant expedition excelled at this practice though it nevertheless brought together several South Carolinians who would go on to prominent roles in the American Revolution, among them Henry Laurens, Isaac Huger, Andrew Williamson, and Andrew Pickens. And these men were now acquainted with the service and cool courage of Francis Marion. Of this period, Marion's captain, William Moultrie, would write of him, "He was an active, brave and hardy soldier, and an excellent partisan officer," and his biographer Hugh Rankin adds "accounts of his behavior had filtered back, and from this time on he was accorded greater respect by the people along the Santee."[19]

After the Grant expedition, Marion returned to a life of planting and farming on his family property, accumulating enough wealth to purchase his own plantation in 1773. The property was located on the Santee River, just four miles below Eutaw Springs, a natural spring that flowed into the Santee, not far from Nelson's Ferry and the property of Thomas Sumter. Marion called his plantation Pond Bluff because of a pond at the foot of a bluff facing the river, and for history's sake we note that he owned slaves and employed slave labor on his farm.

Little else is known about Francis Marion's life in the period between the First Cherokee War and the American Revolution. He remained a bachelor and was apparently content living the life of a modest farmer, for there is no record of his serving in political roles until the elections for the First Provincial Congress in 1774, when both Francis and his brother, Job, were elected delegates from St. John's Parish. But his military service during the First Cherokee War was apparently still well remembered, for when the Provincial Congress voted to raise three regiments of state troops in the summer of 1775, Francis Marion was elected a captain of the Second Regiment, under overall command of William Moultrie.[20] The officers for these new regiments were assigned seniority according to the ballots they received. Marion was tied for third overall, and in the Second Regiment was ranked second captain.

Peter Horry was voted fifth captain of the Second Regiment. Like Marion, Horry was born to a family of Huguenot rice planters on Winyah Bay and later acquired property on the Santee River. Born in 1743 or 1744 (the records aren't clear), Horry was approximately twelve years younger than Marion, though the two would go on to form a close relationship during the American Revolution, with Horry serving as one of Marion's most trusted officers. Today, Horry may be best remembered for the biography of Marion he published in 1809 titled *The Life of General Francis Marion*, written in collaboration with Mason Locke "Parson" Weems, a popular author of the time. By then, Weems was well-known for his biography of George Washington, which included popular but unsubstantiated accounts of Washington's early life such as the chopping down of the cherry tree.[21]

With little literary skill of his own, Horry turned over to Weems a vast collection of Marion-related documents and letters, along with a simply written memorial. True, he had given Weems permission to "embellish the work," but he was infuriated with the liberties Weems took with the finished product. "You have carved and mutilated it with so many erroneous statements your embellishments, observations, and remarks, must necessarily be erroneous as proceeding from false grounds," Horry later fumed to Weems, upon reading the published work. "Can you suppose I can be pleased with reading particulars (though so elevated, by you) of Marion and myself, when I know such never existed."[22] Accordingly, the work is used sparingly here, except for its references to Marion's outlook and character, or when its anecdotes are too delicious to resist, such as his characterization of the infant Marion as "not larger than a New England lobster." Yet despite its embellishments, Horry and Weems's work played a significant role in transforming Marion's remarkable military achievements into the American myth of the "Swamp Fox" still venerated today.

This exercise in mythmaking, however, was still decades away. For now, Marion and Horry were junior officers in South Carolina's newly formed Second Regiment, a body with a strong mythology of its own. After receiving his captain's commission, Marion returned to St. John's Parish, where he recruited among the Huguenots, Scots-Irish, and English along the Santee, Black, and Pee Dee Rivers. For a taciturn, introverted man, Marion was a surprisingly talented recruiter, though he lacked Sumter's personal charisma, and he was able to recruit sixty men for the Second Regiment, among them his nephew, Gabriel. But soon enough he was back in Charleston, preparing to defend the city in the winter and spring of 1776 against a rumored English attack.

It was while helping his commandant, William Moultrie, construct defenses at the mouth of Charleston Harbor that Marion received a promotion to major. That January, Moultrie was ordered by the Council of Safety to make a flag "for the purpose of signals" from the coastal defenses he was constructing, though there "was no national or state flag at that time." Moultrie was inspired by the men of the First and Second Regiments, "who wore a silver crescent on the front of their caps." Though its origins are unclear, the crescent was probably inspired by the crescent-shaped "gorgets" worn as ornamental, symbolic accessories on military uniforms of the time, a derivation of the earlier crescent-shaped gorgets worn as armor to protect the neck and throat during the medieval era. At approximately the same time, Moultrie received a large shipment of dark blue material, and so a famous symbol of South Carolina was born. "I had a large blue flag made with the crescent in the dexter corner, to be in uniform with the troops: This was the first American flag which was displayed in South Carolina," Moultrie recalled. The flag's association with the Whig concept of "Liberty" perhaps came from the British, whose navy was then plying the waters off Charleston Harbor, keeping a close watch on Patriot activities. "They said it had the appearance of a declaration of war," Moultrie recalled, with British captain Thornborough of the war sloop *Tamar* declaring it "an insult, and a flag of defiance."[23]

That Marion still wore the crescent symbol on his own hat during his days as a partisan, or guerilla, commander, we shall soon have eyewitness accounts. Surely, he wore it proudly as he and his Second Regiment participated in the construction of the soon-to-be-famous Fort Sullivan on the south end of Sullivan's Island, guarding the northern mouth of Charleston Harbor. The walls facing the harbor were constructed of two parallel rows of logs, spaced sixteen feet apart and cut from the spongy Palmetto tree (*sabal palmetto*) native to the South Carolina coast, the space between rows then filled with sand.

Though its rear defenses were awkward and unfinished on June 28, 1776, the day of the British assault, Fort Moultrie, as it was now called, in honor of its commanding officer, contained several pieces of artillery, though only limited gunpowder. The men under Marion's command were temporarily converted to an artillery unit and manned an artillery battery on Fort Moultrie's left side that day. Firing slowly and deliberately due to the lack of gunpowder, the guns of Fort Moultrie were nevertheless deadly, disabling the British sloop *Bristol* and defending Charleston Harbor so furiously the British naval attack eventually withdrew.

In one account, during a lull in the fighting that day, Marion led a small party of soldiers to remove powder from the armed schooner *Defence* then lying disabled in Stop Gap Creek. In another famous anecdote from the battle, Sgt. William Jasper of the Second Regiment raced outside the fort to recover the Moultrie flag, which had been blown onto the ground in front of the fort by a British cannonball. Fastening the flag to a sponge staff used to swab the inside of the cannons, Jasper climbed back into the fort and lifted the flag above its walls, thrilling the townspeople watching the battle from the Charleston battery, who feared the garrison had struck its colors.[24]

During the attack, Fort Moultrie's walls of sand and palmetto logs absorbed at least seven thousand British cannonballs, leading to a loss of ten killed and twenty-three wounded in the Second Regiment, but preserving the fate of the city it defended. Meanwhile, Henry Clinton and Charles Cornwallis's amphibious assault force attempted to attack Fort Moultrie's inferior rear defenses. Clinton had chosen to land his force on adjacent Long Island based on an unsubstantiated intelligence report that the channel between the two islands could easily be forded. The attack failed, however, when the British found the channel too deep to cross on foot, leaving Clinton and his men stranded on the wrong side.[25]

Thanks largely to Fort Moultrie's defense at the mouth of Charleston Harbor, the day turned to a glorious American victory, with the defeated British fleet slipping away in the night, and Clinton left fuming on Long Island. The next day, Marion and the Second Regiment marched in parade in front of Continental general Henry Lee. A few days later, on July 4, while the Continental Congress far away in Philadelphia was declaring America's independence from England, John Rutledge, president of South Carolina's Provincial Congress, inspected the garrison at Fort Moultrie and presented to Sgt. Jasper his personal short sword. The regiment was also presented with an "Elegant" set of "Collours" crafted by Mrs. Barnard Elliot, whose words Marion recorded in his orderly book: "Your gallant behavior in Defense of Liberty & your Country Entitles you to the Highest Honours, Accept these two Standards as Reward Justly due to your Regiment & I make not the Least Doubt under heavens protection you will stand by them as Long as they can wave in the Air of Liberty."[26]

Even if Marion had not gone onto his career as a partisan general and master of guerilla tactics, his participation in this Battle of Sullivan's Island would have been enough to cement a place for him in South Carolina lore, thanks in part to the battle's association with South Carolina's distinctive state flag. Perhaps due to their important role at Fort Moultrie, Marion and the Second Regiment were spared duty in the Second Cherokee War and the brutal atrocities of the Williamson expedition. Instead, Marion and the Second remained on the coast, where they were matriculated into the Continental army later that fall. As part of the transition from state troops to Continental ones, Marion was promoted to lieutenant colonel of the Second Regiment, while Peter Horry was promoted to major. For the following two years, Marion and his men were mostly stationed around Charleston, where Marion earned a reputation as a tough but fair disciplinarian, requiring his men to parade and attend church regularly and maintain an orderly, groomed appearance.

"Francis Marion showed an instinctive feeling for discipline," writes Bass, with his officers apparently receiving his most strident attention.[27] "The truth is, Marion wished his officers to be gentlemen. And whenever he saw one of them acting below that character, he would generously attempt his reformation," agrees Horry, who attributes to Marion the unique characteristic of being that rare officer who could maintain both strict discipline and the respect and regard of his troops. Of the leadership of his men, Horry writes, "he seemed to come forward to the discharge of them with the familiarity and alertness of one . . . who was a born soldier. . . . Indeed, I am not afraid to say that Marion was the 'architect' of the second regiment."[28]

During this period there was a slight change in the regiment's uniforms, when Gen. Moultrie ordered that all officers were to acquire leather caps according to a pattern developed by a saddler in Charleston named Callahan. Also during this time, Marion developed one of his more curious habits. Under Moultrie's command, it was standard practice for the men of the Second Regiment to be issued regular portions of vinegar to be drunk for some presumed medicinal value. From this time forward, Marion's favorite drink became a mixture of vinegar and water, sometimes called the "drink of the Roman soldier" for its alleged restorative powers.[29]

Marion's disciplined approach to garrison life was rewarded in September 1778, when the Second Regiment's colonel, Isaac Motte, resigned, making Marion the regiment's new overall commander, or commandant. However, a promotion in rank did not accompany this increase in responsibility—because British regiments were commanded by lieutenant colonels, Congress had halted promotions to the full rank of colonel in the Continental army to facilitate prisoner exchanges.

Also around this time, there was a change in the overall command at Charleston, when Continental general Robert Howe was recalled. Howe had angered a number of South Carolina politicians, including Christopher Gadsden, a firebrand merchant, soldier, and politician perhaps most famously known today as the designer of the Gadsden flag, depicting a snake on a yellow background and the famous logo, "Don't Tread on Me." In 1777, Gadsden resigned his Continental commission in an argument with Howe, and in August 1778, the dispute resulted in a duel between the two men, with Howe's bullet reportedly grazing Gadsden's ear while Gadsden was said to have fired in the air. In December 1778, Howe was replaced by Benjamin Lincoln, an elderly general perhaps best known as a leader of Massachusetts militia, though he had performed well in a number of campaigns since being commissioned a major general in the Continental army in 1777, thus earning George Washington's trust and approval.[30]

Although elements of the Second Regiment took part in the campaigning around Stono Ferry in spring of 1779 to counter a British expeditionary force led by Gen. Augustine Prévost, Marion remained behind to participate in the defense of Charleston. However, Marion did march south later that fall as part of an ill-conceived expedition against the British defenses at Savannah. Recall Savannah had been captured by British forces under command of Lt. Col. Archibald Campbell the previous winter, to the delighted surprise of Henry Clinton. Concerned about the threat to Charleston and security of South Carolina this occupation represented, Gen. Lincoln, Governor Rutledge, Monsieur Plombard, the French consul at Charleston, and even the Continental Congress had been sending urgent appeals for assistance to French admiral-general Count Charles-Hector Théodat d'Estaing, commanding the French fleet in the West Indies.

As part of France's alliance with America, d'Estaing had standing orders to help the Americans at his discretion, but this discretion was subject to whims and sudden impulses. After ignoring Charleston's pleas for support from his base in the West Indies for much of the year, d'Estaing finally sent word that he would arrive in Savannah with thirty-three naval vessels and about four thousand troops in early September, although he could only remain in American waters for a limited time due to the threats of the hurricane season.

Rising from a sickbed at news of d'Estaing's approach, Lincoln hurriedly assembled a threadbare American force of 1,500 for the unexpected joint attack. Marion's command was the 214 men of the Second Regiment and ninety North Carolina Continentals of whom he complained were "Interly Naked, non have any Shirts or Shoes."[31] Nevertheless, the Americans marched south, only to find the French forces already surrounding Savannah, and d'Estaing having already demanded the British garrison's surrender, omitting any reference to his American allies. According to some accounts, relations between the French and Americans were frigid throughout the joint operation, with the French refusing to allow Americans in their camps.

Commanding Savannah now was British general Augustine Prévost, who delayed negotiations with d'Estaing long enough to improve his defenses. This delay also permitted eight hundred reinforcements from Beaufort, South Carolina, under command of British Lieutenant Colonel John Maitland to sneak into the city, raising the total British force to approximately 3,200 men, opposing the Franco-American force of approximately 5,000 (3,500 French).

Deciding the British position was too strong for an assault, d'Estaing instead decided to initiate a siege of the city. Approaches were initiated on the night of September 23, and bombardments began the night of October 3. But the temperamental Frenchman soon grew nervous about the position of his navy sitting in blockade around the city's harbor. Writes historian Mark M. Boatner, "d'Estaing was under pressure from his naval captains to abandon the expedition. . . . The fleet was in need of repairs, the hurricane season was approaching, they were vulnerable to attack by the British fleet, and their men were dying of scurvy at a rate of thirty-five a day."[32]

D'Estaing now threatened to abandon the siege he had ordered just two weeks before, so a hastily arranged attack on Savannah was planned for October 9. Marion and his Second Regiment spearheaded the American column led by Col. John Laurens (who was portrayed in a starring role in the twenty-first-century Broadway smash *Hamilton*), in a direct assault on the redoubt at Spring Hill. This redoubt was commanded by the Loyalist Lieutenant Colonel Thomas Brown, the same "Burnfoot" Brown whom the Whigs had tarred and feathered in Augusta earlier in the war. Like the rest of the "Siege of Savannah," the assault was a disaster. "Many gallant men were the victims of count D'Estaing's folly in this affair," remembered Horry.[33]

Rankin reports the South Carolinians lost about one-quarter of their men in the attack. Casualties from Marion's Second Regiment included Sgt. William Jasper, the hero of Fort Moultrie. Allied casualties were approximately eight hundred, including 650 French. British casualties were approximately 150 killed and wounded.[34]

After the disastrous assault, Lincoln wanted to continue the siege, but d'Estaing could not be convinced, and by October 20, the French assault force had returned to their boats, soon to return to their bases in the West Indies. For Marion, it was back to the drudgeries of garrison duty in Charleston, although Rankin finds a silver lining in the failures of Savannah: "In retrospect, had the attack succeeded and the enemy been forced to give up Savannah, Francis Marion would still probably have received little notice except as the capable commanding officer of a South Carolina Continental regiment. Without Savannah, the British might well have abandoned their plans for a southern campaign."[35]

An interesting perspective, enriched by hindsight, but in the present, the Americans appeared heedless of the renewed threat to the American South. Despite the danger posed by the British at Savannah, essentially giving them control of Georgia, South Carolina could not keep their six Continental regiments fully complemented. Facing a cascading debt, the Continental Congress ordered South Carolina governor John Rutledge to reduce the six South Carolina regiments on the Continental establishment down to three. Marion remained commander of the Second Regiment, becoming South Carolina's most senior Continental officer, though Horry was dismissed and returned to his plantation on the Santee.

The timing of this reduction could not have been worse, for bolstered by their successes in Georgia, and swayed by their Loyalist sycophants, the British now launched their full-scale implementation of the "Southern Strategy," with Henry Clinton, Charles Cornwallis, Banastre Tarleton, and 8,700 British troops setting sail from New York on December 26, 1779.

As rumors of this impending attack reached General Lincoln, he attempted to concentrate American forces in Charleston, where Governor John Rutledge had adopted a resolution to defend the city "to the last extremity," calling on militia from throughout South Carolina to bolster the city's defenses. And it was in this capacity that Lt. Col. Francis Marion and his Second Regiment were employed when he attended the fateful dinner party at the home of Alexander McQueen.

His service to the city's defenses now limited by his broken ankle, Marion evacuated the city sometime around early April, carried out of town on a litter, according to Rankin. "When the story got about in Charleston, most people said he was a great fool for his pains," recalled Horry, and indeed, the proud Continental officer probably felt a bit foolish as he was "obliged to sculk from house to house" among his family's property on the Santee, "and sometimes hid in the bushes." Surely his disgrace was most poignant when he received news of the surrender of Charleston on May 12, 1780, followed perhaps by word of Tarleton's humiliation of Buford on May 29. "But the event soon proved Marion was in the right," Horry continued, "and there is no policy like sticking to a man's duty."[36] Sequestered in the swamps and river plantations of the Santee, Marion would heal soon enough. A competent, successful American officer before the surrender, Marion's great role as the "Swamp Fox" of the American Revolution was now set to begin.

SEVEN

TURNED
to FLOOD

WHETHER MASSACRE OR NOT, Tarleton's victory at the Waxhaws set the Carolinas awash in a panic that soon turned to flood as thousands of British regulars and Provincials marched their way into the backcountry after the surrender of Charleston. Cornwallis and Rawdon arrived at Camden on June 1, three days after Buford's defeat. With them were the remainder of the 2,500 British troops not including the seven hundred sent forward with Tarleton on his relentless hunt for Rutledge. Toward Ninety Six marched a similar corps of six hundred British regulars and Provincials under Lt. Col. Nisbet Balfour. With him was his fellow Scottish officer, Patrick Ferguson, and Ferguson's Provincial Regiment, the "American volunteers," raised in New York and New Jersey in 1779.[1]

Much to Balfour's chagrin, Clinton had appointed Ferguson Inspector of Militia before returning to New York. Ferguson's new appointment gave him broad authority to organize and lead militia in the Carolinas. Never a

Ferguson fan, Balfour would complain to Cornwallis, "As to Ferguson, his ideas are so wild and sanguine that I doubt it would be dangerous to entrust him with the conduct of any plan,"[2] using the word "doubt" in an archaic sense to mean fear. Balfour's doubts, or fears, would, of course, prove true four months later at Kings Mountain.

Similar garrisons were established in Cheraw in northeastern South Carolina and Augusta, Georgia. At Cheraw was posted Maj. Archibald McArthur and two battalions of British regulars from the 71st. Cornwallis was counting on Cheraw to anchor South Carolina's Pee Dee region on his eastern flank and provide a link with the Loyalist settlement at Cross Creek, near current-day Fayetteville, North Carolina, which was home to the same community of Scots Highlanders who had disappointed Clinton four years before. But hope springs anew, and Cornwallis had important plans for this Loyalist enclave later in the campaign.

Commanding at Augusta was the indomitable Thomas "Burnfoot" Brown, whose talent for both finding and escaping trouble had somehow seen him through the war. Brown was the Scottish Loyalist who had been tortured by Augusta's Whigs before the war, spoiled William Henry Drayton's Whig recruitment efforts in the backcountry in 1775, escaped jail by fleeing to East Florida, and helped beat Francis Marion, the Americans, and French, at Savannah. Like a bad penny, Brown kept turning up in the hot spots of the American South. At Augusta, Brown would also be appointed Indian agent to the Cherokee and Creeks living in that part of the frontier.

To Georgetown, the fourteen-gun sloop HMS *Loyalist*, under the command of Capt. John Plumer Ardesoife, was dispatched to control the important port there on Winyah Bay.[3] On the west side of the Wateree River, Cornwallis and Rawdon established a fortified outpost at Rocky Mount, guarding the communication line between Camden and Ninety Six. Commanding there was Lt. Col. George Turnbull, another veteran Scottish officer, if a reluctant one. Earlier in the war, Turnbull had married the daughter of a New York Loyalist and now commanded the New York Volunteers, yet another Provincial regiment, along with some Loyalist militia. But Turnbull was unhappy in his post and kept threatening Cornwallis that he would soon resign his commission and return to New York.[4] Provincial captain Christian Huck commanded a detachment of dragoons from the British Legion to serve as Turnbull's mounted platoon. Soon another British outpost would be established at Hanging Rock, defending the important northern route on the Great Wagon Road leading from Camden into the Waxhaws and southern North Carolina. All in all, this occupation force amounted to approximately four thousand men, not including British troops still stationed in Charleston.[5]

The arrival of this British occupation force so soon after the surrender of Charleston temporarily stunned and demoralized the countryside. But four thousand men to control a territory the size of South Carolina was hardly enough, and England's plan for the "Southern Strategy" always depended on recruiting Loyalist militia to supplement its forces. With the capture of Charleston complete, it was time to see if these passive supporters would now rise up to support the Loyalist cause, as the British ministry had presumed.

And at places like Alexander's Old Field in Chester County near the Catawba River and Mobley's Meeting House, about twelve miles north of Shirer's Ferry on the Broad River, and also Ramseur's Mill just across the North Carolina state line near modern-day Lincolnton, the Carolina's Loyalists did gather to pledge their support and organize militia regiments. In the Orangeburg District, twelve Loyalist militia companies were organized for six-month service, approximately five hundred men in all, and Patrick Ferguson similarly raised seven Loyalist regiments of as many as 1,500 men total in the Ninety Six District. One of these was the Long Cane Regiment, consisting of 230 officers and men, most from settlements along the Little River of the Savannah and Long Cane Creek. In the Little River District, home of the Cunningham brothers, three hundred men enlisted in the newly raised Loyalist regiment, and Patrick Cunningham was named its commander. Robert Cunningham did not receive a militia commission at this time, though he would eventually be named the Ninety Six District's brigadier general after Ferguson's defeat and death at Kings Mountain.

Some of the men recruited for these regiments were, like the Cunninghams, prominent citizens who truly supported British rule. One such Loyalist was Henry Houseman. Believed by historian Michael C. Scoggins to be a Charleston attorney during the early 1770s, Houseman had moved to the Camden district in 1780 and lived on Cedar Creek, on the east side of the Catawba River directly across from the British outpost at Rocky Mount.[6] There, George Turnbull appointed him captain of a Loyalist regiment, reporting that Houseman "was the Choice of the People and I thought him deserving."[7] Daniel Harper was a local physician in the Camden District who had immigrated to South Carolina from Ireland in 1767 and married a prosperous Camden widow. Dependent on the local Whig community to support his medical practice, Harper had little incentive to join the Loyalist militia except true commitment to its cause. Indeed, he would suffer for his allegiances, for eventually his property would be plundered and seized by American forces.[8]

And then there's Henry Rugeley. We last encountered Rugeley at his plantation twelve miles north of Camden on the night before the Battle of the Waxhaws, when he had awakened his houseguest, South Carolina governor-in-exile John Rutledge, to warn him of Banastre Tarleton's pursuit. Deeply in debt after the death of his brother/business partner, Rugeley was a merchant and businessman who appears to have been always more profiteer than Loyalist proselytizer. But for the time being, the British were eager to take advantage of Rugeley's mercantile contacts and his property's strategic location on the Great Wagon Road, putting aside any doubts about his allegiances to name him first an officer in Camden's Loyalist regiment and eventually its colonel.[9]

However, men of means like Cunningham, Houseman, Harper, and Rugeley, were more the exception than the rule, for many of those who pledged to the Crown were from poorer and less prestigious backgrounds who seemed to have done so reluctantly. In his memoir of the war, James P. Collins recalled the effect of these unwilling recruits: "In order to expedite the business, there were officers sent out in various directions, with guards or companies of men, to receive the submission of the people. Vast numbers flocked in and submitted; some through fear, some through willingness, and others, perhaps, through a hope that all things would settle down and war cease."[10]

The historian James H. Saye categorizes those pledged to the Loyalist cause after Charleston's surrender into six principal types. One category thought "the fleets and armies of Great Britian were perfectly invincible, while defeat and utter ruin to all engaged in it must follow rebellion against the King."[11]

To this class we can attribute the militia of Andrew Williamson in the Long Canes settlement, along the Savannah River basin in the far western portion of the state, not far from Ninety Six. Williamson had been one of South Carolina's most prominent Whig militia officers throughout the war, commanding Patriot forces in the Battle of Ninety Six in November 1775. On June 5, 1780, Williamson assembled three hundred of his militia and volunteered to lead his men into the mountains, where they could continue their fight for the Patriot cause. But with Charleston captured and Ninety Six soon to be occupied, these Whigs showed little enthusiasm for leaving their farms and families, and voted to accept British parole. Among them was Andrew Pickens, himself an able militia commander who had commanded with distinction at the Battle of Kettle Creek in February 1779, stalking and surprising a superior force of Loyalists. An exceptionally able commander, well respected by both Loyalist and Patriot, Pickens would later renounce his parole, winning a congressional award for his service at the Battle of Cowpens on January 17, 1781. But for now, he agreed there seemed little point to continuing the fight, sitting out the conflict for the ensuing six months.[12]

Other Tory classes described by Saye included those conscientiously opposed to war, such as the region's small but not insignificant population of Quakers and other passivist religions, and those who "thought the Government of George the Third too good to exchange for an uncertainty." And then there were those "who claimed no little credential for shrewdness and management; who prided themselves on being genteel and philosophical. . . . If they had a sport of patriotism or love for their King, it could only be kindled by fuel from the Government coffers."[13]

Probably it was a mix of all these types that now pledged their support to the Crown across South Carolina. In the region south of Charleston, Patriot militia sent a flag to the British outpost at Beaufort submitting their parole, and most citizens of Camden also negotiated a capitulation. "The total rout of all the continental troops of the southern states . . . together with the universal panick occasioned by the surrender of Charleston, suspended . . . all military opposition to the progress of the British army," wrote Ramsay. Briefly, at least, Clinton and Cornwallis had good reason to consider "the spirit of rebellion in South Carolina" subdued.[14]

Historian Robert S. Lambert reports British officers authorized eighteen militia regiments in the two months after the fall of Charleston, originally mustered of at least 2,500 officers and men. However, recruitment in some regions of the state were far less than expected. Like James P. Collins, Loyalist officer Robert Gray believed many enrolled in the Loyalist militia "because they believed the war to be at an end in the Southern provinces & partly to ingratiate themselves with the conquerors." Gray estimated that, at the time, no more than one-third of the state's population were truly "loyal" inhabitants and those "by no means the wealthiest" part.[15]

And certainly, among these recruits were those bent on revenge, along with some outright criminals, men whom Saye describes as "a disappointed, roguish, revengeful class. It must not be supposed that these characteristics were never combined. Several of them had a natural affinity for each other, and were almost invariably found united in the same person."[16] And if the

British at first had good reason to be optimistic about Loyalist recruits such as Houseman and Harper, they would soon enough become all too familiar with these roguish and revengeful types, with calamitous outcomes on their designs for a southern strategy.

In South Carolina's vast coastal plain, the British and their Loyalist agents received a particularly cool reception. As with the rest of South Carolina, the region was characterized by its rivers, with the Pee Dee, or "Great" Pee Dee, at its center. Rising in the North Carolina mountains, where it is known as the Yadkin River, the Pee Dee crossed into South Carolina near the town of Cheraw, which was also its fall line. Below Cheraw, the Pee Dee was navigable all the way down to Winyah Bay, where it emptied into the Atlantic Ocean at Georgetown. Historian William S. Powell writes that the river's unusual name may be derived from the Catawba Indian word *pi'ri*, for "something good," although most sources attribute it to the Pee Dee Indians, whom early American settlers found living and traveling among its waters.[17]

Major tributaries to the Pee Dee included the Little Pee Dee, the Lynches, the Black River, and the Waccamaw River, among others. For convenience, we shall call this the Pee Dee watershed, essentially the whole of South Carolina's eastern plain, though not quite, and separate from the watershed that contains Charleston, the "Pee Dee Region," or simply the "Pee Dee," for it will play an increasingly important role in our story.

In an attempt to plan its interior settlement, South Carolina's royal administration established a series of townships in 1759. They were centered around its navigable rivers, most within a hundred miles of the coast, created in the hope they would draw white settlers to the colony's interior, where they were needed for defense against the ever-shifting confederations of Native Americans, French, and Spanish threatening the western frontier. Whites were also needed to balance out the exploding slave population. By 1761, roughly 66 percent of South Carolina's population were slaves, and perhaps the guilty consciences of Charleston's gentry class fueled long-standing fears of a slave uprising.

So, townships were established at Purrysburg and New Windsor on the Savannah, Saxe Gotha on the Congaree, Amelia on the Santee, and Fredericksburg on the Wateree. In the Pee Dee, the townships were Williamsburg on the Black River, Queensborough on the Pee Dee (south of present-day Florence), and Kingston in the Waccamaw basin, along with the "semi-township" known as the "Welsh Tract" adjacent to Queensborough.

However, as with many efforts at regional planning, the flood of settlers coming down the Great Wagon Road disrupted these administrative plans, and the colony's interior never quite developed as its officials intended. Nevertheless, these townships were, for the most part, settled along ethnic lines, providing an opportunity to explore the ethnic composition of the Pee Dee region. In Kingston and Williamsburg, the settlers were predominantly Scots-Irish, "a tightly knit group characterized by 'their National Adherence to each other,' family ties, and the Presbyterian Church," writes Walter Edgar. Queensborough, however, and obviously, the adjacent "Welsh Tract," where settled by the Welsh, whom Edgar characterizes as primarily Baptist.[18]

Historian William W. Boddie describes the settlers of Williamsburg Township as originating from "England, Ireland, Scotland, Germany, Holland, and from the New England States, Pennsylvania and Virginia," though he admits the "greater number of them had lived in Ireland for many years before coming to America. . . . They had migrated from England and from Scotland to Ireland on account of fair promises on the part of the English King. These failing them, they sought refuge in America." They "were all about the same class of men," writes Boddie. "They were people who had been non-conformists as to State-Church religion."[19]

No matter their nationality, these settlers took advantage of what Edgar describes as "some of the best agricultural lands in the colony." Not that those first few decades were easy. "For many years, these people fought the forest and swamps, enduring and overcoming handicaps inconceivable. Slowly they prospered," writes Boddie. This backbreaking work included establishing the vast system of dikes, levees, ditches, and causeways necessary for controlling the Pee Dee region's vast network of swamps and wetlands.[20]

Eventually, the Pee Dee's farmers established thriving crops of indigo, wheat, hemp, flax, and rice. And like the plantations of the low country, these farms relied on slave labor. Boddie estimates the average citizen of the Williamsburg township "owned not more than five" slaves, for the region's relative remoteness, the challenges of its geography, and its reliance on waterborne transportation to transport its crops to market kept the scale of these farms modest in both production and slave populations, at least in comparison to the low country plantations.[21]

Romantically, Boddie also attributes this modesty to the nomadic heritage of the Scots-Irish. "The people of this community have elected to live in modest comfortable homes, although many of them might have erected splendid mansions. . . . Is it that the cryptomnesic content of forty generations of nomad life on the continent and a thousand years of warring and wandering in Ireland and Scotland deter them?" he wondered. "Is there an unconscious yet determining instinct in them that 'something might happen to move me and I could not carry a mansion?'"[22]

Psychological speculation aside (and what does that say then about the residential habits of today's Scots-Irish descendants?), the settlers of the Pee Dee did enjoy some ties of society and commerce to Charleston and had displayed little of the Ninety Six region's Loyalist sentiment in the years leading up to the revolution. But like perhaps most South Carolinians, what these farmers of the Pee Dee region wanted most was to be left alone. "Williamsburg was peaceful and happy in 1775," agrees Boddie, left alone by the "Mother Country" for the most part "to work out its own political and social and religious salvation."

However, in Williamsburg, at least, that ambivalence turned to Whig sentiment once the British attacked Charleston in 1776. After that, the region's young men "sniffed the noise of battle from afar and volunteered for service in the first South Carolina troops." And following the surrender of Charleston on May 12, 1780, when some of those young men were among the militia captured and made prisoner in that city's defense, that sentiment hardened to passion. There were "no brass bands playing martial music, no eloquent orators sounding striking climaxes, no raising of liberty poles, and nothing of the spectacular," writes Boddie. "But somehow every Scotchman determined on 'liberty or death.'"[23]

One of those men was John James. Already an early Whig supporter, James was from one of Williamsburg's most prominent Scots-Irish families and had been elected to the First Provincial Congress of 1776. Described by Boddie as an ardent Presbyterian, James was said to be also a faithful attendant at Williamsburg's popular semiannual Sunday horse races, which were despised by local ministers as "ungodly," but apparently enjoyed very much by James, who "sometimes swore a combination of Scotch and Welsh oaths, and occasionally drank himself to dreamland before the night came."[24] In war, however, James was deadly serious. By 1780, he already had served in the Williamsburg militia, campaigning with William Moultrie around Charleston in spring of 1779.

Certainly, as in other areas of the state, the Pee Dee was not entirely Whig, and many of its Loyalists were also among its prominent citizens. This included William Henry Mills, who owned two thousand acres along the Pee Dee River. A former surgeon in the British army, Mills had retired to South Carolina in 1764. Despite his Loyalist sympathies, he was appointed sheriff of the newly formed Cheraw District in 1773. He also was elected to the Provincial Congress of 1776 and later returned to the South Carolina legislature as a representative for St. David's Parish. Also from the Cheraw region was Loyalist Robert Gray. Though little is known about Gray's background, he was clearly respected among his peers, named a justice of the peace in Cheraw in 1776, and described by British officer Archibald McArthur as a "Scotch gentlemen," and by Cornwallis as a "very sensible, serious man."[25]

Men like Mills and Grey were the exception, however, rather than the rule, and sources unanimously describe the Pee Dee region as fervently Whig. "With very few exceptions, the intelligent and influential habitats were the ardent friends of their country," writes historian Alexander Gregg in *History of Old Cheraws*. "They believed their liberties to be in danger. Roused by this apprehension, they were animated to the most self-denying exertions."[26] And the truth was, after the Whig persecutions of the previous six years, many of the Pee Dee region's Loyalist were gone, either returned to England or relocated to British colonies in Florida or the West Indies. Many of those who remained might be classified more as "opportunists" than "Royalists," despite the reluctant faith the British army was preparing to put in them. From Cheraw, McArthur would write Cornwallis, "the inhabitants appear much pleased with the terms offered by the Commissioners," though it was an assessment McArthur would very soon reevaluate.[27]

THE COMMISSIONERS IN QUESTION WERE Henry Clinton and his naval counterpart, Adm. Mariot Arbuthnot, who had been empowered to regulate civil affairs, negotiate peace, and reestablish royal authority in territories restored to the Crown. The "terms" were Clinton and Arbuthnot's conditions for parole after the capture of Charleston, communicated through a series of proclamations issued by them in late May and early June before they returned to New York.[28]

The first proclamation was issued on May 22. It promised "effectual countenance, protection and support" for the King's "faithful and peaceable support" but also required "all persons whatever to be aiding and assisting to" the King's forces "whenever they shall be required." Those "endeavouring to support the flame of rebellion," meanwhile, would be "treated with that severity so hardened and criminal an obstinacy will deserve, and his or their estates will be immediately seized to be confiscated."[29]

Hardly an example of narrative clarity, the May 22 proclamation nevertheless appeared to require from South Carolina's Whigs nothing more than their passive submission, so long as they didn't actively oppose British army rule. And in the last days of May, Clinton seemed to lean toward clemency, optimistically believing "the spirit of rebellion in South Carolina now very nearly subdued." In a May 30 letter to William Eden, a Clinton confidante in the British cabinet, Clinton reported: "All the rebel grandees are come in. . . . They put on a good face. They own honestly they have been always in arms against us. They confess their dread of the backcountry people, who they say are all up to join us, as well in North Carolina as South. The tyranny of their late government, their hopes of a better under us and conviction that the rebels can never recover this country, have induced them to surrender themselves."[30]

As May turned to June, however, Clinton's sanguine disposition soured, and he began to second-guess his conciliatory approach. He may have been influenced by a report from James Simpson, South Carolina's former royal attorney general. Simpson was one of those former royal officials who had been exiled from the state earlier in the war. But he had returned with the expedition under Clinton, who dispatched him among his former Charleston associates after the surrender to take gauge of their sentiment. Simpson reported this sentiment fell into four categories: those loyal by principle; those demoralized by war who saw royal administration as a return to peace and stability; those who supported the revolutionary cause but now saw no option other than to accept royal authority; and those who were willing to continue the struggle. And within this fourth group was an important subset: those who had fled to the backcountry earlier in the war to escape Whig persecution in Charleston and the low country. "These men were numerous and, having been driven from their homes, they had no intention of letting peace return to the province until the guilty had been punished," observes historian John Shy.[31]

And although Simpson found many were willing to return their allegiances to the Crown, he admitted "the Loyalists who have always adhered to the King's Government are not so numerous" as he had anticipated. Meanwhile, officers in the field reported that many South Carolinians who took an oath of allegiance did so "on the condition that they will not be compelled to fight against their own countrymen," and Clinton himself had doubts about trusting new Loyalist recruits "till they have given me more convincing proofs of their Loyalty than have appeared in so short a time."[32]

So, before departing for New York on June 8, Clinton and Arbuthnot issued two more proclamations. Their demands increasingly strident, the final one, issued June 3, now required all of the state's residents to "take an active part in settling and securing His Majesty's government." And those who neglected to "return their allegiance" to His Majesty "will be considered as enemies and rebels to the same, and treated accordingly."[33]

Here was something different. Ignoring, for now, the confusion created by their conflicting terms, the later proclamations appeared to require that all citizens of the state proactively support the Crown. Passive obedience would no longer be enough, and significantly, this appeared to mean all eligible men must join the Loyalist militia if called upon. And those who refused to take arms against their formal rebel colleagues would be considered guilty by association. "Thus tyrannical measures were advanced step by step till the poor paroled people could no longer be protected as they had been promised . . . but must take up arms in defence of the Government they abhorred, and which was forging chains for their perpetual enslavement," writes the nineteenth-century historian Lyman Draper.[34]

In his memoir, Clinton admitted the adverse effects of the June 3 proclamation: "But, as I did not remain there myself to watch its progress and assist its operation, I shall not take upon me to disprove the evil consequences ascribed to it since, as from the powers I gave Lord Cornwallis I cannot think myself responsible for them."[35] Clinton's biographer, William Willcox, deems this argument unconvincing. "Sir Henry was normally sensitive to political factors . . . but in this case he seems to have suffered a bad lapse of judgment."[36]

Cornwallis did alter those terms, instructing his subordinates to enlist into the Loyalist militia only those "of undoubtful attachment to the cause of Great Britain or whose behavior has always been moderate." The "rest of those that were notoriously disaffected" could remain home on parole, provided they were disarmed and furnished to the British "moderate contributions of provisions, waggons, and horses etc." when called upon.[37]

However, with South Carolina's Whigs eager for evidence of British treachery, and rumors of the Waxhaws "massacre" swirling the countryside, the damage had been done. "If it was proper policy at first to hold a middle course" by offering Whig supporters unconditional parole, "the same policy required that it should have been continued for some time longer," wrote Stedman. "Thus the foundation of mutual jealousy and distrust was laid among the inhabitants themselves. The revolutionists complained their condition was altered without their concurrence."[38]

At Georgetown, British captain John Plumer Ardesoife published the commissioner's second and third proclamations and issued an ultimatum that all the region's inhabitants come there to reaffirm their allegiance to the Crown. In Williamsburg, a public meeting was held, and Maj. John James was selected by his countrymen to travel to Georgetown to determine if the proclamation "meant that they should take up arms against their countrymen." Traveling there in the "plain garb of a country planter," James found Ardesoife at his lodgings, where the British captain admonished James that "although you have rebelled against his majesty, he offers you a free pardon, of which you are undeserving, for you ought all to be hanged, but as he offers you a free pardon, you must take up arms in support of his cause."[39]

When James suggested "the people he came to represent would not submit on such terms," Ardresoife, irritated at James's "republican language . . . replied, 'you damned rebel, if you speak in such language, I will immediately order you to be hanged up to the yard-arm.'" According to his son, William Dobein James, James seized the chair he was sitting in and "brandished it in the face of the captain, and making his retreat good through the back door of the house," escaped into the country. But confusion over the proclamation, and British arrogance in its administration, would have important long-term consequences. "This circumstance, apparently trivial, certainly hastened the rise of Marion's brigade," Dobein James would later recall.[40]

PART TWO

REFUGEES

EIGHT

WHAT
WE CALL
REFUGEES

I F CORNWALLIS HAD DOUBTS about the quantity, or quality, of the Loyalist militia recruited in South Carolina, he was determined not to let it interfere with his plans for the fall campaign. "I think with the force at present under my command (except there should be a considerable foreign interference) I can leave South Carolina in security and march about the beginning of September with a body of troops into the back part of North Carolina," he wrote Clinton at the end of June 1780.[1]

Finally with an independent command, Cornwallis wanted to avoid the quagmire of entrenched positions that had lately characterized the northern theater, and which many blamed on Clinton's crippling indecision. And though well aware of Cornwallis's plans for a fall campaign in North Carolina, and subsequent plans to move into the Chesapeake region of Virginia should all go well, Clinton's ideas about the Southern Strategy never aligned with Cornwallis's, a discrepancy that would lead to their postwar feud, played out in the style of the age through a series of endless attacks and reprisals published in newspapers and pamphlets. In his parting orders to Cornwallis, Clinton had stressed that the defense of Charleston "is always to be considered as the principal object," and in one of these published tracts would complain that had Cornwallis returned to South Carolina after meeting stiff resistance from a combined Continental and militia force at North Carolina's Guilford Courthouse in March 1781, "South Carolina would have been saved, and the fatal catastrophe which afterwards happened to his army in the Chesapeake avoided."[2]

Such bickering was far in the future, however, and for now, both Cornwallis and Clinton had ample motive to be optimistic about South Carolina's interior security. Almost from the start, though, the British had trouble maintaining discipline in these new Loyalist regiments. With good reason, because as these Loyalist regiments formed and spread out over the countryside, years of abuse boiled over into vengeful retribution, and many initiated campaigns of terror against Whig leaders and neighbors considered instruments of their recent repression.

In the Camden and New Acquisition districts, Loyalists began plundering Whig plantations and arresting their prominent Whig leaders. Near Orangeburg, Col. Alexander Innes arrested Whig leaders as he marched his militia north toward Ninety Six.[3] Some, like Thomas Sumter and Francis Marion, were able to avoid these search parties by hiding in the swamps and woods, but many weren't as lucky. In the region around Shirer's Ferry, on the east bank of the Broad River opposite the Dutch Fork, Loyalists under the command of militia colonel Charles Coleman embodied in camp at Mobley's Meeting House, a small church, and then set out in bands to maraud and terrorize Whigs in the surrounding countryside. One of these bands encountered John and Henry Hampton "on the road," presumably as the well-known Whig militia officers were trying to flee the region. The Loyalists seized "thirty negroes, two or three wagons and teams and thirty valuable horses and a large quantity of household goods" before sending the brothers to jail in Camden under guard.[4]

Other Whig homes were looted by hungry Loyalist militia seeking food and forage for their horses. "There was no restraint upon private rapine," writes the historian Lyman Draper. "The silver plate of the planters was carried off" and "all negroes that had belonged to the Rebels were seized."[5]

Samuel McCalla lived near Bechhamville in modern-day Chester County, part of the New Acquisition District. "The Tories collected at

Bechamville and began to plunder everybody suspected of disloyalty, taking horses & cattle and household goods," he recalled.[6]

In some cases, this looting was sanctioned by the British army, which required feed and forage from the surrounding countryside to sustain its newly established occupation force. Charles Stedman, who would later write a significant historical account of the American Revolution from a Loyalist perspective, was at this time serving on Cornwallis's staff at Camden as commissary officer. "From the time that the British army entered Camden . . . it was wholly supported by supplies from the neighbouring district," he wrote, a duty in which British and Loyalist soldiers "were frequently opposed."[7] In some cases, payment or certificates were issued for confiscated goods, but if the homestead was considered Whig, or "avowedly hostile," they were just as frequently raided and looted without compensation. At Rocky Creek near Shirer's Ferry, Loyalist militia under command of John and Richard Featherstone seized horses, confiscations their Whig neighbors deemed little more than horse stealing. In Camden, mills belonging to Whig colonel Joseph Kershaw and his brother, Eli, were raided of rice, coffee, sugar, flour, and other goods. "Lord Cornwallis ordered the commissaries to give no receipt to colonel Kershaw for the property taken from him, as he was deemed a very violent man, and who was said to have persecuted the loyalists," wrote Stedman.[8]

As LOYALIST MILITIA TERRORIZED THE Whig countryside, three Whig militia leaders from the west side of the Broad River held a secret meeting on June 4 somewhere in what is now Union County to discuss rumors and next steps. Whig colonel John Thomas commanded the Spartan Regiment from the upper Spartan District, what is now modern-day Spartanburg County, South Carolina. His companions were Col. Thomas Brandon, militia commander of the Fair Forest Regiment from the lower part of modern-day Spartanburg County, and Col. James Lisle, commander of the Dutch Fork Regiment from the forks of the Enoree and Tyger Rivers, in what is now Newberry County.

All three men were veteran militia leaders. They had fought the Cherokee earlier in the war, and also campaigned against the Loyalists in Georgia and eastern Florida, but never before had they experienced anything like this British occupation of their home regions. With Charleston surrendered and Buford defeated, the odds were stacked against them like never before. But they resolved to fight and agreed to gather their forces at a camp on Fair Forest Creek near the modern-day city of Union, South Carolina, where they would organize and decide their next steps.[9]

Richard Winn was a prominent planter, merchant, and land speculator of Welsh ancestry who had migrated to the western part of the Camden District from Fauquier County, Virginia, in the mid-1760s, acquiring vast tracts of property and establishing the town of Winnsboro with his brother, John. Like Thomas, Brandon, and Lisle, Winn had commanded Whig militia in numerous campaigns during the early part of the revolution. After learning of the Loyalist muster at nearby Mobeley's Meeting House, Winn tried to gather the region's Patriot militia, but found "he could not raise one single person to oppose them."[10] So, on June 7, he left his plantation and traveled north, into the upper New Acquisition District, seeking to join Patriot militia there.

To James Williams we have already been introduced. He was the prominent merchant, militia leader, politician, and landowner from the Little River District who had scuffled with Robert Cunningham during the 1778 General Assembly campaign. Like the others, Williams had served for years in the Whig militia. But now fearing Loyalist reprisals, he left his home on Little River to move his slaves and personal property to safety at the farm of his brother in Caswell County, North Carolina.[11]

The Whig militia leaders had good reason to fear Loyalist reprisal. After five long years of enduring Whig supremacy, South Carolina's Loyalists now spread through the countryside, eager for retribution. Just a few days after escaping to North Carolina, James Williams's property was confiscated by Loyalist militia on or around June 10 and would remain a Tory outpost for the next several months. Meanwhile, perhaps that same day, Brandon's muster camp on Fairforest Creek was routed by Loyalist militia under command of William Cunningham, later to become known as the infamous "Bloody Bill." One of those killed was Robert Young, whose brother Thomas was not at Brandon's camp that day but left a valuable memoir of his American Revolution experience. "I shall never forget my feelings when told of his [Robert's] death," Thomas Young recalled. "I do not believe I had ever used an oath before that day, but then I tore open my bosom, and swore that I would never rest till I had avenged his death. Subsequently a hundred Tories felt the weight of my arm for the deed."[12]

Scattered by this Loyalist persecution, Brandon and several of his men, including Joseph McJunkin, who left an important account of this portion of the conflict, fled the Fair Forest region, seeking to join with other elements of Whig militia in the New Acquisition District. Lisle and some of his Dutch Fork Regiment also headed north toward New Acquisition, while John Thomas Sr. was arrested and incarcerated in the jail at Ninety

Six, to be replaced in leadership of the Spartan Regiment by his son, John Thomas Jr.

Much of the Patriot resistance in the Waxhaws and New Acquistion districts centered in local Presbyterian churches. In 1775, Presbyterian minister William Tennent from the New Acquisition District had joined with prominent Charleston Whig William Henry Drayton to canvas the region in support of the Whig cause. Thanks in part to Tennent's success, several Whig militia units had been recruited from the New Acquisition District. Almost all of the men who emerged as Whig militia leaders from these efforts were Scots-Irish members of either Bethel, Beersheba, Bullock's Creek, or Bethesda Presbyterian churches, the "Four Bs," in what is now York County.

Leading the Bullock's Creek church was Reverend Joseph Alexander, who had grown up under the ministry of Reverend Alexander Craighead, a Mecklenburg County, North Carolina, Presbyterian who preached against British authority long before the American Revolution. Bethel Church, where William Hill attended, was led by staunch Whig reverends James McRee and Francis Cummins.

Most prominent among these Presbyterian minister Whigs perhaps was the Reverend John Simpson, who led the Upper Fishing Creek Presbyterian Church, also known as Simpson's Meeting House, near William Hill's Ironworks. The church served a large community of Scots Irish who had immigrated to the area from Philadelphia. Simpson served several other Presbyterian churches in the area as well, including Bethesda Presbyterian Church and Lower Fishing Creek Presbyterian Church, located near the modern-day town of Lewisville in Chester County. Of Scots-Irish ancestry, Simpson was educated at Princeton University (then the College of New Jersey) and had been a staunch supporter of the revolutionary cause throughout the war, preaching of it often from the pulpit. Many members of Simpson's congregations served in prominent roles in the local Whig militia. And nearby was Rocky Creek Presbyterian Church, pastored by the Reverend William Martin. Only eight years earlier, Martin had led many of his congregation from Ulster, Ireland, to escape the injustices of their English landlords. In the aftermath of the slaughter at Waxhaws, Martin preached a fiery sermon to a congregation so large they had to meet outdoors instead of the log cabin church the community had built together. In recounting the cruelties of the Waxhaws, Martin commanded, "My hearers, talk and angry words will do no good. We must fight!"[13]

His congregation listened, the men of the community meeting the next day to form a new regiment of Patriot militia. "These frontier preachers wielded great influence over their congregations and were one of the reasons why antagonism toward the British was so strong in this part of the Backcountry," writes historian Michael Coggins.[14]

Perhaps inspired by these exhortations, thirty-two Whig militia under the command of Capt. John McClure attacked a Loyalist assembly at a place called Alexander's Old Field, near the present-day community of Great Falls, South Carolina, on the morning of June 6. There, Loyalist officer Henry Houseman had set up a camp a few days before to recruit Loyalist militia and pillage Whig farms in the vicinity. Houseman was administering the oath of allegiance to Loyalist recruits when McClure's company opened fire, scattering the assembly in a "general stampede." Houseman escaped, but four Loyalists were killed and several wounded, in comparison to two Whig casualties. After the attack, several men renounced the oath of allegiance they had just sworn and joined McClure's company.[15]

A few days later, a similar scene took place at Mobley's Meeting House. After finding he could "not raise one single person" around Shirer's Ferry to attack the Loyalists at Mobley's Meeting House, Richard Winn had successfully recruited around one hundred militia in the New Acquisition District, including John McClure and the militia who had attacked Loyalists at Alexander's Old Field, as well as Whig militia from the Bethesda community in present-day York County under command of militia colonel William Bratton. With these men, all on horse, Winn returned to Mobley's, surrounded the meeting house on three sides, for the fourth side backed up to a steep bluff, and attacked the Loyalists at daybreak on June 8. "In a few minutes this body of Tories" was "totally defeated with a small loss of killed and wounded," Winn recalled, with many of the escaping Tories wounded as they leapt down the precipice at the back of the church to escape.[16]

News of the Whig attacks at Alexander's Old Field and Mobley's Meeting House set off new rounds of British and Loyalist reprisal. Though he was not at home, Winn's houses and buildings were burned "to the ground, and every negro plundered, together with every other property he possessed in the world. His wife was plundered of her clothes and she was drove off with two infant children." Learning of this retribution in the New Acquisition District, where he had fled after the attack at Mobley's, Winn replied, "It is no more than I expected."[17]

From his base at Rocky Mount, where he had been posted only days before, British lieutenant colonel George Turnbull received news of the Patriot attacks at Alexander's and Mobley's. A fifty-year-old Scot, Turnbull had vast service in Canada, the West Indies, and the American frontier. Beginning in 1776, he began to serve on the Provincial establishment, becoming lieutenant colonel of the New York Volunteers in October 1777 and traveling south with that regiment in 1778 to take part in the capture of Savannah, then serving with Clinton during the siege of Charleston before traveling to Camden with Cornwallis in late May.[18]

Turnbull was disconsolate in the South Carolina wilderness and longed to return to his family in New York. Still, he could not ignore the rebel activity in his theater, so he ordered his mounted dragoons under Capt. Christian Huck to travel into the New Acquisition District, where his intelligence indicated Whig resistance was headquartered in Presbyterian congregation houses at Fishing Creek and Bethesda, both of which were pastored by the avowed Whig supporter John Simpson. On Sunday, June 11, as they made their way to Fishing Creek Meeting House, where they expected to find the Whigs embodied in Sunday service, Huck and his men stopped at the plantation of Janet Strong, a widow whose family were well known as staunch Whigs. When her oldest son, Christopher, twenty, and other son William, seventeen, attempted to escape, they were shot down by Huck's men, killing William and wounding Christopher.

Huck and his dragoons then proceeded to the Fishing Creek Meeting House, which they found empty and may have burned. Next, they traveled to the home of John Simpson, which they also looted and burned. "The people in that Quarter [of] Fishing Creek immediately cried out they wanted protection from such a set as burnt churches & the word of God," Winn recalled.[19] But in conjunction with the successful Whig attacks at Alexander's Old Field and Mobley's Meeting House, Huck's abuses in Fishing Creek only galvanized Whig resistance.

On June 12, scattered Whigs from the west side of the Broad River began to collect at Bullock's Creek Meeting House. Among them were Thomas Brandon and his Fair Forest regiment, just two days after their defeat by William Cunningham. John Thomas Jr., now commanding the Spartan Regiment after his father's arrest, and Col. James Lisle, with some militia from the Dutch Fork District, were also there, along with some Whig refugees from Georgia who had found their way east. This meeting was later recalled by Joseph McJunkin: "Here after enumerating our dangers and trials past, & thinking of our future danger and hardships, with the offers of British protection before us—the question came up, what shall be done?" According to McJunkin, John Thomas Jr. stood up and said, "Shall we declare ourselves cowards and traitors or shall we pursue the prize, Liberty, as long as life continues." Those in favor of fighting were to throw their hats in the air. "The hats flew upwards, and the air resounded with the ... shouts of defiance to the armies of Britain and the foes of Liberty."[20]

A similar meeting took place the same day at Hill's Ironworks in the northern portion of the New Acquisition District. According to Hill's memoir, a British representative arrived at the meeting, reading a proclamation from Lord Rawdon that Congress had abandoned the southern states and that "he was empowered to take their submissions & give paroles & protections to all that chose to become British subjects." Hill then interrupted the British representative, informing those gathered that Congress had not given up on any of the states and reminding them "we had all taken an oath to defend & maintain the Independence of the state to the utmost of our power." Hill recalled his speech had a "visible animation" on those gathered, forcing Rawdon's emissary to flee the meeting "for fear of being accosted by the audience."[21] Afterward, those assembled decided to remain together as a regiment, embodying as the New Acquisition District Militia, or a reconstituted version of it, electing Hill their lieutenant colonel and Andrew Neal their senior colonel.

ABOUT THIRTY MILES NORTH OF Hill's Ironworks, across the North Carolina border, Loyalist militia was gathering at a place called Ramsour's Mill on the Little Catawba River (today called the South Fork Catawba River) just outside modern-day Lincolnton, North Carolina. A few days earlier, John Moore had returned to his father's home about six miles away, claiming he was a lieutenant colonel in the Royal Volunteers of North Carolina, a Provincial regiment formed in 1779 made up of North Carolina Loyalists who had fled to Georgia.

Although he claimed knowledge of the Charleston campaign, Moore's actual status and rank are unclear. Nevertheless, he issued a call for local Loyalists to muster at a place called Indian Creek near Ramsour's Mill on June 10. According to North Carolina partisan Joseph Graham, "Forty men assembled, and Moore told them it was not the wish of Lord Cornwallis that they should embody at that time, but that they and all other loyal subjects should hold themselves in readiness." Before the meeting broke up, however, they received news that Whig major Joseph McDowell of Burke County was in the vicinity with twenty men, "in search of some of the principal persons of their party." A search for McDowell the following day proved fruitless, but Moore's Loyalists were now spirited, and Moore ordered them to muster at Ramsour's Mill on June 13 for further orders.[22]

Acting with dubious authority, Moore, "whom I know nothing of," Cornwallis would later complain,[23] succeeded in mustering a force of over 1,300 Loyalists at Ramsour's Mill by June 18. Although only one-third of these men were armed, the size of this force quickly attracted the attention of several Whig militia leaders in the vicinity, including Thomas Sumter.

When we last read of Sumter, he was riding off to North Carolina to gather men and resources for a return to South Carolina. Along the way, Sumter had stopped in the Waxhaws to recruit some veterans of the Sixth South Carolina Regiment he had commanded earlier in the war as a Continental officer, including some Catawba Native Americans. At that time Salisbury was the largest, most active town in the North Carolina frontier, thanks to its strategic location on the Great Wagon Road just south of a popular ford on the Yadkin River. The town was also a well-known Whig stronghold. Headquartered there were the Rowan County militia along with some North Carolina civil and military authorities. Sumter's reputation among these officials was apparently strong, for on June 1, 1780, he was issued nineteen United States Loan Office certificates of $1,000 each to organize a resistance force. At Salisbury, Sumter also drew to his command others who had escaped from the Waxhaws, Charlotte, and New Acquisition regions. There Sumter received word North Carolina militia general Griffith Rutherford was mustering at Tuckaseegee Ford west of Charlotte to oppose the Loyalists at Ramsour's Mill. Shortly thereafter, with the small group of men he had assembled at Salisbury, Sumter headed south toward Tuckaseegee Ford to join Rutherford.[24]

Now headquartered at Hill's Ironworks, Col. Neal of the New Acquisition District militia received news the Loyalist militia of Matthew Floyd was intimidating Whig settlers along the Broad River. By now, news of Hill's confrontation with Rawdon's ambassador on June 12 had spread through the countryside, drawing more South Carolina and Georgia Whig refugees to Hill's Ironworks. On June 14, Neal set out in search of Floyd with most of these men, leaving Hill and only a small guard of twelve men to guard the ironworks.

The next day, Floyd and thirty Loyalist militia from the Broad, Tyger, and Enoree Rivers arrived at Rocky Mount. Floyd was a prominent landowner and Loyalist in the New Acquisition District who had been arrested and jailed in Charleston earlier in the war. Impressed with Floyd's credentials, Turnbull appointed him colonel in charge of the Spartan District Loyalist militia of modern-day Spartanburg and Cherokee Counties. By now, Turnbull had heard about the reception Rawdon's representative had received at Hill's Ironworks, and that same day he received news that Neal's Patriot regiment was now wreaking havoc on the homesteads of Floyd and his men. "I immediately order'd Captain Hook [Huck] of the Legion to get ready, that with Captain Floyd's company and the other militia which we cou'd assemble it was necessary to give these fellows a check. . . . I have taken the liberty to give Captain Hook orders to destroy the iron works. They are the property of Mr. Hill, a great rebell," Turnbull wrote to Cornwallis on June 16.[25]

By now, Hill and the New Acquisition militia had received news of Moore's Loyalist muster at Ramsour's Mill and Rutherford's Whig muster at Tuckaseegee Ford. "I was then informed that Col. Sumter was then in Salisbury with a few men waiting for a reinforcement," Hill recalled. "I then wrote to him, informing him of our situation & . . . that we were about to form a junction with Genl. Rutherford in North Carolina."[26]

Probably that same day, Huck and Floyd left Rocky Mount, establishing a camp at crossroads near modern-day Lando, South Carolina, where they could pillage and forage in the surrounding countryside. The next day, June 17, Huck set out for Hill's Ironworks, looting and burning the plantation of Whig militiaman James Simril along the way. Apprised of Huck's approach, Hill valiantly set up defenses with his small guard along the road from the south. Two of William Hill's sons set up a one-pound swivel gun forged at the ironworks atop a hill overlooking the road, where they planned to give Huck a warm reception. But Huck circled around the camp and attacked from the north, avoiding ambush.

Caught off guard, Hill and his militiamen traded a few volleys with Huck's troops before attempting to make their escape, but Huck's mounted dragoons overtook Hill's rear guard. In his report to Turnbull, Huck claimed he killed seven and took four prisoners as he overtook the fleeing Patriot militia. "The rest fled to the mountains," Turnbull later reported to Cornwallis. "I am likewise to inform your Lordship that Captain Huck has compleatly destroy'd the iron works, which has been the head quarters of the rebells in arms for some time past."[27] In his memoir, Hill recalled Huck "burned the forge furnace, grist and saw mills together with all other buildings even to the negro huts, & bore away about 90 negroes."[28] Later that day, after Huck had left, Neal returned to the now burned iron works from his expedition to the Broad River, and the New Acquisition District militia decided to march immediately for Tuckaseegee Ford.

TODAY, THE CATAWBA RIVER WEST OF Charlotte has been altered irrevocably by dams and development, but when historian Benson Lossing visited the region in 1849, the Tuckaseegee Ford probably looked much as it had during the summer of 1780. "The country is very hilly," wrote Lossing of his journey. "I crossed the Catawba at Tuckaseegee Ford, the place where General Rutherford and his little army passed. . . . The distance from shore to shore, in the direction of the ford, is more than half a mile, the water varying in depth from ten inches to three feet, and running in quite a rapid current." Lossing also published a sketch of the ford, depicting a dirt road running down to the river, bookended on either side by small, shrubby trees.[29]

The ford linked Charlotte to points west into the Blue Ridge Mountains along the Tuckaseegee Trail, first established by the region's Native American tribes, and later a significant spur of the Great Wagon Road. Thus, it was a well-known meeting spot for militia general Griffith Rutherford to muster the region's Whig militia against the Loyalists gathered at nearby Ramsour's Mill on or around June 18, 1780.[30]

Among these men, camped according to their militia or regional affiliation, were a large contingent of South Carolinians, along with a handful of Georgians, awaiting Rutherford's arrival. Along with Thomas Brandon's Fair Forest regiment was militia officer Joseph McJunkin, who had been at Brandon's muster on or around June 10 when it was routed and dispersed by Loyalists under William Cunningham. McJunkin had also been at the meeting of Whig militia at Bullock's Creek Meeting House on June 12. Also now at Tuckaseegee Ford were most of the other Whig regiments that had gathered at Bullock's Creek, including James Lisle with his Dutch Fork Regiment, the Spartan Regiment now under command of John Thomas Jr., and the New Acquisition District militia under command of Andrew Neal and William Hill.[31] Richard Winn was there and also camped nearby were approximately two hundred Catawba Indians, whose villages were in the vicinity, and who, according to one account, were so terrified by reports of Tarleton's atrocities against Buford, they stretched cowhides between the trees as a barrier against surprise.[32]

"We was what we Call Refugees," McJunkin recalled. "Not taking protection as many did but retreated from place to place and was continually on the Alert."[33] Certainly, they looked the part. Aside from the Catawbas, most were Scots-Irish immigrants, dressed in the handmade clothes they had been wearing when chased from their farms, most probably without shoes and many carrying for weapons only crude farm implements or old mill saws, crafted perhaps at the nearby forge of Isaac Price.[34] Of those who carried firearms, few had ammunition. According to historian David Ramsay, these militia soldiers "sometimes came to battle when they had not three rounds a man, and some were obliged to keep at a distance, till, by the fall of others, they were supplied with arms."[35]

Poor they were, but they didn't lack the spirit to fight, a fire in the blood, these South Carolinians. Now they needed only a commander of stature suitable to lead them all. In the tradition of the time, each community's militia regiment had their own "colonel," of which many were present, but only one was perhaps suitable for command of the whole.

Thomas Sumter was now also arrived at Tuckaseegee Ford with the band of men he had recruited on his travels to Salisbury. Among them were several veterans of his Sixth Regiment, and according to Sumter's biographer Robert D. Bass, two hundred Catawba Indians. At forty-five years of age, Sumter was older than most of his fellow militia officers, and his service as a Continental officer endowed him with natural authority. Bass suggests he may have even worn his old Continental army colonel's uniform on his journeys. Beyond that there was a charisma and spirit of industry about Thomas Sumter that drew men to him and also a shrewd insight into the psychological character of these backcountry settlers.[36]

It was the custom of the time for militia leaders to be chosen by democratic process, sometimes a formal vote, or sometimes by simple consensus. In his memoir, Winn recalled the South Carolinians "got together and had a consultation. Nothwithstanding the smallness of our number, it was unanimously agreed on to oppose the British and Tories . . . the next question rose, who should command." It was Winn who was first chosen, "without a dissenting voice," at least according to him. However, observing that Sumter was on the ground, "an old experienced officer,"[37] Winn deferred, stating Sumter was "surely the most proper person to take command."

To this proposal, according to Winn's memoir, some of the colonels objected, though Winn provides no insight on the nature of these concerns. This was democracy after all, a messy, quarrelsome process, where opinion and dissent are like seeds blowing in the hay fields of June, or the memories of old men, floating into the ether of time. In the memory of Winn, he and Col. Robert Patton retired from the group to consult Sumter on the subject. "After some conversation and explination, Col. Sumter accepted the nomination."[38]

McJunkin recalled this referendum somewhat differently: "After some consultation and various efforts to collect scattered comrades, the party said to Col. Sumter, 'If we choose you our leader, will you direct our operations?' He replied, 'Our interests are the same. With me it is liberty or death.' An election was held and Sumter unanimously chosen General."³⁹

That this "election" held no official authority, everyone involved would readily admit. Yet in the custom of the time, Thomas Sumter was now the general of these refugees. "It is interesting to note that Cornwallis in his letters at once accorded him" the title of "General," observes Sumter biographer Anne King Gregorie, even "if Rutledge and other South Carolinians punctiliously kept to the old title of colonel."⁴⁰

This was the first large-scale embodiment of the South Carolina militia since the fall of Charleston, and without doubt or dissension, whether elected or conferred, Sumter was now their leader. The men agreed "with solemn obligation to place themselves under the command of Genl. Thomas Sumter and to continue in a body and serve under his command until the war was at an end or until their services were no longer necessary," recalled militia soldier John Adair, who was at Tuckaseegee and observed Sumter's election.⁴¹

In truth, this was no army. Only a volunteer militia corps, of the type that had been formed and reformed, banded with others and dispersed with equal efficiency, since the earliest settlements on the American frontier. But "this was the first organization of the militia after the fall of Charleston," recalled militia soldier Robert Wilson, who was also on the banks of the Catawba that June day.⁴² And that primacy would confer on it, and its "general," a measure of status in the warfare soon to come.

NINE

HUCK'S WAR

With help from Hollywood, Banastre Tarleton is a stereotype of the American Revolution. His role, the vain and ruthless British officer. This is the "Bloody Ban" of Whig propaganda, perpetuated in fiction, television, and film as the sneering, preening villain, his lecherous eye turned on our hero's gal, his innate cruelty foiled by our hero's guile.

And like many stereotypes, there must be some element of truth in this version of the man. Certainly, the real Banastre Tarleton had a scoundrel side. In his portrait by Joshua Reynolds and appearance as one of Mischianza's dashing black knights is evidence of his vanity. Sources agree that in London he dropped out of college to pursue a life of iniquity and gambled away a small family fortune, forsaking a career in the law. In Philadelphia, he seduced another man's mistress. On the outskirts of Charleston, his Legion troops burned, pillaged, and perhaps raped. And on the field at the Waxhaws, he condoned a violent ruthlessness bordering on massacre, if not crossing that line.

Yet clearly Banastre Tarleton was more than just some villainous stereotype. In battle and cavalry operations he displayed a courage bordering on recklessness, but also an initiative and intelligence impeccably suited to eighteenth-century war. True, Tarleton had the advantages of social status that were almost prerequisite for success in the British officer corps, but no mere rake could rise through it as rapidly as Tarleton, nor earn the confidence of Clinton and, especially, Cornwallis without some qualities of character and leadership Tarleton indubitably possessed. His postwar memoir, *A History of the Campaigns of 1780 and 1781, in the Southern Provinces of North America*, reveals him as a talented, if sometimes unreliable, writer and intellect, with prescient insights into the strengths and weaknesses of British strategy. And after the notoriety of his wartime exploits finally waned, Tarleton eventually settled down into a respectable, if not particularly noteworthy, career as a politician and career British officer.

Tarleton's biographer Anthony J. Scotti Jr. believes the stereotype unfair. "To heap the most heinous acts upon the British Legion and its commandant is not realistic," he argues. "As a field commander, Tarleton was no more guilty or innocent than any other British or American officer."[1] Here, too, is a bit of hyperbole, for clearly there were officers on both sides who scorned the excesses Tarleton practiced or accommodated. But war is a brutal profession in any age, and the eighteenth century was no different. Both British *and* Americans officers either condoned or committed atrocious acts during the American Revolution. That Tarleton has become the poster boy for such atrocities only suggests he did it with more panache, and in more critical circumstances.

Historian Stephen Conway depicts the British officer corps in the American Revolution as divided into two camps by the latter stages of the war. On one side were the conciliators. "Officers who recommended or practiced restraint did so, in some instances, for moral reasons associated with humanitarian values of the Enlightenment, or from an older sense of chivalry. Others were primarily motivated by more immediate practical considerations. They believed that mild treatment would pay political dividends," Conway writes. On the other side were the hard-liners. "When the supporters of severity urged a harsh approach, they meant above all, much greater destruction of private property." Dubbed the "Fire and sword men," these officers believed that only by inflicting large-scale psychological trauma on the countryside would American Whigs be battered into submission, finally pressuring the Continental Congress to submit again to British rule.[2]

Banastre Tarleton was clearly in the latter camp. "Nothing will secure the People but Fire & Sword," he would write to Cornwallis later in the campaign.[3] But Tarleton was among good company. Earlier in the war, Rawdon proposed "we should (when we get further into the country) give free liberty to the soldiers to ravage at will, that these infatuated wretches may feel what a calamity war is."[4] And even Patrick Ferguson, who condemned the excesses of Tarleton's British Legion outside Charleston, personally arresting its soldiers accused of rape, proposed at one point in the war that an expedition into New England should "destroy all the houses, grains & fodder throughout that fertile and populous tract . . . after which it is possible that the general distress and destruction of the Country . . . would prevent the rebel Army from throwing any great impediment in its way."[5]

Even for men like Rawdon, Ferguson, and Tarleton, however, these positions were rarely absolute, and Conway acknowledges it was quite common for British officers to express conciliatory outlooks at some points during the war and propose "Fire and Sword" at others. Indeed, Cornwallis is often depicted as the prototype of the conciliatory officer yet condoned "Fire and Sword" as a necessary evil at various times in the Backcountry War. And for some of the same complex psychological motivations that fueled the bitterness between Whig and Loyalist, the most vicious proponents of "Fire and Sword" were often the Provincial soldiers and officers of America's Loyalist class.

Such was the case for Christian Huck, whose name also appears as Huyck or Hook (among other variations). A German immigrant, probably born in 1748, Huck came to America and by 1775 was a Philadelphia attorney. When the American Revolution erupted, Huck chose to remain loyal to the Crown, and like many Loyalists, was persecuted for his choice. In 1778, the Pennsylvania legislature branded him a traitor and his property was confiscated. Seeking retribution, Huck raised his own company of Loyalist volunteers that July and joined the British army in New York. There, he was commissioned a captain in Emmerick's Chasseurs, a "Legion" of dragoons and light infantry commanded by the German officer Lt. Col. Andreas Emmerick, but the following year, Clinton disbanded the Chasseurs due to discipline and morale problems. Briefly, Huck then commanded his own dragoon corps before Clinton attached it to Tarleton's British Legion in August 1779.[6]

It was in this service that Huck and his company of dragoons was assigned to the outpost at Rocky Mount in mid-June. While the Legion infantry was posted at guard duty around Camden, its dragoons were portioned to Camden's outer defensive outposts, Rocky Mount and Hanging Rock guarding the northern frontier with North Carolina, and Cheraws on the Pee Dee River. Remember the British only ever sent two of its regular cavalry regiments to the American Revolution and relied heavily on Provincial regiments for mounted support throughout the war. In the Backcountry War, cavalry operations were handled primarily by Tarleton's Legion, and during the first part of that summer its dragoons were "directed to keep the communications open between the principal posts" of the British defenses as their principal duty.[7]

Meanwhile, Tarleton returned to Charleston with Cornwallis to recruit and reequip his regiment in preparation for Cornwallis's planned invasion of North Carolina that fall, departing from Camden on June 21. In Charleston, Tarleton's behavior contributed to his roguish reputation: Bass writes that he was quartered in the home of a leading Whig, who was fighting with the American troops, and there confined the man's wife and children to a single room of the house; when the women requested another room, he replied "that enemies should not be allowed any conveniences."[8]

Tarleton's departure from the backcountry allowed Christian Huck to act as Tarleton's surrogate, at least for a brief period between mid-June and mid-July 1780. Just six years older than Tarleton, Huck shared many characteristics with his commanding officer. Both were educated to some degree. Both were dragoon commanders in the Carolina backcountry, and both shared a taste for "Fire and Sword." Both could be accused of arrogance. Indeed, to one who knows the southern campaigns only from popular media a man like Christian Huck and a man like Banastre Tarleton might appear to be one and the same. For if it is true that Banastre Tarleton is the poster boy for that sneering, preening British villain of television and film, exemplified by the dastardly "Colonel Tavington" of Mel Gibson's 2000 film *The Patriot,* many of the atrocities attributed to him during the American Revolution are in fact an amalgamation of his own actions and those of others, with officers like Christian Huck occasionally serving in his stead.

This type of confusion only adds to Banastre Tarleton's notoriety, but Banastre Tarleton and Christian Huck were *not* one and the same. While Tarleton carefully cultivated the air of a British gentlemen, and adhered closely to British army social conventions, Huck was unburdened by such constraints. Perhaps fueled by the persecutions he had endured earlier in the war, Huck openly disdained the backcountry's Whigs, particularly the

Scots-Irish Presbyterians, whom he never failed "on convenient occasions, to curse."[9] In fact, Huck's reputation for cursing earned him the nickname the "Swearing Captain," and by July 1780, his profane arrogance, accompanied with the reputation for "Fire and Sword" he had achieved with the burning of homes, churches, and Hill's Ironworks, had made him public enemy number one throughout the Carolina countryside, or at least the part of it where Thomas Sumter and his refugees now patrolled.

AFTER SELECTED AS GENERAL AT Tuckaseegee Ford, Sumter and the men of his new command traveled with Rutherford toward Ramsour's Mill on the morning of June 20. They had waited out a heavy rain the day before, and before commencing their attack on the approximately 1,300 Loyalists mustered at Ramsour's Mill, Rutherford had ordered a junction with a body of approximately four hundred militia from North Carolina's Rowan County under command of Francis Locke later that day.

But Rutherford's orders were either lost or ignored, and at a council meeting on the night of June 19, Locke's officers decided to proceed with the attack on Ramsour's Mill at dawn, with or without Rutherford. Their plan was to approach the Tory camp in three companies on horseback early the next morning, with the unmounted militia following behind. "No other arrangements were made, and it was left to the officer to be governed by circumstances after they should reach the enemy,"[10] reported American militia officer Joseph Graham, a witness to the action.

The Loyalists were camped on a hill three hundred yards east of Ramsour's Mill. When the Whig horsemen came within sight of the Tory guards, "they plainly perceived that their approach had not been anticipated," reported Graham. The pickets fled back to the camp, Rebel horsemen in close pursuit, firing at the Tories from "within thirty steps." Some of the Loyalists fled camp during this initial charge, but others formed a disorganized line and started to return the Whig fire, forcing the rangers to retreat back into the ranks of their own infantry, which was following close behind.

What followed was a disorganized melee, as much street brawl as battle. Graham reported that in some places, the Tories were "crowded together in each other's way; in other places there was none ... the action became close, and the parties mixed together in two instances; and having no bayonets, they struck at each other with the butts of their guns. In this strange contest several of the Tories were taken prisoners, and others of them ... intermixed with the Whigs, and all being in their common dress, escape unnoticed."

Locke and his men finally drove the Loyalists from the ridge where they had established their defenses, but the effort came at a huge cost—littering its slope were fifty-six dead; other dead from both sides "lay scattered on the flanks and over the ridge toward the mill." Some of the Loyalists assembled on the other side of the mill, apparently forming for a counterattack, but only eighty-six of Locke's Whigs could be collected for another round of fighting; the rest deserted the battlefield, aghast at the day's already bloody toll.

After the two sides agreed to a temporary truce to tend to the wounded and dead, most of the Loyalists fled as well. Graham reported that each side lost approximately seventy men killed and a hundred wounded. Finally arriving with his seven hundred men shortly after the battle, including Sumter's corps, Rutherford ordered a young officer of the North Carolina state militia named William R. Davie and his mounted rangers to sweep the countryside for straggling Loyalists. Davie reported many Loyalists "came and surrendered voluntarily and a great number were taken prisoners, some flying to South Carolina, others at their plantations, and in a few days that district of country lying between the river, the mountains and their [South Carolina] line was entirely cleared of the enemy."

In terms of the body count, the Battle of Ramsour's Mill was no Patriot victory, though the outcome had a rousing effect on the Whigs of the western Carolinas. Cornwallis and his officers certainly understood its negative implications. "Mr. Moore, in spite of your Lordship's earnest advice and in contradiction to your express direction, has called forth the loyalists in Tryon County," Rawdon informed Cornwallis in a letter dated June 22, 1780. In that time, Tryon County encompassed the entire southwestern corner of North Carolina, extending from the Catawba River to the Cherokee Indian Territory in what is now modern-day Lincoln, Gaston, Cleveland, and Rutherford Counties. The region was named after William Tryon, royal governor of North Carolina from 1765 to 1771. "The consequence was that early on the 20th . . . they were attacked near the south fork of the Catawba River . . . and entirely dispersed."[11]

Cornwallis was furious after receiving the news. "The affair of Tryon County has given me great concern," he responded to Rawdon. "The folly and impudence of our friends is unpardonable." To Clinton he admitted, "I am sorry to say that a considerable number of loyal inhabitants of Tryon County, encouraged and headed by a Colonel Moore . . . rose . . . without order or caution and were in a few days defeated by a General Rutherford with some loss." But Cornwallis assured Clinton plans for a North Carolina invasion were not jeopardized: "I still hope this unlucky business will not materially affect the general plan. . . . I think that with the force present under my command . . . I can leave South Carolina in security and march about the beginning of September with a body of troops into the back part of North Carolina."[12]

Eager to put a positive spin on this negative development, Cornwallis shared with Clinton an account of Huck's destruction at Hill's Ironworks in this same report. "The dispersion of a party of rebels, who had assembled at an iron work on the north west border of the province, by a detachment of dragoons and militia from Lt. Colonel Turnbull put an end to all resistance in South Carolina," he boasted optimistically. Underneath this sanguine assessment, however, Cornwallis knew the countryside was far from pacified. A prominent concern was what appeared to be the reformation of the Continental army, in the vicinity of Hillsborough, North Carolina. By the time of his June 30 report to Clinton, Cornwallis had received news that Maryland and Delaware reinforcements had arrived there under command of "Major General de Calbe."[13]

Though he called himself "Baron de Kalb," Johann Kalb was not European nobility, but the son of a Bavarian peasant, born in 1737, who left his home at the age of sixteen to become a soldier of fortune. After a successful career in the French army and marriage to the heiress of a prosperous French estate, his quest took him to America in 1777.

Promised a major general's commission in the Continental army as part of American envoy Silas Deane's effort to recruit European officers, Kalb sailed to America with Lafayette in 1777, temporarily serving as Lafayette's second in command while he squabbled with Congress over the terms of Deane's promises. But the problems were political, not personal. Unlike some of the officers Deane recruited from Europe, Kalb was every inch the professional soldier, accomplished in war and liked by his soldiers and fellow officers. "In person De Kalb had distinction," writes the historian Christopher Ward, who quotes one of Kalb's staff officers to describe him: "A perfect Ariovistus, more than six feet tall," with an engaging countenance and a "temperance, sobriety, and prudence" others found noteworthy. He was said to work a full day only on water and a slice of bread for breakfast and bowl of soup for dinner. And he bore the hardships of war with "patience, long-suffering strength of constitution . . . and a cheerful submission to every inconvenience. . . . Brave to the point of temerity, he was an ideal leaver of a combat force in action."[14]

Finally, on September 15, 1777, Kalb received his major general's commission, but it wasn't until the Backcountry War of 1780 that he received his first independent command, taking charge of the first and second Maryland brigades, along with the Delaware Regiment. With this small army, Kalb was ordered to relieve Charleston, much like Abraham Buford's Virginia troops. Kalb then marched from Morristown, New Jersey, on April 16, passing through Philadelphia before sailing down the Chesapeake Bay to Petersburg, Virginia, where he received news of Charleston's surrender.

Kalb's secondary orders from Washington were to gather Patriot militia as he approached Charleston and keep the British from taking South Carolina. With both Charleston and most of South Carolina now under British control, Kalb wasn't sure what to do, though he was reinforced in Petersburg with the 1st Artillery and eighteen field pieces, bringing his total force to about 1,400 soldiers. Kalb decided to march on. "The country was not yet conquered," remarked Maryland colonel Otho Holland Williams, serving as Kalb's adjutant general. "It was presumed that the countenance of a body of regular troops, however small, would constitute more than anything the fortitude of the militia."[15]

They marched on to Hillsborough, North Carolina. At that time, the village served as the seat of North Carolina's Whig government, and Kalb had received assurances from North Carolina officials his army would be provisioned there. The village was also home to some Continental army magazines, or supply depots. Arriving at Hillsborough on June 22, Kalb's presence was soon reported to Cornwallis. However, the food and provisions promised by North Carolina never arrived at Hillsborough, and after a week Kalb's army moved on, reaching Cox's Mill on Deep River, in modern-day Randolph County, North Carolina, south of today's Ramseur community, on July 6. At Deep River, "the baron found himself under the necessity of halting for want of provisions."

THOUGH THEY HAD MISSED THE FIGHTING at Ramsour's Mill, Sumter and his men were galvanized by its outcome. After the battle, Sumter returned to South Carolina and established camp on Hagler's Branch, a tributary of Sugar Creek in the northeast corner of the New Acquisition District. There he was joined by additional South Carolina militia, as well as another small body of Georgians, altogether about five hundred men. According to Joseph McJunkin, Sumter called a council of his officers on or about June 22 to decide next steps. "Sumter said, 'Gentlemen, you may depend upon it, that in order to regain our country, we must expect to fight hard, & the force must repel force, or otherwise we need not attempt to regain our beloved country.'" The point was well taken. "The conclusion was to gain our point, or die in the attempt," McJunkin recalled.[16]

Meanwhile, Christian Huck and his dragoons had also returned to the New Acquisition District. Huck ordered the region's Loyalists to assemble at upper Fishing Creek on June 22. This meeting was colorfully recounted in the memoir of William Hill, who recalled that Huck harangued the Loyalists "on the certainty of his majesty reducing all the Colonies to obedience." Though "God almighty" might have become a rebel, Huck assured the gathered, that even if "there were 20 gods on that side, they would all be conquered." And while Huck was engaged in this "impious blasphemy he had his officers & men taking all the horses fit for his purpose, so that many of the aged men had to walk many miles home afoot."

Huck's "ill behavior . . . made an impression on the minds" of Sumter and his men, Hill continued, "and raised their courage under the belief that they would be made instruments in the hand of Heaven to punish this enemy for his wickedness and blasphemy—and no doubt the recent injuries that many of their families received from the said Hook and his party had an effect to stimulate this little band to a proper courage."[17]

With men streaming into his camp, Sumter established a new base on July 1 at Catawba Old Town, an old, unused field of the Catawba Indians situated about fourteen miles south of Charlotte on Clem's Branch of Sugar Creek. There he sought food, forage, and supplies for his troops. Many of the men now joining Sumter were known to him from his earlier service in the war, including about eighty veterans of his Sixth South Carolina Regiment. By July 4, Sumter had moved again, establishing camp on the east side of the Catawba River about four miles from the Old Nation Ford, an ancient crossing place on the Catawba River.[18]

There Sumter was joined by Colonel James Williams and a small party from the Little River Militia. This was the same James Williams who had brawled with Robert Cunningham during the 1778 General Assembly campaign and was by now a well-known Whig politician and militia commander. Recall that after escaping his plantation on Little River in early June, Williams had moved some of his personal property and valuables to family property in Caswell County in northern North Carolina before returning to South Carolina and joining with some of his militia troops. "On the whole, I expect we will shortly meet the tories, when they must give an account of their late conduct," Williams wrote to his wife on July 4, 1780, informing her of his arrival at Sumter's camp.[19]

In response to the disaster at Ramsour's Mill, Turnbull marched north from Rocky Mount on June 22 with a detachment of New York volunteers and Loyalist militia, rendezvousing with Captain Huck and his Legion dragoons on June 24. Probably that same day, Huck and his dragoons ran into a small body of Whig militia while on patrol at Bullock's Creek. A sharp skirmish ensued, with Huck's troops killing at least one Whig. As ever, exaggerated rumors of the skirmish soon swept the countryside, agitating the local Whig community.

Turnbull set up a forward base at Brown's Crossroads, where he received frequent and exaggerated reports of Sumter's growing force. There on July 5, he received news Sumter was marching toward Rocky Mount with a force of five hundred men. In fact, Sumter had sent only a small force toward Rocky Mount, but his feint had worked, forcing Turnbull to evacuate Brown's Crossroads that day.[20]

Meanwhile, Rawdon had dispatched some infantry under Maj. Thomas Mecan to subdue the Waxhaws and collect wheat from the vicinity.[21] In response, Sumter broke camp at Old Nation Ford and moved down to intercept Mecan with his entire force of five to six hundred men. Finding no British at the Waxhaws, however, Sumter and his officers decided to temporarily disband his army, allowing the men to return home to gather provisions, recruit, tend to their families, and most importantly, harvest their wheat.[22]

Leaving a small guard at Old Nation Ford, Sumter himself traveled into North Carolina to procure supplies and rifles. It is from this period he may have received his famous "Gamecock" nickname. According to lore, Sumter traveled to the home of the Gillespies in western North Carolina, who may have been gunsmiths, though other versions portray them only as potential recruits. Reaching the Gillespie settlement, Sumter found them watching a blue hen cock named "Tuck" engaging in a cock fight, a popular pastime of the era. "Fight with me," Sumter reportedly told the Gillespies, "and I'll show you a battle of men." Impressed with Sumter's martial spirit, the Gillespies hailed him as "Tuck," and from this encounter the "Gamecock" nickname supposedly was born.[23]

When Turnbull discovered Sumter's corps was temporarily disbanding, he sensed an opportunity to apprehend some of its most egregious offenders, particularly John McClure and William Bratton, whom he accused of recruiting others to the Patriot cause. Again, the mission of apprehending them and pushing "the rebels of the frontier as far as you may deem convenient," was assigned to Captain Christian Huck with a force of thirty-five Legion dragoons, twenty New York Volunteers, and fifty mounted militia.[24]

Leaving the British camp at Rocky Mount on July 10, Huck camped that night at the home of Nicholas Bishop, a known Whig whose four eldest sons were also veterans of earlier campaigns. Prior to Huck's arrival, the Bishops fled to Sumter's camp, informing its remaining men Huck was in the vicinity. The following morning Huck and his troops proceeded to upper Fishing Creek, first stopping at John McClure's home, in what is now the Rodman community of northeastern Chester County. McClure was not there, but several of his family members were. Storming into the house, Huck quickly arrested two men engaged in the production of ammunition, and according to local tradition, looted and attempted to burn the property, though McClure's wife was eventually able to put out the fire.[25]

After sacking the McClure's, Huck looted several other Whig homes in the vicinity, confiscating wheat and horses and taking several prisoners. By late afternoon he reached the home of William Bratton. Though Bratton was still at Sumter's camp, his wife, Martha, was home, along with several neighbors who had gathered there to help collect the wheat harvest. According to family lore, Martha dispatched a family slave to warn her husband of Huck's raid. Finding Bratton away, Huck's soldiers terrorized Martha Bratton, placing a sword at her neck when she refused to divulge her husband's whereabouts, before a British officer finally intervened in the terror.

After Huck himself interrogated Martha harshly, he ordered her to prepare dinner for him and his men, then arrested the elderly men who had been assisting in the wheat harvest and confined all of the women and children to the home's garret. Huck planned to spend the night at the Bratton plantation but changed his mind sometime during the course of the evening and moved his camp to the nearby home of James Williamson, perhaps because there was an oat field at Williamson's where Huck could forage his horses.

Meanwhile, the small garrison remaining at Sumter's camp had been receiving news of Huck's raid all day and was now preparing to move against him. With Sumter away, command fell to Richard Winn and the other militia commanders who remained at the camp, among them Bratton, McClure, and William Hill. The militia set out in the late afternoon and by evening received news that Huck was camped at Bratton's. At this point, some of the Whig militia in the rear of the column dispersed, apparently receiving false news that the British were attacking in front, leaving Winn, Bratton, and McClure with approximately 130 men.

They proceeded to Bratton's, where they planned an early morning assault, but William Bratton soon got cold feet, afraid for his family captured inside the house. However, scouts sent forward to reconnoiter Huck's position soon learned he was camped instead at the nearby Williamson property. The Whigs split their force, deciding to attack Williamson's at break of day from both ends of the road that passed by the property. The men of the northern New Acquisition District, what is now York County, would attack from the west end of the lane. This group was under the command of Bratton, Hill, and Winn. The men from the lower district, what is now Chester County, would attack from the east under command of McClure and Col. Edward Lacey. The plan was to begin the attack as soon as either group fired the first shot, raising a war whoop as they stormed the farm.

Lacey and McClure had the tougher assignment, for they had to sweep through the woods around Williamson's farm in the dark to reach the east end of the lane. Thus, they were not in position when Winn, Hill, and Bratton's men started firing at Huck's guards at the break of dawn. Huck was still inside the Williamson house, where he had slept the previous night, and allegedly took time to harangue Williamson and his family during the early moments of the attack. "We have driven the Regulars out of the country," he boasted, according to tradition, "and I swear that if it rained militia from the Heavens, I would not value them."[26] However, after Huck stormed out to investigate the shooting, Williamson barricaded the home's doors, separating Huck from his jacket and accoutrement, still inside the house.

By this time, the Whig attack had commenced, Bratton's men raising the war whoop, though McClure and Lacey's men were still not in position. Using a nearby fence for cover, Whig riflemen took deadly aim at the Loyalist militia camped on the outskirts of the farm, killing a Loyalist officer named James Ferguson (no direct relation to Patrick Ferguson). With Ferguson dead, much of the remaining Loyalist militia dispersed, with several escaping down the east end of the lane, where McClure had still not yet taken position. Those who could not escape surrendered.

The Patriots now turned their attention to the area around Williamson's house, where the Legion dragoons were positioned. Witnessing this portion of the fight from a nearby peach orchard was James Collins, a sixteen-year-old from Bullock's Creek who was participating in his first battle. According to Collins's memoir, the dragoons mounted and paraded in front of the Patriots. "This, I confess, was a very imposing sight, at least to me, for I had never seen a troop of British horse before." Leading the dragoons by now was Huck, dressed in his white shirt, for his jacket was still locked inside Williamson's house. "The leader drew his sword, mounted his horse, and began to storm and rave, and advanced on us; but we kept close to the peach orchard," Collins recalled. "When they had got pretty near the peach trees, their leader called out, 'disperse you d——d rebels, or I will put every man of you to the sword.' Our rifle balls began to whistle among them, and in a few minutes my Lord Hook [Huck] was shot off his horse and fell at full length."[27]

Huck was dead, and despite another charge at the Whig position, the rest of the Legion dragoons soon fled. Meanwhile, McClure and Lacey's militia had finally broken through to the east side of the road and now pursued some of the fleeing Loyalists and dragoons. According to some accounts, the fighting lasted as little as five minutes. Whig casualties were light, perhaps as little as one man. Legion and Loyalist casualties are unclear, although in an account sent to Gen. Kalb, Thomas Sumter claimed their losses were two officers and twelve privates dead, and two officers and twenty-seven privates captured.[28]

More important than the body count was the effect Huck's Defeat had on the surrounding countryside. In the aftermath of the action, Sumter received so many new recruits he had to move his camp yet again, this time a few miles north of the Old Nation Ford on Steel Creek. One of the new recruits was John Lisle, second in command of the Upper District Loyalist Militia Regiment, who arrived at Sumter's camp with several of his fellow Loyalists, along with their arms and ammunition newly issued from the British army. Writing of the betrayal in his memoir, Tarleton said Lisle's defection "ruined all confidence between the regulars and the militia."[29]

Though he did not participate in the engagement, Sumter's power expanded in the aftermath of Huck's Defeat. According to the memoir of Richard Winn, "as the laws of the State had subsided about this time, it was thought necessary to call a convention of the people, which met in or near the Catawba Indian land." After Winn was elected president, "it was then moved and seconded that Col. Thomas Sumter should be appointed a brigadier-general and that the President be directed to make out a commission to that effect." Though Sumter's commission obviously had little "official" standing, it would bolster later arguments of his status over other partisan Whig leaders.[30]

Sumter certainly portrayed himself as South Carolina's militia commander in chief in a long letter he composed to Gen. Kalb on July 17, 1780, the only correspondence Kalb received from any South Carolina officer in the field after arriving in North Carolina. In it, Sumter gave a detailed breakdown of British troops in the state, revealing his talent for intelligence and reconnaissance operations. Sumter assured Kalb "the enemy is by being so Detached in small parties, and the Impossibility of their being collected in a Short Time," that a party of "one thousand or fifteen hundred Troops"[31] sent to capture the Santee River crossings at Nelson's and Manigault's Ferry would cut off access between Charleston and the British army's northern outposts, disrupting Loyalist recruitment efforts and forcing a retreat toward Georgia. Though an optimistic assessment, the letter reveals Sumter's predilection for partisan operations and decisive attack. Kalb would hand the letter to his successor, Gen. Horatio Gates, upon Gates's arrival in North Carolina, and evidence suggests it had a profound influence on Gates's plans for the Camden campaign to come.

From his quarters in Charleston, Tarleton was furious at Huck, whom he accused of neglecting his duty "in placing his party carelessly, at a plantation, without advancing any pickets, or sending out patroles." But he was also angry with Rawdon, whom he believed was jeopardizing his Legion dragoons in dangerous and undermanned detachments. "Ever since the affair at Waxhaw, the Troops of the Legion (not withstanding my Remonstrances, Petition, & openly pointing out the dangers of Detachment into N. Carolina) have been sent out at great hazard," Tarleton complained of Rawdon's administration of the Legion troops in a July 16 letter to John André, now serving as Clinton's adjutant general back in New York. "I have had the mortification to hear that 70 men of the Legion have never been kept together—Detachment after Detachment either by my Lord Cornwallis or my Lord Rawdon to the great Detriment of the Corps."[32]

Cornwallis's sharp letter to Rawdon of July 15, in which he cautions his junior officer that "cavalry acts chiefly upon the nerves, and if once it loses its terror, it loses its greatest force," may have been written in response to Tarleton's complaints. "Let me conjure you to take care of the cavalry, and to give the most positive orders against small detachments; they are always dangerous, especially under ignorant and careless officers."[33]

In the same letter, Cornwallis announced to Rawdon, "Tarleton will join you in a few days." It seems the British general realized his most talented cavalry officer was needed more desperately in command of his dragoons than in Charleston. But shortly after Huck's Defeat, perhaps as he was preparing to rejoin the Legion in Camden, Tarleton fell sick, encountering a first bout with the malaria that would plague him throughout the summer and fall. It would not be for another two weeks until he would return to the backcountry.[34]

If Cornwallis felt frustration at his officers' carelessness, and concern over burgeoning Whig resistance, Huck's Defeat convinced him primarily that he must move as soon as possible into North Carolina. "I foresee that it will be absolutely necessary to act offensively very soon to save our friends in North Carolina and to preserve the confidence, in which is included the friendship, of the South Carolinians." In a letter informing Clinton of Huck's defeat, he wrote similarly, "This little blow will, I fear, much encourage the enemy and greatly increase the difficulty of protecting our borders. I see no safety in this province but in moving forward as soon as possible."[35]

Charles Cornwallis. The Battle of Camden was his greatest victory of the American Revolution, but Cornwallis could never gain complete control of South Carolina in 1780 thanks to the campaigns of Thomas Sumter, Francis Marion, and other talented militia leaders. Sumter, in particular, was a thorn in Cornwallis's side, leading to his authorization of a failed assassination attempt on the Gamecock at Fishdam Ford.

Francis Marion. No known portrait exists taken from Marion's life. This one, at least, captures the Swamp Fox's sharply angled nose. The writer William Dobein James, who knew him, described Marion as possessing "a countenance remarkably steady; his nose was aquiline; his chin projecting; his forehead was large and high; and his black eyes piercing.

Banastre Tarleton. Still in his mid-twenties during the Backcountry War, Tarleton and his green-coated dragoons were Cornwallis's preferred instrument of war, even if he is often confused with lesser "Tarletons" such as James Wemyss and Christian Huck. Though artists such as Sir Joshua Reynolds romanticized his appearance, an observer in 1777 described him as "rather below middle size, stout, strong, and heavily made. . . . His complexion dark, and his eyes small, dark, and piercing."

Thomas Sumter. Bold and enterprising, with a natural charisma, the Gamecock possessed an acute understanding of backcountry militia psychology. He was a talented recruiter, spymaster, and strategist but also prone to baffling security breakdowns, as at Fishdam Ford and Fishing Creek. At Blackstocks, he defeated British regulars under Banastre Tarleton two months before Daniel Morgan more famously achieved the same feat at Cowpens.

Horatio Gates. Although a historic reevaluation suggests Gates's defeat at the Battle of Camden was as much bad luck as bad leadership, his 180-mile flight from the battlefield to Continental Army headquarters in Hillsborough, North Carolina, was a disgrace from which his military career could not recover. Still, Gates recognized the talents of Sumter and Marion and attempted to incorporate them into his plans to capture Camden.

William R. Davie. A talented partisan commander, Davie's militia legacy was undermined by his later service as Nathanael Greene's commissary general, or chief supply officer. He played an important leadership role during the Battle of Hanging Rock and other militia engagements during the Backcountry War but is perhaps better remembered today as a governor of North Carolina and founder of the University of North Carolina at Chapel Hill.

TEN

PROVIDENCE
and MOTION

O N THE BANKS OF DEEP RIVER in central North Carolina, Maj. Gen. Johann Kalb waited. Mostly he waited for the provisions he had been promised by the Continental army and the Whig governments of North Carolina and Virginia. His men were starving; their clothes and equipment were in tatters. Yet Kalb and his senior officers now realized provisions were scarce everywhere in the South, and such promises were not to be trusted.

He also waited for reinforcements. By now he had been joined by scattered elements of the Continental army that had escaped Charleston, mostly a small band of mounted dragoons and light infantry under the command of the French officer Charles Armand, the remnants of Pulaski's Legion, no more than 120 men. Portions of other cavalry regiments under Continental officers Anthony White and William Washington were refitting near Halifax and were expected in the next few weeks. But promised militia reinforcements from Virginia and North Carolina had still not arrived.

Mostly, though, he waited for Horatio Gates. After Continental general Benjamin Lincoln was captured at Charleston, the Southern Department needed a new commander in chief. Though he was now a major general, a talented officer with enough experience for the job, at least in the Continental army, where any experience was a premium, any experience at all, Kalb's foreign émigré status disqualified him politically from overall command. George Washington wanted his protégé, Nathanael Greene, but Washington only had influence in this particular decision. Congress had the final say, and Congress wanted Gates.

Gates's appointment made sense. Despite his feuds and political missteps, Gates was still the "Hero of Saratoga," general at the most important American victory of the war, even if talented subordinates like Daniel Morgan and Benedict Arnold had also played important roles in the victory. In fact, Gates forte was always staff work, not combat leadership, but that doesn't mean he wasn't a talented officer. He was born in England on July 26, 1727, his mother a servant in aristocratic households. Though bred to humble circumstances, the young Gates gained powerful benefactors, probably through his mother's employers. From them, "he learned to mingle with aristocracy on terms of easy familiarity. He exuded a sense of competence and dependability. Acquaintances felt at home with him and gave him their trust. . . . He conveyed the feeling that he not only gave but needed friendship. . . . He tried, perhaps too hard, to please." With assistance of his patrons, Gates was commissioned a lieutenant in the British army, serving in Germany during the War of Austrian Succession before traveling to Nova Scotia in 1749 to join the staff of its military governor, Col. Edward Cornwallis, an uncle to Charles Cornwallis. "Young Gates made himself an expert in organizational minutiae and parade-ground technique," writes historian Max Mintz. "Regiments depended on the few such officers who applied themselves to detail."[1]

In Nova Scotia, Gates courted the pretty but domineering Elizabeth Phillips. Eventually, they married, settling briefly in New York City, where Gates befriended members of the Whig Club, early proponents of an American republic, and was influenced by their ideals. By now he had purchased a captain's commission on credit, which brought him to the ill-fated Braddock expedition into the Pennsylvania frontier. There he joined a mixed British and American force that included other American Revolution notables like George Washington and Daniel Morgan. Braddock's defeat at the Battle of Monongahela on July 9, 1755, was a disaster of epic proportions, perhaps foretelling future disasters to come for Gates, but his reputation emerged from it unscathed. In 1765, after a successful if unremarkable career, and a burgeoning reputation as a "red hot republican," he retired from the British army as a major and, with assistance from George Washington, settled in Virginia in 1772.

The relationship between Gates and Washington was a complicated one. Sensing opportunity in the American Revolution for a man of his professional experience, Gates came out of retirement to accept a commission as brigadier general and joined Washington's staff as adjutant general, or chief administrative officer, a rank someone of his social status could have never obtained in the British army. In councils of war, Gates typically counseled toward caution, but his politics were by now radical, and his ambitions were ravenous, if not always refined. By 1777, Gates was a major general, and as British general John Burgoyne led an invasion force down the Hudson Valley, attempting to drive a wedge between New England and the rest of the American colonies, Gates political lobbying gained him command of the Northern Army, though these machinations "brought out the worst side of Gates's nature by showing him to be petty and vindictive where matters of rank and authority were concerned."[2]

Nevertheless, Gates's administrative skills served him well in the Hudson Valley, and he showed there a true flair for managing militia. "Unlike most American generals, he had great confidence in short-term soldiers and showed a keen understanding of their temper," observes historian George A. Billias.[3] As temperamental as he could be with his fellow officers, Gates displayed true concern for the welfare of his troops, and with militia, especially, believed in mustering them only when necessary, and using them expediently before returning them to their homes and families.

This approach paid off in the successful campaign around Saratoga in September and October 1777, although Gates was afterward sensitive to criticisms that he'd left the actual fighting to his subordinates Arnold and Morgan. Nevertheless, the victory positioned him as a true rival to Washington, and even if history suggests Gates was never an active participant in the Conway Cabal, a muddled plot attributed to the machinations of the Irish-French officer Thomas Conway, but perhaps also supported by leading Whigs such as Samuel Adams, Richard Henry Lee, and Dr. Benjamin Rush, Gates at the least insinuated he was ready, willing, and able to take Washington's job, if the opportunity was presented to him.

Washington never forgave this betrayal, however, and their relationship continued to sour after Gates was appointed president of the Board of War, an ill-fated attempt by the Continental Congress to reorganize the Continental army. Technically, the post made him Washington's superior, though the administrative body never achieved the oversight function Congress intended for it, and its standing soon dissipated. After an unsuccessful stint there, Gates was assigned again to command of the Northern Department in Upstate New York, and then the Eastern Department in Boston, where he saw little action.

Returned to active command in 1778, his posts were mostly administrative, and in 1779 he requested an extended furlough due to failing health. By June 1780, the now fifty-three-year-old Gates was convalescing at his farm called Traveller's Rest, located in what is now Jefferson County, West Virginia, when Benjamin Lincoln was captured at Charleston. If Washington wanted Greene to replace Lincoln, Gates was, after all, not only a known quantity, but also available and relatively nearby. So, on June 13, 1780, he was appointed the new commander of the Southern Department by the Continental Congress. Clearly, Gates's heroic reputation had survived his personality conflicts with Washington. Also influential to Congress was his reputation for commanding militia, upon which success in the southern theater depended. And the appointment appealed to Gates's pretensions.

While Kalb waited on Gates to relieve him, Gates spent the end of June and first of July in Virginia pleading for supplies and reinforcement for his new command from state and federal officials, including North Carolina governor Abner Nash and Virginia governor Thomas Jefferson. Promises and assurances he successfully received, which he had little choice but to optimistically believe, an optimism he would find in short supply at Deep River, as in everything else an army needs to campaign.[4]

AT DEEP RIVER, KALB WAS certainly *not* waiting on Francis Marion, but there he arrived, sometime around the first of July, perhaps in response to a proclamation Gates had issued from Virginia, calling on all Continental officers still at liberty in the South to join him in North Carolina. With Marion were about twenty men, both Black and white, some wearing the distinctive black leather cap of South Carolina's Second Regiment adorned with the silver crescent symbol denoting "Liberty." At Deep River, Marion was greeted by his friend and former officer Peter Horry, who had already arrived and was volunteering as an aide on Kalb's staff.

For clarity's sake, let us note the different reactions of Sumter and Marion to the British occupation. Sumter had settled on the militia approach, determined at once, it appears, to raise his own paramilitary resistance force, if not coalesce the militia commands of others around him. In contrast, Marion's arrival at Deep River suggests his ambition was limited to continued service in the Continental army, to which he still considered himself an obedient officer. True, the militias of the Pee Dee region had not organized as quickly as those in the northern and western portions of the state, limiting Marion's opportunities to react as Sumter had. And true, Sumter had resigned his Continental army commission two years before, with little reason to still consider himself bound to its terms and obligations, although historian Robert D. Bass suggests Sumter sported his old Continental uniform as he recruited across the Carolinas.

Even as a more established militia leader later in the war, Marion would almost always honor his allegiance and obedience to the Continental army, reluctantly sometimes, as his power and independence grew, but always ultimately. Sumter, meanwhile, almost always acted on his own initiative, coordinating with the Continental army when it suited him, ignoring its orders and strategies otherwise. According to historian Charles Royster, many of the Continental army's officers had adopted a fraternal, almost cultish, outlook by the end of the war, after years of enduring the harshness of prolonged campaigning and the seeming indifference of the American public. And although "their separation from civilian society and their pride in their officer corps encouraged the first step in identifying the class of public-spirited men who could save independence," these officers often showed signs they "felt separated from civilian society" and only they possessed the "true revolutionary spirit of virtuous effort."[5]

Let us not commit ourselves too deeply to Royster's theory here, however, for neither Thomas Sumter nor Francis Marion are perfect examples of it. Sumter obviously valued his service as a Continental officer, and Marion could be temperamental and independent-minded with his Continental army superiors. It is presented only as a difference of outlook between the two men, measurable in degrees, not absolutes, to emphasize the discrepancies between Sumter's initial impulses and Marion's.

Nevertheless, with little to feed extra mouths, Kalb sometime around July 10 sent Marion to Cole's Bridge on Drowning Creek between modern-day Pinehurst and Rockingham, North Carolina, to gather intelligence and search for supplies in the Pee Dee region. Meanwhile, recruits were streaming into Sumter's camp in the aftermath of Huck's Defeat. And while Sumter was fomenting revolution in the New Acquisition District, North Carolina militia general Griffith Rutherford ordered one of his talented officers across the border to establish camp near the Waxhaws "to prevent the enemy from foraging on the borders of the state . . . and check the depredations of the Loyalists who infested that part of the Country."[6]

That officer's name was William Richardson Davie, and though he was commissioned by the state of North Carolina, Davie was raised in the Waxhaws community of north-central South Carolina, with many strong ties there. Davie was born in Egremont Parish, County Cumberland, England, in June 1756, though both of his parents were Scots immigrants. His mother was from a substantial family in Dumfriesshire, Scotland, but his father, William, moved the family to Egremont, near Whitehaven, Cumberland County, England, to start a textile operation. By the 1760s, Mary's brother William Richardson had established himself in the Waxhaws as minister of the Old Waxhaw Presbyterian Meeting House, a religious mecca for the region, and it was probably William who convinced Mary and Archibald to emigrate to the New World.

In the Waxhaws, William's uncle became a patron of his namesake, arranging for Davie to study at Queen's Museum, later Liberty Hall, in Charlotte, and then the College of New Jersey, later Princeton University, where Davie graduated with honors in 1776. After briefly studying law in Salisbury, he soon joined the Patriot cause as a partisan soldier, fighting under North Carolina militia general Allen Jones from 1777–1778.

From the beginning, Davie proved himself a talented officer, rising to the rank of major and eventually raising his own cavalry regiment. Clearly, he was a charismatic young man, considered refined due to his upbringing and education. An early biography describes him as "tall, graceful and strikingly handsome, he had those graces of person which would have made him the favorite in the clanging lists of feudal days. To this he added elegant culture, thrilling eloquence, and graciousness of manner which was to charm in after days the salons of Paris,"[7] a reference to Davie's postwar service as a diplomat in France.

When fighting moved to the region around Savannah, Georgia, in 1779, Davie's mounted militia joined with Pulaski's Continental cavalry at the Battle of Stono Ferry on June 20, where Davie was seriously wounded. Some sources suggest he resumed his study of law in Salisbury during his convalescence, but with Charleston defeated, Davie was once more well enough to take the field, joining with the North Carolina troops of Gen. Griffith Rutherford. This was the same body of militia that, after joining with Sumter and his South Carolina and Georgia refugees at Tuckaseegee Ford, arrived too late to participate in the Battle of Ramsour's Mill.[8]

Now, Davie's forward camp on the north side of Waxhaw Creek placed him only eighteen miles from the Loyalist encampment at Hanging Rock. "Here he was in the neighborhood in which he had been reared and in which he knew every road and by-path, and which was now to be the scene of his most brilliant exploits," wrote the nineteenth-century historian Edward McCrady.[9]

At this camp Davie and his approximately forty mounted militia were joined by additional North and South Carolina militia, as well as thirty-four Catawba Indian warriors under Chief General Newriver. "Skirmishes happened every day for some time," Davie recounted in his memoir. "The Tories were all soon driven into the lines, and the enemy effectually prevented from foraging."[10]

According to Davie, the British forces camped at Hanging Rock had "improvidently consumed all the grain between that post and Camden" and were now relying on supplies from Camden to survive. "To cut off these became an object of importance." On July 20, he set out from his base with some of his dragoons and mounted militia to intercept a supply convoy headed to Hanging Rock. Passing by the British base at Hanging Rock in the night, they set up an ambush at the "Flat-rock," about five miles south of Hanging Rock, where they captured the British supply convoy later that afternoon "with little trouble."

Assuming they would be pursued by the British after the raid, Davie and his men mounted the captured escorts and wagoneers two to a horse and placed them at the head of their column, then set off through the woods to avoid the enemy's pursuit. At two o'clock in the morning, they came to a ford on Beaver Creek, where there was a small settlement, and where Davie anticipated an enemy ambush. He sent a Capt. Petit forward with an advance guard to "examine the Houses and a narrow lane through which the road led." When Petit reported back that all was clear, Davie moved his convoy forward, right into the ambush he had anticipated. But absorbing the brunt of the attack were Davie's prisoners, still mixed in with the advanced guard. "It was owing to these circumstances that the prisoners were all killed or wounded except three or four," wrote Davie, who blamed the incident on Petit, "a misfortune solely occasioned by the officer of the advance guard not having executed his orders; this may furnish a useful lesson to the officers of a partizan corps ... who should never forget that every officer of a detachment or command may at some moment have its safety and reputation committed to him."[11]

While Davie harassed the patrols and foraging parties sent out from Camden, Joseph Graham was among the Mecklenburg County militia stationed with Sumter during the latter part of July, now at a camp on Clem's Branch, near the main road from Camden to Charlotte. Despite initial enthusiasm after Huck's Defeat, Sumter's militia soon grew restless, and the Gamecock struggled to maintain his small army. "The numbers of his men daily diminished," reported Graham. "While he kept moving, and they expected to meet the enemy, they kept with him; but whenever they camp to attend only to the dull routine of camp duty, such as mounting, relieving and standing guard and enduring privations, they became discontented, and those in convenient distance went home, and others to the houses of their acquaintances. . . . This was the first practical lesson to our commanders of militia, showing that while they kept in motion and the men expected that something would be achieved, they continued with the army."[12]

To keep his men mustered, Sumter resolved to attack the outpost at Rocky Mount, despite its robust fortifications. Located just south of modern-day Great Falls, South Carolina, on the west side of the Catawba River, the outpost consisted of two or three log buildings, "calculated for defense" and "loop-holed" for shooting, surrounded by an abatis, which were field fortifications typically consisting of sharpened logs pointed outward, interlaced, or tied together by wire and brush. The fortification stood on top of a hill, bounded by the Catawba River on the east and a creek on the north.[13]

The base had been a thorn in the Patriot's side all summer. From it, Lt. Col. George Turnbull threatened most of the New Acquisition, Dutch Fork, and western Camden districts. Calling his men back to camp, Sumter was able to gather about six hundred, including approximately three hundred from Joseph Graham's Mecklenburg Militia. At a council with Davie on July 30, it was decided that Sumter would attack Rocky Mount while Davie created a diversion at Hanging Rock, sixteen miles to the east.

Davie arrived near Hanging Rock around one o'clock in the afternoon on August 1 with a party of eighty men, his forty mounted dragoons and another forty mounted militia riflemen. Scouting the camp, he discovered three companies of mounted Loyalist infantry, probably around sixty or seventy riders, "returning from some excursion, had halted at a farmers house, situated in full view of the camp."[14] Acting decisively, Davie immediately formulated a bold plan to attack the detachment. As both the Loyalist and Patriots there were volunteers, they were all dressed in their regular clothes, with no uniforms or markings to distinguish one side from the other. Davie ordered his forty riflemen to ride past the Loyalists on the lane that ran in front of the house. "As the riflemen were not distinguishable from the Loyalist," Davie recalled, they "passed the camp sentries without being challenged," it being assumed they were simply another company of Loyalists headed to muster at the main part of the camp.

Meanwhile, Davie divided his dragoons, placing twenty in the road on the opposite side of the house from his riflemen and twenty into the woods, to attack from behind. Once past the house, the riflemen stopped in the lane, turned, and opened fire on the Loyalists. "The astonished Loyalists fled instantly the other way," Davie recalled in his memoir, "and were immediately charged by the dragoons in full gallop," from the opposite end of the road. Driven back toward the house, the Loyalists then tried to take cover at a fence, where they were "literally cut to pieces" by the dragoons Davie had ordered to attack from the field behind the house. The encounter was a rout—a stunning, bloody victory for the dashing young commander. "As this was done under the eye of the British camp no prisoners could be safely taken which may apologize for the slaughter that took place," Davie explained. During the fighting, the rest of the nearby camp at Hanging Rock was beat to order, but by the time they could respond, Davie had vanished back into the countryside, taking sixty horses and "one hundred muskets and rifles" with him.

Meanwhile, Sumter was having less success at Rocky Mount. Although his six hundred men considerably outnumbered the 150 Provincial and Loyalist troops under Turnbull's command inside, Sumter lost any element of surprise when his approach was encountered by a band of Loyalists patrolling outside the base. This patrol quickly retreated into the fortifications, alerting those inside. Finding Rocky Mount better defended than he'd been led to believe, and without any artillery to support his assault, Sumter first demanded Turnbull's surrender, which was defiantly rejected. Then, with an impulsive boldness that would come to define his field leadership style, Sumter ordered the fortifications attacked. "A brisk fired commenced on both sides, which lasted a considerable time," recalled Graham, but "the enemy were under cover in the fortified buildings, and sustained but little damage."[15]

According to William Hill's memoir, he and another officer named Johnson volunteered to try to set the buildings on fire, racing a hundred yards across the open ground with "lightwood" and torches through heavy gunfire. Eventually, the flames took and Hill and Johnson raced back to the Patriot defenses through the same hail of bullets. "And here I beg leave to remark that Providence so protected us both, that neither of us lost a drop of blood, altho' locks of hair was cut from our heads and our garments riddled with balls," Hill recalled. But just then, a "heavy a storm of rain fell," dousing the flames.[16] Sumter eventually retreated, after what may have been as long as eight hours of fighting. Despite the failed frontal assault and Hill's heroics, Sumter lost only six killed and eight wounded before he retreated back to the Catawba River.

WHILE SUMTER AND DAVIE WERE CAMPAIGNING against the British outposts, Gates had finally arrived at Deep River on July 25, and immediately put his forces in order for a march on Camden, considered the key to the British occupation of South Carolina for its strategic position on the Great Wagon Road. Documenting this arrival was Col. Otho Holland Williams, the Maryland officer who had been serving as Kalb's adjutant general.

Born to Welsh immigrants, Williams had risen through the Maryland ranks from his initial rank of lieutenant in the Frederick City rifle corps. Taken prisoner during the defense of Fort Washington on Manhattan Island in November 1776, he was promoted to colonel of the Maryland line while still a prisoner and finally exchanged in 1778. Now commanding the 6th Maryland Regiment, he served with distinction during the Monmouth campaign and also, briefly, as the Continental army's acting adjutant general from December 1779–April 1780, before marching south with Kalb and taking on the familiar role of adjutant general with Kalb's southern corps.[17]

The Virginia cavalry officer Henry Lee described Williams as "elegant in form . . . his countenance was expressive and the faithful index of his warm and honest heart." But he did have his severe side. "He was cordial to his friends, but cold to all whose correctness in moral principle became questionable in his mind,"[18] writes Lee. Perhaps this explains the narrative he left of Gates's Camden campaign.

Written at some point after the events it describes, possibly late in 1780, and unpublished until 1822, when it appeared as an appendix to William Johnson's *Sketches of the Life and Correspondence of Nathanael Greene*, Williams's version of Gates's march finds its way into many contemporary American Revolution accounts, including the influential *War of the Revolution* by Christopher Ward and *The Road to Guilford Courthouse* by John Buchanan. But his narrative often appears crafted to depict Gates's management of the campaign in its worst light, and several of his harshest criticisms are contradicted by others.

According to Williams, after being received in the Continental camp with "respectful ceremony," Gates "as if actuated by a spirit of great activity and enterprise, ordered the troops to hold themselves in readiness *to march at a moment's warning* [italics original]" toward Camden, for a go at Rawdon and the British defenses there. According to Williams, the orders baffled Kalb and his officers, who knew the Maryland and Continental troops they commanded, now joined by scattered Continental soldiers escaped from Charleston, were famished and had not been adequately resupplied in over a month. "But all difficulties were removed by the general's assurances, that plentiful supplies of rum and rations were on the route, and would overtake them in a day or two," Williams reports, "assurances that were certainly too fallacious, and that never were verified."[19]

Here, Gates seem to have been relying on the assurances of supply and reinforcement he had received from Continental, Virginia, and North Carolina officials prior to his arrival at Deep River. He told his officers "articles of salt, rum, & c.," would soon follow him to Deep River from the Continental magazines in Hillsborough. And Gates also anticipated receiving supplies and reinforcements from the North Carolina militia. General Griffith Rutherford was waiting for him at a forward position near Cheraw, on South Carolina's Pee Dee River, with "A Quantity of provision." And marching toward Cheraw with 1,200 militia and "a plentiful supply of provisions" was former North Carolina governor Richard Caswell. True, Kalb warned him, "I have struggled with a good many difficulties for Provisions" ever since arriving in North Carolina. No fool, Gates surely had his own doubts about these promises, but even if he regarded them skeptically, he had good reason to promote them optimistically to his troops, as the new American commander appeared motivated to launch a campaign against the British defenses posthaste.[20]

Another astonishment to Williams was the route Gates proposed. By now wary of false promises, Kalb had intended to march south on a westerly route, essentially along the Great Wagon Road, through the pro-Whig region around Salisbury and Charlotte, if he intended to march at all. To Williams fell the task of convincing Gates the countryside on the route he proposed to Cheraw was "by nature barren, abounding with sandy plains, intersected by swamps, and very thinly inhabited," with a population mostly hostile to the American cause, while the route through Salisbury and Charlotte was "in the midst of a fertile country and inhabited by a people zealous in the cause America."[21]

But Thomas Pinckney, another observer on the scene, argues convincingly Gates had little option but march to Cheraw, even though the route took him through the Carolinas' infamous Pine Barrens, now better marketed as North Carolina's Pinehurst/Southern Pines region. Pinckney suggested Gates's route was in response to what was essentially the blackmail of Caswell and Rutherford, whose safety at Cheraw was threatened by nearby British forces. Therefore, the only means of preserving them "from defeat & destruction, was to form a junction as rapidly as possible," Pinckney wrote. "Could Genl. Gates under these circumstances have retired to refresh his Army in summer quarters at Charlotte or Salisbury, leaving this body of Militia, the only hope of immediate support from the State in which he was acting, to be sacrificed by the imprudence or misconduct of their commanding Officer? Sound policy forbade it."[22]

In Pinckney's commentary are allusions to Gates's militia strategy from earlier in the war—that once embodied, militia must be used quickly, and toward expedient purpose. Historian Paul David Nelson believes Gates had been stung by criticisms of his strategy during the Saratoga campaign, where he had established a defensive position and won victory largely by capitalizing on British mistakes. "In the Carolinas he apparently intended to prove to his critics that he could be aggressive if he chose." And probably also true was Pinckney's assertion that Gates believed his Continentals "may as well march on and starve, as starve lying" at Cox's Mill.[23]

Whatever his reasoning, Gates was resolute, marching his small, hungry army toward the Pine Barrens on July 27, just two days after his arrival. With him now was Francis Marion, who had returned to Deep River around the time of Gates's arrival, attended "by a very few followers, distinguished by small black leather caps and the wretchedness of their attire," according to Williams, who again seems eager to cast Gates's reception of the Swamp Fox in an unfavorable light. "Their number did not exceed twenty men and boys, some white, some black, and all mounted, but most of them miserably equipped; their appearance was in fact so burlesque, that it was with much difficulty the diversion of the regular soldiery was restrained by the officers."[24]

No doubt, after hiding out in the swamps and coastal plain of the Carolinas for two months, Marion's appearance was "burlesque." With his hooked nose and misshaped legs, he cut an odd figure even under the best circumstances. But Gates was at his best with these types of irregular troops. According to Williams, Marion requested leave from Gates after "only a few days," to take command of militia in the Williamsburg District in eastern South Carolina, and Gates was "glad of an opportunity of detaching Colonel Marion."[25]

However, this account does not correspond with later scholarship. According to Marion biographer Hugh Rankin, Marion joined Gates sometime around July 27 and did not leave his command until August 14 or 15, serving with him for almost the entire march toward Camden. And though Williams admits Gate's orders to Marion included instructions "to watch the motions of the enemy, and furnish intelligence,"[26] he implies Gates saw little value in Marion's service, a considerable exaggeration. In fact, Gates would eventually assign Marion an important role in his strategy to take Camden.

Undeniable, however, is the starvation and deprivation the Continental soldiers experienced on their march through the Pine Barrens. "The country exceeded the representation that had been made of it," continues Williams. "Scarcely had it emerged from a state of sterile nature," a characterization affirmed by William Seymour, a sergeant in the Delaware Regiment who left a valuable journal of his experiences in the Carolinas. "At this time we were so much distressed for want of provisions, that we were fourteen days and drew but one half pound of flour," he remembered of the march to South Carolina. "Sometimes we drew half a pound of beef per man, and that so miserably poor that scarce any mortal could make use of it."[27]

Despite the deprivation of his men, however, Gates's march toward Cheraw was having a significant propaganda effect on the people of the Pee Dee region. Gates's "name and former good fortune re-animated the exertions of the country," recalled Tarleton.[28] In response to Gates's approach, Rawdon ordered the 71st Highlanders to evacuate their outpost at Cheraw and retreat to a defensive position on Lynches Creek, sending forward Lt. Col. Alexander Webster and the 33rd Regiment to support their withdrawal, though he admitted to Cornwallis the retreat only fueled the fire of Whig sentiment already consuming the Pee Dee region. "This the active incendiaries of the enemy represented as an act of fear and so encouraged the disaffected and terrified the wavering that the whole country between Pedee and Black River openly avowed the principles of rebellion, and collecting in parties commenced acts of hostility," Cornwallis later admitted to Germain.[29]

Arriving at the Pee Dee River on August 4, Gates issued there a proclamation announcing the approach of his "numerous, well-appointed, and formidable army," which would soon "compel our late triumphant and insulting foes to retreat from the most advantageous posts with precipitation and dismay."[30] Though such assurances were pure propaganda, they nevertheless electrified the countryside, evidence of Gates's gift of a common touch. After Gates's proclamation, "the spirit of revolt, which had been hitherto restrained by the distance of the continental force now advancing to the southward, burst forth into action," reported the Loyalist officer Charles Stedman, still serving as Cornwallis's commissary officer. "Almost all the inhabitants between Black River and Pedee had openly revolted and joined the Americans."[31]

After his confrontation with British naval officer John Plumer Ardesoife in Georgetown, and with news of Gates's approach animating the Pee Dee, John James was chosen as leader of four Whig militia companies in Kingstree totaling four hundred men. This included the regiment of Henry Mouzon, already formed, and shortly thereafter, two more recently formed companies under Maj. Hugh Giles of Pee Dee. With such a large body of troops now organized, James and his officers sent Gates a request for one of his own Continental officers to command them.[32]

In the meantime, James's Whigs captured a Loyalist officer named Amos Gaskens, who had been put in charge of the Loyalist militia in Williamsburg, South Carolina. They then took post on Lynch's Creek, at Witherspoon's Ferry, four miles above the junction with the Pee Dee between present-day Williamsburg and Marion County.

News of these actions quickly reached Cornwallis. To quell these flames of insurrection, he dispatched to the Pee Dee region his most efficient weapon, Lt. Col. Banastre Tarleton, who, though still in Charleston, had now recovered enough from his bout with malaria to return to action. Tarleton's orders were "to encourage our friends and intimidate the enemy" in the Pee Dee region aroused by the 71st's retreat, specifically dispersing the militia of John James before then heading toward Camden to resume his command of the British Legion.[33]

With thirty dragoons and forty mounted militia, Tarleton left Charleston on August 1 and headed toward the Pee Dee "in order to punish the inhabitants in that quarter for their late breach of paroles and perfidious revolt." But his mission was delayed by rains and high waters, and they didn't reach Lenud's Ferry until August 5, traveling only forty miles.[34]

Tarleton was deeply disturbed by the conditions he found there. "The country, My Lord, I found *scared* [italics original]," he confided in a letter to Cornwallis written that evening. Having quartered in Charleston for the last two months, Tarleton had not yet experienced the shift in momentum that was sweeping the South Carolina countryside since his victory at the Waxhaws. "The revolt was spreading," wrote historian Charles McCrady. "Those who were before indifferent were now siding with the Whigs, and many who had joined the Royal standard were deserting to the Americans."[35]

Not only was James taking Tory captives and seizing territory in the Pee Dee, but Huck's Defeat and the joint attacks on Hanging Rock and Rocky Mount were energizing the Whigs of the Camden and New Acquisition District. And the Ninety Six District was equally violent with revolt. On the night of July 12, the Spartan Militia of John Thomas Jr. surprised and ambushed about 150 Loyalists at Cedar Springs, just south of modern-day Spartanburg. The next day, July 13, Georgia militia, under the command of Col. John Jones of Burke County, surprised and dispersed Loyalist militia at Gowen's Old Fort, near modern-day Landrum, including some of the Loyalists who had been ambushed at Cedar Spring the night before. This Georgia militia, under overall command of Col. Elijah Clarke, now joined the North Carolina militia at Earle's Ford on the North Pacolet River, in present-day Polk County, North Carolina, near the South Carolina line.

On the night of July 15, this combined North Carolina-Georgia militia was attacked by Loyalist militia stationed at nearby Prince's Fort, near modern-day Lyman, South Carolina. The attack was repulsed, and the next morning a small squad of the North Carolina Whig militia in turn pursued the Tories, routing their camp and chasing them all the way back to Prince's Fort. "It is not a little remarkable that three successive night fights should have occurred within a few miles of each other," wrote the nineteenth-century historian Lyman C. Draper. "And in all three of these affairs, the Tories got the worst of it."[36]

At Lenud's Ferry, Tarleton was just beginning to comprehend the consequences of Whig victories such as these across South Carolina. Undoubtedly, he found parallels to Whig impudence from earlier in the war, and his thoughts turned darkly to the tactics of Fire and Sword. "Many of the insurgents, having taken certificates and paroles, don't deserve lenity," he brooded to Cornwallis. "None shall they experience." Like his fellow officers of the "Fire and Sword" outlook, Tarleton believed only the destruction and devastation of total warfare could quell the Patriot revolt, and his feelings were strident enough, his rapport close enough, to express his feelings to Cornwallis: "I have promis'd the young men who chuse to assist me in this expedition the plunder of the leaders of the faction. If warfare allows me, I shall give these disturbers of the peace no quarter. . . . Fire and confiscation must take place on their effects etc. I must discriminate with severity."[37]

ELEVEN

ENTERPRISE
and
EMPLOYMENT

O N AUGUST 5, THE SAME NIGHT Tarleton was writing Cornwallis from Lenud's Ferry, promising "fire and confiscation" for the people of the Pee Dee, Sumter and Davie were meeting at Sumter's latest camp at Lands Ford on the Catawba River, contemplating another attack on Hanging Rock. Whig militias were again streaming into their camps after Davie's successful action at Hanging Rock just four days before, and Sumter had discovered "that his men, while marching and fighting, and fighting and marching, would keep with him," recalled Joseph Graham.[1] "But to encamp and remain stationary, he might calculate with certainty his force would diminish." Tarleton, in his memoir, somewhat grudgingly admired this same quality in Sumter: "The active partisan was thoroughly sensible, that the minds of men are influenced by enterprize, and that to keep undisciplined people together, it is necessary to employ them."[2]

This meeting was captured in some detail by Davie in his memoirs, which he describes in the third person: "Major Davie numbered about five hundred effective men Officers and privates, and about three hundred South Carolinians remained with Colonels Sumpter, Hill, Lacey and others." Their eyes still set on both Rocky Mount and Hanging Rock, "it was supposed if one of them was taken the other would be evacuated; and upon a meeting of the Officers, it was resolved to attack the Hanging-Rock the next day."[3]

Unmentioned in Davie's account, however, were the operations of Rawdon. Having already ordered the evacuation of the British 71st from the Cheraws in advance of Gates approach, Rawdon had sent forward Lt. Col. James Webster and the 33rd Regiment to reinforce the 71st's position on Lynches Creek. Now he moved toward Lynches Creek himself with reinforcements from Camden, his collected force totaling 1,100 men, "all regulars and provincials," his object "to retard the progress of Gates' . . . or to reduce the enemy to hazard an action where my peculiar advantages of situation would compensate for my disparity in numbers."[4]

The British garrison at Hanging Rock now consisted of some "400 provincials and 800 militia," and because "Sumter menaced that road to Camden," Rawdon reinforced it with 160 infantries from Tarleton's British Legion and 180 from the Prince of Wales American Regiment, raised in New York largely of Connecticut recruits in 1777.[5]

Rawdon had good reason to be apprehensive about the security of Hanging Rock. At a surprise inspection of the outpost on July 29, Rawdon discovered its commanding officer, Thomas Pattinson, drunk. Once described by a fellow British officer as a "dead weight," Pattinson was immediately arrested and relieved of his command, Rawdon replacing him with John Carden, an untested Provincial officer from the Prince of Wales's American Regiment.[6] The success of Davie's attack clearly demonstrated the outposts vulnerability, and in addition to the approach of Gates to the east, the menace of Sumter to the north, and lack of trust in his officers, men such as the inexperienced Carden and the disconsolate Turnbull at Rocky Mount, Rawdon was battling an even more deadly foe within his own army—malaria. On July 31, Rawdon reported to Cornwallis from Camden that three of his senior officers were withdrawn from their outposts and "sick in this town" with the scourge. Two weeks later, on August 13, a return of his troops counted 756 rank and file sick, almost 25 percent of his command.[7]

A talented and tenacious intelligence officer, Sumter kept minute details of Rawdon's troop movements and personnel issues, which undoubtedly were part of the conversation with Davie and his officers on the night of August 5. There's no historical evidence Sumter and Davie were operating in conjunction with Gates at this time. Indeed, Rawdon reported to Cornwallis on August 2 that "the enemy are moving about me but, as far as I can see, not with any combined plan."[8] But Sumter was also undoubtedly keeping track of both Rawdon's and Gates's movements, as well as the movements of the North Carolina militia under the command of Gen. Richard Caswell, now camping at the Lynches River in advance of Gates's approach. Some sources suggest Sumter had learned that three hundred British soldiers from Hanging Rock had been recently detached to Rocky Mount in anticipation of another attack there by Sumter, inspiring the Patriots to target Hanging Rock instead.[9] Also influential, no doubt, was the success of Davie's previous attack on Hanging Rock on August 1, and intelligence about the camp he gathered then. All of these contingencies would've played a role in the discussion on the night of August 5, when it was resolved to attack Hanging Rock the next day.[10]

The camp at Hanging Rock was named for a nearby boulder that precariously jutted over a ravine above Hanging Rock Creek. The site was located just above the fall line of the Catawba River, near the present-day South Carolina community of Heath Springs, which had once been the shoreline of an ancient, primordial ocean. Historian Benson J. Lossing described the region memorably during his travels there in 1849. "I was approaching the verge of the Lowlands, the apparent shore of the ancient ocean, along which are strewn huge boulders—chiefly conglomerates—the mighty pebbles cast upon the beach, when, perhaps the mammoth and the mastodon slaked their thirst in the waters of the Catawba. . . . For several miles the road passed among erratic rocks and curiously shaped conglomerates."[11]

The British outpost was set up in an open formation in three separate encampments stretching about a half mile along the west side of the Great Wagon Road, just south of where the road crossed Hanging Rock Creek. According to Davie, "a Creek with a deep ravine covered the whole front of the Tory Camp." In the northern encampment, separated from the rest of the outpost by a "skirt of wood," was the North Carolina Loyalist militia of Col. Morgan Bryan, the regiment whom Davie had routed elements of on August 1. In the center encampment were the British Legion infantry, under command of captains Kenneth McCulloch and John Rousselet, along with a regiment of North Carolina Loyalists under command of Col. John Hamilton. Some of Thomas "Burnfoot" Brown's King's Rangers were also camped in this center area, although Brown himself was not present. In the southern encampment was probably Carden's detachment from the Prince of Wales American Regiment, as well as other assorted units. These were perhaps as many as 1,400 men in all, although accounts differ, all under the command of the inexperienced Carden following the arrest of Pattinson.[12] Despite their advantage in numbers, this outpost was at a keen disadvantage. "They did not know Sumter's whereabouts or intentions, whereas he knew not only where they were but how their units were deployed."[13]

After Sumter, Davie, and the other Whig officers resolved to attack Hanging Rock again, the decision to attack was placed in front of the body of militia soldiers for consideration, in militia custom. Their "appropriation" was received with "great spirit & cheerfulness," Davie recalled. The Whigs marched through the night, arriving about two miles outside the camp around midnight. "A council was now called to settle the mode of attack," recalled Davie, still writing in third person. At the council, Sumter proposed the Whigs divide into three units, each detachment attacking one of the separate encampments. To cross the open fields, Sumter proposed the Patriots ride their horses, then dismount and form for battle in front of the enemy. "This plan was approved by all the officers except Major Davie, who insisted on the necessity of leaving horses at that place, and marching to the attack on foot, urging the confusion always consequent on dismounting under a fire and the certainty of losing the effect of a sudden and vigorous attack."

His logic sound, Davie was overruled, a decision some historians use to criticize the Gamecock's weakness in military tactics. Surely, however, other Whig officers had influence in this decision. Throughout the American Revolution, the Whig militia of the Carolinas remained devoted to their horses. Here, Davie was perhaps the more prudent tactician, but Sumter, as usual, was the master psychologist.

The strategy was settled in the council: Davie was to attack the southern encampment, Hill the North Carolina militia of Morgan Bryan on the north end of the outpost, and Sumter, "as the Senior officer," the middle. Their attack was to commence "as the day broke"[14] on the morning of August 6. However, when the entire army of Patriot militia left the road to avoid the enemy's patrols, they became lost and discombobulated, with all three divisions stumbling upon the northern encampment of Bryan's North Carolina militia just as the Loyalists there were finishing up their breakfasts.

In the confusion, all three Whig detachments commenced attacking Bryan's position from different sides around the same time. Surprised and quickly routed, the North Carolina Loyalist militia fled toward the camp of the Legion in the center of the outpost. The Legion infantry and some of the retreated North Carolina Loyalist Volunteers soon formed and took cover at a fence, but the Patriots' "impetuosity was not checked a moment by this unexpected discharge." Flushed with impulsive momentum, the Patriots surged forward, overrunning the Legion Infantry, "who immediately broke and mingled in the flight of the Loyalists," writes Bass.

The experienced King's Rangers of Thomas "Burnfoot" Brown, however, did not retreat, and instead set up formation in the woods just behind the camp, where they now started sniping at the Whigs, then advanced in platoons, perhaps joined by some of the regrouped Legion infantry. But Sumter's militia included experienced soldiers as well, and "these brave men took instinctively to the trees and bush heaps and returned the fire with deadly effect," wrote Sumter biographer Robert D. Bass, who depicts his subject colorfully during this portion of the battle: "The Gamecock was magnificent. Recklessly sitting his foaming charger, his long hair flying and his golden epaulettes a shining target for enemy sharpshooters . . . he was Old Tuck. Like the gamest slasher cock, he neither shrank nor cowered when a rifle ball ripped into his thigh. Scorning the pain before his men, he continued to ride, cheering, animating, and directing the fighting."[15]

Despite such romanticisms, the fighting was fierce during this portion of the battle, the two sides firing at each other from covered positions for perhaps as long as an hour, exhausting the Whig ammunition and causing the inexperienced Carden to panic and turn over command to Capt. Rousslet of the Legion.[16] In a later report to Thomas Pinckney, Sumter admitted he was wounded in the thigh during this firefight, though Bass reports he hid his injury from his men until after the fighting.[17]

While the Whigs were occupied with the King's Rangers, some of the British Legion infantry and Loyalists who had retreated during the initial Whig charge reformed into a hollow square in the center of the cleared grounds at the middle encampment. Though Sumter and his officers urged an attack on the square, disorder had now settled on the Whig militia, many of whom were diverted by plundering the camps they had overrun and indulging in the liquor discovered there. Sumter was finally able to organize "as many stragglers as he could" for a counterattack against the Legion formation, but when he inspected their ammunition, he found that most "had not on average three rounds per man, which was the true cause of his retreating."[18]

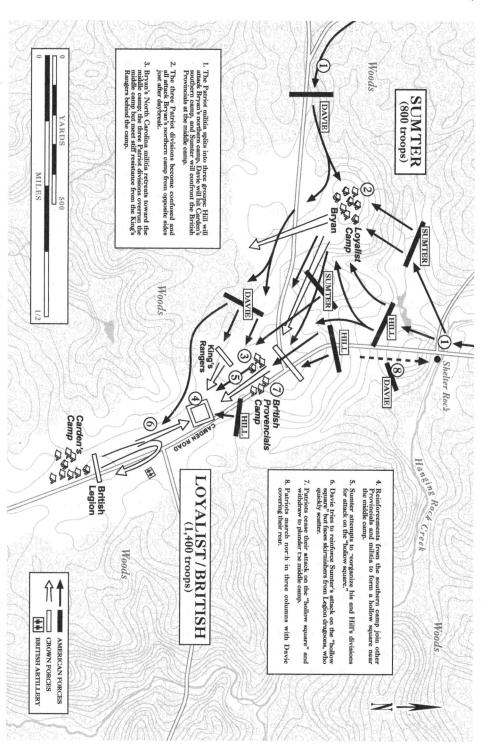

SUMTER
(800 troops)

LOYALIST/BRITISH
(1,400 troops)

1. The Patriot militia splits into three groups; Hill will attack Bryan's northern camp, Davie will hit Carden's southern camp, and Sumter will confront the British Provincials at the middle camp.

2. The three Patriot divisions become confused and all attack Bryan's northern camp from opposite sides just after daybreak.

3. Bryan's North Carolina militia retreats toward the middle camp; the three Patriot divisions overrun the middle camp but meet stiff resistance from the King's Rangers behind the camp.

4. Reinforcements from the southern camp join other Provincials and militia to form a hollow square near the middle camp.

5. Sumter attempts to "reorganize his and Hill's divisions for attack on the "hollow square."

6. Davie tries to reinforce Sumter's attack on the "hollow square" but faces skirmishers from Legion dragoons, who quickly scatter.

7. Patriots cease their attack on the "hollow square" and withdraw to plunder the middle camp.

8. Patriots march north in three columns with Davie covering their rear.

YARDS

MILES

AMERICAN FORCES
CROWN FORCES
BRITISH ARTILLERY

While Sumter's men continued their looting, Davie organized his dragoons and about two hundred infantries advanced in a flanking action from the woods against the re-formed Loyalists. As they approached, Davie's dragoons scattered a "large body of the Tories," who were "rallying and forming in the edge of the woods" on the opposite side of the British camp, but "the distance of the square from the woods and the constant fire of two pieces of field artillery" made Davie's counterattack on the Legion infantry ineffectual.

Meanwhile, a party of about forty Legion dragoons, passing through the vicinity as they returned to Camden from Hanging Rock, heard the shooting and rode toward the battle. As Davie and his dragoons returned toward Sumter's position, they encountered the Legion Cavalry "drawn up on the Camden road, with a countenance as if they meant to keep their position." However, they quickly dispersed when charged by Davie's horsemen. "The Legion without Tarleton, both foot and horse, had not lived up to its reputation," observed historian John Buchanan.[19]

Upon Davie's return, "it was agreed to plunder the encampments and retire." Thus ensued a burlesque scene, the Patriot militia looting the Loyalist encampments, tending to the wounded, and getting increasingly drunk, all while the Loyalist forces watched the debauchery from a short distance away. To console themselves, the Loyalists played music and gave three cheers for King George, which were immediately answered by three cheers for "Liberty." "The militia at length got into a line of march in three columns, Davie's corps covering the rear," Davie recounted with no small degree of chagrin. "But as they were loaded with plunder, encumbered with their wounded friends, and many of them intoxicated, it is easy to conceive this retreat could not be performed under the rules of the most approved tacticks."[20]

Despite a vaudevillian conclusion, the attack on Hanging Rock was a stunning American victory, considered by many the greatest of Sumter's partisan career. Tory casualties were estimated at two hundred, while the Americans lost only twelve killed and forty-one wounded. Sumter later reported to Gates's aide, Thomas Pinckney, that he "brought off one hundred horses & fifty Stand of arms, with other articles of Considerable value."[21] Most importantly, the attack showed that American militia could effectively fight the trained Tory militia upon whom the British were counting to hold territory in their rear as they advanced forward to other theaters. And as the first American victory under the Gamecock's leadership, it secured his status as the Backcountry War's first great Patriot militia leader.

Davie, obviously, also led courageously, with perhaps more tactical acumen, begging the question as to why his leadership does not enjoy the same historical status as that of Sumter and Marion, along with the later militia leadership of Andrew Pickens, who rose to prominence in the battle of Cowpens in January 1781. The simple answer is that Davie would soon join the staff of Continental army general Nathanael Greene, confining him to a staff officer's role for the latter part of the American Revolution's southern campaigns, while the reputations of Sumter, Marion, and Pickens would only grow in the fighting to come. But we shall not leave Davie behind quite yet, for he still has an important role to play in the Backcountry War.

Learning of Sumter's victory, British officers were dismayed. "The post at Hanging Rock was attacked by General Sumpter a few days after his repulse from Rocky Mount and very nearly carried," Cornwallis admitted glumly to Germain.[22] More disconcerting than Sumter and Davie's success, however, was the feeble performance of the Loyalist militia. Reporting the defeat to Clinton on August 10, Cornwallis admitted, "these accounts, added to the infidelity which we have experienced of our militia, are not pleasing."[23] The back country of South Carolina in early August was far from the subdued province Cornwallis and his officers believed it to be in late June, and the Loyalists depended on to hold the countryside were proving far from the "silent majority" of which they had been depicted, as events both in the vicinity of Camden and in the Ninety Six District to the west were making clear.

To Rawdon and his junior officers, now positioned at Lynches River awaiting the approach of Gates, the attack on Hanging Rock had the effect of a coordinated attack by the American forces, whether it was intended as one or not. "It appeared a clear consequence that Sumpter, whose men were all mounted, would lose no time in pushing for Camden," Rawdon later recalled. "I addressed the Officers around me, who seemed struck with the obvious magnitude of evil. I told them . . . that we were in a scrape from which nothing but courage could extricate us, & that we must march instantly to crush Sumpter before he could further co-operate with Gates."[24]

Learning of Sumter and Davie's attack, Rawdon immediately ordered a retreat back toward Camden, but the following morning he received intelligence that Hanging Rock was still in the hands of Loyalist forces. This diminished his fears of a Sumter raid on Camden, so Rawdon now ordered his men to establish a defensive position at a strategic causeway on Little Lynches Creek, which he later described in an 1801 narrative: "Lynche's

Creek runs thro' swamps of perhaps a mile in breadth on each side; impenetrable, except where a causeway has been made at the passing-places on the great road."[25]

Sumter was not marching on Camden, however, but retired with Davie to Davie's camp at the Waxhaws. There, according to Bass, Sumter "called in Soldier Tom," his manservant and slave, to "dress his wounded thigh" in secrecy. Then Sumter, Davie, and their collected men spent the following two days recuperating.[26] By August 9, Sumter was recovered enough from his wound to write a letter to Pinckney, again suggesting a rearguard action against the Santee River crossings at the High Hills or Nelson's Ferry. This action would "inevitably Ruin" Rawdon's Camden headquarters, Sumter believed, as it "could by no means effect a retreat without going far to the Westward."[27] This was in essence, a reiteration of the strategy he had sent to Kalb in July, proposing not only to cut off Camden's supply lines from the south, but also potential reinforcements, leaving Rawdon isolated and vulnerable to attack.

The imminent campaign against Camden was clearly on everyone's mind, including James Williams, colonel of the Whig Little River militia. Recall that Williams and some of his militia had joined Sumter's forces in early July, after Williams returned from a trip to North Carolina to secure property and his slaves. At Sumter's camp, Williams had reunited with Thomas Brandon and other militia soldiers of the Ninety-Six District. At the time, with their own district seemingly overrun by the British and the Loyalist militia commanded by Maj. Patrick Ferguson, and with Loyalist leaders like Robert and Patrick Cunningham resurgent, these refugees had voted to join with Sumter for the summer campaign.

However, things had changed drastically within the last month, and the Ninety-Six District was once more in play. This was where the Americans had defeated the Loyalists in a string of victories in the vicinity of modern-day Spartanburg in mid-July, and where now a talented duo of militia leaders—Isaac Shelby from North Carolina and Elijah Clarke from Georgia—were in the midst of one the most spectacularly successful campaigns of the Backcountry War.

Although little is known of Elijah Clarke, what is known positions him as one of the great unsung militia leaders of the American Revolution. Nineteenth-century historian Lyman Draper reported Clarke was a native of Virginia, who settled briefly on the Pacolet River in the Spartanburg, South Carolina, region, before pushing into Wilkes County, Georgia, "where the Revolutionary out-break found him. He was one of those sturdy patriots, well fitted for a leader of the people—one who would scorn to take protection, or yield one iota to arbitrary power."[28]

Prior to the British occupation, Clarke's finest moment had been at Kettle Creek on February 14, 1779, when he had teamed up with Andrew Pickens and other Georgia and South Carolina militia to defeat a superior force of Loyalist Militia in the vicinity of modern-day Athens, Georgia. However, his most significant contributions to the American Revolution were beginning now, in the Spartan District, where he had once lived. Within the next month, he would launch a bitter and bloody attack on everyone's favorite nemesis, Thomas "Burnfoot" Brown, at Augusta. And although that campaign would end unsuccessfully, with Clarke and his Georgians again on the run, he would play a significant role in the circumstances that allowed Patrick Ferguson to be caught and defeated at Kings Mountain.

For now, Clarke was joined with Isaac Shelby under the overall leadership of North Carolina militia general Charles McDowell, who commanded from his outposts in the northeast corner of the Ninety-Six District on the Broad River in what is now Cherokee County, South Carolina, but with Shelby acting as McDowell's field commander. Shelby would go on to become the future first governor of Kentucky. In 1780, at age thirty, Shelby was already an experienced frontiersman and talented militia leader. Though he had served in various military capacities during the American Revolution, he was then serving as colonel of the North Carolina militia of Sullivan County, which is now the westernmost corner of Tennessee. Shelby and his Sullivan County militia had answered a call for reinforcements from McDowell to keep Ferguson's Loyalist militia from extending their conquest of western South Carolina into western North Carolina.

So far, that effort had been a rousing success. On July 30, just two days before Sumter's unsuccessful attack on Rocky Mount, the combined militias of Clarke and Shelby had captured the Loyalist outpost at Fort Thicketty, outside modern-day Gaffney, capturing ninety-three Loyalist militia and a sergeant from Ferguson's American Volunteers, the Provincial regiment placed under Ferguson's command prior to the Charleston campaign. In this effort they were assisted substantially by the Loyalist commander, Patrick Moore, who despite occupying a notoriously impenetrable position inside the blockhouse, apparently panicked at the sight of Shelby and Clarke's superior force of six hundred men and surrendered without a fight, in some accounts deceiving his men to convince them to give up their arms.

Despite its unheroic conclusion, Fort Thicketty's surrender raised Patriot morale, and also alerted the attention of Patrick Ferguson.[29]

On August 8, just two days after the Patriot victory at Hanging Rock, Clarke and Shelby were on patrol in the vicinity of modern-day Spartanburg with approximately six hundred men when they learned a large body of Ferguson's Loyalist militia was nearby. They began to retreat along the road east toward Wofford's Ironworks on nearby Lawson's Fork, a tributary of the Pacolet River. Like William Hill's ironworks in the New Acquisition District, Wofford's Ironworks was a well-known meeting place in the community, where settlers would congregate to acquire or barter for iron hardware and share news and gossip.

As Clarke and Shelby retreated, they soon encountered the pursuing major James Dunlap with fourteen American Volunteers and 130 Loyalist militia, all mounted. At Wofford's Ironworks, the Americans set up an ambush. During the ensuing skirmish, Clarke received two saber wounds in hand-to-hand combat, one on the back of his neck and the other on his head, his life perhaps saved only by a stock-buckle that diminished the impact of the saber blow. He was briefly captured, before overpowering his guards and returning safely to the American lines. After the fighting subsided, the Americans retreated again to the east side of the Pacolet River. By now Ferugson himself had come up with additional Loyalist troops, though with the American holding the river's eastern bank, all he could do was scowl at Clarke and Shelby on the other side, perhaps vowing later revenge. This skirmish has become known as the Second Battle of Cedar Springs, or the Battle of Wofford's Ironworks, and although it was hardly an American victory, the Patriots had displayed military skill and order in their retreat, earning a victory of morale against the increasingly notorious Patrick Ferguson.[30]

Eager for revenge against Cunningham and Ferguson, who had seized his estate to use it as a Loyalist outpost, Williams was keeping close tabs on the action back home from Sumter's camp. Now, rather than commit himself to the Camden campaign, Williams informed Sumter he "preferred a return toward Ninety Six to a march down the Wateree," and that he was taking Thomas Brandon, Joseph McJunkin, and the rest of the Ninety Six District militia with him.[31] The matter apparently led to some kind of dispute. According to the account of Joseph McJunkin, Sumter "having a disposition to go Southward," and Williams "towards the West," the two men disagreed "in their notions, the troops joined with Sumter or Williams just as their own inclinations led them."[32]

There is little else known or documented about the nature of this conflict, though its consequences spread throughout the future events of the Backcountry War. Some insist there's no proof any conflict existed at all, though William Hill, for one, recalled it vividly in his wartime memoir, ascribing its origins and consequences squarely to the actions of James Williams. Those consequences pertain to the Battle of Kings Mountain, often considered the greatest militia victory of the American Revolution, and the reasons why Sumter did not fight there.

Hill's memoir was written in his old age and is believed by many to have been composed chiefly as a defense of Thomas Sumter for his absence at Kings Mountain. In it, Hill claims that after the attack on Hanging Rock, it was discovered that James Williams and Thomas Brandon "had eloped and had taken a great number of the public horses & a considerable quantity of provisions with the camp equipage and a number of men,"[33] suggesting Sumter was neither advised of nor had authorized this procurement.

Hill may have been bitter because, according to his own account, it was he who had convinced Sumter to appoint James Williams as commissary, or chief supply officer, for Sumter's battalion. Hill clearly insinuates Williams stole the supplies from Sumter, but according to Williams's biographer, William T. Graves, the supplies, including much of the ammunition, may have been provided by the Ninety Six militia in the first place, and "it is difficult to believe that the men who had provided the supplies would not have felt entitled to take some, if not all, of those supplies with them when they decided to part company with Sumter."[34]

Here we see evidence of the loose discipline and command hierarchy of the southern militia, where decisions were often made by consensus. Though Sumter was "elected" general of this militia army, each regiment still operated according to their own internal politics, pledging their allegiance to the cause, not necessarily their commanding officers. Whether it was improper for Williams and the Ninety Six militia to take their supplies with them when they left Sumter's camp is an evaluation now lost to time, based on the subjective circumstances of the moment.

Whatever the true circumstances of the event, Hill recalls in his memoir that Sumter sent Col. Edward Lacey with a small party of men to recover the horses and equipment taken by Williams and his subordinates. Lacey found Williams and Brandon camped on the west side of the Catawba River, where their party was too strong to be coerced by force. Instead, Lacey asked Williams for a meeting in private, and once alone, pulled a gun on him, coercing a pledge from Williams to return the supplies taken from

Sumter's camp. But once returned to the security of his men, Williams disregarded this promise and continued west to join with McDowell, Clarke, and Shelby in the Ninety Six District. More of this affair will soon be told.[35]

WHILE SUMTER WAS DEALING WITH Williams's alleged insubordination, Gates had united with the North Carolina militia under Richard Caswell on Lynches Creek. His force now consisted of approximately 3,500 men, including Caswell's 2,100 North Carolina militia and a recently arrived one hundred experienced Virginia State Troops under command of Lt. Col. Charles Porterfield. With this army, Gates now continued his march toward Camden, finding Rawdon's expeditionary force opposing him at the causeway over Little Lynches River Creek on August 11. Though Rawdon's force totaled only 1,100 men, he had taken up a strong defensive position at the east end of the only causeway leading through the vast and impenetrable swamp.

So Gates turned his army north, marching around the swamps of Lynches River toward Hanging Rock, where he could approach Camden from the Great Wagon Road. A necessary detour, though Otho Holland Williams suggests he should've detoured even farther north, to the Waxhaws, where he could feed and rest his army, though Williams admits that "movement would look like retreating from the enemy."[36] As Gates marched north, Rawdon withdrew toward Camden, where he called in most of his detachments and awaited reinforcement from four companies of light infantry sent from the British garrison at Ninety Six.[37]

Ever industrious, and with his forces swelling after the successful attack on Hanging Rock,[38] Sumter wrote Pinckney on August 12. After providing a detailed report of British troop movements, Sumter assured Gates (via Pinckney) that Camden was "altogether defenseless" and suggested yet again that if "Gen'l Gates, thenk proper to Send a Party over pinteree Creek to fall in their Rear . . . it Woud Totally Ruen them, and Nothing is more Certain then that their Retreat woud be Rendered exceedingly precareous."[39] Here was yet another version of the plan Sumter had submitted to Kalb back in July, and more recently to Pinckney on August 9—to cut off Camden from the south and west, rendering it vulnerable to siege or attack, forcing Rawdon either into retreat or attack under unfavorable circumstances. Sumter's persistence would soon pay off, for Gates, it shall be argued, was swayed by Sumter's arguments.

After a detour of thirty-four miles, Gates and his army arrived on August 13 at Rugeley's Mill, about twelve miles north of Camden. This was the plantation and business compound of Henry Rugeley, the enterprising Loyalist who had warned South Carolina governor-in-exile John Rutledge about the pursuit of Banastre Tarleton two months before. Gates was next joined by approximately seven hundred soldiers under Gen. Edward Stevens, a former Continental army officer now commanding Virginia militia, who had been following behind Gates on his march south.[40]

It was around this time, or perhaps a few days earlier, depending on different accounts, that Gates detached Francis Marion from the main body of his army. As he marched toward Camden, Gates had received John James's request for an American officer to command the Whig militia of the Pee Dee.[41] Despite his "burlesque" appearance, at least according to Otho Holland Williams's description, Marion was the obvious candidate for the job. An experienced, decorated Continental army officer, he possessed many ties, both professional and personal, in the Pee Dee region. And Gates likely had gained confidence in Marion's capacity during their march south. Despite his many faults, Gates's affinity for militia now served him well, and he assigned Marion to command of the Pee Dee, cementing Marion's famous role in American history.

Accompanied by Major Peter Horry and some other militia officers, Marion arrived at James's headquarters on Lynch's Creek sometime around August 17, "and took command of the country there and of the large extent of the country on the east side of the Santee."[42] According to William Dobein James, John James's son, who knew Marion and campaigned with him during this part of the war, Marion

was a stranger to the officers and men, and they flocked about him to obtain a sight of their future commander. He was rather below middle stature of men, lean and swarthy. His body was well set, but his knees and ankles were badly formed; and he still limped upon one leg. He had a countenance remarkably steady; his nose was aquiline; his chin projecting; his forehead was large and high, and his black eyes piercing. He was now forty-eight years of age; but still even at this age his frame was capable of enduring fatigue and every privation, necessary for a partisan. . . . He was dressed in a close round bodied crimson jacket, of a coarse texture, and wore a leather cap, part of the uniform of the second regiment, with a silver crescent in front, inscribed with the words, "Liberty or death."[43]

It is hardly a flattering sketch, though as close to a true portrait of Marion as any we have, drawn from an eyewitness account, for even if the sixteen-year-old James was not in his father's camp at this moment, he was with Marion numerous times thereafter. Marion was now united with the militia with which he would gain his fame, though he was not quite yet the famous "Swamp Fox."

Marion's orders from Gates were to "go Down the Country to Destroy all boats & Craft of any kind" in order to prevent British troops from escaping Camden from the east.[44] A later account from Thomas Pinckney said Marion was "expressly instructed for that purpose" of scouting for the approach of Charles Cornwallis, with reinforcements from Charleston.[45] Pausing briefly to organize his new command, Marion did immediately send Peter Horry with three companies of militia down to the Lower Santee, ordering them to gather men and ammunition as they worked their way to Lenud's Ferry in response to Gates's orders. That the effort was too little too late Marion would not discover for another few days. In the interim, Cornwallis and a small guard had slipped past Patriot scouts in a race to Camden, with disastrous consequences for Gates and the American Army.

WHEN WE LAST LEFT BANASTRE TARLETON, he was also at Lenud's Ferry, writing to Charles Cornwallis on August 5, promising the rebels of the Pee Dee "no quarter . . . Fire and confiscation must take place on their effects etc. I must discriminate with severity."[46]

By the next day, the floodwaters of the Santee had subsided enough for Tarleton and his small band of thirty dragoons and forty mounted infantries, along with approximately twenty-five Loyalist militias, to finally cross into the Pee Dee region, their mission "to punish the inhabitants in that quarter for their late breach of paroles and perfidious revolt."[47]

Crossing the Black River later that day, Tarleton's detachment went into bivouac on the village green in Kingstree, home of John James, in order to "punish the inhabitants in that quarter. . . . The vicinity of the rivers Santee and Wateree, and of all the Charlestown communications with the royal army, made it highly proper to strike terror into the inhabitants of that district."[48]

But Tarleton had little opportunity to punish Kingtree's inhabitants, for later that night a Loyalist informant told him Patriot militia commander William McCottry was advancing toward his position with five hundred men. In fact, McCottry only had fifty men, but the exaggerated report upended Tarleton's plans for Kingstree. He broke camp at midnight and headed back to the west side of the Black River. Tarleton then put out word he "intended to join the British army by the main road over the Santee hills," but in fact he doubled back over the Black River again "to gain intelligence of General Gates's operations."[49]

On their way north, Tarleton and his detachment passed through the now-vanished community of Salem, South Carolina, approximately ten miles northwest of Kingstree, where they came upon the plantation of the well-known Whig Henry Mouzon. Born to a family of French Huguenots, Mouzon had been educated in France, graduating from the Sorbonne as a civil engineer and trained surveyor. In 1771, he had been commissioned by Lord Charles Montagu to produce a map of South Carolina, which eventually also included North Carolina and was published in 1775. Some sources even suggest Tarleton and Mouzon were acquainted from their early school days in England.[50] If true, the acquaintance didn't spare Mouzon's plantation. After rousing Mouzon's sleeping family and slaves, and finding Mouzon absent, Tarleton burned all fourteen buildings on Mouzon's property before continuing his ride north.[51]

Next, Tarleton headed toward the plantation of James Bradley, another prominent Whig who had served as a representative in the South Carolina General Assembly. By now, Tarleton had learned from local Loyalists that the Whigs were awaiting the arrival of a Continental officer to lead them. Local rumors suggested this officer would be the Continental cavalry officer William Washington, the cousin of George Washington whom Tarleton had humiliated both at Biggin's Bridge and Lenud's Ferry earlier in the campaign.

Always an enthusiastic thespian, Tarleton decided to play a cruel trick, posing as Washington when he arrived at Bradley's plantation. According to Tarleton's memoir, he convinced the elderly Bradley he was on a mission from Gates to attack the rear elements of Rawdon's position at Little Lynches Creek, and asked Bradley and some of his neighbors to guide him through the countryside. Completely duped, or so Tarleton claimed, Bradley agreed, gathering some of his Whig neighbors. After Bradley and his Whigs guided Tarleton through a nearby swamp, "Tarleton undeceived his late host, and conducted him and his volunteers prisoners to Camden."[52]

Despite the burning of Mouzon's plantation and the capture of Bradley, Tarleton's first expedition to the Pee Dee region had hardly been the campaign of "fire and confiscation" he had promised to Cornwallis in his letter of August 5. The delay at Lenud's Ferry and the circumstances of Gates's approach toward Camden had limited his time and options for fulfilling such promises. He was eager to reunite with his Legion dragoons, whom he worried had been mistreated by the "constant duties of detachment and patrole"[53] during his absence in the long, eventful summer. After depositing his prisoners at Camden, and collecting all the dragoons at that post, he joined Rawdon at Little Lynches Creek on August 10, before falling back to Camden to participate in the preparations for Gates's attack.

PART THREE

FIRE
and
SWORD

TWELVE

COOL
INTREPIDITY

F ROM HIS HEADQUARTERS IN CHARLESTON, Cornwallis had been
monitoring Gates's march toward Camden through the dispatches of
Rawdon. On August 9, Rawdon reported that Gates was approaching with
an army of six thousand and "that the disaffected country between Pedee
and Black River had actually revolted; and that Lord Rawdon was con-
tracting his posts and preparing to assemble the force at Camden."[1]

Threatened by these exaggerated accounts of Gates's strength (his real
number was considerably less than six thousand) and the deteriorating security throughout northern South Carolina, Cornwallis decided to take
command at Camden himself, leaving Charleston on the evening of August
10 and arriving at Camden early in the morning of August 14. Traveling
only with a small personal escort, Cornwallis's party "eluded the known vig-
ilance of Marion," who Gates ordered to keep an eye out for the British
general.[2]

Much has been written about Gates's inept leadership during the Camden campaign, and although many of these criticisms are deserved, the disastrous consequences of his decision to march toward Camden on the night of August 15 appear more a case of bad luck than bad leadership. Again, much of this criticism emanates from the memoir of Otho Holland Williams, who described the moments leading up to that fateful march both colorfully and caustically in his influential memoir of the campaign.

Recall Gates had finally arrived at Rugeley's Mill, twelve miles north of Camden on the Great Wagon Road, on August 13, just hours before Cornwallis arrived at Camden the following morning. On August 14, Gates sent forward Lt. Col. John Christian Senf, a Swedish born engineer, to scout "for the purpose of occupying a strong position" so near to Rawdon at Camden as "to cut off his supplies of Provision, from the upper part of the Wateree & Pedee Rivers & to harass him with detachments of light Troops, & to oblige him either to retreat and come out & attack up upon our own ground, in a situation where the Militia which constituted our principal numerical force, might act to the best advantage." Meanwhile, other American scouts reconnoitered Rawdon's position, determining "the Enemy at Camden inferior to our Army."[3]

Or that was how Thomas Pinckney recalled it, writing almost forty years after the fact. However, Pinckney's account is supported by Senf, who also recalled this mission to scout a forward position for Gates's army. This appears to have been an adaptation of the plan Sumter had been proposing since July—to cut off Camden from below and behind, forcing Rawdon to attack or retreat. Evidence of this strategy comes from Gates himself, who in his account of the battle to Samuel Huntington, president of the Continental Congress, reported that at daybreak on August 15, he "reinforced Colonel Sumpter with 300 North Carolina militia, 100 of the Maryland Line, and two Three-pounders from the Artillery" and directed the South Carolina general "to proceed down the Wateree opposite to Camden, intercept any Stores coming to the Enemy," and stop British reinforcements attempting to join Rawdon from Ninety Six and the west.[4]

Gates's decision to support Sumter with this detachment is typically included in the criticisms of his conduct in the Camden campaign, especially the decision to include artillery and the one hundred Maryland Continentals, the cream of his troops. "The reasonable thing was to send for Sumter and add his troops to the army," complains historian Christopher Ward, "but Gates did the unreasonable thing."[5] This sentiment was echoed by historian John Buchanan, who called the decision to send troops and cannon to Sumter yet "another foolish decision" by Gates.[6]

However, those criticisms argue from the presumption that Gates intended to attack Camden immediately, which evidence suggests was not Gates's plan. And given a chance to organize effectively, the Sumter/Gates strategy to cut off Camden's supply lines from behind might have worked. Sumter certainly did his part. He immediately marched to Rocky Mount, eager for another attempt at that outpost now that he was equipped with artillery, only to find it deserted, the ever-disconsolate Turnbull and his Provincials having fled to Ninety Six.

Sumter then took possession of all the passes on the west side of the Wateree River, "from Elkenses foard to Mr. Whitecan's ferry, five Miles below Camden," finding all of the passes deserted except the Wateree Ferry, or Camden Ferry, just three miles from Camden.[7] There a Patriot detachment under the command of Col. Thomas Taylor surprised the British redoubt guarding the west side of the river, killing seven, and taking thirty to forty prisoners, including the commanding officer, a militia colonel named Carey, along with "40 waggons with Drivers, 4 Horses & Waggon, loaded with Rum, Flour, Corn, &c., 300 head of cattle & some Sheep."[8] And later that day, a detachment of seventy British regulars from the 71st and 33rd Regiments who were marching from Ninety Six to reinforce Camden were also captured by Taylor as they approached the Wateree Ferry unawares.

By the end of August 15, Sumter commanded the west side of the Wateree, although the British had collected their boats safely on the east side. Writing from Wateree Ferry that night, Sumter informed Gates the British kept up a "constant fier" at the Patriots from the other side, but that he intended to keep possession of the ferry crossing until "I am honoured with your farther Commands."[9] Later in the night however, he retreated up the Wateree ten miles after a party of British soldiers crossed the river below him and advanced on his position, although not before sending Senf back to report his successes to Gates.[10]

If Sumter's part of the plan was working, Gates's was not. It is at this point many histories of the Battle of Camden jump ahead to Gates's decision to march toward Camden on the night of August 15. Again, Otho Holland Williams's narrative proves influential in these versions. According to Williams, that evening Gates issued orders for the army to march toward Camden at ten o'clock that night, providing Williams with "a rough estimate of the forces under his command, marking them upwards of seven thousand."[11]

Though not explicit, Williams's insinuation is clear, that Gates formed this plan without consulting his officers. Astounded by Gates's exaggerated estimate of his troops, Williams recalled that he requested an immediate field return, reporting only 3,052 present and fit for duty. "These are enough for our purpose," responded Gates enigmatically. According to Williams, this remark astonished the American officers, who "could not imagine how it could be conceived, that an army, consisting of more than two-thirds militia, and which had never been once exercised in arms together, could form columns, and perform other maneuvers in the night, and in the face of the enemy."[12]

Gates's bogus belief in his numerical superiority, therefore, became motivation for his foolish expedience in launching a nighttime attack on Camden. This, at least, is the contention of Otho Holland Williams, who has been cited repeatedly by subsequent historians deeply influenced by his account. "On August 15, Gates ordered a night march which he expected would bring his army into position to trap a much smaller British force," wrote historian Robert Middlekauff in his popular American Revolution history, *The Glorious Cause*. Similarly, historian John Ferling states that "Gates's haste for battle had led him into a deadly predicament, a snare that he only began to comprehend on August 15."[13]

These criticisms, however, assume it was Gates's intention to attack. Not the case, according to the recollections of Pinckney. Indeed, from Pinckney's perspective, Sumter's raid on the Wateree Ferry was depicted as a successful stroke in the strategy to cut off Rawdon's supply lines to Charleston, an effort to provoke Rawdon into retreat or attack. Given more time, Marion likely would have played a significant role in this plan also by preventing British supplies and reinforcements from crossing lower on the Santee. Worth noting is that Nathanael Greene would employ an almost identical strategy in his own effort to take Camden in April the following year. And supporting Pinckney's version is the account of Senf, who claimed he attended a council of Gate's officers the afternoon of August 15 to discuss "taking another position for the Army, as the Ground where they were upon was by no means tenable. On reconoitering a Deep Creek,[14] 7 miles in front, was found impassable 7 miles to the Right, & about the same distance to the left, except only in the place where the Ford intersects the great road." By marching there, Senf recounted, Gates's army "would get a more secure Encampment, come nearer Genl. Sumpter, occupy the road on the East side of the Wateree river, and would be able to get nearer intelligence of the Enemy."[15]

But if Gates's plan was to set up a defensive position closer to Camden as part of an effort to isolate Rawdon and tempt him into attack, why wasn't Otho Holland Williams notified of it? "It is possible that Col. Williams, who does not mention it, may not have known the transactions," reports Pinckney, "but I have the most perfect recollection of it." A perfect recollection shared by Senf and also Gates's aide, Maj. Charles Magill, who also recalled discussing the movement of the Army "to an advantageous post with a swamp in our front, fordable only at the Road" at a council of officers on the evening of August 15.[16] Referring to Williams's quote, that Gates deemed the number of troops "enough for our purpose," Pinckney believed this was in reference only to the effort to establish a strong defensive position north of town, not in reference to a nighttime attack, as Williams insinuates.[17]

Gates's failure, perhaps, was not strategy but hesitation. By the evening of the fifteenth, Gates had received the news that Cornwallis was at Camden.[18] What he didn't know was that Cornwallis and Rawdon also recognized the vulnerability of their position, and just as Gates was preparing his night march toward the defensive position north of Camden identified by Senf, Cornwallis was also preparing his troops for a desperate nighttime attack.

"I now had my option to make, either to retire or attack the enemy, for the position at Camden was a bad one to be attacked in, and by General Sumpter's advancing down the Wateree my supplies must have failed me in a few days," Cornwallis explained in his report to Germain. Retreat to Charleston was an option, "but in taking that resolution I must have not only left near 800 sick and a great quantity of stores at this place but I clearly saw the loss of the whole province except Charleston, and of all Georgia except Savannah."[19]

And Tarleton reported in his memoir that while on patrol earlier that day, he captured three American soldiers, convalescents rejoining the army from Lynche's Creek, who revealed to him they "were directed to join the American army on the high road that night," for the march toward Camden. Interpreting this as Gates's intention to attack, Tarleton conveyed the prisoners to Cornwallis, who deemed "their story credible, and confirmed all the other intelligence of the day."[20]

Cornwallis was invested too heavily in his plans for a fall invasion of North Carolina to turn back now. "After consulting some intelligent people well acquainted with the ground, I determined to march at ten o'clock on the night of the 15th," his destination the American position at Rugeley's Mill.[21]

Fated to collide with each other, the two armies set out at almost the same time, Gates marching south along the Great Wagon Road, Cornwallis marching north. Gates had placed the mounted dragoons of Armand's legion at the advance of his columns, and at around two o'clock the morning of August 16, Armand's horsemen encountered elements of Cornwallis's vanguard—mounted infantry and dragoons along with British light infantry under the command of British lieutenant colonel James Webster. A "smart salutation of small arms fire" ensued, scattering Armand's legion and throwing Gates's columns into disorder.[22]

The Virginia state troops of Lt. Col. Charles Porterfield, however, maintained their position in the panic and instituted a disciplined crossfire at the British position. "The enemy, no less astonished than ourselves, seemed to acquiesce in a sudden suspension of hostilities," reported Williams, allowing the American officers to regain control of their troops. On the British side, Cornwallis immediately halted his troops after the initial skirmishing. Though "the ground on which both armies stood, being narrowed by swamps on the right and left, was extremely favourable for my numbers, I did not chuse to hazard the great stake for which I was going to fight to the uncertainty and confusion to which an action in the dark is so particularly liable," Cornwallis recalled, but "confiding in the disciplined courage of His Majesty's troops," he "resolved to defer the attack 'till day."[23]

Gates and his officers were less resolute. After the initial skirmishing was halted, and the two sides withdrew to set up positions approximately five hundred yards apart, Gates called another council of war. There, according to Otho Holland Williams, Gates's "astonishment could not be concealed" when presented with the intelligence that Cornwallis and the main body of his force were positioned opposite him in the night. "All the general officers immediately assembled in the rear of the line; the unwelcome news was communicated to them," Williams recalled. "General Gates said, 'Gentlemen, what is best to be done?' All were mute for a few minutes—when the gallant Stevens exclaimed, 'Gentlemen, is it not too late now to do any thing but fight?'" Hardly an adamant response, but "no other advice was offered, and the general desired the gentlemen would repair to their respective commands."[24]

Skirmishing continued throughout the night, as the two generals arranged their sides for the battle coming at dawn. On his right wing, along the right side of the Great Wagon Road, Gates placed the Delaware Continental regiment and three Maryland Continental regiments under overall command of Kalb. On the left (or east) side of the road, Gates placed the

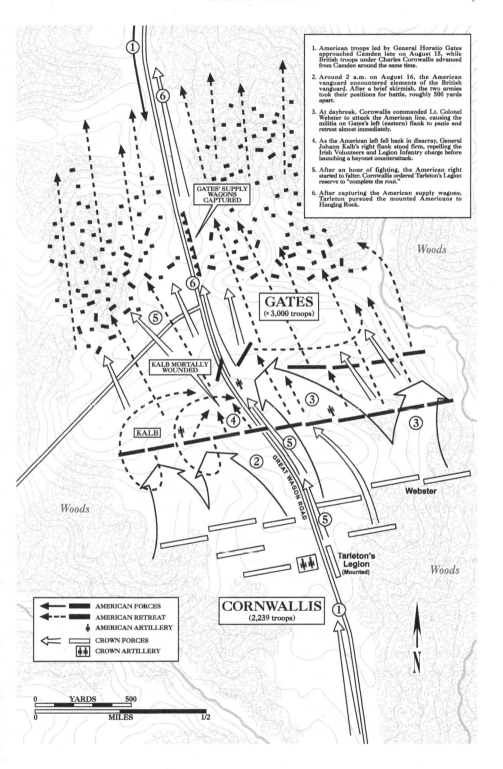

1. American troops led by General Horatio Gates approached Camden late on August 15, while British troops under Charles Cornwallis advanced from Camden around the same time.

2. Around 2 a.m. on August 16, the American vanguard encountered elements of the British vanguard. After a brief skirmish, the two armies took their positions for battle, roughly 500 yards apart.

3. At daybreak, Cornwallis commanded Lt. Colonel Webster to attack the American line, causing the militia on Gates's left (eastern) flank to panic and retreat almost immediately.

4. As the American left fell back in disarray, General Johann Kalb's right flank stood firm, repelling the Irish Volunteers and Legion Infantry charge before launching a bayonet counterattack.

5. After an hour of fighting, the American right started to falter. Cornwallis ordered Tarleton's Legion reserve to "complete the rout."

6. After capturing the American supply wagons, Tarleton pursued the mounted Americans to Hanging Rock.

Woods

GATES'S SUPPLY WAGONS CAPTURED

GATES
(≈ 3,000 troops)

KALB MORTALLY WOUNDED

KALB

Woods

GREAT WAGON ROAD

Webster

Woods

Tarleton's Legion
(Mounted)

CORNWALLIS
(2,239 troops)

N

AMERICAN FORCES
AMERICAN RETREAT
AMERICAN ARTILLERY
CROWN FORCES
CROWN ARTILLERY

YARDS   500
0
MILES   1/2
0

North Carolina militia under Caswell along with the Virginia militia under Stevens and the Virginia state troops of Porterfield. Armand's Legion, including sixty mounted dragoons and approximately the same amount of light infantry, were placed on the far eastern flank, and Maryland general William Smallwood's 1st Maryland Brigade was held in reserve along the Great Wagon Road. As memorably recounted by Williams, the American army, present and fit for duty, consisted of just over three thousand men (Williams field return earlier in the evening came in at 3,052), but only nine hundred of these were the experienced Continental veterans of Maryland, Delaware, and Armand's Legion. Aside from Porterfield's hundred experienced Virginia state troops, the rest were mostly untrained and untried militia from Virginia and North Carolina. Stevens Virginians had been given bayonets prior to the battle but had no training or experience in using them. The artillery was placed at the front of the formation in between the North Carolina and Virginia militia, while Gates and his staff were positioned six hundred yards back from the line, roughly in the middle of the formation.

On the right, or east, side of his line, Cornwallis placed the 33rd and 23rd Regiments along with five companies of light infantry regulars, his most experienced troops. Commanding the right wing was Lt. Col. James Webster, one of Cornwallis's best and most experienced officers. On the left side of the road were the Volunteers of Ireland and the infantry of Tarleton's British Legion, both under the command of Rawdon. Also on the left were regiments of North Carolina militia and provincial regiments. Like Gates, Cornwallis set up his artillery in the center of the formation, along the road. In reserve was the British 71st Highlanders, another experienced regiment of British regulars, with two cannons. Tarleton and his Legion dragoons were also in reserve, near the 71st, "with orders to act offensively against the enemy, or in defence of the British troops, as opportunity or necessity required."[25] Altogether, the British forces totaled 2,239, over eight hundred fewer than the Americans. But these two thousand plus possessed a decided advantage in experience and training over Gates's Americans.

At dawn on the morning of August 16, the two armies aligned in their battle formations. The morning light finally revealed the setting for the battle to come, an open forest of pines narrowly bordered by swamps on both sides, with the American's terrain slightly higher than the British, though the dry ground widened behind the American position, exposing the American flanks in the case of a retreat.

Perceiving some movement on the American's left flank, Cornwallis "directed Lt. Colonel Webster to begin the attack."[26] The British regulars under Webster initiated the battle, marching forward in columns that were preparatory to forming into their lines of battle, the two or three lines formed for coordinated musket fire. An American artillery officer reported the movement to Otho Holland Williams, positioned near the front of the American formation, who immediately ordered the artillery to open their battery. Williams then rode to Gates's position in the rear, reporting the British right appeared to be advancing and recommending a counterattack by Stevens's Virginia militia.

"'Sir,' Gates responded, "that's right—let it be done,'" which Williams reported "was the last order the deputy adjutant general received."[27] In the centuries since, Gates has been criticized for his failure to recognize the British were fighting "right-handed," concentrating their best, most experienced soldiers on the right side of their line. A former British officer himself, Gates should've recognized this tactic and placed his most experienced troops—his Maryland and Delaware Continentals—on his left to meet the British challenge, this line of criticism contends. In this matter, historical evidence offers no insight into Gates's thinking. One could argue Gates attempted to employ the same tactic himself, placing his most experienced soldiers on his own right side, facing the British Provincials and militia under Rawdon. Convinced of his own numerical superiority, Gates perhaps intended for his militia to simply hold their position on the left, while his Continentals on the right attacked Cornwallis's weaker left flank.

There's no evidence to support this supposition. To the contrary, it appears that Gates's confidence in the American militia let him down. To quote Otho Holland Williams, how could it be "conceived, that an army, consisting of more than two-thirds militia, and which had never been once exercised in arms together,"[28] could form columns and fight with regular order in the face of an experienced and disciplined enemy attack? Gates himself offers little insight into this point. "At day Light the Enemy attacked, and drove in our Light Parties in Front, when I ordered our Left to advance and attack the enemy."[29]

Almost immediately, the consequences of that decision turned disastrous. "To my astonishment," reported Gates, "the Left Wing and North Carolina Militia Gave Way."[30] Things would only get worse from there. After his consultation with Gates, Williams raced back to the front line and gave Stevens the order to attack, which Stevens conveyed to his men. But with British regulars already advancing in front of them, the Virginians resisted. Indeed, it was already too late, for Webster instituted the attack with "great vigour, and in a few minutes the action was general along the whole front," described Cornwallis.[31]

Though Stevens tried to order his men to their bayonets to counter the British charge, Williams described "the impetuosity with which the British advanced, firing and huzzaing, threw the whole body of the militia into such a panic, that they generally threw down their loaded arms and fled in the utmost consternation." And to make matters worse, "the unworthy example of the Virginians was almost instantly followed by the North Carolinians," reported Williams.[32]

On the American left, chaos ensued. "Our line continued to advance in good order and with the cool intrepidity of experienced British soldiers, keeping up a constant fire or making use of bayonets as opportunities offered . . . threw them into total confusion and forced them to give way," reported Cornwallis.[33]

The American militia retreated in waves in the face of this cool intrepidity. "They ran like a torrent, and bore all before them,"[34] reported Gates. Here, for once, Williams agrees with his commanding officer. "The great majority of the militia, (at least two-thirds of the army) fled without firing a shot. The writer avers it of his own knowledge, have seen and observed every part of the army, from left to right, during the action. He who has never seen the effect of a panic upon a multitude, can have but an imperfect idea of such a thing," Williams describes eloquently. "The best disciplined troops have been enervated, and made cowards by it. . . . Like electricity it operates instantaneously."[35]

It was an electricity that caught Gates in its charge. In his report to Huntington, Gates claimed he and Gen. Caswell attempted to rally the militia but were obliged to retreat with them in the overwhelming chaos. "The torrent of unarmed militia, bore away with it, General Gates, Caswell, and a number of others," agreed Williams, who tried to rally the retreating American troops at Rugeley's Mill, "but the farther they fled, the more they were dispersed; and the generals soon found themselves abandoned by all but their aides."[36]

On the American right, however, Kalb and the American Continentals fought on, at first unaware of the total disintegration of the American left. Indeed, their vision may have been impaired by the haze of gun powder smoke, which "occasioned so thick a darkness that it was difficult to see the effect" of the British advance.[37] Twice they repulsed the charge of the Irish Volunteers and Legion Infantry under Rawdon, then counterattacked with bayonet. During the fighting, Kalb called for the Maryland reserves, who were now under the command of Williams, but by then it was too late, the chasm between the two brigades was filled with British soldiers, and Williams and his men "were obliged to give way."[38]

Already wounded, the gallant Kalb fought for almost an hour more, his experienced Continentals stoutly resisting Rawdon's British Provincials. According to one British soldier, Cornwallis rode toward Rawdon's troops "in the midst of a heavier fire than the oldest soldier remembers," calling out "Volunteers of Ireland, you are fine fellows! Charge the rascals. By heaven you behave nobly."[39] The British held, and Kalb was wounded repeatedly, finally falling on the battlefield only after his eleventh wound from bullets, bayonet, and saber.

Now Cornwallis delivered the coup de grace, ordering Tarleton and his dragoons into the fray to "complete the rout, which was performed with their usual promptitude." Tarleton remembered that

"rout and slaughter ensued in every quarter. . . . The continentals, the state troops, and the militia abandoned their arms, their colours, and their cannons to seek protection in flight. . . . The legion dragoons advanced with great rapidity towards Rugeley's mills: On the road, General Rutherford, with many other officers and men, were made prisoners."[40]

But was Bloody Ban up to his old tricks, allowing the slaughter to turn indiscriminate during the pursuit? In descriptions of the ensuing chaos, Tarleton's dragoons largely escape such accusations, although it is probably true the confusion was so great, the slaughter so indiscriminate in all cases, that no one thought to note or transcribe the individual transgressions of Tarleton and his dragoons. "Every corps was broken and dispersed," wrote Williams of this chaos. "The cries of the women and the wounded in the rear, and the consternation of the flying troops, so alarmed some of the waggoners, that they cut out their teams, and taking each a horse, left the rest for the next that should come . . . the whole road, for many miles, was strewed with signals of distress, confusion and dismay."[41]

Tarleton concurred, reporting the chase did not terminate until the Americans were entirely dispersed, "and fatigue overpowered the British," the pursuit of over twenty miles for Tarleton and his riders producing "many prisoners of all ranks, twenty ammunition wagons, and one hundred and fifty carriages, containing the baggage, stores and camp equipage of the

American army." Finally, "sated with blood and death, horses and riders overcome by exhaustion," Tarleton halted at Hanging Rock.[42]

The American losses were disastrous. "Never was victory more complete, or a defeat more total," described the American historian John Marshall.[43] Given the total chaos and carnage of the encounter, a true count of the American losses will never be known, but historian Christopher Ward estimates 650 Continentals were killed, wounded, and/or captured. This toll included three killed Continental officers and twenty wounded, fourteen of whom were captured, including Kalb, who somehow survived his eleven wounds on the battlefield only to die three days later. About one hundred North Carolina militia were killed, and three hundred captured. In his battle report, Cornwallis reported between eight and nine hundred American killed, and about eight hundred prisoners, many of them wounded, a report undoubtedly exaggerated for positive effect, but still indicative of the scale of the American defeat.[44]

Despite the "compleat victory" he reported to Germain, however, Cornwallis did not escape the day unscathed. His own losses were reported at 324 killed and wounded, including two officers and sixty-six men killed, eighteen officers and 227 wounded, and eleven missing—roughly 15 percent of his fighting strength.[45] And with the size of his South Carolina occupation force already limited, and much of the rest decimated by malaria, this was a significant loss despite the victorious outcome, given his plans to invade North Carolina in just a few short weeks. Indeed, after the total collapse of American discipline and order, Cornwallis has been criticized for not pursuing the retreating Continentals into North Carolina, eradicating American resistance and taking control of the northern province in the momentum of his Camden victory. "His lordship certainly gave the world another instance in proof of the assertion, that it is not every general, upon whom fortune bestows her favours, who knows how to avail of all the advantages which are presented to him," Otho Holland Williams observed acidly.[46] Here Cornwallis's innate compassion may have let him down, with disastrous consequences for the Southern Strategy's implementation, though he can hardly be criticized for pausing to tend to his dead and wounded.[47]

Cornwallis perhaps believed he had little to fear from Gates, who completed his humiliation in the aftermath of the battle. In his report to Huntington, Gates wrote that, after failing to rally the militia at Rugeley's Mill, "I concluded to retire towards Charlotte."[48] He neglected to tell Huntington he rode atop the fastest charger in his army, a racer sired by the famous stud Fearnaught, leaving the rest of his officers and soldiers behind. Gates's biographer, Paul David Nelson, attributes the decision to abandon Kalb and the Continental soldiers to strategic considerations. "Had he lingered near Camden, quite likely he could not have assisted Kalb and the Continentals, but he would have risked capture by Tarleton's men. Needless to say, such a consequence would have had implications far greater than merely his own safety, for the enemy would have used his seizure for propaganda purposes."[49]

William R. Davie was riding south on the Great Wagon Road from the Waxhaws with some of his dragoons, still hoping to join with Gates's army before the fighting, when he encountered "General Gates himself, in full flight. General Gates desired Major Davie to fall back on Charlotte, or the dragoons would soon be on him,"[50] Davie recalled in his memoir. But Davie replied cooly to Gates that "his men were accustomed to Tarleton and did not fear him. Gates had no time to argue, but passed on," while Davie and his dragoons continued south, hoping to be useful in saving soldiers, baggage, and stores in the retreat.

A while later, Davie encountered the South Carolina general Isaac Huger, fleeing in the same direction, and inquired of him "how far the directions of Gates ought to be obeyed." Huger replied, "Just as far as you please, for you will never see him again."[51] Gates and Caswell arrived at Charlotte after a ride of sixty miles. Sleeping in Charlotte that night, "the ensuing morning presented nothing to them but an open village, with few inhabitants," Otho Holland Williams observed sourly.[52] In his report to Huntington, Gates said "reflecting that there was neither Army, Ammunition, nor any prospect of collecting any Force" at Charlotte, he decided to ride on to the North Carolina capital at Hillsborough, where he could "endeavor to fall upon some Plan, in conjunction with the legislature of this State, for the Defense of so much thereof as it is yet possible to save from the Enemy." He arrived there on August 19, having ridden 180 miles in the three days since being swept from the fields of Camden.[53]

It was a flight for which his historic reputation still suffers. From some perspectives, this embarrassment is just desserts for a man with the temerity to challenge George Washington's status, if not through the inflated intrigues of the Conway Cabal, then certainly through his other schemes and machinations undermining Washington's character. And no one captured the acidic nature of this opinion better than Alexander Hamilton, Washington's most famous Federalist ally, who noted, "Was there ever an instance of a general running away as Gates has done from his whole army? And was there ever so precipitous a flight? One hundred and eighty miles in three days and a half! It does admirable credit to the activity of a man at his time of life. But it disgraces the general and the soldier."[54]

GATES WOULD EVENTUALLY RECOVER command of his army, if not his dignity, before eventually being relieved by Nathanael Greene in December. But the outcomes of August were not all doom and gloom for the American side.

When we last left James Williams, Thomas Brandon, and the Ninety Six refugees, they had departed Thomas Sumter's camp (or deserted it, according to William Hill) and were headed toward North Carolina militia colonel Charles McDowell's base on the Broad River with a quantity of horses and supplies they may or may not have inappropriately taken from Thomas Sumter's brigade. When they arrived at McDowell's, on or about August 16, they discovered plans were already in process to attack Musgrove's Mill, a Loyalist outpost guarding a ford on the Enoree River some forty miles away. Today, the site is located on South Carolina Highway 56, just a few miles north of the Clinton and Laurens communities and is operated as a park and historic site by the State of South Carolina.

At this time, news of Gates's defeat two days before had not yet reached McDowell's camp, but the militia commitment of Isaac Shelby's Overmountain regiment was expiring, and Shelby and Georgia militia leader Elijah Clarke desired one last operation before ending their summer campaign. At Musgrove's Mill, they believed, approximately two hundred Loyalist militia were guarding a strategic road crossing on the Enoree River. Musgrove's Mill also served as a Loyalist field hospital, and in some accounts, rumors that a British payroll chest had recently arrived there swirled through McDowell's camp, increasing its desirability as a target for the Whig militia. The site was not far from the homes of either Williams or Brandon, and their arrival proved fortuitous, for they could guide the Patriots along the backroads through the night for an early morning attack.

With James Williams and the Ninety Six refugees guiding the way, the combined party of South Carolina, Georgia, and North Carolina militia, approximately two hundred men in all, set off from McDowell's base at Cherokee Ford on the Broad River an hour before sundown. "They traveled through the woods until dark," writes historian Lyman Draper, "when they fell into a road, and proceeded on all night . . . crossing Gilky's and Thicketty creeks, Pacolet, Fair Forest, and Tyger, with other lesser streams," a route one can approximate today by riding south from Spartanburg on Highway 56.[55]

Arriving at the north bank of the Enoree River around dawn on August 18, Patriot scouts soon discovered Musgrove's Mill had been reinforced the night before with two hundred Provincial troops and one hundred mounted South Carolina rangers riding from Ninety Six, all under the command of Colonel Alexander Innes. On their way to report back to Williams, Shelby, and Clarke, the Patriot scouts skirmished with a Loyalist patrol, putting the garrison at Musgrove's Mill under alert.

Their horses now too exhausted to retreat to Broad River, the Americans decided to set up an ambush along the crest of a ridge farther north, where they hastily assembled a breastwork in the form of a semicircle extending approximately three hundred yards across the left and right side of the road. According to historian Lyman Draper, "Shelby occupied the right" of this defense, "Clarke the left; and Williams in the center, though with no special command, for the whole force formed one extended line."[56]

Meanwhile, the Loyalists under Innes had organized an expedition of approximately four hundred men, leaving one hundred at Musgrove's Mill as a reserve, to pursue the Patriots across the river and up the road. From their defensive position, the Patriots sent forward Capt. Shadrach Inman with a small party of twenty-five men to entice Innes's force into attack. The plan worked to perfection. After skirmishing with the Loyalists, Inman fell back, and the Loyalists charged after him, blundering into a sheet of rifle fire about seventy yards from the Patriot ambush.

Staggered but not broken, the Loyalists recovered, and advanced on Shelby's position with a bayonet charge. But Clarke sent his reserves to re-inforce Shelby's position, and when Innes was shot from his horse, the Loyalists' order was broken. In the melee, the Americans charged from their lines with "a regular frontier Indian yell,"[57] sending the Loyalists racing back across the Enoree River into the defenses of Musgrove's Mill.

In fighting that probably lasted about an hour, sixty-three Loyalists were killed and ninety wounded, compared to only four Patriots killed and seven wounded. Seventy Loyalists were taken prisoners. Elated with their victory, the Americans planned to ride on to Ninety Six, just twenty-five miles away, which was rumored to be in a weakened condition, but around this time they received a dispatch from Charles McDowell informing them of Gates's defeat at Camden. This news chilled their initiative, convincing the American commanders to go their separate ways. Shelby and his men re-turned to the Holston River settlements in what is now eastern Tennessee, while Clarke and his militia set off toward their homes in Georgia. Williams volunteered to march with the prisoners back to Hillsborough, which was not far away from his property in North Carolina's Caswell County. Though the Patriot victory at Musgrove's Mill paled in comparison to the British one at Camden, it was proof that Cornwallis's great victory had not entirely doused the flame of Patriot resistance in South Carolina. And Williams's arrival in Hillsborough a few days later would soon lead to further intrigues in the Backcountry War.[58]

THIRTEEN

CONSPICUOUS
MANEUVERS

E NCUMBERED WITH THE BAGGAGE, wagons, and the prisoners his
troops had captured at Camden Ferry, Sumter marched north along
the west bank of the Catawba River on August 16. During the morning,
he heard the cannon and musket fire of the battle across the river, but he
was apparently unaware of Gates's defeat until later in the day, when a messenger from Davie arrived, informing him of Cornwallis's victory and suggesting a rendezvous in Charlotte, where other elements of the American
forces were gathering.[1]

Sumter and his eight hundred men—approximately seven hundred militia, the rest Maryland Continentals who remained with Sumter's brigade,
along with the two cannon Gates had sent him—continued marching north
throughout the night but moved slowly, his troops sapped by the heat and
the extra burden of their plunder and prisoners, their horses exhausted. In

addition to the seventy British regulars Sumter had captured at Camden Ferry, he had also captured Loyalist militia during his raid. With him were perhaps as many as 150 prisoners in total. Probably influenced by the intelligence that Turnbull and a part of Ferguson's corps was pursuing him from the west, Sumter hung close to the Catawba River, despite its proximity to Cornwallis and Tarleton on the other side. Sumter's forced march continued throughout the following day, August 17, but upon reaching an old camp site near Rocky Mount that evening, he stopped to camp for the night. "Incautious and unafraid, he allowed his troops to light campfires, cook and eat, and then sleep until dawn," writes Bass.[2]

Sumter's incaution would soon betray him, for earlier that day Cornwallis had ordered Tarleton to "harass or strike at Colonel Sumpter, as he should find it most advisable when approached by him." With Tarleton for this mission was a force of approximately 350 men, including the British Legion and the light infantry of the British 71st, along with a single cannon. By late afternoon, Tarleton had intelligence of Sumter's position. That night, he and his men watched Sumter's campfires from across the Catawba River. "Immediate care was taken to secure the boats, and instant orders were given to the light troops to pass the night without fires," Tarleton recalled in his memoir. "No alarm happened and at daybreak it was apparent that the Americans had decamped."[3]

Accounts differ as to whether Sumter had knowledge of Tarleton's pursuit. Davie reported that on the morning of August 18 Sumpter received reports that the British Legion had crossed the river at Rocky Mount and was hanging on his rear. Others, including Henry Lee, who left a detailed account of the incident in his own history of the war, though he was not there, suggest that Sumter was unaware of Tarleton's nearby position, a supposition Sumter's biographers Bass and Gregorie also support. But if unawares, it was a surprising oversight from a commander whose intelligence operations were rarely matched in the Backcountry War.[4]

Sumter arrived at another old campsite after midday on August 18. This was the camp he had used after being repulsed by Turnbull at Rocky Mount earlier that month. Despite having marched only eight miles that morning, Sumter again ordered his men to set up camp, posting only a few scouts and vedettes in his rear for security. "The Detachment was halted in the line of march upon an open ridge," Davie later complained. "No advantage was taken of the waggons . . . the army should have been posted or formed in the order of battle, and the waggons so disposed to have covered the troops from the charge of the British Cavalry, these precautions dictated by common practice and common prudence would have enabled him to have repelled five times the Enemy's force."[5]

Sumter ignored the wisdom of such measures and "exhausted from herding his undisciplined troops and from lack of sleep," he took off his jacket and boots, crawling under the shade of a wagon to sleep while his men stacked their arms and started to cook and clean in camp.[6]

It was this scene of "listless and slumbering security"[7] Tarleton and his troopers encountered upon arriving at the outskirts of Sumter's camp shortly thereafter. Earlier in the day, around noon, Tarleton had "found the greatest part of his command overpowered by fatigue; the corps could no longer therefore be moved forwards in a compact and serviceable state."[8] In response, the relentless Tarleton left about two hundred of his corps behind and continued his pursuit with one hundred Legion dragoons and around fifty infantries, comprised mostly from the British 71st.

Tarleton and his reduced force continued their march for five miles, receiving no intelligence of Sumter "except the recent tracks upon the road," until two of Sumter's scouts shot a dragoon, a "circumstance which irritated the foremost of his comrades to such a degree, that they dispatched the two Americans with their sabres before Lieutenant-colonel Tarleton could interpose." Sumter claimed to have heard the shots but was told by an officer it was simply the militia slaughtering cattle. It was an unfortunate assumption, for a few minutes later, Tarleton "plainly discovered over the crest of the hill the front of the American camp, perfectly quiet, and not the least alarmed by the firing of the vedettes."[9]

Determining strategy for the next steps was no problem for the hard-charging Tarleton. "The decision, and the preparation for the attack, were momentary. The cavalry and infantry were formed into one line, and giving a general shout, advanced to the charge."[10] Sumter's camp was caught completely by surprise; the American artillery and many of their arms were seized by the charging British before the Americans could assemble. During the ensuing panic, the main guard ran, and Sumter's British prisoners were instantly released. Tarleton reported some opposition was made from behind the wagons, and "the numbers, and extensive encampment of the enemy, occasioned several conflicts before the action was decided."

But most of the Americans fled, either to the river or the nearby woods. Of the men in the river, some were drowned, floating "like the corks of a fishing seine."[11] Although Sumter's biographer Anne King Gregorie claims Sumter briefly tried to rally his troops, there's little evidence he did anything but flee for his life, perhaps still bootless and undressed.

The outcome was disastrous for Sumter and his militia army, and given the timing, so soon after the defeat at Camden, demoralizing to the American cause. Tarleton captured three hundred of the Americans, including most of the Continentals, and reported 150 of Sumter's Americans were killed or wounded. In addition, Tarleton captured the two cannons on loan to Sumter from Gates, along with two wagons of ammunition, a thousand "stand of arms," and forty-four carriages loaded with baggage, rum, and other stores. In contrast, he suffered only sixteen casualties, including one officer killed.[12]

After a momentous summer, Tarleton's heroics at Camden and Fishing Creek finally brought him the ultimate praise—recognition by King George. In a letter to Cornwallis dated November 19, 1780, Germain conveyed the congratulations of the king, "signifying to your Lordship His Royal Pleasure that you do acquaint the Officers and Soldiers of the brave Army under your Command . . . is highly approved by the Sovereign, and you will particularly express to Lord Rawdon, Lieutenant colonels Webster and Tarleton His Majesty's approbation."[13] And when Germain published Cornwallis's report in a London paper that October 9, the hero of Fishing Creek became a hero to the people of England.

WHILE DAVIE, SUMTER, AND THE REMNANTS of Gates's army tried to reorganize at Charlotte, Francis Marion was having better luck on the eastern bank of the Wateree and Santee. After arriving with the Pee Dee militia at Witherspoon's Ferry on Lynches Creek on or about August 17, where today Highway 51 crosses Lynches River just outside of Johnsonville, South Carolina, Marion took a few days to organize his new command. Marion sent Col. Peter Horry with a small detachment of sixteen men to destroy boats on the Santee River, part of Gates and Sumter's strategy to cut off a British retreat from Camden. Still unaware of Gates's defeat the previous day, he instructed Horry to "post guards on each crossing place and prevent any persons crossing to or from Charles Town on either side of the river," giving "all intelligence necessary."[14]

Marion then marched to Kingstree, gathering seventy men, before heading south to the Santee himself, destroying boats as he rode upriver from Lenud's Ferry. Finally, on August 19, he received news of Gates's and Sumter's defeats. However, Marion kept this news to himself. "To keep the men together, and with nothing better to do, he continued destroying boats and canoes," surmises Marion biographer Hugh Rankin.[15]

Marion was camped near Nelson's Ferry later that same day when he learned from a Loyalist deserter that approximately 150 American prisoners and their escort were bivouacked at Thomas Sumter's nearby plantation on Great Savannah, six miles east. This was Sumter's main plantation house, the one he built after marrying Mary Cantey, not the summer house in the High Hills of the Santee that had been burned by Tarleton's Legion.

Resolving to rescue the prisoners, Marion roused his regiment early on the morning of August 20 and traveled through the swamps and backroads toward Sumter's plantation.[16] As they approached Great Savannah, Marion ordered Peter Horry's brother, Hugh, and a detachment of sixteen men to take the pass at Horse Creek, preventing reinforcement from the British outpost at Nelson's Ferry. Meanwhile, Marion and the rest of his regiment circled around the swamp to attack Sumter's house from behind.

In the darkness, however, Horry's detachment encountered a British scout, who fired blindly at the Whig militia. Believing the surprise attack ruined, Horry charged the British guards stationed at Sumter's house. With arms stacked carelessly next to the plantation and even jackets and accoutrement scattered across the yard, the guards were taken completely by surprise. As Marion and the rest of the militia charged toward the house, a brief skirmish ensued during which a British officer, two Tory guides, and twenty-two regulars of the 63rd Regiment and Provincial Prince of Wales Regiment were either killed, wounded, or captured. Marion's losses were only one killed and one wounded.[17]

If Marion and his Whig militia expected gratitude from the 147 prisoners they had just rescued, they were sorely disappointed. Most of these men were the Maryland Continentals who had marched south with Kalb earlier that spring and suffered a brutal summer of heat, starvation, and defeat under Gates. Rather than subject themselves to more abuse under their American commanders, approximately seventy of these men refused Marion's assistance and demanded that they be allowed to continue to Charleston as prisoners.

Nevertheless, Marion gained immediate notoriety from the successful raid at Great Savannah, and his success there helped raise sagging American morale in the wake of the Camden debacle. After sending a report of the action to Gates on August 29, Gates included details of it in his own report to the Continental Congress, written September 5: "I also have information on which I can depend that 140 of our prisoners coming from Camden to Orangeburgh have been released by Colonel Marien; and the guard of forty Regulars, escorting them, taken by our party." Though Gates may have misspelled Marion's name, his account was soon reprinted in Whig newspapers across the country.[18] "For the first time patriots from

Maine to Georgia read the name of Francis Marion," wrote Bass. "But from that perversity which ever dogs military dispatches, it was spelled 'Marien.'"[19]

The American Whig press was not alone in noticing Marion. In a letter to British officer John Harris Cruger, Cornwallis wrote, "the first division of the rebel prisoners consisting of 150 under the escort of 36 men, regulars, Provincials, and militia were attacked . . . at Sumpter's house near Nelson's Ferry and taken by a Colonel Marion." It was the first time Cornwallis mentioned Marion's name in correspondence, though far from the last.[20]

Cornwallis was already in a sour mood, and the addition of a new Whig threat on his eastern flank wouldn't improve it. Staggered by the loss of three hundred at the Battle of Camden, his army continued to struggle with malaria. To bolster his manpower, Cornwallis transferred many of the prisoners he housed at Charleston to prison hulks in the harbor, allowing the remainder of the British 71st to join him in the field. Meanwhile, his patience finally snapped with the Whigs of Charleston. Accusing them of advancing in the "most publick and insolent manner the grossest falsehoods tending to encourage the disaffected," he sent almost sixty of them, including Lt. Gov. Christopher Gadsden, to exile in St. Augustine. A few weeks later he appointed Provincial officer John Cruden commissioner of sequestered estates, authorizing the confiscation of the estates of those accused of Whig sympathies.[21]

This new Whig incursion in the Pee Dee was an insult Cornwallis could not tolerate. Although Tarleton was his preferred instrument for this type of blunt operation, Cornwallis was already in the middle of planning his move into North Carolina; he needed to keep Tarleton operating on his left flank, guarding his advance into Charlotte from the threat of Thomas Sumter and other Whig militia in the west. And so, on August 28, he ordered British major James Wemyss (pronounced "Weems") to lead a retaliatory expedition into the Pee Dee.

Born in Edinburgh, Scotland, in 1748, Wemyss joined the British army as an ensign at age seventeen and arrived in America in 1775 as a captain in the 40th Regiment of Foot. In 1777, he was promoted to major, and given command of the Queen's Rangers, a Provincial unit raised around New York and western Connecticut. With them he fought at Brandywine and Germantown in 1777 before transferring to the 63rd in 1778 and later joining the expedition to South Carolina.[22]

By August 1780, Wemyss and his brigade were stationed at the High Hills of the Santee, guarding the supply route from Charleston to Camden.

For Cornwallis, this location made Wemyss an attractive option for operations in the nearby Pee Dee. Furthermore, Wemyss was familiar with the region, having served briefly as commander of the Georgetown garrison earlier in the campaign, though he had found the majority of people there hostile to the Crown's cause. "The principal inhabitants of this place have been the most violent and persecuting rebels and . . . ought, I think, to be treated with some marks of disscouragement," he wrote Cornwallis from Georgetown on July 11, 1780. In contrast, "the friends of Government" were "much inferior to the other party both in numbers and consequences."[23]

With smallpox threatening his troops, Wemyss's position at Georgetown was barely secure, and when the British evacuated Cheraw in the face of Gates's advance, it became untenable. At the end of July, Cornwallis ordered him to march with "much secrecy from Georgetown" to the "High Hills of the Santee, . . . and when we are ready to move [into North Carolina], you shall join the army."[24]

Although there is little in the historic record about Wemyss's appearance or personality, Cornwallis considered him an "intelligent" officer. Clearly, he had a talent for "fire and sword"—prior to his posting at Georgetown, Wemyss and his troops had swept through the region toward Cheraw, "destroying property of every description, and treating the inhabitants with relentless cruelty."[25] Like Christian Huck, he now becomes a surrogate to Banastre Tarleton, the stereotype of the merciless, destructive British dragoon, even if his own name has been mostly lost to the ages.

With orders from Cornwallis to sweep the country from Kingstree to Cheraw, disarming "in the most rigid manner all persons who cannot be depended on and punish the concealment of arms and ammunition with the total demolition of the plantation,"[26] Wemyss now had his general's permission to institute the type of wanton destruction and psychological terror he preferred. Subsequent orders commanded Wemyss to "establish some trusty militia . . . at the Cheraws," under the overall command of William Henry Mills, the former British officer who had emerged as a prominent Loyalist landowner and public official in the Cheraws District. And although Cornwallis's orders instructed that those loyal or acquiescent to the "King's Government" were to be spared, anyone who had joined the revolt "must have their property entirely taken from them or destroy'd and themselves taken as prisoners of war." Those who had joined the Loyalists militia and then deserted to the rebels "must be instantly hanged up."[27]

These are hardly ineffectual orders from a general occasionally accused of being too humane to win the American Revolution, yet something about the Whigs of the Pee Dee incited Cornwallis's cruel streak. And in Wemyss, he had an enthusiastic instrument for his savagery. From the High Hills, Wemyss responded ominously to Cornwallis's instructions: "I was honored with yours of this day . . . and shall proceed without loss of time to execute with greatest pleasure every part of your Lordship's commands."[28]

Yet it would take a few days for Wemyss to organize his expedition, and in the interim, Marion remained active. After the raid at Great Savannah, he retreated to Witherspoon's Ferry on August 26. From Lynch's River, he wrote Peter Horry, informing him of the action at Great Savannah and Gates's defeat, begging Horry to "retreat as immediately as you receive this, for I expect the enemy will send their Horse in this part of the country."[29] Along the way, all but three of the Continental soldiers he'd released at Great Savannah deserted him, and only about sixty eventually rejoined the Continental army in North Carolina, the rest drifting away as deserters.[30]

In the region around present-day Dillon, South Carolina, not far from where I-95 crosses from North Carolina into South Carolina, Loyalists on Catfish Creek, the Little Pee Dee, and the tributaries of Drowning Creek joined with North Carolina Loyalists from Bladen County and organized into a substantial militia body under the command of a Loyalist militia officer named Micajah Gainey (also spelled Ganey). Formerly a soldier in Marion's Second Regiment, Gainey had switched sides after Whigs stole some of his horses. Jesse Barefield was another former Continental army soldier who joined this new Loyalist corps after becoming disenchanted with the Patriot cause.

Learning that Marion and his regiment were bivouacked on Britton's Neck, the isthmus lying between the junction of the Pee Dee and Little Pee Dee Rivers, not far east from modern-day Conway, South Carolina, Gainey and Barfield mustered 250 Loyalist militia and set out to surprise Marion's camp. But Marion's scouts alerted him of Gainey's approach on September 3. Outnumbered roughly five to one, for he now had with him only fifty-three men, Marion decided to turn the tables on Gainey. Early in the morning of September 4, he mustered his troops, ordering them to place white cockades, or ribbons, on their hats, so they could be distinguished from the Loyalists. Otherwise, he did not inform his men of his plans. Already Marion instinctively understood security and secrecy would be key to his operations in the Pee Dee.

"The morning was warm, and the road wound across sand ridge covered with scrub oaks and partridge peas and through swamps flaming with leaves of black gum trees,"[31] wrote Bass. Then, the morning was interrupted abruptly by one of Marion's scouts, reporting an armed party on the road ahead. At the news, Maj. John James, atop his mount Thunder, immediately raced forward to confront the Tories, taking several of Marion's regiment with him. What Marion thought of this breach in discipline he did not record. In his report to Gates, he noted only, "On the 4th in the morning I surprised a party of 45 men."[32] James's son, William Dobein James, left a more colorful account. According to him, the charging James and his detachment now engaged the Tory patrol, led by Gainey himself, wounding or killing all but fifteen. During the fighting, James pursued the fleeing Gainey down the road, not realizing the other members of his platoon had dropped off from the chase, until he ran into the reformed Tories a half mile down the road. "Not at all intimidated, but with great presence of mind, Major James called out, 'Come on my boys!—Here they are!'" The ruse worked, at least according to his son: "And the whole body of tories broke again and pushed into little Peedee swamp."[33]

From the prisoners, Marion learned Barefield and the main body of the Tory militia were about three miles away. He continued down the road, soon coming up on Barefield, who had placed his approximately two hundred men in a line across the road formed for battle. Ever cautious, the wily Marion ordered a retreat, feigning fear, withdrawing back up the road to the Blue Savannah. This was a marshy, sandy-rimmed depression known as a Carolina "bay," not for the water it collects, but for the bay trees frequently found growing there. Typically, elliptical or oval in shape, Carolina bays are likely caused by ancient meteor impacts. Blue Savannah was named for the bluish-gray mud that stuck to the boots and wagon wheels of those crossing it.[34]

This was prime habitat for a fox, and Marion ordered his men concealed in Blue Savannah's tangled underbrush while the impetuous Barefield soon rode right into Marion's trap. "I Directly Attack them & put them to flight," Marion reported to Gates. "I had one man wounded in the first action, & 3 in the second, & two horses killed."[35] Marion gave no account of the Loyalist casualties in the second encounter, though of the ambush at Blue Savannah, William Dobein James noted, "This was the first manouevre of the kind, for which he afterwards became so conspicuous."[36]

After his success at Blue Savannah, Marion's notoriety soared throughout the Pee Dee, increasing the urgency of Wemyss's mission. Requiring mounts for his men, Wemyss ordered the planters of the Santee and High Hill settlements to a meeting while his men raided horses on their farms. Finally mounted and ready for his pursuit of Marion, Wemyss set out from the High Hills on September 6 with eighty to one hundred men of the British 63rd. They rode to Kingstree, where they were joined by approximately one hundred Loyalist militia recruited from the Carolinas.[37]

Almost immediately, Wemyss began implementing Cornwallis's orders, laying down a brutal path of destruction marked by flame and carnage. The raid was vividly recounted by William Dobein James, a victim of its brutality. "The country through which Wemyss marched, for seventy miles in length, and at places for fifteen miles in width, exhibited one continuous scene of destruction," he wrote.[38] With growing concern about the reports he was hearing from his hideout at Port's Ferry, Marion sent Capt. John James (perhaps William Dobein James's brother) to reconnoiter the Kingstree area, while he moved with about one hundred men toward Indian Town to oppose those "Burning all the houses of those who had Joined me."

Near Kingstree, James and his detachment took a Loyalist prisoner and returned to Marion's camp at Indian Town. The prisoner told Marion that he was with a party of "200 British & a number of Toreys, and that Majr. Wemyss with 200 more was to Join them that night." In the prisoner's belongings Marion found an orderly book stating, "their intention was to remove me & proceed to the Cheraws,"[39] he would later write to Gates. Marion also received intelligence that two hundred British regulars had been posted at Georgetown, threatening the outpost at Port's Ferry, which Marion had left defended with about fifty men.

Though the prisoner's report was an exaggeration, Marion believed himself outnumbered again and threatened on two flanks. He decided to retreat into North Carolina, but with many of his men anxious about the fate of their homes and families, he dismissed most of his regiment. With the approximately sixty men who continued to serve, he collected the two cannons he had left at Port's Ferry and retreated into the Great White Marsh in what is now Columbus County, North Carolina.[40]

Although Wemyss claimed he did everything in his power to "get at Mr. Merrion," he "never could come up with" him.[41] That did not prevent him from implementing other elements of Cornwallis's orders, however, in a manner that would quickly gain him infamy. "On most of the plantations every house was burnt to the ground, the negroes were carried off, the inhabitants plundered, the stock, especially sheep wantonly killed; and all the provisions, which could be come at, destroyed,"[42] reported William Dobein James.

When a local Whig named Adam Cusan fired at the "black servant of a Tory officer" in Wemyss's corps, he was taken prisoner, tried by court martial, and ordered to hang. As Wemyss supervised the execution, Cusan's "wife and children prostrated themselves before Wemyss, on horseback, for a pardon; and he would have rode over them, had not one of his own officers prevented the foul deed," James wrote.[43] Perhaps most shockingly, Wemyss burned the Presbyterian church at Indian Town, calling it a "sedition shop." This atrocity was approximated in *The Patriot*, though its violence was exaggerated for cinematic effect, and of course, its supervision attributed to the film's Tarleton surrogate, "Tavington."

Among the houses burned by Wemyss was that of Maj. John James, Willliam Dobein James's father, leaving a lasting impact on his son. "I felt an early inclination to record these events," James wrote in the preface to his *Sketch of Marion*, "but Major Wemyss burnt all my stock of paper, and my little classical library in my father's house; and for two years and a half afterwards, I had not the common implements of writing or of reading."[44]

Cornwallis intended for the term of Wemyss's mission to be limited. "Don't stay longer in that country than is actually necessary to do your business effectually," Cornwallis had instructed him.[45] By September 20, Wemyss had reached Cheraw on his march of destruction, and although "Merrion" had escaped him, he clearly believed he had done all he could do to pacify the region's Whigs. "I have burnt and laid waste about 50 houses and plantations mostly belonging to people who have either broke their paroles or oath of allegiance and are now in arms against us,"[46] he informed his commanding officer.

Not surprisingly, however, Wemyss found little for the British to be optimistic about in the Pee Dee region. "It is impossible for me to give your Lordship an idea of the disaffection of this country. Every inhabitant has been or is concerned in the rebellion, and most of them very deeply." Subsequently, his efforts to bolster the Loyalist militia under William Henry Mills were ineffectual. Few recruits turned out, "and even most of them of such suspicious characters as to convince both him and me of impracticability of such a scheme." Mills was so discouraged he was "determined to leave this part of the country at least for a time," requesting from Cornwallis permission to abandon his post as commander of the local Loyalist militia and retreat with his family and belongings to the Savannah River.[47]

It was hardly an encouraging report, and in his response, Cornwallis admitted he found it "not so agreeable." Nevertheless, other strategies were in motion, and Cornwallis needed Wemyss and the British 63rd back at Camden to support his long-planned march into North Carolina. Efforts to establish a Loyalist militia presence in the Pee Dee remained desultory, but there was little more that Cornwallis could do for the time being, except resort to threats and extortions. "I wish you to publish to the country that all persons ... return to the habitations, where they will be suffered to live quietly, provided they deliver up their arms and give their military parole neither to say or do any thing contrary to His Majesty's interest,"[48] wrote Cornwallis. But even in their tone, these orders conveyed Cornwallis's increasing doubts about security in the Pee Dee region. Though he would try to pacify it again, he was beginning to believe the Loyalist cause there hopeless, and his strategy was shifting with those beliefs.

FOURTEEN

The
HORNET'S
NEST

A T LEAST BRIEFLY, SEPTEMBER BLEW in a wind of change for Cornwallis, Tarleton, and the British-aligned forces occupying the South. If July had been ominous, with Huck's defeat and a string of setbacks in the Spartan region of the Ninety Six District, and the beginning of August disastrous with the emergence of Sumter and Davie on his northern front, Shelby and Clarke on his west, and the approach of Gates and a reconstituted Continental army on his east, the victory at Camden had not only steadied the ship, permitting Cornwallis to instigate his long-planned North Carolina expedition, but also the storm winds surrounding him. Gates was banished and humiliated, attempting to reestablish his command, if not his dignity, in Hillsborough, North Carolina. And despite their victory at Musgrove's Mill, Shelby, Clarke, and James Williams were all on the run.

And for the moment, even Cornwallis's biggest headache du jour, Thomas Sumter, appeared pacified, thanks to the beating Banastre Tarleton handed him at Fishing Creek. "It is impossible there can be any enemy openly in arms near the frontier after the total rout of Gates and Sumpter," Cornwallis wrote optimistically on August 24, expressing the confidence he had earned at Camden and Fishing Creek a few days before.[1]

Indeed, Cornwallis's assessment of Sumter's status after Camden would prove optimistic, despite the Continental army's panic generated by news of Sumter's defeat. With Gates already back in Hillsborough, the news hit Charlotte on August 19, when Otho Holland Williams, and what was left of the Continental army, received news that "Colonel Sumpter, whose arrival they looked for every moment, was *completely surprised* the preceding day, and the whole party *killed, captured, or dispersed.*" Disappeared in the fighting, Sumter's condition was unknown. And though there was "no council, nor regular poll taken, respecting this irksome situation," Williams and the rest of the Continental officers found the unfortunate news aggravating. "Dead or alive, he was censured for *suffering a surprise.*"[2]

Dead or alive, however, Sumter's fate could do little to dissuade the Continental officers from agreeing that

Charlotte, an open wooded village, without magazines of any sort, without a second cartridge per man, and without a second ration, was not tenable for an hour against superior numbers, which might enter at every quarter. Moreover, it was estimated by those who knew the geography of the country, that even then the victorious enemy might be in the vicinity of the place. It was admitted, by everyone, that no place could be more *defenseless.*[3]

Under the command of Maryland general William Smallwood, who "leisurely put himself at the head of the party," the remnants of the Continental army marched off toward Salisbury that same afternoon, August 19. Trailing behind was a cohort of terrified women, children, and elderly. These were the refugees of the Waxhaws/Charlotte region, residents of the two states now united in the miseries of war. "By noon a very lengthy line of march, occupied the road from Charlotte to Salisbury," Williams recounted. "It consisted of the wretched remnants of the late southern army; a great number of distressed Whig families, and the whole tribe of Catawba Indians (about three hundred in number; about fifty or sixty of whom were warriors, but indifferently armed)." Among this wretched parade were six wounded of Buford's Brigade, still recovering from the atrocities they en-

dured at the Waxhaws earlier in the summer, now forced to flee like everyone else. They "had but two sound arms among them; indeed, four of them
had not one arm among them; and two only an arm a piece." Williams's
account of the march's misery goes on. "The distresses of the women and
children . . . the nakedness of the Indians . . . and the disorder of the whole
line of march, conspired to render it a scene too picturesque and complicated for description . . . care, anxiety, pain, poverty, hurry, confusion, humiliation and dejection would be characteristic traits in this mortifying
picture."[4] After a brief delay at Salisbury, below the Yadkin River, and then
at Guilford Courthouse, outside modern-day Greensboro, North Carolina,
Smallwood and the remnants of the Continental army's Southern Department were reunited with Gates at Hillsborough in early September. "Thus
ended the campaign of 1780," decreed Williams.[5]

Strangely, however, the Continental army's retreat proved a windfall to
the indefatigable Sumter, who arrived in Charlotte at William Davie's camp
a day later, on August 20, without a single follower. From Charlotte, on the
evening of August 16, North Carolina general Richard Caswell had issued
a call for the local militia to embody under him there, calling in "upwards
of one thousand fresh men." But when Caswell abandoned Charlotte on
August 18 in advance of the rest of the American forces, the remnants of
the North Carolina militia who had answered his summons were left without a commanding officer, and these men were added to Sumter's command.[6]

Sumter's militia bounty just as quickly diminished after William L.
Davidson, a lieutenant colonel in the Continental army (and future namesake of Davidson College north of Charlotte) was appointed brigadier general of the Salisbury militia in place of Griffith Rutherford, who had been
captured at Camden, and set up his own camp nearby on McAlpine's
Creek. A veteran of Germantown and Valley Forge, Davidson had been on
furlough for the first half of 1780, and thus escaped capture when the rest
of his North Carolina Continental regiment had surrendered at
Charleston.[7]

Nevertheless, Sumter's command remained bolstered by the circumstances following Camden. "Notwithstanding the *bruit* made in history
about this defeat of Sumter," asserts William Dobein James, employing an
archaic word for "rumor," "the author can re-assert . . . that Sumter was *in
three days* at the head of a very respectable force."[8] But with little momentum or initiative for the Whig cause in the battle's aftermath, it doesn't appear Sumter was able to hold the bulk of these men in his service for long.

A few weeks later, on September 24, North Carolina general Jethro Sumner reported to Gates that Sumter was camped near the Catawba Indian nation with about three hundred troops.

With harvest time approaching, the bulk of Sumter's men probably drifted back to their farms. Also discouraging the muster was news that Cornwallis was finally on the move north. He left Camden on September 8, with an invasion force of 2,200 men and thirty-eight wagons, headed up the Great Wagon Road toward Charlotte.

In his correspondence, Cornwallis lamented the delay between this march and the victory at Camden. "The great sickness of the army, the intense heat, and the necessity of totally subduing the rebel country between the Santee and Pedee have detained me longer than I could have wished on the frontiers of this province," he wrote to Germain.[9]

And though Cornwallis attributed the delay in part to the "great fatigue which the cavalry underwent during the violent heat of the summer" and "their great exertions in the action and pursuit of the 16th,"[10] it was one regretted by Tarleton. "The immediate advance of the King's troops into North Carolina" following the victory at Camden, "would undoubtedly, at this critical period have been productive of various and important advantages," Tarleton wrote in his memoir, though he admitted, "But however useful and beneficial such an expedition may have proved, many material requisites and necessary arrangements were not in convenient state or sufficient forwardness to warrant the undertaking."[11] The malaria and sickness that had overwhelmed Tarleton earlier in the summer and limited Cornwallis's fighting force at Camden was a critical consideration, and Cornwallis hoped the cooler weather of September might provide some relief.

Although Cornwallis undoubtedly lost some momentum in the three weeks since his victory at Camden, he had not wasted the time entirely. "Emissaries were again sent into North Carolina, with instructions to the friends of government to take arms, and seize the most violent of their persecutors . . . under an assurance the British army would march without loss of time to their support," reported Loyalist historian Charles Stedman, who accompanied Cornwallis on this march.[12]

Meanwhile, British major Patrick Ferguson was under orders to prepare an expeditionary force of Loyalist militia from the Ninety Six district to support Cornwallis's western flank and "hold communication with the inhabitants of Tryon County," the vast region that now encompasses several western North Carolina counties (none of them named Tryon, though a town of that name, with a famous equestrian community, still exists) "till the King's troops under Earl Cornwallis were in condition to advance."[13] Ferguson's appointment as Inspector of Militia had been forced on Cornwallis by Clinton in the aftermath of Charleston, and it appears Cornwallis was never much of a Ferguson fan. In particular, his summer correspondence with Nisbet Balfour, now commanding the British garrison at Charleston, includes several derogatory comments about Ferguson. "As to Ferguson, his ideas are so wild and sanguine that . . . it would be dangerous to entrust him with the conduct of any plan," Balfour had written to Cornwallis earlier in the summer, to which Cornwallis replied, "I beg you will continue to mention your opinions freely to me," mentioning the opinion of another officer who did not think Ferguson "can give me much assistance in regulating the militia."[14]

But over the course of the summer, Ferguson's diligence in organizing the Loyalist militia of western South Carolina appears to have earned some measure of Cornwallis's respect, along with an important role in the strategy for the North Carolina campaign. On September 20, Cornwallis wrote to Ferguson, "I wish you joy of the success of your expedition, which, considering all things, has been as prosperous as we could have expected."[15] Little did Cornwallis or Ferguson suspect such prosperity would soon end in utter catastrophe.

As Cornwallis marched along the Great Wagon Road toward Camden, Tarleton with "the British dragoons, the light and legion infantry, with a three-pounder," crossed to the west side of the Catawba River, moving through the same territory where he had defeated Sumter at Fishing Creek less than a month before. Tarleton attributed this detachment to the "scarcity of forage"[16] in the Waxhaws District, and Cornwallis's need to spread his hungry army across the countryside, eating and foraging as it traveled north. However, there can be little doubt Tarleton had his keen eye trained to the movements of the Gamecock. But camped farther north at the Catawba Indian nation, Sumter showed little inclination to try his luck again against his opponent from Fishing Creek.

It was not Sumter who plagued Tarleton on the march north, but an even more tenacious enemy. After foraging the country on the west side of the Catawba for several days, Tarleton again fell victim to the malaria that had incapacitated him throughout the summer. In the vicinity of Fishing Creek, Tarleton became violently ill. And Tarleton was far from the only one struck down by the dreaded yellow fever. Along the way, so many men contracted malaria that Cornwallis was forced to leave behind McArthur and the 71st in charge of a field hospital at a place called Blair's Mill on the Catawba River, near modern-day Landsford, South Carolina.[17] Too ill to travel, Tarleton was carried to the home of a nearby Loyalist on the west side of the river, where he lay helpless and delirious for several days. "He cannot be moved," wrote Cornwallis to Balfour on September 20, "and I am obliged to leave his Corps there for protection."[18]

By the following day, however, Tarleton had improved. "His fever has now intermitted and I hope he is safe," Cornwallis reported. Still, Tarleton's illness inconvenienced Cornwallis's plans. "I not only lose his services but the whole corps must remain quite useless in order to protect him."[19] But Cornwallis could not afford to delay his fall campaign for the illness of one man, and on September 22, he sent McArthur and the 71st to guard Tarleton while Major George Hanger was given temporary command of the British Legion and ordered to cross the Catawba at Blair's Ferry to guard Cornwallis's advance into Charlotte. As Hanger and the Legion rode north, Tarleton was well enough to be moved across the Catawba in a litter to the field hospital at Blair's Mill by September 23.

Though plagued by the illness of his troops, Cornwallis's mind was ever on the Gamecock. "Sumter is with 3 or 400 militia on Allison's Creek at the head of the Indian settlement," he reported to Balfour on September 21.[20] With Sumter now camped ten miles from Charlotte, the British offered twenty guineas to anyone who would betray the Gamecock and lead them to his camp, but Sumter kept well informed of the British movements. On September 24, while Sumter lay at Bigger's Ferry, now submerged under Lake Wylie in northern York County, South Carolina, the Legion dragoons were detached to search for Sumter, but being in a "friendly neighborhood," Sumter had information of the "approach, and instantly . . . passed the South Branch up into the forks."[21]

Also proving ineffectual was the North Carolina militia under William Davidson and Jethro Sumner, another North Carolina Continental officer pressed into militia service following the American defeat at Camden. As Cornwallis advanced on Charlotte, Davidson and Sumner's militia retreated north. Sumner retreated all the way to the north side of the Yadkin River while he attempted to call in militia from outlying regions in Rowan and Surry Counties, though Davidson's corps fell back only to Mallard's Creek, about eight miles northeast of Charlotte.

But that industrious horseman, Maj. William Davie, refused to concede, harassing Cornwallis's flanks as the British army moved north through the Waxhaws, his former home. Around September 20, Davie surprised a party of approximately 130 Tories, killed twelve to fourteen men, and made off with about fifty horses.[22] Notable from this portion of Davie's wartime memoir is his description of the British practice of burning homes and property of suspected Patriot sympathizers as they marched north through the Waxhaws. "This barbarous practice was uniformly enacted by the British officers in the Southern States," Davie writes, perhaps referencing the Pee Dee region raid of James Wemyss, which was also occurring at this time. "However casual the rencounter might be, when it happened at a plantation, their remaining in possession of the grounds was always marked by commmtting the Houses to the flames."[23]

Also still in the field, threatening Cornwallis's far western flank, was Elijah Clarke. After returning to Georgia following the victory at Musgrove Mill, Clarke planned a joint operation with South Carolina militia colonel James McCall of the Long Canes District against his old nemesis Thomas "Burnfoot" Brown at Augusta. But the one thousand men Clarke and Mc-Call planned to raise for the campaign in the end amounted to only a little less than five hundred. Nevertheless, Clarke attacked the town boldly on September 14, marching through the middle of Augusta and chasing the surprised Brown into a local trading post, where he was eventually reinforced by some Cherokee Indians and managed to resist Clarke's siege for four days. Clarke retreated only after receiving news that five hundred men under the command of John Harris Cruger, the British commandant at Ninety Six, were marching toward Augusta to relieve Brown.

Forced to leave behind twenty-nine wounded, Clarke retreated quickly in advance of the approaching British column, fleeing into the safety of the North Carolina mountains. Though Cornwallis showed satisfaction with Cruger's "quick and judicious movement," the incident left him wary of the security on his far western flank and the isolated position his North Carolina campaign imposed on Cruger at Ninety Six and Brown at Augusta.[24] Cruger briefly pursued Clarke toward the mountains before passing the assignment onto Patrick Ferguson, already moving into western North Carolina to support Cornwallis's march on Charlotte. Thinking the "direction which he had taken toward Gilbertown perfectly consonant" to this purpose, "Ferguson unfortunately adhered to the plan of striking at Clarke," recounted Tarleton in his memoir, with knowledge of the disaster to come.[25]

THOUGH DAVIE AND CLARKE REMAINED ACTIVE, Sumter was curiously dormant, his attention at this time perhaps diverted by what his biographer Anne Gregorie King calls a "curious affair."[26] Remember that after the battle of Musgrove Mill on August 19, militia colonel James Williams had volunteered to march the Loyalist prisoners captured there to Continental army headquarters, now in Hillsborough, North Carolina. Also in Hillsborough when Williams arrived was South Carolina governor John Rutledge, having recently returned from a trip to Pennsylvania, where he had lobbied the Continental Congress for troops and support.

Prior to the fall of Charleston, Rutledge had been invested with what were essentially dictatorial powers by South Carolina's Whig legislature. Now, with Gates and Sumter recently defeated, Rutledge undoubtedly was eager to reestablish resistance operations in South Carolina, perhaps vesting Williams with some official designation to recruit and lead troops. But what that designation was, precisely, remains lost to history. According to William Hill's memoir, it was a brigadier general's commission, "the governor not knowing that General Sumter had the command of all the South Carolinians then in arms in defence of their country."[27] But James Williams's biographer, William Graves, notes there is no historical proof Rutledge ever promoted Hill to brigadier general, no official record or document of the promotion, nor any reference to it in official correspondence, leaving Hill's memoir as the primary evidence to the claim.[28]

True, there is evidence Williams held some official designation, the most substantial being a letter of authorization from North Carolina governor Abner Nash dated September 8 authorizing Williams to recruit and command up to one hundred soldiers from Caswell County "and to proceed with them to such parts as you judge proper, and to act against the enemy."[29] And in a letter dated September 20, Rutledge noted that he had placed Williams under the command of General William Smallwood, a Continental officer who had been appointed commandant of all North Carolina militia. This letter suggests that, through this chain of command, Williams had some official rank or authorization to command South Carolina militia.[30]

His status historically unclear but certainly elevated, Williams returned to the New Acquisition District sometime around September 20 with the small company he had recruited in North Carolina. According to William Hill's memoir, Williams "had the assurance to march into Sumter's Camp" and had his brigadier general's commission "publicly read & required all the officers & me to fall under his immediate command."[31] Important to note there is no evidence corroborating Hill's account, just as there is no corroborating evidence to support Hill's account of Williams leaving Sumter's camp earlier that summer with unofficially procured horses and provisions. Williams's biographer, William Graves, for one, refutes Hill's account. After an extensive review of pension applications of the men who served with Sumter and Williams during the fall of 1780, Graves declares, "Not one of these men states that Williams came in Sumter's camp after the Battle of Musgrove Mill and tried to usurp command from Sumter."[32]

Yet clearly there was some conflict between the two militia leaders, if not directly, as Hill recalled in his account of Williams appearing ostentatiously in Sumter's camp and attempting to assert authority over Sumter's men, then indirectly, for Sumter and some of his officers chose this moment to call on Rutledge themselves in Hillsborough.

Hill's memoir stated that the purpose of this trip was "in order to deliberate on some plan respecting General Sumter's commission as it was protested by Williams," although this is the only known historical account making this assertion.[33] Nevertheless, in a letter to congressional delegates, John Rutledge admitted Sumter and Williams "will never agree." And even British spies were reporting on the conflict; in a letter dated October 1, Cornwallis informs Ferguson that "Sumter has had a quarrel with Williams about command and gone to Hillsborough to refer it to Gates."[34]

Though evidence indicates Sumter traveled to Hillsborough in late September to discuss matters of command, Hill's memoir makes considerable, tortuous effort to suggest Sumter played only a passive role in this dispute. Hill recalled that he and a committee of four other men, including Richard Winn and Col. John Thomas Jr. of the Spartan Regiment, were chosen as "commissioners" to discuss the conflict with Rutledge. "Sumter was not to make his appearance until the business was decided,"[35] Hill recalled, suggesting somewhat inconceivably that the brash, confident Gamecock waited impassively in the wings while Hill and the others argued his case. Richard Winn agreed he and Thomas were appointed commissioners to procure from the officials in Hillsborough "arms, ammunition, camp utensils, and cloathing, & etc., in order to enable us more fully to prosecute the war in South Carolina" yet neglects to make any mention of the dispute with Williams.[36]

Nevertheless, it is Hill's version that was recounted in Lyman Draper's *Kings Mountain and Its Heroes*, an influential nineteenth-century history of the American Revolution. And Draper's version was subsequently endorsed by Sumter's biographers Anne Gregorie King and Robert D. Bass. "The militia voted to send a delegation to inform Governor Rutledge that they were determined to serve only under General Sumter," describes Bass, while Sumter "agreed to turn command over to Colonels Hill and Lacey until Rutledge settled the question of rank between him and Williams." And

King agrees that during the absence of the Winn commission, "temporary command was given to Hill and Lacey, for Sumter was to remain in retirement until the matter was settled."[37]

Then why concoct an elaborate pretext to suggest Sumter was not part of this commission sent to Hillsborough, when he clearly was there with it? Or to suggest that during this period Sumter had voluntarily suspended his command? The answer to these questions lies in the events of October 7, when American militia defeated the Loyalist militia of Patrick Ferguson at Kings Mountain, and the decades and centuries of American history that followed after it. "So Sumter was not present at the pivotal battle of the Revolution," admits King, "where, but for the entanglement with Williams, he probably would have been in chief command."[38] And though it is perhaps an obscure controversy from a long-ago moment in history, for the supporters of Thomas Sumter after the war, and even into the twentieth century, Sumter's absence at Kings Mountain was an issue that loomed large.

WHILE SUMTER DID OR DID NOT FEUD with Williams, and then traveled to Hillsborough, Charles Cornwallis continued his invasion of North Carolina, or at least of Charlotte, for he never got much farther than its outskirts this time around.

As if cursed by bad fortune, the invasion started dismally and only got worse. This was thanks in part to the irrepressible William R. Davie and his cavalry corps of 150 men, who were determined to defend Charlotte. With Davie was North Carolina militia major Joseph Graham, who left behind an account of the action that followed.

"Charlotte stands on an eminence of small elevation above the ground, two wide streets crossing each other at right angles; the courthouse was in the centre," begins Graham's account.[39] On the morning of September 26, as into the town rode the advance elements of the British invasion force—the British Legion dragoons commanded by Maj. George Hanger and other mounted British troops—Davie dispersed the main body of his force "in three lines across the street leading to Salisbury," using a stone wall surrounding the courthouse for cover, hidden from the approaching British by a swell in the landscape. On his left and right flanks Davie placed troops of about twenty men each in the cross streets about eighty yards from the courthouse, hidden from the British advance by a house and other structures, while Graham's company and a troop of Rowan militia were placed in reserve near the town's jail.

The British cavalry advanced at a slow pace until fired on by Davie's pickets, then "came on at a brisk trot." Once they were within fifty yards of the courthouse, "our first line moved up to the stone wall and fired," reports Graham, "then wheeled outwards and passed down the flanks of the second line, which was advancing; the enemy, supposing that we were retreating, rushed up to the courthouse and received a full fire on each side from the companies placed on the cross streets. Upon which they immediately wheeled and retreated down the street to their infantry."

At this point, according to Charles Stedman, who also was there, Cornwallis rode up to the front of the column to observe the action just as Hanger and the Legion cavalry returned. Urging the cavalry back into action, Cornwallis said, "Legion, remember you have everything to lose, but nothing to gain," alluding to the regiment's reputation for bold attack gained at Waxhaws and elsewhere.[40] The British now regrouped and advanced en masse. Davie's men retreated in good order, with British lieutenant John Money, Cornwallis's aide de camp, reporting that the "cavalry pursued Major Davy's corps 8 miles from the town."[41]

British casualties from the skirmish were light, but Davie's resistance provided a sharp sting, and an inauspicious beginning to the British occupation of Charlotte. Cornwallis's plans were to establish an outpost there, guarding his supply routes from South Carolina and then move with the main body of his force to Salisbury, "which will open the country sufficiently for us to see what assistance we may really expect from our friends in North Carolina."[42] Ultimately, he planned to join with a Loyalist force in North Carolina's Cross Creek community, near modern-day Fayetteville, before pushing on into southeastern Virginia.

But first he had to build fortifications, bring up his sick and wounded from South Carolina, and collect grain and stores for his planned operations. At first glance, Charlotte seemed an ideal location for all three objectives. "The vicinity of Charlotte abounds with mills," reported Stedman, and from its position on the North and South Carolina border, located on a spur of the Great Wagon Road, it only made sense to establish an outpost and supply depot there. Cornwallis had ample reason to believe "the post at Charlottetown will be a great security to all this frontier of South Carolina."[43] However, Cornwallis underestimated the "hostile disposition" of the Charlotte region's inhabitants. "So inveterate was their rancour, that the messengers, with expresses for the commander in chief, were frequently murdered," wrote Stedman. "The inhabitants" of Charlotte, he continued, "instead of remaining quietly at home to receive payment for the produce

of their plantations, made it a practice to way-lay the British foraging parties, fire their rifles from concealed places, and then fly into the woods."

Graham described two of these raids in his memoir of the war. In one,
a Maj. Dickson from Davie's command attacked a place called Polk's Mill,
approximately two miles outside Charlotte, "which was kept grinding night
and day." Dickson waited until evening, attacking the mill's fifty-man
British garrison with his own squad of sixty. "Major Dickson was repulsed,"
reports Graham, "with the loss of one man killed and several horses
wounded," after the British took cover in a nearby house. The British lost
only two wounded but began to realize no outpost was safe in Charlotte.

The second skirmish described by Graham took place at McIntyre's
Farm on October 3, where a party of only fourteen Patriot militia under
the command of a Capt. James Thompson ambushed the rear guard of a
five-hundred-man British foraging party, including sixty cavalry and forty
wagons. British Major Doyle had left a reaguard of about one hundred
men at McIntyre's Farm, about seven miles from Charlotte, while the rest
of his British detachment "continued their march three or four miles to the
farms further up" to forage for food and supplies. With the British rearguard at McIntyre's "much out of order, some at the barn throwing down
oats for the wagons, others racing down the chickens, ducks and pigs; a
squad robbing the bee-house, others pillaging the dwelling house," Thompson and his thirteen militiamen quietly stalked toward the farm before
opening fire, wounding several British, including the "captain of the party,"
before retreating off in the woods.

Hearing the skirmish, Doyle and the rest of the party returned to McIntyre's then set out through the woods with cavalry in pursuit of Thompson,
who had taken up a defensive position on the opposite bank of a creek.
When the British came up to the creek, Thompson and his men ambushed
again, before escaping through the thick and hilly countryside without casualties. "Major Doyle's party moved on from the ford of the creek and
formed a junction with those at McIntyre's farm, took up their dead (eight)
and wounded (twelve), put them in their wagons and retreated to Charlotte
in great haste, not carrying more forage than could have been carried in
two wagons," reported Graham. "On their arrival they reported they had
found a 'rebel in every bush.'"[44]

For Cornwallis, skirmishes such as these made his post at Charlotte increasingly untenable. "The town and environs abounded with inveterate
enemies," described Tarleton. "The plantations in the neigbourhood were
small and uncultivated; the roads narrow and crossed in every direction; and

the whole face of their country covered with close and thick woods. . . . It was evident, and it had been frequently mentioned to the King's officers, that the counties of Mecklenburg and Rowan were more hostile to England than any others in America."[45] With his couriers and detachments subject to unrelenting ambush and sniping, Cornwallis was finding it impossible not only to raise support from the region's Loyalists, but also to establish any kind of communications or reconnaissance at all. "No British officer could obtain any information in that position, which would facilitate his designs, or guide his future conduct . . . accounts of the preparations of the militia could only be vague and uncertain,"[46] wrote Tarleton, though to the west, Patrick Ferguson was beginning to receive credible reports of a large militia force gathering to oppose him. These reports would soon become more than credible, leading to one of the most important American victories in the Backcountry War.

FIFTEEN

A STEP TOO FAR

O N SEPTEMBER 24, TWO DAYS BEFORE Cornwallis rode into Charlotte on September 26, Francis Marion departed his hideout at North Carolina's Great White Marsh. The departure was precipitated by the arrival of Maj. John James, bringing accounts of Wemyss's ride of terror and destruction through the Pee Dee. Recall that Marion had escaped into North Carolina after receiving exaggerated reports of Wemyss's mission against him from the south, and also reports of a Loyalist regiment of two hundred riding against him from the Georgetown vicinity to his east. His own force now dwindled to only sixty men, Marion had sought refuge in the swamps of North Carolina, awaiting further orders from Horatio Gates.[1]

By all accounts it had been a miserable bivouac. Marion biographer Hugh Rankin describes the "hum of the mosquito in the swamp" as a "constant irritant." "It had been a wet summer, and the turgid water ran deeper than usual. The men became sickly; some fell ill of malaria . . . the camp in the Great White Marsh began to take on the semblance of a primitive hospital."[2]

While his father Maj. John James returned to South Carolina to scout, young William Dobein James was in camp with Marion, and

had the honour to be invited to dine with the general. The dinner was set before the company by the general's servant, Oscar, partly on a pin log, and partly on the ground; it was lean beef, without salt, and sweet potatoes. . . . The general said but little, and that was chiefly what a son would be most likely to be gratified by, in the praise of a father. They had nothing to drink but bad water; and all the company appeared to be rather grave.[3]

The return of Major James with news of Wemyss's raid gave ample reason for this miserable party's return to the Pee Dee, although William Dobein James would be left behind in North Carolina to recover from the malaria that he also had contracted. Wemyss's "acts of wantonness and cruelty had roused the militia," the younger James recalled, "and Major James reported they were ready to join the general."[4]

Though Marion's force had dipped to as low as twenty or thirty men, at times, during his refuge at Great White Marsh, and he longed for instruction from Horatio Gates, Marion was eager both to reassemble his corps and escape the miseries of Great White Marsh, and with news of Wemyss moving off to Camden, the timing was right for Marion to resume operations in the Pee Dee. He and his militia left Great White Marsh on the evening of September 24 and traveled about sixty miles in two days, camping on the east side of the Little Pee Dee River the night of September 26. During the journey they were forced to swim the Little Pee Dee on their horses, always a harrowing experience for Marion, who did not know how to swim. James recounts that in such situations Marion often relied on the services of a young man named Bob James, who "being an excellent swimmer . . . was generally by Marion's side when swimming rivers, or paddled him over in a canoe if they had one."[5]

Marion's party reached Porte's Ferry on the afternoon of September 28 and crossed the Pee Dee in flatboats, a scene eloquently captured by the American artist William Tylee Ranney in his 1851 painting titled *Marion Crossing the Pedee* (or if not a depiction of this moment, one just like it). From there, it was on to Lynches Creek, where they were met by the patrol of Capt. John James and ten men after crossing at Witherspoon's Ferry, who reported that the Loyalist militia commander John Coming Ball was camped about fifteen miles away at a tavern on the bank of Black Mingo Creek near Sheppard's Ferry.

Ball and his regiment were well-known to Marion, hailing from the same Santee River settlements as Marion himself and others of South Carolina's French Huguenot lineage. In fact, Marion's family was connected through marriage to the family of Ball's second-in-command, Peter Gaillard. Other members of Ball's militia had joined Wemyss through his raid of the Pee Dee. Though Marion's scouts knew Ball's position, they apparently did not have accurate reports about the strength of Ball's force. Nevertheless, Marion's men were eager to attack, though they numbered only about sixty, and Marion the tactician must've seen some advantage in the Loyalist position his scouts reported to him. He knew both the disposition of his enemy's leaders and the ground upon which they camped. He decided to attack, though waited for night before setting out for Black Mingo Creek through the Pee Dee countryside.

According to Horry and Weems's account, Marion's approach was betrayed by the sound of his horses' hooves on the nearby Willtown Bridge, one of the many causeways traversing the Pee Dee region's swampy terrain. "Marion never afterwards suffered us to cross a bridge in the night, until we had first spread our blankets on it, to prevent noise," Horry and Weems write.[6] Marion biographer John Oller disputes this account, noting that at least four separate pension applications of Marion's regiment state Marion did spread blankets on Willtown Bridge before crossing it, one of the Swamp Fox's many ingenious tactics. Likely Marion's approach was betrayed by a local Loyalist sympathizer, for he wrote in his report to Gates that Ball's Loyalist "had intelligence of our coming."[7]

Marion biographer Hugh Rankin writes that a shot sent out by one of Ball's sentries alerted the Loyalists at Black Mingo Creek.[8] Whatever the case, Marion believed Ball's men probably were fortified for attack inside the tavern when he arrived a short time later. Therefore, he ordered most of his men to dismount and attack on foot, giving Hugh Horry command of a column that would approach the tavern on foot from the right. Capt. Thomas Waites with a smaller unmounted company was to make a demonstration in front of the house, drawing attention from Horry's flank attack, and on the left, Marion dispatched a small party of mounted troops to sweep in on horseback if and when necessary. Marion himself stayed behind in the rear. The experienced Continental officer rarely engaged in combat, and instead preferred to direct operations from a rear position.

The night was dark, without moonlight, and unknown to Marion and his troops, the alerted Ball had moved his men to a field near the tavern, where they faced the flanking attack of the unsuspecting Horry. At thirty yards, Ball's men opened fire on Horry's company, killing a Capt. Logan and wounding Henry Mouzon. Some of Marion's men panicked, but Capt. John James rallied his own men and those of Mouzon's company with them. Meanwhile, Waites and his dismounted men had come up on the Loyalist flank and also opened fire. Attacked from two sides, Ball's men panicked and "took into their swamp," but not before Marion collected thirteen prisoners, as well as all the Loyalists' horses and baggage. Marion took the captured horse of John Coming Ball for his own mount, naming it Ball in a rare display of humor. He would ride Ball for the rest of the war. To Gates, Marion reported three Loyalists dead in the action, and passed on a report that "several of their men has been found Dead & wd. [wounded] in the Swamp and adjoining woods." As to his own casualties, Marion reported the death of Logan and another "private," along with eight wounded, including Henry Mouzon, the gifted engineer and mapmaker, who would never fight again.[9]

As a battle, Black Mingo's propaganda value far exceeded its strategic one. Though Ball escaped, the prominent Loyalist refused to take the field again until late in the war. Meanwhile, Peter Gaillard and several of Ball's captured Loyalists now joined Marion's brigade, taking an oath to the Patriot cause. "The Toreys are so Affrighted with my Little Excursions that many is moving off to Georgia with their Effects," Marion reported to Gates. "Others are runned into Swamps."[10]

Robert Gray, the newly appointed commander of the Loyalist militia at Cheraw, saw little hope for the Loyalist cause in the Pee Dee region. "The second rebellion had been so general in this district that at least three fourths of the inhabitants upon this river had taken active parts in it, and this number must be included almost every person of influence or popularity here," he complained to Cornwallis in a letter dated September 30, the day after Marion's victory at Black Mingo. "No dependance therefore can be placed upon the militia here, but as the restoration of the British Government in this district . . . to effect this it will be necessary to have a force, independent of the militia, established here until Cape Fear River is the boundary."[11]

British lieutenant colonel Nisbet Balfour, now commandant at Charleston, was among those whose chief object of concern was "driving off Mr. Marion." Receiving news of Black Mingo, Balfour feared Marion's next move would be for Georgetown, which had been temporarily abandoned by the Loyalist militia assigned to defend it. In response, he quickly assembled a collective force of about ninety men, including thirty "convalescents," and sent them on a British galley to reinforce the town.[12]

But the fact was Cornwallis did not have the troops to spare for the type of operation Gray recommended, not if he hoped to pacify North Carolina in a fall campaign. Reports such as Gray's only confirmed Cornwallis's growing suspicion that the Loyalist support promised by Germain, North, and the Loyalist sycophants of London and Philadelphia were merely propaganda of their own kind, conjecture based mostly on wishful thinking. "I have found the militia to fail so totally when put to trial in this country," Cornwallis complained in a letter to Clinton, written a few days before Black Mingo. Increasingly, he believed his only chance to complete the Southern Strategy rested on moving forward, pacifying North Carolina in a display of power whose effects would "prevent insurrections in this country, which is very disaffected."[13]

Even Wemyss, writing to Cornwallis from Cheraw, the day before he set out to return to Camden, admitted the effect of his raid was, at best, temporary, that "fire and sword" could do little to quell the Patriot resistance of the Pee Dee. "I think I may safely venture to assure your Lordship that as long as this country continues a fronter it cannot be kept by militia," and that even those "who have not broke our oath of allegiance . . . are deluded in a most extraordinary manner by reports of a large army coming from the northward, the arrival of a French fleet and army etc. etc."[14]

Cornwallis, Wemyss, and Gray were not the only ones concerned about the security of the Pee Dee. Beginning with his surprise of the British guards at Big Savannah on August 20, Marion had won three victories in just over a month—including Blue Savannah on September 4 and Black Mingo on September 28—rising from relative obscurity (at least to Cornwallis and his officers) to exalted status as one of the Whig's most effective partisan commanders.

But Marion's success, coupled with Wemyss's brutal raid of terror and destruction, followed almost immediately by his departure for Camden, created a vacuum, allowing other Whigs of less moral standing to execute their own reprisals against neighboring Loyalists. To Marion was often attributed the antics of a Capt. Maurice Murphy, whom Marion's biographer Hugh Rankin describes as "an evil and sadistic man, whose greatest pleasure came from the sufferings of others." Murphy was known for burning Tory houses after he evicted their residents, and at one point, shot down in cold blood an uncle who had the temerity to criticize him in front of the man's own sons and the rest of Murphy's regiment. A former Marion officer named Col. Hugh Ervin was another Whig partisan who now "burnt a Great Number of Houses" and intended "to go on that Abominable work," which Marion feared "may be Laid to me." Indeed, Wemyss attributed this marauding to Marion in his letter to Cornwallis of September 30. But Marion assured Gates, "there is not one house Burnt by my Orders, or by any of my people. It is what I detest to Distress poor Women & Children" he complained.[15]

In fact, Marion was considering a move against Georgetown, but after Black Mingo, he wrote "so many of my followers was Desirous to see their wifes & family, which have been burnt out,"[16] that he found it necessary to retreat across the Big Pee Dee the next day at Britton's Ferry, camping in relative safety at Ami's Mill on Drowning Creek, which historian Robert D. Bass placed on the south side of the Lumber River, not far from the modern community of Nichols, South Carolina. This placed Marion approximately halfway between the British outposts at Cheraw and Georgetown.[17] There, Marion would spend the following two weeks, waiting for further instructions from Horatio Gates.

At this point, Marion's reputation was more dangerous than his attacks, for even in camp he was arousing the attention of Cornwallis. Indeed, Cornwallis's distress over the condition of the Pee Dee was so great, that he took the unusual step of ordering Wemyss back to the Pee Dee from Camden on October 7, despite his own issues with manpower and security at Charlotte. "The state of the lower country, and the absolute necessity of preventing the enemy from being in quiet possession of the east bank of Santee, obliges me to change the destination of the 63rd Regiment," he wrote that day to Wemyss, who was then at Camden. "I would have you mount your whole regiment." His orders required Wemyss "to prevent the enemy from being thorough masters of the country you have left." Therefore, Wemyss should "act, according to your discretion and the intelligence you may receive, either offensively or defensively."[18] Given the tactics of Wemyss's previous mission to the Pee Dee less than two weeks before, there can be little doubt Cornwallis condoned the use of "fire and sword," if not authorizing it.

At this point Cornwallis still intended to march north by northeast, through Salisbury and Hillsborough toward Cross Creek. He hoped that Wemyss and his mounted raiders could keep the insurgency on his southern flank subdued until he reached eastern North Carolina in a few weeks. In hindsight, through the lens of history, it seems a desperate plan, born of insufficient manpower and resources to hold a vast and hostile country, akin to American strategy in Vietnam. That it would fail seems almost a foregone conclusion, even if there wasn't a glitch in it by the name of Patrick Ferguson.

INSPECTOR OF MILITIA: IT IS A TITLE worthy of a Chekhov story, or perhaps a minor Italian opera. If so, it is a work by Henry Clinton, orchestrated in a melancholy strain, with an overture of which Charles Cornwallis was never much of a fan.

Clinton had appointed Maj. Patrick Ferguson "Inspector of Militia" on May 22, 1781, as he made preparations to return to New York. It was a broad commission authorizing Ferguson to recruit, enlist, and train militia under his own authority throughout "the provinces of Georgia and the two Carolinas, as opportunity shall offer."[19] And though Ferguson's orders didn't circumvent the overall authority of Cornwallis, they did circumvent his consultation, as the feud between Clinton and Cornwallis was in full flame at this time, and the two men barely communicated at all, except through emissaries.

For Ferguson, the appointment was the supreme "high" in a military career that had already seen its fair share of highs and lows. Already thirty-five, holding commissions in the British army since the age of twelve, there was a sense about Ferguson that his was a career derailed, undermined by bad health and a string of bad luck. Certainly, he was an intelligent, if not ingenious officer. Trained at the Royal Military Academy at Woolwich, in southeast London, where the curriculum focused on engineering and artillery, Ferguson had devised a breech-loading rifle in the early stages of the war. Both the smooth-bore muskets and more accurate rifles of the time required loading from the barrel, a cumbersome process that required the soldier to stand, exposing himself to enemy fire during the loading process.

Ferguson's rifle could be loaded from the breech, or rear part of the barrel near the stock, and though his design was actually a modification of an earlier breech-loading schematic, Ferguson's modification minimized fouling with better threading and a greased groove, improving the concept for battlefield conditions. He also added a folding rear sight to enhance the accuracy of the original design.

But his real achievement was getting the weapon adopted by the British army, at least on an experimental basis. In this effort he employed a series of public exhibitions that also displayed his exceptional marksmanship and eventually caught the attention of King George III. This public relations campaign paid off when Ferguson was placed in command of a special corps, trained and outfitted with his experimental rifle, and sent to America to test the design under combat conditions.

Now seemingly ascendent, Ferguson's luck just as quickly turned sour. Arriving in America in time to participate in Howe's 1777 campaign against Philadelphia, Ferguson was seriously wounded in the right arm during the Battle of Brandywine on September 11. Sent to New York for a long convalescence, in which his right arm was saved but rendered forever useless, Ferguson eventually learned to write and handle a saber with his left hand, but in the interim his rifle corps dissolved and was absorbed into other units, and with it the army's interest in Ferguson's experimental design.

By happenstance, his convalescence roughly corresponded to Clinton's replacement of Howe as commander in chief, and the ever-resilient Ferguson put his down time to good use, courting Clinton's favor with a prolonged correspondence. A bit of an oddball himself, Clinton seemed to appreciate or at least read Ferguson's letters seriously, though to the modern reader they can often seem impractical and pedantic. Strangely, though Ferguson is generally regarded as a relatively humanistic officer, his bark almost always fiercer than his bite, some of these letters depict him as an advocate of "Fire and Sword."

"America has never yet felt us in Earnest," he advised Clinton in a letter dated August 1, 1778. In it, Ferguson recommends the destruction "of all houses, grains & fodder throughout that fertile" province of New England. "The general distress and destruction of the Country join'd to the want of subsistence would prevent the rebel Army from throwing any great impediment" in this expedition's way.[20] Though Clinton never enacted this plan, Ferguson was certainly capable of Fire and Sword when the situation called for it. On a mission to rout out American profiteers at Little Egg Harbor, New Jersey, Ferguson discovered the infantry of Casimir Pulaski's Legion sleeping and lightly guarded nearby. Leading a charge of approximately three hundred men in the early morning of October 5, 1778, Ferguson stormed the Legion's barracks, killing fifty officers and men with the bayonet, before reinforcements chased them away. Though the Americans depicted the assault as a massacre, the Loyalist press in New York published a favorable account of the raid, and the action earned Clinton's esteem.[21]

His allegiance to Clinton confirmed, Ferguson was selected to sail south with the Charleston expedition of 1780. And likely it was the success of Little Egg Harbor and the tactics Ferguson advocated in his correspondence to Clinton that garnered him the "Inspector of Militia" title, though Cornwallis was clearly miffed by the appointment. For the reason why, we have mostly the insinuations of Nisbet Balfour, captured in his letters to Cornwallis around this time. Ferguson served briefly under Balfour's command during the beginning of the campaign, when Balfour was assigned commandant of the outpost at Ninety Six, and from this time Balfour writes, "As to Ferguson, his ideas are so wild and sanguine that . . . it would be dangerous to entrust him with the conduct of any plan."[22] And from June 9, Balfour snipes, "I imagine we can expect but little assistance from him [Ferguson] than bare inspection."[23]

If Ferguson was aware of Balfour's attempts at character assassination, he had the good sense to ignore them. And by the end of the summer, Ferguson appears to have garnered some measure of respect from Cornwallis, though perhaps old prejudices still remained. Of all the efforts to raise dependable local Loyalist militia across the state, Ferguson's had proven the most successful. By fall he had a trained and relatively disciplined force of one thousand men, including about 125 trained Provincials from the King's American Rangers, the Queen's Rangers, and the New Jersey Volunteers. It was with this force that Cornwallis had ordered him into western North Carolina, the vast Tryon County consisting of most of the land due west of Charlotte, to protect his western flank as Cornwallis marched to Charlotte.

But Ferguson drifted into the mountains of western North Carolina in search of the fugitive Elijah Clarke, who had recently attacked Augusta, antagonizing the local populace. And he went a step too far when he issued a proclamation to the "Overmountain" settlements of the Watauga, Nolichucky, and Holston Rivers in present-day western North Carolina and Virginia and East Tennessee that "if they did not desist from their opposition to the British arms, he would march his army over the mountains, hang their leaders, and lay their country waste with fire and sword."[24] In response, the militias of the Overmountain settlements mobilized for battle, and by September 19, Ferguson had confirmed reports the "Overmountain Men" were marching his way. However, he underestimated their numbers and lingered in the far reaches of Tryon County too long, collecting cattle and provisions from western North Carolina homesteads and searching for Clarke.[25]

Also organizing against Ferguson were the South Carolina regiments of the Ninety Six and New Acquisition districts, among them James Williams and the small corps he had raised in North Carolina and also William Hill with the New Acquisition Regiment, along with other assorted regiments from the North Carolina and South Carolina Piedmont. Seeking a junction with the Overmountain Men, this collection of militia marched into what is now Rutherford County, North Carolina, camping at Flint Hill on October 2.

With Sumter still in Hillsborough, lobbying for command, the Hill memoir here goes off the rails in its efforts to denigrate Williams. According to Hill, Williams again tried to assert his authority over the militia assembled at Flint Hill by reading the general's commission he claimed to have received from John Rutledge. "Upon this he was told to absent himself & not attempt to march with us or the North Carolinians, as the consequences would be serious," Hill recounted. A day or two later, on or about October 5, Williams and his associate, Thomas Brandon, militia commander of the Fair Forest Regiment, were noticed missing from camp, and Hill said he was informed they "had taken a pathway that led to the mountain." When they got back, according to Hill, Williams reluctantly admitted he had met with the Overmountain Men and deceived them into believing Ferguson was heading toward Ninety Six, which not coincidentally, was also in the vicinity of Williams's confiscated property. "In the course of the conversation he said with a considerable degree of warmth, that the North Carolinians might fight Ferguson or let it alone, & that our business was to fight for our own country." Hill reported that he replied that Ferguson was most certainly not headed toward Ninety Six and was by all accounts retreating toward Charlotte, then rode off to inform the Overmountain Men of Williams's attempted deception.[26]

Meanwhile, Patrick Ferguson was beginning to have misgivings about the Patriot force assembling against him. On September 27, Ferguson began marching back toward the safer confines of South Carolina. On September 30, Ferguson sent Cornwallis a dispatch, advising his commander of the threat rising in the west and requesting reinforcement from the British Legion. On the following day, October 1, Ferguson finally began a serious retreat, moving east by southeast from the region around Columbus, North Carolina, toward Charlotte. In response, Cornwallis ordered Ferguson to march toward "Armour's Ford," near the mouth of the Catawba River's South Fork, south of present-day Gastonia. There he was to be reinforced by elements of the 71st Regiment under Maj. Archibald McArthur.[27] But Ferguson either never received Cornwallis's orders or believed them imprudent, for by October 6, he reported he had "taken a post where I do not think I can be forced by a stronger enemy than that against us" at a place called Kings Mountain.[28]

By that time, about 1,100 men, including not only the Overmountain Men but also other North Carolina militia from the counties of Wilkes and Surry, Georgia refugees from Clarke's band (though not Clarke himself), and South Carolina militia under both James Williams and Sumter's militia now commanded by William Hill and Col. Edward Lacey, gathered at a local meeting placed called the "Cowpens" in what is now western Cherokee County, South Carolina. A few months later this same field would serve as the site of another famous Revolutionary War battle on January 17, 1781, where Continental general Daniel Morgan would achieve one of the most important American victories of the war over Banastre Tarleton. For now, it was a convenient place to muster the American militia assembled against Patrick Ferguson. However, on the march to Cowpens, Hill reported, Williams was shunned, "obliged to keep at such a distance as required by our rear guard, who held him & his men in such unfavorable light that they were throwing stones & otherwise affronting them the whole day."[29]

At Cowpens on October 6, the collected American militia selected an advance force of approximately nine hundred men to pursue Ferguson, whose position at Kings Mountain was approximately thirty miles away. The selected men were probably those with the best mounts, and notably did not include William Hill, who was left with the rearguard because of a lingering injury (and therefore was not present to witness the battle he described in his memoir).

These nine hundred men came upon Ferguson's defensive position atop Kings Mountain on the afternoon of October 7. With Ferguson at this time were about eight hundred militia and one hundred Provincials, since he had sent about two hundred of his men on a foraging expedition earlier in the day. Of the almost two thousand men gathered on Kings Mountain that afternoon, Ferguson was the only Englishman. The rest Loyalist and Patriot, all Americans. Curiously, despite ample time, Ferguson neglected to construct breastworks or battlefield defenses for his troops. Instead, it appears Ferguson intended to rely for defense on the field drilling and training he'd instilled in his militia to considerable effort earlier in the summer.

The Patriot army surrounded Kings Mountain and approached Ferguson from all sides, taking cover in the trees and boulders that dotted the slopes. Ferguson counterattacked with a bayonet charge against the troops of Isaac Shelby, the North Carolina patriot and future governor of Tennessee who had skirmished with Ferguson at Wofford's Ironworks two months before. Shelby gave ground, but meanwhile other Patriots were scoring casualties with their accurate hunting rifles. Ferguson tried desperately to rally his men, racing from one position to the next on his mount, blowing the silver whistle he used to drill his troops.

But the Patriots were better shots, or perhaps more motivated than their Loyalist counterparts, and Ferguson's position was inferior to theirs. After almost an hour of fighting, Ferguson was shot from atop his horse and died on the slopes of Kings Mountain with seven bullets in his body. It was a hero's end for a man who appeared to crave posterity, but possibly an unnecessary death, as he probably had time to complete his retreat to Charlotte, and instead made a conscious decision to stand and fight. Why we will never know, though Ferguson's concern for his honor, still a popular conception in the Hanoverian age, undoubtedly played some role.[30]

Around the same time Ferguson was killed, James Williams was also shot as he led his men up the slopes of Kings Mountain and died the next day. Even in death, William Hill could not resist disparaging his rival, insisting "it is generally supposed & believed that it was done by some of the Americans, as many of them had been heard to promise on oath that they would do it when they had the opportunity."[31] It is an account in striking opposition to that of Thomas Young, a teenage boy fighting in Williams's regiment, who was actually at the battle that day. "On the top of the mountain, in the thickest of the fight, I saw Col. Williams fall," he remembered in his memoir of the war. "A braver or better man never died upon the field of battle."

Despite Williams's death, Kings Mountain was a momentous American victory. Ferguson's entire command was either killed (157), wounded (163), or captured (698 prisoners), while Patriot losses were twenty-eight killed and sixty-four wounded. Dishonorably, some of the Loyalist casualties were received after their surrender, with some of the Patriot atrocities attributed to revenge for Tarleton's alleged "slaughter" at the Waxhaws earlier that summer. Other Loyalists were executed at a kangaroo court held a few days later at a place called Biggerstaff's Old Field in what is now Rutherford County, North Carolina.[32]

In the days and hours before the battle, Ferguson continued to send messages to Cornwallis, pleading for reinforcements. On October 3, after crossing the Broad River, Ferguson wrote Cornwallis requesting reinforcements, as he did also on October 5 and again on October 6. But Cornwallis appears to have underestimated Ferguson's plight. On October 6, he sent Ferguson a letter advising him Tarleton was headed his way "but for the present he and his corps want a few days' rest."[33] If Tarleton had set out for

Ferguson that day on horseback, he could've easily covered the twenty-five miles separating Ferguson from British headquarters at Charlotte.

But Tarleton delayed, claiming weakness from the malaria that had wracked him and his Legion troops, a claim even Cornwallis found difficult to accept. After the war, Tarleton's memoir criticized Cornwallis's management of the North Carolina invasion, including a failure to support Ferguson. By then the governor-general of India, Cornwallis vented his frustrations over Tarleton's accusations in a letter to his brother:

Tarleton's is a most malicious and false attack; he knew and approved the reasons for the measures which he now blames. My not sending relief to Colonel Ferguson, although he was positively ordered to retire, was entirely owing to Tarleton himself; he pleaded weakness from the remains of a fever, and refused to make the attempt, although I used the most earnest entreaties.[34]

Although these recriminations are perhaps the inevitable aftershocks of a lost war, there is also in them the hint of class and personality conflicts that still afflicted the British army. Ferguson was not only from a lower social class, and a Scot at that, he was also known to be a "Clinton" man, and although there is nothing in the historical record to suggest Cornwallis and Tarleton betrayed him as such, this factor perhaps explains their lackluster response to his pleas. If so, it was a treachery they would both soon regret, for Ferguson's defeat at Kings Mountain was a tragic reversal of the British momentum Cornwallis had seized at Camden, and the beginning of a series of British defeats and miscalculations that would within the next year lose them the war.

PART FOUR

The
BRIGADIERS

SIXTEEN

A GENERAL RETREATS, A GENERAL RETURNS

I F THE LIVES, MISCALCULATIONS, AND DEATHS of James Williams and Patrick Ferguson are but the subplots of this tale, they were major plotlines in the lives of at least two of our main players. For Sumter, it was most significantly an impact of historic legacy. No doubt, James Williams was an important though obscure figure in the history of the American Revolution, but his death had little strategic significance in the war. In fact, if not for William Hill's vindictive memoir, he probably would barely be known at all.

But the American victory at Kings Mountain had *huge* significance, and as the years passed, and its legends became more prominent than its facts, the question of Sumter's absence from it became an issue. Fought entirely with volunteer militia, the battle became a metaphor for American grit, courage, and democratic spirit after the war. And many of the American militia leaders who were at Kings Mountain went on to prominent political careers, especially John Sevier, elected the first governor of Tennessee, and Isaac Shelby, elected the same for the state of Kentucky.

Sumter himself would go on to become both a United States congressman and senator, enjoying a long political career before eventually dying in 1832 at the age of ninety-seven, reputedly the last living American general of the American Revolution. But Sumter's wartime legacy was more complicated than that of his militia contemporaries. In 1781, during the latter stages of the war, he had feuded with both Continental general Nathanael Greene, who by that time had replaced Gates, and Francis Marion. Eventually, these feuds, and others, led him to resign from the field in order to defend himself and his wartime actions in South Carolina's General Assembly. And by the 1800s, accounts of this contentious behavior started to appear in published histories of the war, tarnishing Sumter's wartime legacy.

Nevertheless, Sumter still enjoyed the loyal support of many of his old militia soldiers. He was, after all, the great South Carolina "Gamecock," a living symbol of his state's grit and defiance during the American Revolution, and an early proponent of the states rights' activism that would eventually lead to the American Civil War. But his legendary status only made his absence at Kings Mountain more mysterious. Hill, among many, remained fiercely loyal to Sumter, and perhaps these questions about Kings Mountain rankled this ardent Sumter devotee.

Hill dictated his wartime "memoir" to his young grandson, William R. Hill, while he was in his seventies, "in his old age & indeed dotage," and sent the only known copy of it to Thomas Sumter in 1815. Included were the many accusations against James Williams described in this book. But these accusations were either unsubstantiated or refuted by other significant American leaders at Kings Mountain, including Isaac Shelby and Col. William Campbell, who had served as overall commander of the battle's Whig forces. According to the comprehensive review of Williams's biographer, William T. Graves, none of Hill's accusations were repeated in any of the surviving pension applications of militia soldiers who fought in the battle. Hill died in 1816 and Sumter kept the memoir manuscript in his possession, unpublished, until his own death in 1832. Graves suggests Sumter's retention of the manuscript is evidence he did not want Hill's accusations made public.[1]

There the controversy may have died, if not for the research of a Wisconsin historian named Lyman Draper. A prolific folklorist and documentarian, Draper spent much of the 1850s, 1860, and 1870s collecting letters, personal narratives, and family documents about prominent American soldiers and frontiersman of the eighteenth century, including George Rogers Clark and Daniel Boone. In the 1870s, his fascination turned to Thomas Sumter, and during this period he was sent a copy of Hill's manuscript by Susan Brownfield, Sumter's great-granddaughter. In 1881, Draper published his great work (a gifted researcher, Draper published relatively little), *King's Mountain and Its Heroes*, a comprehensive history of the battle based on his large collection of documents. His treasure trove of Sumter material, known collectively as the "Sumter Papers," remains unpublished, and today is only available on microfilm.

Given Draper's own fascination with Sumter's legacy, he may have tried to safeguard it. In Hill's memoir, he had a previously unpublished primary source with outstanding provenance that not only explained Sumter's absence at Kings Mountain but also spun a juicy tale of conflict and intrigue. As with any book-writing historian, Draper had both scholarly and commercial ambitions. For these reasons and perhaps others, Draper relied heavily on Hill's memoir as a reference for *King's Mountain and Its Heroes*, presenting Hill's accusations as fact, without caveats or disclaimers.

Scholar William B. Hesseltine, who researched Draper's career and works, writes that *King's Mountain and Its Heroes* "had no success. Sold by subscription, it found no subscribers, and it was difficult to find agents to handle it."[2] But Hesseltine's evaluation ignores the book's influence on subsequent American Revolution historians. The story of Williams's deceptions and intrigues soon began appearing in other histories of the war, typically citing Draper as a reference, including the comprehensive two-volume *The History of South Carolina in the Revolution* by Edward McCrady published in 1901 and 1902. Professor Anne King Gregorie repeated many of them in her 1931 biography of Thomas Sumter, still the only scholarly work published on Sumter's life. "So Sumter was not present at the pivotal battle of the Revolution," she writes, explaining her subject's absence from Kings Mountain, "where, but for the entanglement with Williams, he would probably have been in chief command."[3] Popular South Carolina historian Robert D. Bass made similar claims in his 1961 biography of Sumter, and today Hill's memoir stills shows up as a reference in books and articles, though typically with some disclaimer, as included here.[4] For many writers, including this one, it is a tale too intriguing to ignore.

SIDENOTES AND DISCLAIMERS ASIDE, James Williams's death enabled Sumter to consolidate his command at the moment he was absent from it.

For Cornwallis and Tarleton, the aftershocks of Ferguson's defeat at Kings Mountain sent every flank except their rear into a renewed state of revolt. To the west, from his outpost at Ninety Six, Lt. Col. Cruger sent word to Cornwallis that the American victory had enflamed the Whig population, and that the "whole country had determined to submit as soon as the rebels should enter it." Though the Overmountain Men returned north and west after the battle, the Whig militias of the Ninety Six and New Acquisition districts were reinvigorated after the battle's success.[5]

Meanwhile, Loyalist militia colonel James Cassells had evacuated Georgetown, apparently in a panic after hearing word of Francis Marion's victory at Black Mingo. Cornwallis had already begun to worry about Cassels resolve, ordering a detachment of Provincials and Loyalist militia from Camden to reinforce him on October 2, 1780.[6] But the effort was too late, for Cassells had already fled Georgetown. "This kind of behavior is too bad," lamented Balfour, "but it is no more than I expected from these militia." Nevertheless, Balfour now had to detach troops from Charleston to "repossess George Town, where it is not possible to allow them to remain for obvious consequences."

The consequence was Francis Marion, and although he had contemplated an attack on Georgetown after Black Mingo, he was instead in camp on Drowning Creek. Yet Balfour's concern illustrates the propaganda effect Marion's success was starting to take on the Loyalists of the Pee Dee.

Back in Charlotte, Cornwallis was still threatened by about five hundred members of the Salisbury militia under William Davidson's command. Davidson was posted on the Salisbury Road at Rocky River, today on the outskirts of Charlotte near the Lowe's Motor Speedway on U.S. Highway 29. And in Salisbury proper, Brig. Gen. Jethro Sumner commanded about eight hundred Patriot militia from the Hillsborough District. Though William R. Davie was sick and temporarily retired from the field, his subordinates Capt. Joseph Dickson and a Capt. Rutledge still patrolled Charlotte's perimeter, threatening British patrols and scouts.[7]

As he anxiously awaited news of Ferguson on his west, eager to escape Charlotte and the "hornet's nest" of Patriot partisans, Cornwallis planned an offensive action against Sumner and Davidson to the north. On October 8, Davidson learned Cornwallis had ordered his army in Charlotte to draw provisions for two days. "I find he is determined to surprise me & I am as determined to disappoint him," Davidson wrote.[8] Tarleton confirms that "in the beginning of October, it was intended to send a corps from Charlotte town, under the orders of Lieutenant-colonel Webster, to attack a party of Americans ... at Alexander's Mill, on a branch of Rocky river ... But the design was laid aside, on account of the news from the Westward," of Ferguson's defeat.[9]

On October 9, Cornwallis finally learned definitively of Ferguson's defeat, and by all accounts, the news convinced Cornwallis to retreat. With his western frontiers "now exposed to the incursions of the mountaineers ... it became necessary for Cornwallis to fall back for their protection, and to wait for a reinforcement before he could proceed farther upon his expedition," explained Charles Stedman.[10] Although this explanation ignores the vulnerability of the British position at Charlotte, and the struggles they faced there with security and supply, it provided political coverage for a strategic retreat.

But where to go? After months of stripping the local countryside bare of provision and forage, Camden could no longer subsist both his division and the existing outpost there. The small South Carolina settlement of Winnsboro, located on the west side of the Catawba/Wateree River between Ninety Six and Camden, with roads leading to either, offered a better strategic position. "Wynnesborough presented the most numerous advantages," wrote Tarleton. "Its spacious plantations yield a tolerable post; its centrical situation between the Broad river and the Wateree afforded protection to Ninety Six and Camden; and its vicinity to the Dutch forks, and a rich country in the rear, promised abundant supplies of flour, forage, and cattle."[11]

Cornwallis himself is strangely quiet at this low point of the campaign, for right around the time he learned of Ferguson's defeat, he contracted the malaria that had already afflicted his army earlier in the summer and fall. Cornwallis was a British aristocrat to the bone. Yet despite his aristocrat's heritage and demeanor, Cornwallis's leadership endeared him to his troops. "The Earl's sense of discipline, justice, and compassion made him, more than Howe or Clinton, a part of the British army in America. He did not consider himself above it. If it prospered, he prospered, if it failed, he failed. He could never maintain that detachment from it that many of his fellows could," Tarleton wrote.[12]

"He worked hard at being a successful commander, studied tactics, strategy, and the ins and outs of administration, and throughout his long, illustrious career paid more attention to his troops than most eighteenth century generals ever dreamed of doing," agrees historian Richard N. Ketchum. "But there was a flaw in his makeup somewhere that kept him from the ultimate success ... he always seemed just to miss bringing the thing off, as if he became bored or distracted during a long period of activity and could not summon up the final dedication necessary to finish the job."[13]

Cornwallis's fugues often occurred when there was an unpleasant task in front of him, as when he pleaded illness at the surrender at Yorktown, sending Brig. Gen. Charles O'Hara to lead the capitulation ceremony in his place. As his troops now departed Charlotte, there is certainly nothing in the historic record to suggest Cornwallis was anything but seriously ill. But his illness allowed him to turn over the unpleasant task of retreat to the command of Lord Rawdon, still only twenty-five years old, though by all accounts one of Cornwallis's best officers in the South. British troops and wagons rolled out of Charlotte on October 12. So anxious were they to leave the town that they marched away around sunset, and there seems to have been an air of disorientation about the retreat from the beginning. "Owing to the badness of the road, the ignorance of the guides, the darkness of the night, or some other unknown cause, the British rear guard destroyed, or left behind, near twenty waggons," reported Tarleton, including a printing press and other public stores, along with the "knapsacks of the light infantry and legion."[14]

The guides may have not been as ignorant as Tarleton presumed. According to the memoir of Joseph Graham, the British had with them as a guide William McCafferty, a Charlotte merchant from Ireland who had stayed in the town during the British occupation "to endeavor to save his property." After leading the main column down a wrong road, McCafferty abandoned the British, leading to "confusion and disorder." The British column "attempted at different places to file to their left along byways, in order to reach the main road," but in the darkness they encountered only "high hills and deep ravines . . . finally most of them got into the woods, were separated into parties, and kept hallooing to find which way their comrades had gone. By midnight they were three or four miles apart, and appeared to be panic struck, lest the Americans should come upon them in the night."[15]

The army finally regrouped the next morning, "seven miles from Charlotte," but "owing to the difficult passes they took, the darkness of the night, and the scare upon them," lost the wagons lamented about by Tarleton, though in Graham's account it was forty wagons, not twenty, filled with "considerable booty."[16]

Things only got worse from there. Rain set in, and the soldiers marched in roads that were "over their shoes in water and mud," according to Charles Stedman. The soldiers had no tents, and slept at night on the ground in damp, wet woods, "a most unhealthy climate; for many days without rum." Provisions were unreliable. "Sometimes the army had beef and no bread; at other times bread and no beef. For five days it was supported upon Indian corn, which was collected as it stood in the field, five ears of which were the allowance for two soldiers for twenty-four hours."[17]

Like the other sick, Tarleton spent at least part of the journey in the back of a wagon. Also making the journey by wagon was Maj. George Hanger, who left a harrowing account of the journey in his memoir. So weak from malaria he couldn't even turn himself, Hanger lay "so long, first on one side, then on the other, then on my back, that the bones of my back and each hip came fairly, or rather freely through the skin." From this gruesome position, fortified with nothing but "opium and port wine," he watched his five fellow passengers die, all "in the first week of our march, and were buried in the woods as the army moved on."[18]

In this desolate wilderness, the miserable column encountered numerous creeks and streams, swelled by continuous rains. Hanger reported streams that normally a "soldier may walk through and not wet him above the ancles," were now flooded to such a height "as to take a man up to the neck," even flooding the straw in the back of the wagons in which the sick like Cornwallis and Hanger lay, impeding the march of the army "for hours."[19]

Though Stedman writes "few armies ever encountered greater difficulties and hardships," he states such hardships only endeared Cornwallis to his soldiers more. "Their attachment to their commander supported them in the day of adversity; knowing as they did, that their officers, and even lords Cornwallis and Rawdon's fare was not better than their own."[20] If from the hindsight of history such assertions appear to border on propaganda, there is little evidence to dispute them. Despite several setbacks during the Backcountry War, Cornwallis does seem to have retained the esteem of his fellow soldiers, at least those who later wrote about it.

Nevertheless, there was collateral damage. If British grand strategy relied on wining the hearts and minds of a mostly Loyalist population, the miserable march to Winnsboro revealed them as their own worst enemies. Encountering a difficult crossing at Sugar Creek, its water "very rapid, its banks nearly perpendicular" and the clay soil "as slippery as ice," the British soldiers spared their exhausted horses and instead harnessed Loyalist militia to the wagons. "We are sorry to say, that, in return for these exertions, the militia were maltreated, by abusive language, and even beaten by some officers." In consequence, several of the militia "left the army next morning, for ever, choosing to run the risk of meeting resentment of their enemies rather than submit to the derision and abuse of those to whom they looked upon as friends."[21]

The army finally reached Winnsboro on October 29, taking fourteen days to travel approximately sixty-five miles, what is little more than an hour in an automobile. Upon reaching their destination, Cornwallis resumed command from Rawdon, although as early as October 19, Rawdon had reported to fellow British officer George Turnbull that Cornwallis's fever was "not violent."[22] Not for the last time, the lord's malaise, seemingly, had lifted with the embarrassing circumstances of the retreat.

So, THOMAS SUMTER WAS NOT AT THE Battle of Kings Mountain. But, with James Williams dead, he emerged from it as the undisputed leader of South Carolina's militia forces, at least for the next few months. On October 6, 1780, he received the commission of brigadier general from South Carolina governor-in-exile John Rutledge. It empowered him to embody as soon as possible "all the Militia of South Carolina" and hold them ready to cooperate with the Continental forces. In the meantime, Sumter was to employ the men he assembled in military service to the state, as Sumter deemed necessary. In a letter accompanying the commission, Rutledge ordered Sumter to liberate people held captive by the British forces and "secure every subject of the state who holds any office or commission under his Britannic Majesty," and hold them for future trial. And he ordered Sumter "that all the enemy's outposts be broken up, and the several parties they have throughout the country cut off . . . that they be harassed and attacked in every quarter of South Carolina and Georgia where they can be to advantage, and with a reasonable prospect of success."[23]

Later in the month, Continental general William Smallwood, then serving as Gates's second-in-command from a forward position at Salisbury, while Gates remained at Continental army headquarters in Hillsborough, authorized Sumter to also command Georgia militia troops operating on the west side of the Catawba.[24]

In short, these were carte blanche powers for Sumter to wage war with militia forces against the British throughout South Carolina, although while in Hillsborough, Sumter coordinated plans against Cornwallis with Gates and other American military personnel, including Continental general Daniel Morgan, who had arrived in Hillsborough in late September.[25] These plans made Sumter's primary responsibility the support of Continental army operations on the west side of the Catawba River; meanwhile North Carolina militia general William Davidson would command Virginia and North Carolina militia defending Cornwallis's northern and eastern flanks on the Catawba's eastern side, and Morgan took command of a "Flying" division of mostly Continental cavalry and light troops operating in the "Advance."[26]

Sumter biographer Anne Gregorie King suggests Sumter and Morgan may have been acquaintances.[27] If so, they would have met decades before, when both served with the British forces fighting the French and Indian War. Born in either New Jersey or Philadelphia around 1735, Morgan had migrated as a young man to Virginia, where he eventually joined British general Edward Braddock's 1755 expedition as a teamster, or "waggoner," traveling with Braddock, Gates, and George Washington to fight in the disastrous Battle of Monongahela on July 9, 1755.

By 1762, the six-foot, two-hundred-pound Morgan had left British service, settling near Winchester, Virginia, where he eventually acquired property and status. In 1775, Morgan was commissioned captain of a Virginia rifle company and assimilated into the Continental army during the siege of Boston. Captured during the failed assault on Quebec in 1775, Morgan was exchanged in 1776, in time to join George Washington as a newly commissioned colonel during the New Jersey campaign of 1777, then detached to Gates's command at Saratoga later that fall. There Morgan had mastered the art of coordinating operations between his sharpshooting riflemen and conventional troops armed with the less accurate musket. At the Battle of Bemis Heights on October 7, the bayonet charge of the Continental infantry formed a protective screen for Morgan's riflemen, allowing them to pour deadly fire from their slow-loading rifles into the British right flank. Though Gates emerged as the "Hero of Saratoga," many attribute his victory there to the talents of Morgan and his fellow officer, Benedict Arnold.

Following Saratoga, Morgan returned to Washington's command, fighting in New Jersey under Nathanael Greene in November and December of 1777 before wintering at Valley Forge. Believing he was owed a promotion, Morgan claimed failing health as an excuse to resign from the Continental army in 1779, retiring to his farm in Virginia. But in June 1780, with Charleston surrendered and the security of the South threatened, his commission was reactivated, and he was ordered to join his old commander Gates in the Carolinas. The orders did not include a promotion, and so Morgan had delayed, but after the disaster at Camden he relented, taking command of Gates's light troops on October 2. And on October 13, Congress awarded him the promotion to brigadier general that he had long sought.[28]

They were similar men, Sumter and Morgan, both from poor, immigrant families, raised in hardscrabble circumstances on the American frontier. Both had natural charisma and an acute understanding of militia psychology. Surely, both pledged their mutual respect and support from the confines of American headquarters in Hillsborough. Yet this was a pledge they would struggle to keep in the theaters of war west of the Catawba, leading to another mysterious Sumter absence on the battlefield at a place called Cowpens.

As he prepared to resume operations in South Carolina, Sumter attempted to raise arms and supplies for his troops in Hillsborough. Mostly these efforts appear unsuccessful, although he did receive $13,000 in loan certificates and some South Carolina funds. By October 10, Sumter had left Hillsborough and was in Salisbury, North Carolina, where he probably received news of the American victory at Kings Mountain.[29] A few days later, he was again operating in the environs of the New Acquisition District, up and down the Catawba, although he apparently struggled to regather his troops. In the Carolina backcountry, it was common for militia units to return home after a major engagement to tend to their farms and families, and this appears the case in the aftermath of Kings Mountain. "General Sumpter lies high up on the Southside of the Catawba," Smallwood reported to Gates on October 31. "He writes me his number is very inconsiderable. The Georgians have not joined him as he expected. The other Parties who defeated Ferguson are dispersed and gone Home."[30]

But if Sumter the brigadier general had returned to South Carolina to find his militia army diminished, he nevertheless indisputably enjoyed its command. Surely, the legacy of Kings Mountain was far from his mind. The month of October may have been lost in administrations and machinations, but Sumter, the irrepressible Gamecock, was now ready to fight.

SEVENTEEN

The
S W A M P
F O X

N EWS OF THE VICTORY AT KINGS MOUNTAIN spread quickly across the Carolinas, invigorating Patriot factions and discouraging the Loyalists. In the Pee Dee, however, Loyalists needed little further evidence the tide of war was turning against them. On October 10, North Carolina brigadier general William Henry Harrington wrote Horatio Gates that the "British & Tories" from the Pee Dee region around Cheraw were retreating to Camden, "& that Post might be yet taken there to advantage."[1]

A former sheriff of the Cheraw District, Harrington had moved to North Carolina after getting married and eventually becoming a brigadier general in the North Carolina militia. He was now posted in the Cross Creek region (around modern-day Fayetteville, North Carolina), where his role was mostly an administrative one, procuring and transporting supplies. Probably through the accolades of North Carolina governor Abner Nash, or others Horatio Gates encountered shortly after arriving in North Carolina, Gates had appointed Harrington commander of all militia regiments on both sides of the Pee Dee extending from Cross Creek into South Carolina.[2]

Though this preceded Marion's posting to the Pee Dee later that month, the appointment created some conflict, for as a Continental officer, Marion did not consider himself subject to Harrington's command. Nevertheless, on October 12, the North Carolina Board of War, acting with the apparent approval of Gates, had authorized Harrington to command Marion and all other Patriot militia in eastern South Carolina, and Harrington believed Marion had been directed to "apply to me for directions how to act."[3]

On October 8, Marion departed camp near the Lumber River for an attack on Georgetown, arriving there on October 12. The port had long been an object of Marion's attention. "If I could raise one hundred men, I Shou'd Certainly pay a Visit to George Town," he had written to Gates on October 4.[4] That he now attempted it with no more than seventy was perhaps at the order or suggestion of Harrington, though these orders have been lost to time.

The following day, October 13, Marion sent forward an advance party under the command of Peter Horry to draw the attention of the town's guards while with his main force he planned to circle the outskirts of Georgetown and attack the Loyalist redoubt inside the town. The first part of the plan worked, for Horry's soldiers soon came upon a group of Tory troopers under the command of Micajah Gainey. This was the same Micajah Gainey whom Marion's regiment had defeated at Blue Savannah on September 4 and who had formerly served as a Continental soldier in Marion's Second Regiment. The two parties skirmished briefly in the road before Gainey ordered a retreat to Georgetown, but a Sgt. McDonald from Horry's detachment pursued Gainey, stabbing him from the back with his bayonet, the thrust strong enough for the point of McDonald's blade to emerge through Gainey's chest. Remarkably, Gainey not only remained on his horse and escaped into town but would survive and recover to fight another day.

Marion, meanwhile, had made it to the Loyalist redoubt located inside Georgetown. "I found Col. Cassell in a redoubt which enclosed the Jail, a brick building," Marion reported to Gates. The redoubt was also supported by an armed British galley in the harbor. "After reconnoitering it around, I found it too strong to Storm it with such men as I had & it was Defended by Seventy men of the militia."[5] Marion's attempt to draw Cassell's force out of the redoubt failed, and when he received word that a large party of

Loyalists were on their way to relieve the town, he suspended the attack. Although not before parading his men through town and seizing some horses and baggage belonging to the Loyalist militia inside, then escaping into the swamps and back roads of South Carolina's coastal plain.

Meanwhile, on October 11, Gates had finally responded to Marion's letter of October 4, having just received news of Ferguson's defeat. "I am extremely pleased with your management & success & request you earnestly to continue your Hostilities against our Tyrannic & cruel Enemies," Gates wrote, informing Marion he was dispatching Harrington to take post against Cheraw. "I desire you to Correspond with the General & as far as for the Benefit of the Common Cause, cooperate with him," Gates wrote to Marion. "The enemy may be much destracted and divided by your different attacks & the Country well covered by your joint endeavors to protect the persons and estates of our Friends the Whiggs."[6]

Though he chafed at being subordinate to Harrington, Marion the obedient soldier immediately broke camp again, motivated by Gates's confidences. Gathering the small corps of men he had with him, Marion moved immediately to his old post at Port's Ferry, on the southwest side of the Great Pee Dee, near the modern-day community of Johnsonville, South Carolina. There he called out his militia for a muster, but his timing was bad. "Things were peaceful enough" in the Pee Dee "for the moment," reflects Marion biographer Hugh Rankin, "and for many it was as though the war had briefly laid its heavy hand upon them and had then passed on its way. Then, too, there were homes to rebuild and personal tragedies to mourn."[7]

A man who always took his military commitments seriously, Marion fumed at his militia's procrastination and apparently threatened to abandon the Pee Dee to join Gates in North Carolina. But his old comrade, Col. Hugh Horry, "who partook more of his confidence than any other,"[8] prevailed on Marion to remain. Within a few days, Marion's spirits revived, as his men gradually started reporting to camp.

On October 24, Marion received reports that the Loyalist militia of the High Hills had been embodied and ordered to the forks of the Black River as part of yet another attempt to restore Loyalist order in the Pee Dee region. This militia was led by a Loyalist named Samuel Tynes, a prominent landowner of the High Hills whom Cornwallis had once referred to as a "weak, well-intentioned man."[9] It could hardly have been an imposing force—when inspected by a British officer on September 4, not a third of Tynes's men had arms.

Nevertheless, the British were desperate to reestablish order in South Carolina's eastern reaches, and before marching into the Pee Dee, Tynes's regiment of approximately two hundred men had been outfitted with new English muskets, ammunition, blankets, and horse tack. "Proud, careless, and completely unmilitary, they were now camping at the old muster field bordering Tearcoat Swamp,"[10] writes Bass. Also written as *Tarcoat* or *Tarcote* swamp in some historic accounts, Tearcoat Swamp was located near today's Interstate 95 east of Sumter, South Carolina.

Sensing opportunity, Marion traveled to Kingstree that day, sending out false information that he was planning to attack another body of Loyalist militia camped at McCallum's Ferry, near modern-day Bishopville, South Carolina. By the time he departed Kingstree the following day, Marion had with him approximately 150 men. Moving decisively, Marion approached Tynes's position that night, receiving news from his scouts that Tynes was encamped just off the main road with his rear flanks protected by Tearcoat Swamp. Although sentinels guarded the road, Marion's scouts reported, camp discipline appeared lax, with men playing fiddles and cards around campfires.

First resting his men, Marion moved off toward Tearcoat Swamp in the early evening. William Dobein James gives us an intriguing portrait of Marion's tactics in these nighttime raids. "The general's favorite time for moving was at the sitting sun, and then it was expected the march would continue all night . . . he had been known to march sixty or seventy miles without taking any other refreshment than a meal of cold potatoes and a drink of cold water, in twenty four hours."[11]

On this particular raid, Marion and his regiment arrived on the outskirts of Tearcoat Swamp early in the morning hours of October 26 to find Tynes's camp lightly guarded as had been reported. As he had done at Black Mingo, Marion divided his men into three parties: one detachment to attack from the right, one from the left, and the largest group to strike at the front. This time, their approach was not detected, and when Marion signaled the attack by firing his pistol, all three groups rushed into the Loyalist camp, taking their quarry by surprise. "The rout was universal," reported James, with Tynes and many of his men fleeing for their lives into the swamp. Marion's forces killed eight and wounded fourteen, while "Gen. Marion lost not a man."[12] Marion took twenty-three Loyalist prisoners. Also captured were eighty horses, along with the new saddles, bridles, and tacks with which they had been outfitted courtesy of the British army.

Marion detached a party led by Capt. William Clay Snipes to pursue Tynes while he collected the spoils and moved back toward Kingstree. Snipes soon returned from his hunt, producing not only Tynes but several other Loyalist militia officers and two justices of the peace. The rout on Tearcoat Swamp was so complete, Snipes's raid against the Loyalist officers so alarming, that James reported "most of Tynes' men, soon after joined Gen. Marion, and fought bravely."[13]

Marion's strength was now great enough to patrol roads heading north from Charleston, threatening British supply lines to Camden and points north. Thanks to his string of victories, from Big Savannah to Black Mingo to Tearcoat Swamp, he was beginning to garner attention in the press, though not always favorable. Loyalist papers like the *South Carolina Gazette* and *American Journal* reported that Marion controlled the countryside with the "most despotic and cruel tyranny." Nevertheless, reports such as these only emboldened other Patriot militia regiments in the region, prompting Balfour from Charleston to report to Rawdon at Winnsboro that the Patriot numbers "betwixt the Peedee and Santee . . . from the best accounts they exceed a thousand." Though he believed these reports exaggerated, Balfour dispatched elements of the British 64th Regiment to guard Nelson's Ferry and begged Cornwallis, through Rawdon, for a "very strong detachment from the army with cavalry" to "shew themselves in that country."[14]

Similarly, from Camden, Turnbull reported that "Colonel Tynes has been surprised and defeated on the forks of Black River. . . . Lost all his arms, so we are now exposed to the east and north, which will prevent our collecting provisions in these quarters. . . . Dragoons or mounted men must be got to check these rebells, which lays waste the country and murders the well affected in cold blood."[15]

Just over a month after Cornwallis had authorized Wemyss's raid of terror into the Pee Dee, he was now faced with dismayingly familiar circumstances. With Ferguson's defeat in the west, and the Pee Dee in constant revolt, the "Southern Strategy" of holding interior territory with Loyalist militia was clearly turning into a failure. Yet his options were limited. Now sufficiently recovered from his bout with malaria, Cornwallis was determined to attempt another expedition into North Carolina. Believing his first attempt had suffered from a lack of manpower, Cornwallis had by now received authorization from Henry Clinton to order British brigadier general Alexander Leslie and his brigade of approximately 1,900 to sail from Virginia to Charleston to support his invasion plans. Cornwallis hoped that by subduing North Carolina, the rebels of South Carolina would realize their cause hopeless, diminishing their revolt. That these expectations were hardly the components of effective military strategy seemed not to bother either Clinton or Cornwallis at the time. "If my wishes are fulfilled, they are that you may establish post at Hillsborough, feed it from Cross Creek . . . and be able to carry on desultory operations in Chesapeake till more solid operations can take place," Clinton informed Cornwallis.[16]

Later, Clinton would have second thoughts, especially after receiving news of another disastrous British defeat at Cowpens on January 17, 1781. But for the moment, both men seemed content to wait for Leslie to join Cornwallis before initiating a winter's push into North Carolina. However, Leslie would not set sail from Portsmouth until November 22 nor arrive in Charleston until December 13, creating a delay that would only allow Whig insurrections in the Backcountry War to foment and prosper.

Unburdened by these larger strategic deliberations, finally recovered from his latest bout with malaria, and probably already bored with camp life in Winnsboro, Tarleton was eager for another crack at Marion. In his memoir, Tarleton even expressed reluctant regard for Marion, writing "Mr. Marion, by his zeal and abilities, shewed himself capable of the trust committed to his charge." So when Tarleton learned of Turnbull's request for "dragoons or mounted men" to "check these rebels" in the Pee Dee region, he eagerly volunteered for the assignment. Reluctant to lose support of his mounted troops in foraging operations around Winnsboro, Cornwallis acquiesced to Tarleton's request, provided "you will of course not be long absent, and let me hear from you constantly."[17]

After first marching to Camden, Tarleton and the bulk of the British Legion (for he had left at least forty dragoons behind at Winnsboro) departed for the Pee Dee region on November 5, raiding horses from the local countryside to mount his infantry as he traveled. Turnbull had passed onto Tarleton intelligence that Marion and other Patriot regiments operating in the vicinity had as many as four thousand men. Nervous about these reports, Tarleton at first moved his corps in a compact body, "lest the Americans should gain any advantages over patroles or detachments." But after his scouts determined Marion's force was much smaller than rumored, he "divided his corps into several small parties, publishing intelligence that each was a patrole, and that the main body of the King's troops had countermarched to Camden." To Cornwallis, he reported, "I kept my numbers concealed, advanced on the roads, fell back again, shew'd tokens of fear, by leaving camps abruptly and provisions cook'd, in order to draw the enemy."

But Tarleton did not underestimate Marion's threat, and "took care that no detachment should be out of the reach of assistance; and that the whole formed, after dusk every evening, a solid and vigilante corps during the night."[18]

Tarleton's main objective was protection of the ferries and supply lines along the Santee River, his destination the strategically vital crossing at Nelson's Ferry, and so he stayed close to the river's east bank, soon riding through the High Hills. What these patrols did during the day as they moved south, we have no primary accounts. However, prior to his mission Tarleton had written Cornwallis that "nothing will serve these people but fire and sword" and that "the only treatment I can propose or think of, if I am spared long enough here, is, according to the ancient scripture, saving only the salt which we cannot spare," presumably to salt his enemies' wounds.[19] From this missive, we can presume that looting, terror, and fire were a part of Tarleton's tactics in the Pee Dee.

Indeed, Marion later reported Tarleton "burned all the houses and barns from Camden down to the Santee." As to his own operations, Marion's focus was also on Nelson's Ferry at this time, with "an intention of dispersing the guards there, which was defended by sixty Hessians and some militia."[20] From there he planned to proceed to Wright's Bluff, another Santee crossing (now mostly submerged under Lake Marion) to intercept boats carrying British supplies.

As he rode south, Tarleton grew increasingly frustrated at the lack of reliable intelligence he could procure from the terrified residents of the High Hills. "No intelligence to be depended upon cou'd I possibly obtain of the enemy's situation,"[21] he reported to Cornwallis. And so he decided to set a trap. Near the Santee River, in modern-day Clarendon County, South Carolina, not far from St. Mark's Episcopal Church, established in 1757, was the home of South Carolina Brigadier General Richard Richardson. Richardson had been an active Patriot earlier in the war, serving in both military and political roles, but had died several weeks before. Here, Tarleton and his four hundred troopers set up camp on November 7. To attract Marion, Tarleton lit bright campfires, intending to light up the sky as if he was burning Richardson's plantation, while setting up his troops and artillery in an ambush on its outskirts.

The plan almost worked. On the way to Nelson's Ferry, Marion learned that Tarleton was camped nearby at Richardson's. That very night, Marion and his regiment raced to Richardson's plantation after receiving reports that it was being burned. But as he approached, he was met by Richardson's son, Capt. Richard Richardson Jr., a former Continental officer who had escaped his father's plantation upon learning of Tarleton's approach and hid in the nearby swamp. Now Richardson Jr. emerged from his hiding place to warn Marion of the trap. "After marching all night, I found, when I came within three miles, that he had 300 infantry one field-piece and a howitzer, and was so advantageously encamped that I could not succeed with so small a number of men as I had, which did not exceed 200," Marion wrote to Harrington.[22]

Marion wheeled and fled, but by morning, Tarleton learned of Marion's aborted approach from one of Marion's prisoners who had escaped in the night. "A pursuit was immediately commenced," wrote Tarleton in his memoir, "for seven hours through swamps and defiles."[23] It was during this unsuccessful chase, allegedly, that an American myth was born. Frustrated yet again by Marion's elusiveness, Tarleton called off the pursuit, allegedly telling his troops, "Come on Boys! Let us go back, and we will find the Gamecock [Thomas Sumter]. But for this damned old fox, the Devil himself could not catch him," thus giving birth to Francis Marion's famous "Swamp Fox" nickname.[24]

Twentieth-century Marion historians Robert D. Bass and Hugh Rankin assert that the nickname was shortly thereafter adopted by "the people along the Santee." Popular historian Bass is particularly effusive on the subject, despite little documentary evidence, writing, "The Whigs along the Santee . . . seized upon Tarleton's epithet, turned it euphemistically into Swamp Fox, and fastened the nickname forever upon their hero."[25] However, spoilsport historian Karl G. Heider observes that the name did not become widely adopted until the story of the nickname was adopted in an 1844 Marion biography by William Gilmore Simms, a popular novelist of the time. It was Simms who modified the earlier anecdote, collected in a volume titled *Anecdotes of the Revolutionary War in America* by Alexander Garden in 1822, from "this damned old fox" to "this damned Swamp Fox."

Indeed, the Marion biography of William Dobein James, considered the most reliable primary account of Marion's campaigns, makes no reference to the Swamp Fox nickname. The Marion biography by Peter Horry with Parson Weems does indicate that Loyalists of the region called Marion a "vile swamp fox," perhaps inspiring the anecdote from Garden, but Heider observes the Horry/Weems reference only accounts for the term in a negative context, not for the famous "sobriquet" that became popular in the decades following the war. "Swamp Fox was a Tory term, not a Whig term at all. So until counterevidence appears, we must credit William Gilmore

Simms, not Whigs along the Santee River in the 1780s, with the friendly use of "Swamp Fox," Heider asserts.[26]

Heider's research suggests the name "Swamp Fox" emerged as part of the folkloric tradition of the American Revolution, with little chance it was a term of endearment used by Marion's troops and followers in reference to their leader, and certainly not a term Marion would ever use to describe himself. But let us not be troubled by such disheartening intellectualizations. If it serves some cultural need to imagine Tarleton's epithet was quickly transformed by the Patriots of the surrounding countryside into an emblem of American cunning and defiance, that the name was adopted by Marion and his men as a badge of honor, what harm can there be in the supposition? Perhaps those who attempt to strip history of all elements of myth and folklore doom it to the dustbins of indifference these same scholars so frequently lament.

According to the account of William Dobein James, Marion attempted to set an ambush for Tarleton at a place called Benbow's Ferry, about ten miles above Kingstree, on the east side of Black River. "In partisan warfare, this position was the best that could have been taken," James writes. "He could now defend himself first at Black river itself, and then at three difficult passes of swamps at his rear. . . . Here then Marion determined to make a stand, and felled trees to across the road to impede the enemy."[27] But if Marion did intend to fight Tarleton at Benbow's, his later account of the action to Harrington makes no mention of it, and instead suggests that Marion considered himself outnumbered from the beginning of the encounter, with no intention to fight.

Nevertheless, Tarleton never made it that far, depriving us of the chance to regard the Swamp Fox and Bloody Ban face-to-face in mortal combat, a situation that never occurred throughout the American Revolution. Instead, after making it as far as Ox Swamp on the Pocotaligo River, Tarleton's horses and men gave out. Tarleton, of course, didn't depict it as such in his memoir, claiming instead he "gained ground very fast," and undoubtedly would've had Marion in his clutches, if not for an urgent express received from Cornwallis on the ride, recalling Tarleton to Winnsboro. Giving up on the chase, Tarleton returned to Richardson's, where he "laid the houses and plantations about Richardson's" to waste.[28] Writing to Harrison on November 9, Marion reported that on the previous evening, Tarleton's detachment was on the Santee, "burning all before them without distinction." But the destruction did not last long, for shortly afterward Tarleton received new orders that he was now urgently needed in the west.

Before leaving, however, he paused to write Cornwallis a report of his raid: "I have the honor to inform you that I am so far returned from my expedition after Colonels Marion, Horry, etc. The insurrection would have been general and dangerous to Camden . . . had it not been nipp'd before it arrived at maturity . . . Thus, my lord, I have used my best ability to settle the affairs of this part of the province."[29]

Despite the sanguine exaggerations of Tarleton's assessment, they were fabrications Cornwallis was eager to believe. "Colonel Marion had so wrought on the minds of the people, partly by the terror of his threats and cruelty of his punishments and partly by the promise of plunder, that there was scarce an inhabitant between the Santee and Pedee that was not in arms against us," he explained to Clinton in a letter dated December 3. "I therefore sent Tarleton, who pursued Marion for several days, obliged his corps to take to the swamps, and, by convincing the inhabitants that there was a power superior to Marion who could likewise reward and punish, so far checked the insurrection that the greatest parts of them have not dared openly to appear in arms against us since his expedition."[30] Clearly, Cornwallis had not yet learned that a Marion forced into the swamps was still a dangerous foe.

OF COURSE, TARLETON HAD NOT quelled Marion's "insurrection" (a fact even Cornwallis realized, suggesting his account to Clinton was the exaggerations of a subordinate desperate to impart some good news, however false). Marion remained as strong, if not stronger than ever, and once he was sure Tarleton had left the vicinity, he returned to Nelson's Ferry, though there was no evidence there of British supply trains.

Then, receiving news the redoubt at Georgetown was now guarded by only fifty British regulars, mostly invalids, he quickly made plans for another assault on the town. "Georgetown, at that period, and afterwards, was often the point to which his views were directed," explains James, "since it was there he expected to take the supplies of ammunition, clothing, and salt, which he sorely needed."[31]

To keep his plans secret, he directed his regiment to travel the back roads, avoiding settled areas as much as possible, crossing the Black River at Potato Ferry then bushwhacking his way through Gapway Swamp.

If once accurate, Marion's intelligence soon turned false. The night before Marion arrived at Georgetown, it had been reinforced by over two hundred militia led by Jesse Barefield from the stronghold Loyalist communities around the Little Pee Dee River. Marion arrived outside Georgetown on November 15 and sent out two scouting parties to reconnoiter the town. The first, led by Peter Horry, set out that night to see if they could gain some advantage over the enemy near the lines of Georgetown. The other, led by Capt. John Melton, was sent to scout the plantation of Col. William Alston, where Marion had received word that a large party of Loyalist militia were encamped. Alston was a respected horse breeder and farmer in the Georgetown area who was also a member of Marion's brigade. In Melton's patrol was Gabriel Marion, Francis Marion's twenty-year-old nephew, serving as a lieutenant in Marion's regiment.[32]

A confirmed bachelor, at least in this part of his life (after the war he would marry a cousin, Mary Esther Videau), Marion's family rarely played a role in his military adventures, except through distant family connections. Gabriel Marion was the son of Francis's late brother, Gabriel, Marion's closest comrade as a boy and young man, and later his business partner. As Melton's detachment rode down the Sampit Road, they were ambushed by a party of Loyalists led by Jesse Barefield himself, and a sharp skirmish ensued. In the fighting, Barefield was wounded by a shotgun blast in the initial round of fire, after which Melton's detachment turned and raced away. The Loyalists now raced after the Patriots, and in the pursuit, Gabriel Marion was shot down. As he lay wounded, he was recognized as Marion's nephew and cruelly beaten. Gabriel recognized one of his attackers and flung himself at the Loyalist, pleading for mercy, but "the angry loyalists shouted to Marion's protector that if he did not thrust the prisoner from him that he too would be shot down. As he was pulled away, a musket was thrust against Gabriel's chest and fired, so close the linen was scorched."[33]

Overall, Melton lost five dead and four wounded in the skirmish but took twelve prisoners. Horry, meanwhile, also encountered a party of about one hundred Loyalists on his patrol. "Instantly we took the road, and clapping spurs to our horses, dashed upon them at full speed," wrote Horry in his biography of Marion. "We pursued. Then you might have seen the wood all covered with armed men; some flying, others pursuing; and with muskets, and pistols, and swords, shooting and cutting down as fast as they could." During the fight, wrote Horry, he was separated from the rest of his patrol with a teenage soldier named Gwinn. As they were approached by a party of ten Loyalists, Gwinn fired his musket, toppling the Loyalist officer and saving Horry's life, allowing Patriot reinforcements to rush to their aid in the confusion that followed, "with several of my troops whooping and huzzaing as they came on," wrote Horry. "The tory party then fired at us, but without effect, and fled."[34] As the skirmish cleared, Marion's men collected the fine horse of the officer Gwinn had killed.

After these skirmishes, most of the Loyalists retreated toward town as Marion brought up the main body of his troops. The Loyalists then attempted to establish a defensive line about one-quarter mile from Georgetown's redoubt but seeing that Marion ordered a flanking maneuver to separate them from the fort, they scurried back to Georgetown, taking cover inside the redoubt's walls. Marion was now in the same position he had been a month before, without artillery or sufficient ammunition to assault the fort, while from inside the fort, the Loyalists had the protection of mortars and swivel guns. "As I had not more than four rounds of ammunition per man, I retreated,"[35] Marion explained in his report on the action to Gates.

Marion's early biographers attempt to portray the loss of Gabriel as one of the war's great emotional crises for the Swamp Fox, though one Marion endured stoically. "As the general had not children, he mourned over his nephew, as would a father over an only son," described William Dobein James. "And shortly after publicly expressed his consolation for himself—that his nephew was a virtuous young man—that he had fallen in the cause of his country, and he would mourn over him no more." In Horry and Weems's version of the death, Marion comments, "As to my nephew . . . I believe he was cruelly murdered: but living virtuously, as he did, and then dying fighting for the rights of man, he is, no doubt, happy: and this is my comfort."[36]

If true, these accounts correspond to others we have of the Marion's demeanor. Though capable of moments of warmth and esprit de corps with his men, he was normally reserved, commanding through discipline and indefatigable concern for his men's safety, not the magnetism that characterized the leadership of contemporaries such as Sumter and Daniel Morgan. To Gates, he reported only that "Our loss was Lt. Gabriel Marion & one private Killed & three wounded."[37]

Another anecdote from this action also sheds light on Marion's character. As Marion's regiment and their prisoners marched away from Georgetown, a mulatto prisoner named Sweat, who was rumored to have been part of the party that murdered Gabriel, was brutally murdered on the march. "Marion was furious and dressed down the officer in command of the prisoner's guard,"[38] writes Rankin, though of the murderer's fate we have no accounts. The next day, Marion called the men into a circle, what Horry and Weems referred to as a "strange manoevre, and a sergeant was seen leading into the circle an elegant horse, under saddle and bridle, with portmanteau, sword, pistols, and muskets." Marion, with great ceremony, then presented the horse to Gwinn, the teenager who had saved Horry's life.

Gwinn "blushed, he chuckled, he looked around and around upon his comrades, as if at a loss how to contain himself, or what to do . . . Marion smiled, and commended him for a good boy," wrote Horry.[39]

Whatever the emotional effect of Gabriel's death, Marion didn't allow it to hinder his campaign, though yet again he was having trouble keeping his regiment intact. "Many of my people has Left me & gone over to the Enemy, for they think that we have no Army coming on, & have been Deceived," he complained to Gates. "As we hear nothing from you a Great while, I hope to have a line from you in what manner to Act, & some Assurance to the people of support."

The command of Harrington was also beginning to rankle. A loyal officer of the Continental army, Marion could be peevish about issues of command, and the independence of his campaign in the Pee Dee only seemed to exacerbate this trait. Even before the raid on Georgetown, Marion had complained to Gates in his letter of November 4 about Harrington's superiority over him, writing, "I cannot think it is your intention I should be under his Command," a sentiment he also expressed to South Carolina governor John Rutledge.[40]

Two weeks later, Harrington had moved into Cheraw, chasing away the Loyalists there under the command of Robert Gray, but Marion found little benefit from having his commanding officer closer to his position. "I have written to Genl. Harrington to spare me his horse to endeavour to remove the post at Kingstree," Marion complained to Gates on November 21. "But from what I know of the Genl., I do not expect he will part with them. I beg leave to mention to you that Genl. Harrington has not done any service with the troops he commands, while I have been obliged to act with so few as not to have it in my power to do any thing Effectual, for want of ammunition & men."[41]

The British viewed Marion as anything but ineffectual, however, and two weeks after Tarleton's operation against him, were still at wit's end to figure out a way to check the success of the Swamp Fox. Despite his assurances to Clinton that he had "checked the insurrection" led by Marion, Cornwallis wrote to Balfour, requesting that he establish a post at Kingstree, "the utility of which I am most thoroughly sensible of."[42] The request was made upon the advice of Tarleton, who suggested a garrison at Kingstree might check the influence of Marion, providing additional security to the strategic Santee crossing at Nelson's Ferry.

To comply with Cornwallis's request, Balfour had to transfer American prisoners from camps on shore to prison hulks in the harbor, releasing their

guards for a detachment under overall command of Maj. Robert McLeroth
of the 64th Regiment. In all, Balfour sent 275 troops to Kingstree under
McLeroth, including the 64th, Loyalist militia, and the British prison
guards, supported by two three-pound field pieces. "I am now quite easy
and satisfied," Cornwallis responded, after learning of McLeroth's detachment. "Indeed I flatter myself that so respectable a force on Black River . . .
will render the whole navigation of the Santee secure." Yet again, it was a
false assumption by the increasingly disconsolate British commander.[43]

EIGHTEEN

FISHDAM
FORD

F OR THE MILITIA REGIMENTS of the Carolina frontier during the
American Revolution, it was common to disembody for a time after
a major engagement, such as Camden or Kings Mountain. Military doctrine might suggest the appropriate course for the Overmountain Men and
their Kings Mountain allies was to advance after victory, leveraging their
psychological advantage with a move against another nearby target, say the
British outpost at Ninety Six, whose occupation created psychological advantages of its own for the British. Indeed, one could argue that if Cornwallis had adhered to such doctrine after his complete victory at Camden,
pushing forward into North Carolina immediately after the victory, today's
South might well fly the Union Jack instead of the Stars and Stripes.

But such doctrine always appears clearer in hindsight. Following their
victory at Kings Mountain, the Americans had good reason to expect the
arrival of British reinforcements. Ferguson had been encamped there for

over twenty-four hours, more than enough time to send for more troops, and Charlotte was a relatively short horse ride away. They were only volunteers after all, every single last one of them, and encumbered as they were with almost seven hundred prisoners, their ranks full of men who wanted to return to their frontier homes in the isolated mountains to protect against the threat of Cherokee attack, retreat and dispersion seemed the more prudent option.

But in the days before aerial reconnaissance or even telegram, the British had only rumor and spies to inform them of their enemies' movements, and among the many British deficiencies in their attempt to conquer the South, an unreliable intelligence network was prominent among them. In such an age, rumor was a powerful weapon, and news of the American victory at Kings Mountain did much to dishearten the Loyalists of the region, causing them to question their allegiances. "The defeat of Major Ferguson had so dispirited this part of the country, and indeed the majority of the loyal subjects were so wearied by the long continuance of the campaign, that Lt. Colonel Cruger commanding at Ninety Six sent information to Lord Cornwallis that the whole country had determined to submit as soon as the rebels should enter it," Rawdon reported to Clinton at the end of October, Cornwallis presumably still too ill to sign the letter himself (or perhaps just sick of delivering bad news).[1] And so Cornwallis—or rather Rawdon acting as Cornwallis's proxy—ordered Maj. James Wemyss west to scout for enemy troops, "secure . . . supplies of grain from being interrupted by small parties of the enemy,"[2] and intimidate the rebel countryside as best they could. With Wemyss went not more than eighty or ninety mounted regulars of the 63rd Regiment, probably supported by some Provincials, a relatively small corps to secure a large swath of South Carolina, highlighting Cornwallis's manpower issues.

Just because the Overmountain Men vanished into the Blue Ridge Mountains does not mean that American forces weren't active, nor that the British weren't tracking them. On October 21, still in the midst of their miserable retreat south from Charlotte, Rawdon reported to Col. Turnbull that American forces under the command of Continental officers William Smallwood and Daniel Morgan were in Salisbury and on the move south. And most of all, the British were on the lookout for their old nemesis, Thomas Sumter, now rumored to be somewhere near McAlpine's Creek, near modern-day Rock Hill, South Carolina.[3]

Indeed, Thomas Sumter had now returned to South Carolina, and with his brigadier general commission from John Rutledge, on behalf of the state of South Carolina, was more powerful than ever, perhaps as powerful in this period of October and November 1780 as he would ever be throughout the course of the American Revolution. Though not as powerful as even the Americans might wish . . . or believe.

Reporting to Continental general Jethro Sumner on October 16, William R. Davie reported that Sumter was on the west side of the Catawba with 2,500 men, a figure reported as "Two Thousand Militia" by the North Carolina Board of War in their "Proceedings" dated October 25, 1780.[4] In truth, his number was far smaller, probably not more than two or three hundred at this time, for he reported to Gen. Smallwood in Charlotte that his "number is very inconsiderable. The Georgians have not joined him as expected. The other Parties who defeated Ferguson are dispersed and gone Home."[5]

Nevertheless, the Americans had good reason to be optimistic, for the British retreat toward Winnsboro not only lifted Patriot sentiment, but it also made the British vulnerable to attack. General William Smallwood was now commanding the advanced detachments at Salisbury, with Gates still attending to logistics and supplies at Hillsborough. By now, the Continentals were well aware that a Congressional inquiry into Gates's defeat at Camden had been held, and that news of Gates's fate would soon be delivered. In fact, Congress had resolved on October 5 that George Washington order a court of inquiry into Gates's conduct at Camden and appoint another officer to take Gates's place until the inquiry could be made. Washington quickly appointed Nathanael Greene, although Greene would not arrive in Charlotte to assume command from Gates until early December.[6]

The uncertainty of Gates's fate was influencing the plans of the Continental officer corps, but with Cornwallis in retreat, they smelled opportunity. At Salisbury, Smallwood formed a plan to shadow Cornwallis's retreat. William Davidson, commanding North Carolina and Virginia militia, was to follow Cornwallis down the east side of the Catawba; Sumter, commanding the "South Carolinians and Georgians," was to follow Cornwallis closely down the Catawba's west side. To muster the Georgians, Smallwood sent letters to Cols. Elijah Clarke and William Candler, the Georgia commanders then in South Carolina, instructing them to receive orders from Sumter. Davidson and Sumter were to "disperse 'till it can be determined whether the Enemy can be attacked with a prospect of Success."[7]

Meanwhile, Daniel Morgan would command the "Advanced Troops," consisting of a corps of Virginia riflemen, the Continental light infantry (hand-picked infantry from the Maryland regiments and Delaware brigade, including its captain, Robert Kirkwood), and the cavalry brigade of William Washington, roughly four hundred infantry and seventy horse, the core of his "Flying Army" that would successfully defeat Tarleton at Cowpens in four months.[8]

Morgan's troops were to reconnoiter the vicinity north of Camden, where there was opportunity with Cornwallis and Rawdon still in retreat. Commanding Camden now was George Turnbull, a reliable, veteran officer. But he was still burdened with a considerable number of sick soldiers and prisoners from the summer campaign, and his defense works were "not in greater forwardness." Writing to Cornwallis on November 3, Turnbull reported, "the Negroes took the small pox, deserted, many died, [so] that the troops have been obliged to work there three weeks. We will do it as fast as we can."[9]

Morgan arrived at Six Mile Creek on October 22, fourteen miles south of Charlotte, where two days before Gen. William Davidson had established a camp near a local meetinghouse called New Providence. According to historian William Lee Anderson, the location of Camp New Providence afforded several benefits, raising the spirits of the Mecklenburg Whigs and providing access to mills, roads, and forage in the Waxhaw region south of Charlotte, while asserting American control on the east side of the Catawba River.[10]

Three days later, on October 25, the Continentals repositioned in advance of the militia to better defend the camp. It was here, on this same day, where Daniel Morgan would receive news of his promotion to brigadier general, a commission for which he had long lobbied and rightfully deserved.[11] However, by then, Smallwood had discovered Cornwallis had crossed to the west side of the Catawba.[12]

Shortly thereafter, in early November, the Continentals learned Maj. Gen. Nathanael Greene had been appointed commander of the Continental army's Southern Department on October 23, effectively putting an end to any major operations contemplated against the British for the fall. Smallwood posted Davie with three hundred mounted troops at Lands Ford on the Catawba River in South Carolina, near the fall line of the Catawba River, south of modern-day Rock Hill, to "inspire the country" and observe the enemy but contemplated no more major actions until Greene's arrival.[13]

If Sumter got the memo about halting operations against Cornwallis, however, he chose to ignore it. By this time, Sumter was in camp at Stallings' (or Stallions') Plantation on Fishing Creek, about two miles southeast of modern-day York, South Carolina, calling in his militia regi-

ments. Joining him there, or shortly thereafter, were men like William Barnet from the Camden District, who had been badly wounded in the Battle
at Ramsour's Mill while serving with the Rowan County militia but was
now well enough to rejoin the fight against the British occupation. Also
returning to Sumter's camp was Samuel Otterson, who had been in
Sumter's brigade earlier that summer, and witnessed Sumter's "election" to
general that June, before suffering a serious wound at Hanging Rock. Edward Strong was a member of Edward Lacey's regiment who was at his
home in Chester County that fall when "again called out" to Sumter's
camp.[14]

For militia colonel Richard Winn, the object of Sumter's campaign was
clear. "As General Sumter and Colo. Winn were together day and night,"
at Stallings, "they conversed together on all confidential points, as well as
other matters as respected war measures," Winn recalled in his postwar
notes. "Lord Cornwallis's headquarters were at Winnsboro," and Winn recalled Sumter saying, "it has been agreed that I shall march as near to
Winnsboro as can be done with safety; this will draw Tarleton and a large
body of infantry after us; this will weaken Cornwallis so much that Gen'l
Smallwood, with the continental troops and, what North Carolinians could
be collected, was to fall on Cornwallis."[15]

This certainly sounds like the plan Smallwood had formulated in late
October, although if Sumter was notified of its suspension as the Continentals waited for the arrival of Greene, it is impossible at this point to say.
As previously noted, Sumter innately understood that his militia were primarily motivated by the promise of impending action, and later in the war,
he would exaggerate claims of Continental support or diminish reports of
British troop's strength in order to justify his own operations, which often
included raid and plunder on Loyalist homesteads. Although there is nothing in the historical record to indicate Sumter was informed of the change
in plans, he was an inveterate intelligence operative and was usually well
informed about all operations in his theater, British and American. Likely
he used the promise of a coordinated attack against Cornwallis to motivate
his militia soldiers to report to camp. Certainly, this was what Winn believed was the object of the fall campaign.[16]

Now on the move, Sumter and his men marched from Stallings west
toward the Broad River, through the small community of Mobley (also
Gibson's Meeting House; in modern-day Fairfield County, South Carolina,
only ten miles west of Winnsboro) "through the Tory country." It was at
Mobley's on June 8 earlier that summer, where a small body of Whig militia

under Richard Winn and William Bratton had attacked the Tory militia encamped there, killing eight, wounding sixteen, and capturing fifteen—one of the first actions of Patriot insurrection after the fall of Charleston. Historian John C. Parker writes that Mobley, and the nearby settlement of Sandy River in Chester County, "was an affluent Loyalist community . . . the residents of the area were said to have the best lands in the entire district and all the Negroes."[17]

Sumter was playing with fire, and he knew it. He was campaigning on the very outskirts of Cornwallis's new headquarters, just ten to fifteen miles away, in prominent Tory settlements. Nevertheless, men were still joining his command, which now consisted of around four hundred. Sumter's biographer Anne Gregorie King states, "Besides collecting militia, breaking up Tory bands, and cutting off supplies from the British, Sumter's more ambitious aim seems to have been to form a junction with Clarke [Georgia militia leader Elijah Clarke] and Brandon [Thomas Brandon, colonel of the Fairforest Militia from just across the Broad] and strike the post at Ninety Six."[18] As he marched he met with Georgia militia officers under the command of Gen. Benjamin Few at a place called Kelly's to discuss joint measures. But on November 8, Few wrote Gates from his camp on Fortenbury's on Tyger River (south of modern-day Spartanburg) announcing he had declined the opportunity to coordinate with Sumter against Winnsboro to instead send Georgia colonels Twiggs and McCall "to the southward, in order to keep up the spirits of the people until it may be practicable for me to make a movement with the main body."[19] Few was far from the last officer who would have reservations about operating in conjunction with Thomas Sumter. As events proceeded into 1781, Francis Marion, among others, would show similar reservations.

Nevertheless, Sumter was proving wildly successful in one of his ambitions, attracting the attention of the British army. By November 7, Sumter was camped at a place called Moore's Mill, five miles from a popular ford on the Broad River called Fishdam Ford, named for a Native American fish dam located there. Today, the Fishdam Ford site is located just south of where S.C. Highway 215 crosses the Broad River on the road between Chester and the small South Carolina community of Carlisle. In 1780, the ford was on a main road leading from Charlotte and Nation's Ford on the Catawba River across the Broad and into the Ninety Six District. Also called a fish weir, a fish dam was an obstruction placed in the river, usually constructed of large stones, to funnel fish into a trap. That day or just before, Wemyss learned Sumter's location. "Major Wemyss, who had just past the Broad River at Byerley's Ferry, came to me on the seventh . . . and told me that he had information that Sumpter had moved to Moore's Mill within Five Miles of Fishdam Ford," Cornwallis later reported to Clinton. Wemyss informed Cornwallis that "he had accurate accounts of his position and good guides, and that he made no doubt of being able to surprise and rout him."[20]

Wemyss's plan appealed to Cornwallis. "As the defeating so daring and troublesome a man as Sumpter [sic] and dispersing such banditte was a great object, I consented to his making the trial on the 9th at day break," Cornwallis reported to Clinton. But why Wemyss and not Tarleton, his preferred instrument for such operations? The reason was that Tarleton was now conducting his raid through the Pee Dee, described in the previous chapter. Not quite a suitable Tarleton substitute, Wemyss was nevertheless detached by Cornwallis with "forty of the dragoons which Tarleton had left with me, desiring him, however, neither to put them in the front nor to make any use of them in the night."[21] The plan was apparently delayed twenty-four hours, made for the early morning of November 9, not November 8, because Wemyss had to return to gather the mounted infantry of the 63rd for the operation, who were then camped about twenty-five miles from Sumter's position. In the interim, probably on November 8, Sumter moved his camp from Moore's Mill to Fishdam Ford.

According to Winn's memoir, Sumter's division arrived at Fishdam Ford "in the evening." Sumter took post "immediately at the ford; Colo. Winn to his left directly on the bank of the river; Colo. Taylor on a square to the left of Colo. Winn, and Lacey Bratton, and Hill in front about three or four hundred yards."[22]

In the *History of Georgia* by Hugh McCall, there is a remarkably detailed description of the layout of Sumter's camp. Generally regarded as Georgia's first historian, McCall published his masterwork in two volumes, in 1811 and 1816. He was also the son of Patriot militia commander James McCall, from the Long Canes community in the Savannah River basin on both the Georgia and South Carolina sides of the community. James McCall, with some of the Long Cane Regiment, arrived in Sumter's camp sometime during that day, and this is how his son describes the layout of his father's camp:

From the fish-dam ford, the road to Charlotte, in North Carolina, runs eastward; and on the right there was a plantation fenced along the road for half a mile, where the Winnsborough road leads out to the right: on the left of the road the ground is open and flat for two hundred yards from the river, and partially enclosed by a fence, and a hill of woodland, with thick undergrowth, commences and continues two hundred yards further along the margin of the road, and thence the high ground diverges to the left; and on the left, about two hundred and fifty yards from the road, a deep gully makes out from the river, and leads nearly parallel to the road, along the left of the high ground. General Sumpter's tent was pitched on the left of the road, at the ford; colonel Richard Winn's troops, one hundred and twenty-five in number, were encamped on the general's left, and upward along the river, colonel Taylor's were encamped along the gully, on the left of Winn; and colonels Lacey, Bratton, and Hills' troops, upward of three hundred men, were encamped on the high ground, in the thick wood, about three hundred and fifty yards in front. During the day . . . colonels Twiggs and Clarke, and majors Chandler and Jackson, with about one hundred Georgia militia; and in the evening, colonel Mc-Call, with a part of the regiment from Longcane, joined the camp. These two re-enforcements occupied the ground between Winn's and Taylor's commands.[23]

During that day, Sumter had ordered Col. Thomas Taylor, with fifty men, to reconnoiter the road to Winnsboro, just twenty-seven miles away, but they returned reporting they had seen no evidence of the enemy. Sumter's position was highly exposed, clearly provocative, and located on a main road directly connected to the headquarters of the British army in the South. His junior officers had a reason to be nervous. Later that night, Sumter called a council of his field, "about eighteen in number" according to Winn, to see what was "best to be done, being altogether in a Tory country—Lord Cornwallis to our left with the British army at Winnsboro at 27 miles . . . and a large British force in our front at Ninety Six." Winn's memoir, edited and compiled by William C. Williams, is too rich in subtle irony not to excerpt at some length: "In this situation of things, it was the opinion of every officer present that Gen'l Sumter ought to cross the river without delay, and particularly so of Colo. Winn who was well acquainted with the people and country. However, after this Gen'l Sumter thought otherwise." In McCall's account, it was only after this meeting, around midnight, that Taylor returned from his reconnaissance mission, reporting no signs of the enemy.[24]

In some later accounts, Sumter is depicted as having ordered no advance scouts or pickets for the night, an almost inconceivable oversight given the events to transpire, the concerns of his officers, or his efforts to provoke the British into attack. In *The Road to Guilford Courthouse*, the great modern-day history of the Charleston-Guilford Courthouse campaign, author John Buchanan insinuates as much.[25] Yet this is conjecture, as far as can be discerned. Indeed, in Winn, there are pickets reported, and other primary sources, including the account of William Hill along with the correspondence of Cornwallis and his officers, make no mention of the matter. But armed with the knowledge of what was to come, deduction suggests the camp was, at the least, poorly secured.

Sumter went to his own tent and fell asleep, but Winn and his compatriots were far more cautious about their situation. "Being so sure of an attack made," Winn ordered his men to sleep with their guns in their arms. "And on the very spot they rose on they were to fight and not fire a single gun until the enemy came up to the fires."[26]

Meanwhile, Wemyss and his mounted 63rd, along with forty Legion Dragoons, were riding through the night. British sources don't list the troop strength of the 63rd, but it was probably the same eighty to one hundred mounted soldiers Wemyss had ridden with on his mission of destruction through the Pee Dee that summer. Wemyss arrived at Moore's Mill "shortly after midnight," only to find that Sumter had moved, though he soon learned through local Tories that he had moved his camp to Fishdam Ford.

Wemyss may have had with him now a Tory spy named "Sealy," who had been in Sumter's camp earlier that day, either "talking Whig" or perhaps captured and interrogated before being released. Sumter biographer Anne Gregorie King reports "it was afterwards thought by Sumter's men that he [i.e., Sealy] acted as a guide and revealed to Wemyss the layout of Sumter's camp, including the location of Sumter's tent."[27]

Wemyss and his dragoons now raced the five miles from Moore's Mill to Fishdam Ford in just a few short hours. In the account of Cornwallis, who was not there, Wemyss arrived at Fishdam Ford around one o'clock in the morning. In the account by Winn, who was there, the attack commenced two hours before daybreak, at around five o'clock. Wemyss apparently came up on Sumter's position so fast, perhaps riding up the main road in the dark, that he charged right into the Patriot pickets on the outskirts of camp and had no chance to form or organize his troops for the attack, let alone deliver to them any final instructions. Recall that Cornwallis had ordered Wemyss to attack at break of day, desiring him not to use the Legion dragoons either "in the front nor to make any use of them during the night," and in a letter to Turnbull, Cornwallis insinuates that had Wemyss waited "for day break," he would have achieved more favorable results.[28]

Nevertheless, by accident or design, Wemyss and his troops now stormed the camp, alerting the pickets but still moving with enough speed to enter into the heart of it mostly undeterred. In his report to Clinton,

Cornwallis wrote, "the major proceeded to attack ... and succeeded so well as to get into his [i.e., Sumter's] camp whilst the men were all sleeping round the fires."[29] Winn agreed the British troopers "made a violent charge" into the camp. However, already on his guard, as he recalled, he put his men "in order" shortly after the "picquets fired alarm guns. . . . As soon as the enemy came up to the fires they halted with surprise. My people poured in on them a well-directed fire."[30]

Seriously wounded in this first round of fire, or perhaps by the pickets, was Wemyss himself, who was shot in the knee and broke his arm in a fall from his horse. Although this wound "put the cavalry into disorder," they still maintained enough discipline after the initial Patriot volley to regroup, dismount, and launch a bayonet attack on some of the Patriot positions. Cornwallis would later accuse Wemyss's second-in-command, Lt. John Stark, "a very young officer who neither knew the ground nor Major Wemyss's plan nor the strength of the enemy" for the mistake of continuing the attack, but such criticism seems unfair given the confusion and disorder of the situation.[31]

Meanwhile, a British assassin team of five or six, perhaps led by Sealy, successfully found Sumter's tent, who McCall reports was still "in profound sleep" during the initial cavalry charge, "and his orderly neglected to awake him on the first alarm." In an account of this part of the battle made the next day, Sumter reported to Smallwood that "there was a party, who had a person acquainted with me, who brought them on through every opposition, and enquired for me upon the alarm posts, and it was with the greatest difficulty that I escaped being cut to pieces."[32]

Winn describes the scene more vividly. "Before he [Sumter] could put on his cloaths, they were up with him. By jumping a fence and running through a briar patch he saved himself, but his service was entirely lost." In the account of McCall, Sumter "ran out, leaped the fence, and escaped by the river bank." In the account of Sumter biographer John D. Bass, Sumter "hatless, barefoot, and without coat or trousers . . . crawled under an overhanging ledge above Broad River." Influenced by Bass's account, John Buchanan reports "Sumter hid from the killers under a cut in the bank along the Broad River while the fighting raged."[33]

Meanwhile, the fighting commenced in camp for at least a brief while between the dismounted British soldiers and the Patriot militia. Winn reported that "the British charged with their bayonet; my men having the advantage of the fire stood the shock and made the second fire. I had only one man bayoneted, through the arm. Major Wimess their commander being badly wounded, the enemy began to retreat."[34]

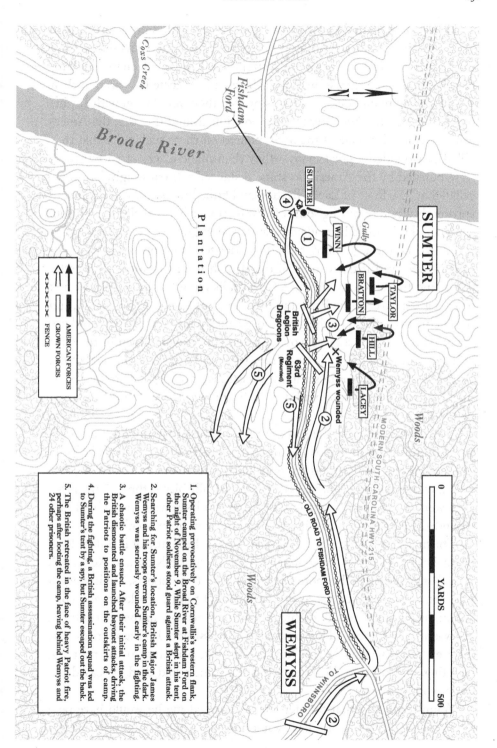

SUMTER

Cox's Creek

Fishdam Ford

Broad River

N

Plantation

SUMTER

WINN

Gully

TAYLOR

BRATTON

HILL

British Legion Dragoons

63rd Regiment (Mounted)

Wemyss wounded

LACEY

Woods

MODERN SOUTH CAROLINA HWY 215

OLD ROAD TO FISHDAM FORD

TO WINNSBORO

WEMYSS

Woods

AMERICAN FORCES
CROWN FORCES
FENCE

0 YARDS 500

1. Operating provocatively on Cornwallis's western flank, Sumter camped on the Broad River at Fishdam Ford on the night of November 9. While Sumter slept in his tent, other Patriot soldiers stood guard against a British attack.

2. Searching for Sumter's location, British Major James Wemyss and his troops overran Sumter's camp in the dark. Wemyss was seriously wounded early in the fighting.

3. A chaotic battle ensued. After their initial attack, the British dismounted and launched bayonet attacks, driving the Patriots to positions on the outskirts of camp.

4. During the fighting, a British assassination squad was led to Sumter's tent by a spy, but Sumter escaped out the back.

5. The British retreated in the face of heavy Patriot fire, perhaps after looting the camp, leaving behind Wemyss and 24 other prisoners.

However, William Hill, who was also in camp with Sumter at Fishdam Ford, remembered the fighting differently: "The Americans retreated in the dark to a commanding ground," after the initial British charge, Hill remembered, "where they waited until the enemy collected . . . around their fires, & began to plunder, not supposing that they would meet with any interruption, & while they were in this position around the fires, the Americans, having advantage of the light, poured on them such a fire that they killed & wounded a great many—they then made a very rapid retreat & were pursued by the Americans some distance."[35] Interestingly, Winn recalled that "the force of Lacey, Bratton and Hill, did not fire a single gun,"[36] apparently afraid of hitting some of Winn's troops in the melee's confusion.

Again, Hill should be read with caution, though in this case, his account seems to echo the account of the battle understood by Cornwallis, who presumably received it from some of the British troops involved. In a letter describing the action to Turnbull, Cornwallis reported the British "at first drove a great part" of the Patriot militia, "but not knowing the ground, and the enemy firing from the heights and swamps where our people could not get at them,"[37] Wemyss was wounded and about twenty men of the 63rd killed or wounded. What is clear from these differing accounts is that the British sustained serious losses in the disastrous attack, including their commanding officer, and soon withdrew into the night, their retreat harassed by Patriot volleys.

"Next morning after the sun got up, Gen'l Sumter from a hill took a view; found his men in possession of the battleground," recalled Winn. Winn is careful not to accuse Sumter of cowardice or dereliction of command, yet here again a subdued sarcasm practically bleeds through the page: "He went to the camp and found the ground strewed with killed and wounded, and the commanding British officer in his power."[38]

The matter of Sumter's whereabouts during the Battle of Fishdam Ford is a delicate one for his biographers, Anne Gregorie King and Robert D. Bass. King, generally the more objective of the two, reports, "Thinking all was lost, as everyone else seems to have thought in the darkness and confusion, he remained out all night, and without his coat in the cold autumn air was nearly frozen." The more unbridled Robert D. Bass writes that Sumter "lay shivering in the November frost, listening to the running, shouting, and firing of his men. After the tumult had died, he eased out and found his horse."[39]

Winn recounted that Sumter later "informed me he would have perished from cold had he not have got a horse; getting on him horsebacked and hugging his neck. He also assured me that from the manner in which the British brought on the attack, he did not expect to hear a single gun fired" by Winn, and "concluded to provide for his own safety."[40]

Sumter's actions at Fishdam Ford are one of those incidents in his military career where his actions are puzzling to his admirers, damning to his critics. At the least, he seems guilty of poor camp security, relying on the assurances of one scouting party that the area was safe, despite a prominent location and a strategy of deliberate provocation. For fleeing the assassin squad sent to his tent he can hardly be blamed, although the presumption that he slept through warning fire of his own pickets is somewhat troubling. And by his own admission to Winn, assuming Winn recalled the exchange accurately, his main concern after he fled from his tent was "his own safety," calling into question his courage and leadership, at least by a chivalric moral code, if not by contemporary and modern military standards.

Nevertheless, Sumter resumed command the following morning. In his letter to Smallwood, Sumter reported, "I have twenty-five prisoners, among which is Major Wemyss, wounded, one surgeon and Sergt. Major, & seven killed. A parcel of excellent horses and arms were taken. My loss was four killed; ten wounded. Officers and men generally behaved with a great deal of bravery, reserving their fire until the Enemy were within ten steps of them."[41] Despite his questionable actions, the skirmish was clearly a Patriot victory, significantly achieved (if that is the correct word) against regular British troops, not Loyalist militia. Such a victory not only cemented Sumter's status as brigadier general of the South Carolina and Georgia troops then campaigning in western South Carolina, it was a provocation Cornwallis simply could not tolerate.

NINETEEN

BLACKSTOCKS

Cornwallis well understood the propaganda problems created by the debacle at Fishdam Ford. Even if it were little more than a skirmish, a blundered raid, it would be viewed as a Sumter "victory," stirring the already emboldened Patriot resistance. Frustratingly, it was a situation that could have easily been avoided, and in the days following the battle, Cornwallis indulged in the futile game of "what ifs." Had Wemyss followed his orders and waited until daybreak to attack, the British would have routed the Patriots, he insinuated in his later correspondence on the attack. Or had Wemyss "not fallen in the first shots, it would have been a very compleat stroke." Adding to the frustration were reports the Americans broke camp immediately after the skirmish, and that "when day broke there was not a rebel to be seen . . . so that if our people had staid till daylight they would have found themselves in full possession of the enemy's camp and would have brought off the major and the rest of the wounded and the victory must have been indisputable, which in this war is of the utmost importance."[1]

Compounding his issues was the loss of Wemyss himself. Though Stark had managed to collect Wemyss and some of the others wounded as he fled Fishdam Ford, he was obliged to leave them at a nearby cabin under a flag of truce before fleeing the field. In the morning, after regaining his command, if not his dignity, Sumter traveled to the cabin himself and took Wemyss prisoner. According to Hill, Wemyss "had in his pocket, the evidence of his having in cold blood hanged several of the Americans," during his raid in the Pee Dee, and "likewise a list of a number of the houses he had burned on Black River," an almost inconceivable anecdote, almost surely apocryphal, though repeated in many subsequent histories, evolving over time to include the addendum that "Sumter generously threw" the list "into the fire," saving the British major from the wrath of the American militia.[2]

Wemyss was no Tarleton, and in the wake of his capture at Fishdam Ford, his ruthless mission to the Pee Dee continued to cause political problems for the Loyalist cause. Writing from the Cheraws on November 12, Loyalist militia general H. W. Harrington would complain that "Major Wemyss here played the petty tyrant . . . Britons have not long been accustomed to countenance such savage acts as these," although he apparently only hanged one person there, making Hill's claim about the list in his pocket even less credible.[3] But Wemyss was one of only a very select handful of officers Cornwallis seemed to trust for these independent missions, after the debacles of Christian Huck at Huck's Defeat and Patrick Ferguson at Kings Mountain, and his loss severely limited Cornwallis's options for these detached missions of "fire and sword."

In the custom of the time, Sumter immediately "paroled" Wemyss, bounding him by his honor and his word to refrain from further service as a British officer until he was officially "exchanged" for an American prisoner of like status. His wounds serious, Wemyss was sent by Cornwallis to Charleston, but never fully recovered, obtaining leave to return to New York that January and taking no further active role in the war. He was promoted to lieutenant colonel in 1783 but sold his commission six years later and returned to his native Scotland. In the late 1790s, financial troubles forced him to immigrate to America, where he acquired a small farm on Long Island and lived the rest of his life as an American, dying in 1833.[4]

With Wemyss defeated at Fishdam Ford and permanently out of commission, Sumter grew more powerful by the day. Following the skirmish

Sumter had moved off to the west, into the Ninety Six District, and British reports suggested his corps was growing steadily. Cornwallis now detached his aide-de-camp, Lt. John Money, with the 63rd and a battalion of the British 71st to Brierley's Ferry on Broad River, today under Parr Shoals Reserve near the town of Newberry, South Carolina, "to cover our mills and to give some check to the enemy's march to Ninety Six," and immediately recalled his number one weapon, Banastre Tarleton, from his "fox" hunting mission in the Pee Dee.[5]

ON NOVEMBER 9, THE MORNING AFTER the skirmish at Fishdam Ford, Thomas Sumter collected his militias and crossed to the west side of Broad River. By the following day, Cornwallis received reports that Sumter had been joined by the militia corps of Elijah Clarke, James McCall, and Thomas Brandon, and that his numbers were swelling.[6] Col. Thomas Brandon of South Carolina's Fair Forest Regiment had been the close associate of James Williams, Sumter's alleged "brigadier general" rival killed at Kings Mountain. It was Brandon, with Williams, who allegedly had been ostracized before the battle, forced to march separately from the rest of the Overmountain Men's corps on the march to Kings Mountain, at least according to William Hill's memoir. That Brandon now joined Sumter does not discredit Hill's account completely—militia units often formed strange bedfellows in the Backcountry War—but it does suggest the earlier animosity between Sumter's New Acquisition militia and the Brandon's Fair Forest militia was exaggerated by Hill.

Serving with the Long Canes militia of James McCall were both South Carolinians and Georgians living along the Upper Savannah River. With them was Maj. Samuel Hammond, whose account of the actions to come will be a primary reference. Hammond was born in Richmond County, Virginia, in 1757, and had served in the Continental army earlier in the war, before immigrating south and joining the Long Canes militia. In that capacity he had already fought at Stono Ferry and Savannah in 1779, and Cedar Spring, Musgrove Mill, and Kings Mountain in 1780. He would go on to fight at Cowpens, Augusta, Ninety Six, and Eutaw Springs, one of the more remarkable records of combat experience in the American Revolution's southern campaigns.[7]

On November 13, Sumter and his militia camped at the plantation of a man named Niam on the Enoree River, in the vicinity of modern-day Whitmire, South Carolina. Sumter biographer Robert D. Bass reports that, at Niam's, Sumter now had "ten colonels and a thousand men in his corps."[8]

Though he was contemplating an attack on the British outpost at Ninety Six, he had no artillery, making the prospects of success unlikely. Instead, Sumter set his sights on the home owned by James Williams on the Little River, located about halfway between modern-day Laurens and Greenwood, South Carolina. This was part of Williams's property that the British had seized and turned into a fortified outpost earlier in the summer. It was now held by about one hundred Loyalist militia under the command of Col. Moses Kirkland.[9]

Meanwhile, British army headquarters was buzzing with reports of Sumter's activity. On November 10, Cornwallis wrote to Balfour in Charleston, reporting Sumter had been joined by Brandon and Clarke, "making all about 6 or 700."[10] The same day, Cornwallis wrote Tarleton with reports that "some of the mountaineers"—the feared and mysterious "Overmountain Men"—were marching to join Sumter.[11] This was only a rumor but shows the effect the Battle of Kings Mountain was still having on the British officer corps.

On November 13, Cornwallis wrote to Rawdon, now back at Camden, reporting that with Sumter menacing Brierly's Ferry, "the whole country is under the utmost terror, and all the loyal subjects instead of thinking of self defence are running as fast as possible to the Congarees. The affair at Fishdam Ford is represented by Sumter as a compleat victory, and it is universally believed." That same day he wrote Tarleton with reports that Sumter was on the Tyger River "with what he calls a thousand men, bragging much of his victory." Despite Cornwallis's obvious derision, this report was remarkably accurate, although the following day, Cornwallis received reports from a "Negro" that Continental general William Smallwood was at Lawson's Iron Works, just outside of present-day Spartanburg, South Carolina, "with three pieces of cannon," a report Rawdon attributed to a deliberate deception by Sumter.[12]

All these reports, false and accurate, were adding to Cornwallis's exasperation with Sumter. After the skirmish at Fish Dam Ford, Cornwallis had accused Sumter of the "inhumanity" of placing the wounded Wemyss "into a waggon" and carrying him off, a false charge he later retracted. Now Cornwallis received news that Sumter's men ambushed a British detachment traveling under a flag of truce, with correspondence for Smallwood, and "by force took away their horses, saddles, pistols and blankets." Seething with rage, Cornwallis wrote Sumter directly about the incident, concluding the letter with "As I am convinced that this outrage must meet with your highest disapprobation, it is needless for me to make any comments upon it, and I can have no doubt you will give immediate orders for the restitution of the horses and effects and the punishment of the offenders." We can imagine Sumter smirking at Cornwallis's rage, though no evidence of the Gamecock's "disapprobation" nor any "restitution" is recorded.[13]

Though his campaign to harass and annoy Cornwallis was working to perfection, Sumter still had to feed his growing militia army. Receiving intelligence that a large store of provisions was stored at a place called Summers' (also seen as Sommers's) Mills, about three miles downstream from Brierley's (or Shirer's) Ferry, Sumter ordered South Carolina colonel Thomas Taylor and Georgia colonel William Candler "down the country" to reconnoiter the site and act "to suite [sic] the circumstances of the times and things." At or around the same time, he ordered a lieutenant-colonel Williamson of Elijah Clarke's Georgia militia, along with Samuel Hammond of the Long Canes militia, to attack a Tory muster at a home owned by a "Captain Faust."[14]

He also sent a detachment to menace Brierly's Ferry on the Broad River, where British major Archibald McArthur was stationed with the 71st Highlanders and eighty men of the 63rd regiment. Commanding this detachment to Brierly's may have been Sumter himself. Richard Winn remembered the Gamecock in command, recalling in his memoir that at Brierly's Sumter delivered a challenge for "the British at that station to come out and fight him."[15] However, accounts differ, and this may have been the detachment of Taylor and Candler reported above. Yet the British clearly considered it a provocation. Reporting the incident to Cornwallis, McArthur wrote, "The rebels had the audacity . . . to come close to the river and fire at our men who were washing in the flatts," wounding a soldier of the 63rd and a waggon horse. "They blackguarded us a great deal."[16]

Also at Brierly's on November 18, was Banastre Tarleton, who had arrived earlier that day with 190 dragoons and mounted infantry after riding four hard days from the Santee, first stopping at Camden then taking a swing north of Winnsboro to rouse the Loyalists and threaten the Patriots in the New Acquisition District.[17] At Brierly's, Tarleton ordered his dragoons to remove their distinctive green jackets while they camped on the east bank of the river "in order to throw the Americans off their guard, and continue their belief of the absence of the British legion."[18]

In Tarleton's account of the Patriot provocation, McArthur fired his cannon at the American party on the western bank, dispersing them, then took possession of both shores with an infantry detachment. Meanwhile, with the American detachment now scattered, Tarleton and his dragoons, passed "at a ford some distance below the ferry, and at ten o'clock the same night, the whole corps assembled three miles beyond Brierly's."[19]

Tarleton's "corps" now consisted of 250 infantries from the 71st Highlanders, under the command of McArthur, his own mounted 190 from the Legion, and the remnants of the 63rd Regiment, eighty mounted infantry now under command of British lieutenant John Money in Wemyss's absence—roughly 520 men in all. That night, Tarleton's scouts reported Sumter was moving in force north toward the Enoree River, perhaps toward the home of James Williams that was now a Loyalist blockhouse. The next morning, Tarleton set out in pursuit of Sumter, marching all day, and camping that night with "secrecy and precaution," his goal to cross the Enoree in advance of Sumter, "which if completed without discovery, would perhaps, give an opportunity of destroying General Sumpter's corps by surprise; or certainly would prevent his accomplishing a retreat without risk of an action." But Tarleton's strategy was destroyed when a soldier from the British 63rd deserted that night. Tarleton assumed the worst, believing Sumter would soon be alerted of his pursuit. Indeed, the deserter from the British 63rd found the Patriot camp around midnight and alerted Sumter of Tarleton's pursuit. Recognizing the danger, Sumter ordered a retreat early that morning, racing north in an attempt to cross the Enoree before Tarleton. Tarleton also "pursued his march at dawn, and before ten o'clock in the morning had information of the retreat of General Sumpter." Bloody Ban had the Gamecock on the run, and he would now relentlessly pursue his quarry.[20]

If the mission to Brierly's had been a provocation, as both British and Patriot accounts suggest, Sumter's strategy remains elusive. Clearly he was spoiling for a fight, and if we recall the "practical lesson" observed by Joseph Graham and attributed by him to Sumter, that while the Patriot militia kept "in motion and the men expected that something would be achieved, they continued with the army," we can acknowledge Sumter had in the previous few days achieved these objectives.[21] Based on the primary evidence, Sumter seems to have no known endgame for his movements up and down the Broad River beyond provocation, nor is there evidence he was coordinating his actions at this time with Smallwood and Morgan at Charlotte.

What was Sumter's plan? In his narrative, Maj. Joseph McJunkin reports Sumter's objective was an attack on Ninety Six. The success of that strategy seems unlikely, given Ninety Six's superior defenses and Sumter's lack of artillery, though Sumter was certainly capable of contemplating such attacks. He had attacked the fortified outpost at Rocky Mount earlier in the summer without artillery and would do the same at Fort Granby and Fort Watson in February of the next year, all with disastrous results.

Winn reveals no insight as to Sumter's motivation, only that he had given a challenge to the British at Brierly's to "come out and fight him." Hammond was still on detachment to raid provisions at Fausts and also provides no strategic insight to this part of the retreat; nor does Hill. Sumter's biographer Anne King Gregorie refuses to speculate.

Sumter biographer Robet D. Bass offers this explanation: "The Gamecock was ready to stand and fight. But could his militia face a charge of the powerful British dragoons? He called in his colonels. They voted to take position behind some strong natural defense." Revered for his popular biographies of famous South Carolina American Revolution figures including Sumter, Banastre Tarleton, and Francis Marion, Bass never referenced or footnoted his work. Here, it appears, he indulges in some supposition, as no primary accounts reference this parley.[22]

A more likely supposition is made by historian John Buchanan, among others, that Tarleton's "reputation for rapid pursuit" was by that time well-known throughout the Carolina countryside and taken into consideration by Sumter and his colonels.[23] Overrunning his retreating enemy, intimidating and slaughtering them with his mounted troops, was a tactic Tarleton had employed to good measure, if not an infamous reputation, at the Waxhaws on May 29, along with similar victories at Lenud's Ferry and Biggin's Bridge in the fighting around Charleston earlier that spring.

And so, retreat. For although the deserter surely must have informed Sumter of Tarleton's troop strength, roughly half of Sumter's own, these were all regular, trained British soldiers, though some of them Provincials, led by perhaps the most feared British officer in the South. The one thing Sumter did not want was to be caught by Tarleton from behind while on the run, essentially as Buford had been at the Waxhaws back in May.

And he still had detachments down river. The party he had sent under Williamson and Samuel Hammond to reconnoiter the home of Capt. Faust had not yet returned, nor according to Hammond's memoir, the party of Taylor and Candler that had been sent to raid provisions at Summers' mill.

"Retreat became necessary," admits Hammond, "but this retreat was not hurried," that the detachments "might have time to rejoin the main body under Sumter."[24] He needed a place nearby where his detachments could find him and where he could, if necessary, form defenses against the pursuing Tarleton. Bass reports Col. Thomas Brandon suggested they march to the plantation of William Blackstocks, not far away on the southern bank of the Tyger River, in what is today Union County, South Carolina, about twenty-five miles due south of modern-day Spartanburg.

Campaigning in his home district, for Sumter and his militia army were now marching through the heart of the Fair Forest militia district, Brandon would've been well acquainted with Blackstock's property. And the story of Brandon's recommendation makes a nice postscript to the tale of the Williams/Sumter feud, suggesting that Brandon, at least, harbored no ill will toward Sumter for their alleged conflict earlier in the fall.

More likely, the site was agreed on by consensus, as it was well-known to many of the colonels gathered under Sumter and offered several advantages to Sumter and his militia. Blackstock's plantation was a poplar landmark throughout the region, so well-known that the main road running through the heart of the Spartan District from the Tyger River forty-five miles north to the South Pacolet River was known as the Blackstock Road, as it still is today.[25]

Its prominence would allow not only Sumter's detachments to find him there but also other militia from throughout the countryside. The hill on which Blackstock's farm was located commanded rising ground, giving tactical advantage over the pursuing Tarleton, and it put the Tyger River at his back. Sumter was more than shrewd enough to understand that if he continued his retreat across the Tyger, most of his troops would probably disperse into the countryside. As historians Oscar and Catherine Gilbert note, "Being chased is never good for morale: in all likelihood Sumter's army would simply disintegrate when the militiamen concluded it was no longer worth the candle."[26] Fighting with the Tyger at his back would also create a psychological barrier for his brave but undisciplined militia, perhaps preventing them from breaking at the first sign of a coordinated British advance, as they had at Camden.

Can it be a coincidence that Daniel Morgan utilized these same tactical advantages in his selection of the Cowpens two months later, where he employed terrain and the psychological ploy of placing a river at his back to motivate his militia troops? We shall explore other similarities between Sumter at Blackstock's and Morgan at Cowpens shortly. But first, Sumter had to cross the Enoree, where he left a party under Capt. Patrick Carr to cover his rear and guard the return of the detachments.

At some point the detachment of Williamson that included Samuel Hammond rejoined Sumter's corps, but "Taylor and Candler were yet in the rear, with a host of the best spirits in our little army," Hammond would recall.[27] Arriving at the Enoree ford two hours after Sumter passed it, Tarleton ordered an advance guard to charge Carr's position, which overtook the rear guard with "considerable slaughter," according to Tarleton's account. From prisoners he took at the Enoree, Tarleton learned "that the sudden movement of the Americans was owing to the treachery of the deserter, by whose information Sumpter had fortunately escaped an unexpected attack, and had now the option to fight or retire."[28]

After passing the Enoree, at around four o'clock in the afternoon, Tarleton made a fateful decision. He had been marching in a single body all day, "unwilling to divide his corps," but concerned that "the enemy would have an opportunity of passing unmolested the Tyger River before dark," he decided to move ahead with his mounted troops, "one hundred and seventy cavalry of the legion, and eighty mounted men of the 63rd." The rest of his infantry—the 250 regulars of the 71st Highlanders, along with a small, "three pounder" cannon—he would leave behind.[29]

Probably around this same time, Sumter arrived at Blackstock's Farm and began employing its defenses. Blackstock's Farm is described here as if approaching it from the south headed north, as Sumter would have approached it on his retreat and also Tarleton in his pursuit. William Blackstock had cleared his tobacco plantation and homestead atop a tall hill. Headed north, the road emerged from the surrounding forest to look up at the cleared hillside, fronted by a small stream that crossed the road at the bottom of the hill. "This water-course formed a half moon," recalled Hammond, "and the ridge corresponded with the shape of the branch."[30] About one hundred yards from the creek, with a climb of approximately fifty feet in elevation, was Blackstock's house, situated on a ridge of the hill. The house was on the west side of the road, or left looking north, and described by McCall as "long and narrow, and of two apartments of eighteen feet square, with eighteen feet space between, and a roof over the whole." Opposite the house, on the east side of the road, was a barn, described by McCall as a "small pole building"[31] and by British soldier Roderick McKenzie (who was not there, but would've crafted his account from soldiers who were), as a "large log barn."[32]

In front of the structures, along the crest of the ridge, ran a fence on both sides of the road. But this was no normal split rail fence, for Blackstocks had constructed it of cut logs, later described by Edward Lacey as "a strong log fence, one notched upon the other."[33] William Hill in his memoir described the fence as "a very large and strong fence not made with common rails but with small trees notched one on the other."[34] In both directions, east and west, the fences ran for several hundred feet, perhaps as far as a quarter mile on the east side of the road, extending all the way to the "low brush wood" near the bottom of the hill. On the west side, in the rear of Blackstock's house, was a second elevation, rising another thirty to forty feet.

Sumter employed these features to his advantage, posting men inside the house and barn and along the log fences. In the woods at the bottom of the hill were his pickets and advanced scouts. In McCall's account, Sumter made a hasty camp atop the high ridge behind the house, allowing his men to cook supper, while he and his officers discussed the disposition of their troops.[35] In one account, collected by the nineteenth-century historian Lyman Draper, Mary Blackstock, wife of William Blackstock (who was away from home at the time), approached Sumter and told him that she would not permit Sumter to fight around her house, although this prohibition was clearly ignored. In another account collected by Draper, Sumter put his horses behind the hill at his rear near the banks of the Tyger River. If true, this also mirrors the actions of Morgan at Cowpens, who placed his militia infantry horses in a rear position, close to the Broad River, in part to prevent the militia from mounting them in the heat of battle and riding away.

In this brief pause while Sumter set up camp, individual or small groups of militias emerged from the countryside to join him as he established his defenses. John Calhoun was one militia soldier who recalled reaching "the army commanded by Brannon [Thomas Brandon] & Sumpter and just joined the army at Blackstock's as the picket guard was fired on [by Tarleton's vedettes]."[36]

Atop the rise above the house, Sumter stationed his reserves, including Richard Winn. He also posted his own command from atop the hill, "high and steep and makes down to the road which passes at its base," as Winn recalled, giving Sumter a clear view overlooking the field of battle. By all accounts, he didn't have long to wait. For shortly after arranging his battle formation, his pickets started firing in the woods at the bottom of the hill, announcing the imminent arrival of the British and Bloody Ban. Tarleton and his mounted troops soon appeared in the clearing near the stream, perhaps pursuing the detachment of Taylor and Candler, which according to Hammond, "at that moment drove in with their wagons loaded with flour & c., passed our rear guard" and climbed the hill to safety. Similarly, Winn recalled, "Colo. Taylor with his party and wagons and the British horse all run in together, which made a great noise. . . . All this took place in a hurry and unexpected, we had only three or four minutes to make disposition of our troops."[37]

Staring up at Sumter's position atop the hill, Tarleton admitted Sumter "made a judicious disposition of his force. He posted the center of his troops in some houses and out-houses, composed of logs, and situated on the middle of an eminence; he extended his right along some rails, which where were flanked by an inaccessible mountain; and he distributed his left on a rugged piece of ground." Tarleton recalled "the whole position was visible, owing to the elevation of the ground, and this formidable appearance made Tarleton halt." Due to Sumter's superior position, Tarleton now decided to await his infantry and his cannon, so he "dismounted the 63rd to take post, and part of the cavalry to ease their horses."[38]

Tarleton recalled that, upon seeing his infantry dismount and take up a defensive position, Sumter ordered "a body of four hundred men to advance," on the east side of the road to attack the position of the 63rd. This body was the Georgia militia under Twiggs and Elijah Clarke, according to the recollections of McJunkin, although accounts differ here, with some of the Americans (Winn and McCall), suggesting that it was the British 63rd that commenced the battle with an attack on the west side of the road. Nevertheless, "a heavy fire and sharp conflict ensued," Tarleton recalled, "the 63rd charged with fixed bayonets." Tarleton would later report to Cornwallis that, "The enemy attack'd the 63rd and forced me to action before the cannon" and his infantry "cou'd be brought up."[39]

Whether attacked or attacking, Twiggs and Clarke's Georgians left their defenses to meet the 63rd but soon fell back to the safety of the log fence. The 63rd pursued, taking a heavy fire. "The ardour of the 63rd carried them too far," Tarleton admitted, "and exposed them to a considerable fire from the buildings and the mountain."[40] During this attack, Cornwallis's aide-de-camp, Lt. John Money, who had recently taken command of the 63rd from the wounded Wemyss, and according to Tarleton led the charge with "great gallantry," was mortally wounded.

Tarleton ordered part of his mounted Legion forward to support the 63rd. As they moved forward against the Patriot defenses, the main part of the battle commenced. From behind their defenses, the Patriots poured a heavy fire on the attacking British cavalry and infantry. "The riflemen, under cover of the hog-pens, and those behind the fence, received them with becoming firmness," recalled Hammond and fired "with extraordinary activity and spirit."[41]

Meanwhile, Col. Edward Lacey and a party of horsemen stationed on the high rise commenced a flanking operation through the woods on the west.

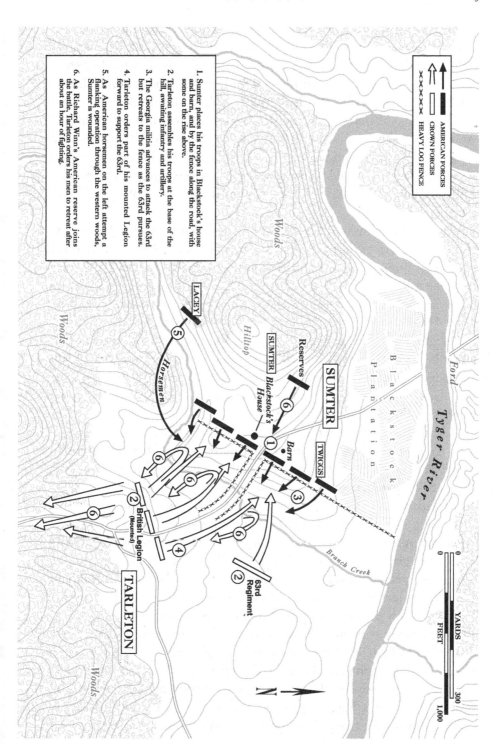

1. Sumter places his troops in Blackstock's house and barn, and by the fence along the road, with some on the rise above.

2. Tarleton assembles his troops at the base of the hill, awaiting infantry and artillery.

3. The Georgia militia advances to attack the 63rd but retreats to the fence as the 63rd pursues.

4. Tarleton orders part of his mounted Legion forward to support the 63rd.

5. As American horsemen on the left attempt a flanking operation through the western woods, Sumter is wounded.

6. As Richard Winn's American reserve joins the battle, Tarleton orders his men to retreat after about an hour of fighting.

AMERICAN FORCES
CROWN FORCES
HEAVY LOG FENCE

Woods

Woods

LACEY

Hilltop

Horsemen

SUMTER Blackstock's House

Reserves

SUMTER

Barn

TWIGGS

British Legion (Mounted)

63rd Regiment

TARLETON

Woods

Blackstock Plantation

Ford

Tyger River

Branch Creek

N

YARDS 300

FEET 1,000

Although Tarleton did not mention this flanking operation in his memoir, nor in his report of the battle to Cornwallis, American accounts do. "Sumter's right, extending along the ridge, advanced upon the flank of the British,"[42] recalled Hammond. During the midst of the heavy fighting in front of Blackstocks' fence, Lacey gained Tarleton's western flank and attacked.

"Tarleton retreated with his cavalry, formed and returned to the charge," wrote McCall, repulsing Lacey's attack. According to Winn, however, Lacey only returned to the cover of the woods, ordered his men to reform and reload their rifles, and then attacked again, "discharging in like manner" and continuing to harass Tarleton's western flank "and so off again," until the end of the battle.[43]

Around this point in the battle, while Lacey conducted his flanking attack, Sumter was seriously wounded with a buckshot blast. This occurred when he was returning by horse path to his command post atop the ridge from the thick woods where Lacey made his attack on Tarleton's western flank. Seeing a British soldier aiming at him at the last moment, Sumter twisted sideways, turning away from the fire to his right, and was hit by six buckshot pellets. Five of the pellets lodged in his chest, and the sixth hit under his right shoulder, chipped his spine as it passed through his body, and lodged under his left shoulder. At first, Sumter gave no sign of receiving the wound, but it was soon noticed by an aide named Robert McKelvey, who was riding with Sumter at the time.

"General—you are wounded!" McKelvey exclaimed.

"I am wounded," agreed Sumter. "Say nothing of it." His right arm too wounded to move, Sumter then asked another aide, Capt. Henry Hampton, to sheath his sword, then asked for assistance leading his horse off the field. As he departed, he passed command to Col. Twigg of Georgia.[44]

In the account by Robert D. Bass, Sumter was taken into Blackstock's home, where he was attended by his manservant slave, Soldier Tom, who was sent to get field surgeon Robert Brownfield. After removing Sumter's bloody coat, Brownfield began probing Sumter for the buckshot without anesthetic, which he successfully removed in a crude operation that Sumter could have only endured in great pain, if he was conscious at all.[45]

As Sumter was being escorted from the field, the fighting continued. According to Richard Winn, whose militia regiment was still stationed in reserve atop the high ridge, he received a report from Georgia major James Jackson that the men on the front line were giving way. "My men was all fresh, as they not being engaged, in a lone on top of the hill," Winn recalled. Forming his troops in a line, Winn ordered them "to jump up, set up the Indian hollo and run down the hill on the enemy and to fire as they run."[46]

Whether it was this final charge of Winn, or Lacey harassing his western flank, Tarleton had endured enough and ordered his men to fall back. In fighting that had lasted about an hour, his soldiers had been cut to pieces, and it was now growing dark. "Thick night came on and for want of infantry I could not pursue the blow," Tarleton reported to Cornwallis the next day.[47] The official American report on the action, filed by Col. Charles Myddelton on Sumter's behalf, listed ninety-two British dead and one hundred wounded left on the field. In contrast, the Americans had lost three killed and three wounded.[48]

Still pursued by Patriot troops, Tarleton and his troops withdrew through the gloaming until he met the rest of his infantry, "who were advancing to sustain" him and set up camp for the night about two miles away. By all accounts, it then began to rain.[49]

After taking possession of the battleground that evening, the Patriot army collected the British dead and tended to the wounded. According to McCall, as many of the wounded as "could be sheltered, were laid in the houses."[50] The wounded Sumter was placed on a makeshift litter, constructed of raw bull's hide attached to poles and slung between two horses, then ridden away from the battlefield under a heavy guard of his New Acquisition militia.

With their general wounded, and the threat of a reinforced Tarleton resuming the attack in the morning, the colonels of the Patriot army decided to disband. "It was thought expedient to retreat that night," recalled Joseph McJunkin. "The troops retreated slowly up the country," wrote McCall, "passing Broad river some distance, and dispersing in small parties to refresh themselves on such viands as they could find." Many of the Patriots undoubtedly returned to their nearby homes, while the Georgians headed westward. Before retreating across the river, the indefatigable Winn "caused a number of fires to be lighted up, as indications of an encampment."[51]

Whether or not Tarleton initiated the attack on the American position with the advance of the 63rd or was lured into it by the advance of the Georgia militia, he nevertheless displayed his trademark disposition at Blackstocks, ordering bold charges against American positions, his apparent strategy to use British discipline and might to overwhelm an inferior opponent. At Waxhaws, Biggin's Bridge, and Lenud's Ferry, the strategy had served him well, solidifying his reputation as one of England's boldest and most able young officers. But at Blackstocks, against a superior defensive position, manned by a larger force, be they militia or not, the strategy had failed. And at Cowpens, under similar conditions, it would fail again, with even more disastrous consequences for the British cause.

Nevertheless, when Tarleton returned to the battlefield the following morning, now reunited with his infantry and his cannon, he found it deserted, allowing him to claim the field of battle and declare victory according to the conventions of the time. A Pyrrhic one, no doubt, and aside from his aggrandized reports to Cornwallis, one he wasted little time trifling over, yet the technicalities allowed him to preserve, for the time being, his record of never being bested in battle in the South.

"My Lord," Tarleton began in his report to Cornwallis written the following day, "I yesterday cut Sumpter's rear guard to pieces on the Enoree. I pursued his trail with great rapidity and had an action on the ground last night with the cavalry and the 63rd only. Sumpter is defeated, his corps dipsersed, and himself dangerously wounded. The ground was difficult. Thick night came on and for want of more infantry I could not immediately pursue the blow."[52]

All of that was true enough, but it hardly conveyed the true outcome or spirit of the action. In his memoir, Tarleton conveyed the action even more obliquely. "The light troops made very great exertions to bring General Sumpter to action, and the hazard incurred by the cavalry and the 63rd, was compensated by the complete dispersion of the enemy," he wrote, before quickly moving on to other topics.[53]

At first, Cornwallis believed his young protégé's deception, or pretended to believe it. "I have no doubt but your victory will be attended with good consequences to our affairs as it is with honor and credit to yourself," Cornwallis replied on November 23, with details of the battle still rather vague at British headquarters.[54] It had been a disastrous fall, and Cornwallis needed some good news to report to Clinton, true or not. "It is not easy for Lt. Colonel Tarleton to add to the reputation he has acquired in this province," he wrote to Clinton in his report of December 3, "but defeating 1,000 men, posted on very strong ground and occupying log houses . . . is a proof of that spirit and talents which must render the most essential services of the country."[55]

Desperate for news of a British success in the South, after the debacle at Charlotte, Cornwallis's fictitious account of a British victory at Blackstock's was received enthusiastically. Tarleton, wrote British lieutenant Roderick Mackenzie, was "for some time hailed as victor, from Wynnesborough to Camden, from Camden to Charlestown, from Charlestown to New

York, and from thence to London. At Liverpool, bonfires are lighted up in honour of their favourite hero."[56]

Tarleton grossly overestimated American losses, reporting "120 kill'd wounded and prisoners of the rebel army," along with the deaths of two of the Patriot colonels, including the notorious Elijah Clarke, an unsubstantiated fiction Cornwallis was only too happy to pass along to Clinton in his report of December 3.[57] "But, my Lord, I have lost men," Tarleton admitted to Cornwallis, knowing he could not long hide his own casualties. In his report, he admitted "50 killed and wounded" along with three officers killed, not including Cornwallis's aide, John Money, who would die later from his wounds, along with "every officer's horse, my own included, kill'd or wounded."[58]

Even if this casualty report was far below the American estimate of ninety-two British killed and one hundred wounded, they were not figures Tarleton could long hide, though Cornwallis seemed sanguine enough in accepting them, perhaps solaced by reports of the wounded Sumter, who had emerged as an archnemesis. Eventually, a truer accounting of the British loss emerged. "Although Tarleton was repulsed at Blackstock's Hill, the immediate effects of the action were nearly the same as those of a victory," wrote Loyalist historian Charles Stedman, somewhat disingenuously, in his history of the engagement.[59]

A far harsher critic was Roderick Mackenzie, a British lieutenant in the 71st regiment who would soon be wounded at Cowpens while serving under Tarleton's command. Following the war, Mackenzie was so incensed by what he considered to be the gross, self-serving exaggerations of Tarleton's memoir, he published his own rebuttal, titled *Strictures on Lt. Col. Tarleton's History of the Campaigns of 1780 and 1781*. Though the bulk of the book is devoted to Tarleton's mistakes at Cowpens, Mackenzie did not spare Tarleton for his false reporting of Blackstocks. "With some men of inventive genius, the sallies of imagination are so exuberant, as only to require frequent repetition to obtrude them on the mind for truths," he complained caustically. However, he noted, "Lieutenant Colonel Tarleton, without waiting for the rest of his detachment, made a precipitate attack . . . upon the enemy" up a "nearly perpendicular" hill. "British valour was conspicuous in this action," he admitted. "But no valour could surmount the obstacles and disadvantages that here stood in its way. . . . The real truth is, that the Americans being well sheltered, sustained very inconsiderable loss in the attack," and the American colonels Tarleton reported killing, "must certainly have been imaginary beings . . . created merely to grace the triumph of a victory, which the British army in Carolina were led to celebrate, admidst the contempt and derision of the inhabitants, who had much better information."[60]

But one truth in the midst of Tarleton's fictions about Blackstocks was the severity of Sumter's wounds. According to Tarleton's report to Cornwallis, "three young men who were of Ferguson's corps . . . promis'd to fix Sumpter immediately," a veiled reference to yet another assassination attempt. As the wounded Sumter was reportedly under a heavy guard, such a scheme seems unlikely, although Tarleton "promis'd them for the deed 50 guineas each in case he falls into my hands." Sumter biographer Anne Gregorie King reported Tarleton himself pursued the wounded Sumter for three days, before turning back at Grindal Shoals on the Pacolet River, though this account seems unlikely, as the distance described was less than a day's ride for the hard-charging Tarleton.[61]

Eager to move on from the debacle in his memoir, Tarleton wastes little time in describing the aftermath, briefly describing his efforts to "remain some time in that quarter of South Carolina" to give protection to Ninety Six before soon returning toward the "neighbourhood of Broad river,"[62] where he had access to the British magazine at Brierly's Ferry and more direct communication with Winnsboro and Charleston.

But this account is not quite accurate either, for after the battle Tarleton did move up the Tyger River, probably pursuing Sumter either himself or with his scouts for one day before turning his ire on the local population. To Cornwallis on November 24, from somewhere upstream of Blackstock's on the Tyger River, Tarleton reported taking thirteen prisoners the previous day. Most likely these were not Patriot militia from Blackstocks, but random settlers the exasperated Tarleton came upon in his pursuit and took prisoner to appease his own wrath. Winn reported that as Tarleton patrolled the countryside in the aftermath of the battle, he hung "Esq'r John Johnston, a respectable citizen with a large family. What was his crime, I know not. . . . He took every old man and stout boy he could find . . . and made them prisoner's at Blackstock's."[63]

A day later, November 25, Tarleton wrote Cornwallis that "Sumter is now reported dead." The countryside was swirling with rumors, and even Cornwallis at Winnsboro received a false report of Sumter's imminent death. "I saw two North Carolina men who met some of Sumpters fugitives, and who learned from them that he was speechless, and certainly past all hopes," Cornwallis wrote optimistically to Balfour on November 25. To Tarleton, Cornwallis confessed, "I shall be very glad to hear that Sumpter is in a condition to give us no farther trouble. He certainly has been our greatest plague in this country."[64]

This was all wishful thinking, for Sumter was now safe at the home of Col. Samuel Watson in the New Acquisition District, about twenty miles from Charlotte, down but certainly not out. The same day Tarleton and Cornwallis were wishing him dead he was scheming attack in a letter to Gen. Gates, now camped at Charlotte. "I am exceedingly happy to find that you have moved forward to with the Continental army, as Tarleton's Legion, 71, 63 and some light companies were sent to destroy my command," Sumter wrote Gates on November 25. He urged Gates to attack Cornwallis at Winnsboro, as Cornwallis "must, therefore, be in a weak situation and easily taken, the advantage of an opportunity which you no doubt sir, would wish to avail yourself of," although he apologized for "being so laconic" due to his wound. "I am without medicine or necessaries of any kind, and feel the want of them much."[65]

It was an attack that would never come . . . at least not from Gates, who was content to await Nathanael Greene's arrival, relieving him of his command. Sumter's wounds were severe enough to incapacitate him for the next two months, and it would be another two months before the Gamecock was ready to again take the offensive in an ill-fated campaign known as "Sumter's Rounds." But the irrepressible Sumter had delivered the British yet another serious blow, making Cornwallis more eager than ever to leave the disaffected populace of the South Carolina Backcountry behind him. While Cornwallis turned his focus toward yet another iteration of his plans for a North Carolina campaign, the Gamecock recuperated and schemed.

TWENTY

The DUEL

I F CHARLES CORNWALLIS is occasionally typecast as the courageous but aloof British lord, the embodiment of the British officer as British aristocrat, and Tarleton the dashing but cruel dragoon, then Maj. Robert McLeroth represents a different British army stereotype—a flawed but honorable officer, the reluctant knight errant in an allegory of character and honor.

He was born in 1738 in Argyll, Scotland, and on January 1, 1766, joined the 64th Regiment as a captain at the relatively old age of twenty-eight, suggesting both a family of means and a directionless youth. He sailed with his regiment to North America in 1768 and was promoted to major on August 28, 1776, commanding the 64th for most of the American Revolution.[1]

After participating in the New York campaign, McLeroth was wounded at Brandywine, where the 64th was in the thick of the fighting and received forty-seven casualties out of a regiment of 420, the highest British casualty rate in the battle.[2] He sailed south with Cornwallis, Clinton, and Tarleton during the winter of 1780 and had spent most of the South Carolina campaign serving garrison duty in Charleston.

Although little biographical information is available on McLeroth, he appears to have had a reputation as a mediocre, if not incompetent, officer, at least in the opinion of Nesbit Balfour, his commander at Charleston. Nevertheless, with the Pee Dee yet again erupting in revolt, Cornwallis ordered Balfour to send a detachment to Kingstree, and with personnel tight in Charleston, McLeroth was most conveniently available for the job. "I must in justice say that he is by no means to be trusted to act for himself," wrote Balfour of the need to detach McLeroth to Kingstree. "With any other good man I should be easy in undertaking such a movement. With *him* [italics original] I am uneasy, I own, till it is over and he returns."[3]

Also a strident critic of Patrick Ferguson, another Scots misfit in the British army, Balfour's criticisms may be linked to the rivalry between Cornwallis and Clinton, for Ferguson was deemed a "Clinton" man, and one wonders if McLeroth suffered the same reputation among Cornwallis and his allies. Whatever the case, the influence of Balfour's aspersions appear reflected in a Cornwallis letter to Rawdon stating, "You will have to keep a constant eye on McLeroth, who by his letters requires much looking after. A blow to any regiment cuts deep."[4] More than any other British officer, perhaps, Rawdon had suffered the consequences of Cornwallis's failure to support Ferguson at Kings Mountain. It was Rawdon who had been forced to command the disastrous British retreat from Charlotte to Winnsboro while Cornwallis suffered through the debilitating case of malaria that not coincidentally happened to coincide with his acute depression over Ferguson's defeat. Perhaps hoping to avoid a similar catastrophe, Rawdon was anxious to counteract the negative influence of Balfour's disdain. "Balfour and McLeroth never liked one another," Rawdon felt forced to explain to Cornwallis.[5]

On or around November 15, McLeroth departed Charleston for Kingstree, marching with an assorted detachment that included two hundred men of the 64th along with Hessians, British prison guards, and Loyalist troops, 275 men in all, supported by two 3-pounder field pieces. By November 20, McLeroth was at Kingstree, where news of his arrival soon reached Marion. But Marion reacted to the news with caution, in part because he had recently intercepted a letter from Rawdon explaining that the New York Volunteers had also been detached from Camden to raid Patriot farms in the Pee Dee and drive off their stock.[6]

He moved down the Pee Dee to Britton's Ferry, but with little news from the Continental army, struggled to maintain his regiment. "Many of my people has Left me & gone over to the Enemy, for they think we have no Army coming on, & have been Deceived. As we hear nothing from you a Great while, I hope to have a line from you in what manner to Act, & some Assruance to the people of Support," Marion complained to Gates in a letter dated November 21, 1780.[7]

Indeed, it was only a day before Marion composed this letter that Rawdon reported to Cornwallis the defection of a Capt. William Richbourg and one hundred men who had recently served with Marion. Richbourg, Rawdon wrote Cornwallis, promised "the best information of Marion's strength, views, and correspondence," in exchange for pardons. Momentarily sanguine, Rawdon believed the betrayal "may produce further defections from the enemy."[8]

With no authority to hold his volunteer militia in camp, and little to either arm or feed them, Marion's frustrations focused up the chain of command, zeroing in on Harrington. In the same letter Marion wrote to Gates complaining about the torpor of the Continental army, he also noted, "I have written to General Harrington to spare me his horse to endeavour to remove the post at King's tree or the Enemy will havé the Intire command of the Country . . . but from what I know of the General I do not expect he will part with them. I beg leave to mention to you that General Harrington has not done any service with the troops he commands, while I have been obliged to act with so few as not to have it in my power to do any thing Effectual, for want of Ammunition & men."[9]

Clearly, Marion's inaction was borne out of these complaints, though the anticipation of a Marion attack soon had McLeroth rethinking his position at Kingstree. And when Loyalist militia failed to muster there as he had anticipated, he moved first to Murray's Ferry on the Santee, then up to Great Savannah, camping near the home of Thomas Sumter. But McLeroth's movements through the Pee Dee and Santee regions displayed none of the burning and looting marked by the previous expeditions of Wemyss and Tarleton. "Major McLeroth was cut from a different bolt of cloth from Tarleton or Wemyss," observes Marion biographer Hugh Rankin. "He took no delight in seeing a home go up in flames. In fact, it might be said that he was something of an anachronism, for he possessed none of that streak of brutality that seemed to characterize the professional soldier of the eighteenth century."[10] Indeed, it was probably this anachronistic quality of mercy, a shared trait with Ferguson, at least in Ferguson's southern campaign, for which he probably enjoyed the disdain of Balfour and the suspicions of Cornwallis and Rawdon. Nevertheless, at Great Savannah, he was finally reinforced with about 125 Loyalist militia, led by the indomitable James Cassells. A Scottish indigo planter on the Waccamaw River, Cassells recently had been appointed a colonel of Loyalist militia and briefly was able to keep Patriot raiding on the Santee subdued.[11]

Marion, meanwhile, was looking for a new base from which to refit and re-organize, and it was at this time he was introduced to his famous hideout on Snow's Island, in the far southeastern corner of present-day Florence County.

Named for William Snow, an early settler of the Williamsburg District, Snow's Island was a low ridge five miles long and two miles wide, bordered on the east by the Pee Dee River and the north by Lynches River, and to the south and west by a network of creeks and swamp. According to Rankin, it was brothers Samuel and Britton Jenkins who told Marion of the place, right around the time he wrote his disconsolate letter to Gates on November 21, though it seems likely he would have known of it from others, if he wasn't already familiar with it himself.

"This island became henceforth the most constant place of his [Marion's] encampment; a secure retreat," observed William Dobein James, who described it as "high river swamp, and large, of itself affording much provision and livestock, as did all the Pedee river swamp at that day. In places there were open cultivated lands on the island; but it was much covered by thick woods and cane brakes."[12]

The cultivated fields James refers to belonged to the island's sole settler, a man named William Goddard, who had built his cabin on the highest point near the middle of the island, where he had cleared a small area for crops. Rankin writes that Marion's camp was in the forest and fields near Goddard's home, where the men pitched crude brush and log shelters to shield them from the elements. Goddard's barn was fortified as a prison, and a redoubt was eventually constructed at the base of a bluff guarding the Pee Dee River approach to the island.[13] In *The Patriot*, Marion's camp is depicted at the very edge of the swamp, a curious setting of campfire and candelabra, set against a murky backdrop of swamp cypress. The cypress were real, no doubt, along with a thick forest of gum, oak, and pine covering the island and nearby land, providing along with the almost impenetrable network of creeks and swamps an excellent natural defense, though the rest of the setting is pure Hollywood fantasy.

At Snow's Island, "reinforcements were now coming in to him [Marion] daily," writes James, and as usual, Marion's spirits rose along with the number of his troops. James's narrative is rich in detail from this period, suggesting an eyewitness account. To secure his position at Snow's Island, James wrote,

Marion secured "what boats he wanted; and burnt those more remote. To prevent the approach of an enemy, he fell upon a plan of insulating as much as possible the country under his command. For this purpose, he broke down bridges, and felled trees across causeways and difficult passes."

Ever cautious, the Swamp Fox ordered a steady stream of scouting parties into the surrounding countryside, securing horses, boats, and provisions, all the while keeping a close eye on British and Loyalist activity. And though he cautioned his men against violence, knowing the negative propaganda effect of terror and looting, away from camp his men found it difficult to stifle the urge for vengeance. "Henceforth, there commenced such a bloody warfare between the whigs and tories, as is seldom recorded in the annals of even civil commotion," observes James, who reported the capture of a Patriot patrol led by Lt. Robert Gordon by a larger party of Tories led by a Capt. Butler. "Gordon capitulated on a promise of quarters; but no sooner had his party grounded their arms, than they were all put to death . . . seldom were prisoners made on either side, and if made, that was no security for their lives; for they were sure to be put to death, either openly or privately, by a few infuriated men, who could be subjected to no subordination."[14]

The atrocities escalated on both sides. Around this time Rawdon reported the assassination of two Loyalist brothers, sick in bed with smallpox, by a "party of rebels." Though the perpetrators of this particular crime probably were not Marion's men, the incident illustrates the vicious nature of South Carolina's revolution. In another incident described by Rawdon, Patriot marauders stripped a Loyalist household of "every thing that could be carried off. Such articles as could not be taken away were destroyed" leaving the woman of the house "standing in her shift, even her stockings and shoes have been pulled off her, and her four children stripped stark naked. These are the enemies who talk of laws and usages of war."[15]

Rumors now swirled through the Pee Dee region that the Loyalist militia commander John Tynes had escaped capture at Harrington's base at Cheraw and was establishing a Loyalist redoubt at Fort Upton, near today's Shaw Air Force Base. Marion sent a patrol under Horry to reconnoiter Tynes's new position, while he moved to Indian Town, about halfway between Kingstree and modern-day Conway, South Carolina.[16]

From Horry's patrol comes an amusing anecdote described in the narrative of Horry and Weems. As Horry and his patrol scouted for Tynes, they came across a tavern owned by a well-known Loyalist, and while Horry interrogated the tavern keeper, Horry's men thoroughly investigated his apple brandy. Back on patrol, despite his men's denials, Horry realized what happened after watching his guide "a jolter-headed fellow," possessed of a great belly, lurching back and forth in his saddle until he finally tumbled to the ground. Back at camp, Horry ruefully confessed the incident to Marion, who he luckily caught in a good mood. "Pray keep a careful eye on the apple water next time,"[17] Marion quipped, agreeing with Horry that it would have been impossible to continue the patrol.

And miraculously, Horry's drunken expedition was an unintentional success. The racket they made in their drunken revelry raised an alarm among the Loyalists of Black River, who spread the false news to Tynes at Fort Upton that General Harrington and his entire command were marching against the post. Most of Tynes men deserted him upon hearing the rumor, forcing Tynes to retreat to Camden, where he submitted his resignation to Rawdon in shame. "Tynes arrived here this morning exceedingly frightened," Rawdon reported to Cornwallis on December 8, 1780. "His militia, upon some report of Harrington's approach, excepting twenty, deserted his new fort. . . . He says that he is convinced he can do nothing with the militia and on that account begged leave to resign his command. I accepted his resignation. That line of interest has failed us; we must not try another."[18]

Meanwhile, Balfour had ordered a detachment under Capt. John Kerr to escort a company of 150 new recruits from the 7th Regiment to Nelson's Ferry. There they would be transferred to McLeroth, who would take them to the High Hills of the Santee, where they would in turn be met by a mounted detachment that would finish their escort to Camden. But Balfour was worried about rebel activity in the "swamp beyond Nelson's" and Cornwallis didn't want the transfer to occur until "Mr. Marion is disposed of."[19]

"Mr. Marion" had already learned of the recruit transfer from his spies, and quickly mustered his battalion for one of his signature surprise attacks. Given the intrigue and violence swirling through the Pee Dee region in this time, we can imagine these plans were implemented in secret, as described memorably by James in this general account of Marion's stratagems on the move:

His plans were laid, and his movements conducted, with the most uncommon secrecy. After making a movement, his most confidential officers and men have had to search for him for days together, perhaps without finding him. . . . At the instance of the secrecy with which Gen. Marion's plans were always adopted and

conducted, the following may be regarded as a specimen of his progress throughout. His men have been several times unexpectedly led out upon long expeditions,
without preparations . . . after some time were in the habit of watching Marion's
cook, and if they saw him unusually busied in preparing any of the frugal fare in
use, they prepared accordingly.[20]

With several hundred presumably hungry men, including Maj. John
James, John Van der Horst, and Hugh Horry, Marion raced across the
Williamsburg District, overtaking McLeroth on the Santee Road to Camden, about twenty miles north of Nelson's Ferry just above Halfway Swamp,
a few miles south of present-day Sumter, South Carolina. "A party of the
Enemy under Major McLeroth with 200 Infantry and 2 field pieces went
up to the High Hills of Santee, with which I skirmaged," Marion would
later report to Gen. Nathanael Greene.[21]

And perhaps it *was* little more than a skirmish. In his report to Greene,
Marion said little more about the incident, aside from stating that the
British suffered six casualties, including a "Captn Kelley of the 64th Regiment."[22] But in his biography of Marion, William Dobein James recounts
a more fantastical encounter. The tale, presented hereafter, is too good to
ignore, though it must be read skeptically.

According to James, as Marion's mounted raiders approached McLeroth's
marching column, they cut off two pickets in McLeroth's rear, wounding or
killing the men, then circled around and attacked McLeroth's column from
the flank and front. Without cavalry, McLeroth's men retreated slowly in
constant skirmish with Marion's troops, until they were able to gain cover
in a field belonging to a nearby farmer, their front defended by a sturdy fence
and their rear defended by the surrounding swamp and forest.

While Marion established his own defenses on the west side of the road,
James wrote, McLeroth was able to send a messenger for help. Riding up
the road, the messenger eventually encountered John Coffin and 140
mounted dragoons, the detachment sent from Camden to relieve McLeroth
of the recruits from the 7th Regiment. However, rather than race to
McLeroth's assistance, Coffin and his men established their own defensive
position at Swift Creek. Coffin later claimed he had received intelligence
that he also was about to be attacked and surmised that since McLeroth
had been able dispatch a messenger, his position was strong enough to defend against Marion without reinforcement.[23]

Still awaiting reinforcements, and plying for time or strategic advantage,
McLeroth sent Marion a flag, reproaching him for shooting the pickets,

"contrary, as he alleged to all the laws of civilized warfare." Then the messenger issued a challenge from McLeroth "defying him to a combat in the open field."

Always sensitive to matters of military decorum and honor, Marion was reportedly outraged at McLeroth's accusations. According to James, Marion replied "that the practice of the British in burning the house of all who would not submit . . . was more indefensible than that of shooting pickets," and "that as long as they persisted in one, he would persevere in the other."[24] Undoubtedly, Marion realized McLeroth's challenge of combat in an open field gave his trained British soldiers an advantage over Marion's volunteer militia, but with his temper up, and his honor insulted, Marion then made an unusual counterproposal, at least according to James's account.

Instead of a combat between the two regiments, Marion supposedly proposed a combat between twenty picked men on each side, essentially a duel en masse. "The offer was accepted" by McLeroth, James writes, "and a place pitched upon to the south of an oak tree."

To lead his "team," Marion appointed Major John Vanderhorst, whom James describes as a "supernumerary officer." According to James, after Vanderhorst assembled his twenty hand-picked men, Marion addressed them with the following speech: "My brave soldiers! You are twenty men picked this day out of my whole brigade. I know you all, and have often witnessed your bravery. In the name of your country, I call upon you once more to show it. . . . Fight like men, fight as you have always done, and you are sure of the victory."

Vanderhorst and his twenty now squared off against their British opposition, but as the two sides approached within one hundred yards of one another, the British retreated to their defenses, apparently having falsely agreed to Marion's terms only as a ruse to gain more time for Coffin's reinforcements to arrive. The two sides then retreated to their previous positions, and in the night, McLeroth managed to slip away from Marion's grasp by leaving his fires burning and abandoning his heavy baggage.

Upon learning of the British escape, Marion ordered Col. Hugh Horry with a party of three hundred to pursue McLeroth. Despite some rearguard skirmishing, Horry's party could not get an advantage on McLeroth, until Horry sent a small detachment under command of John James to race ahead of McLeroth's column. James and his men managed to pass McLeroth's flank and take position in a farmhouse owned by a family named Singleton that commanded a "narrow defile on the road" just before McLeroth and his men reached that point. James and his men took position in the windows and fired one round, until they realized everyone in the house was afflicted with smallpox. Just as quickly they ran out of the house and raced away, no doubt bewildering McLeroth and his soldiers, who were soon afterward finally reinforced by Coffin and his dragoons as they retreated to Camden.[25]

Of course, given the unusual, even fantastical, nature of the "Duel" at Halfway Swamp described by James, it is reasonable to question whether it occurred at all. Although Marion biographers such as Hugh Rankin, writing in the 1970s, and even John Oller in his more recent Marion biography faithfully recount elements of James's account, as has been done to some degree here, the editors of Nathanael Greene's papers distinctly discount it, writing, "According to one later and apparently exaggerated account, which some historians have accepted as true, McLeroth employed several imaginative ruses to escape," although, "Marion said nothing about the ruses."[26] They observe that in his account of the action to Cornwallis on December 15, Rawdon reported only that Marion had been "reconnoitiring" McLeroth and that there was some "loose firing" at McLeroth's "outposts."[27]

Still, Rawdon's account doesn't quite add up, either, for most accounts agree Marion outnumbered McLeroth by nearly two to one (Marion's force is estimated at five hundred in this action, while McLeroth was estimated to have approximately 270 men),[28] and it would be unlike Marion to pass on such a numerical advantage unless perhaps McLeroth's defensive position was markedly superior to his own offensive one, or that Marion thought it inadvisable to engage McLeroth's British regulars in anything other than a surprise ambush.

What is not open for debate is the disgust of Rawdon, who seems to have finally joined Balfour and Cornwallis in their dismal opinion of McLeroth. "I began to be uneasy at not hearing from McLeroth, when to my great surprise I saw him enter the room," Rawdon reported to Cornwallis on December 16. But his surprise quickly turned to dismay upon hearing McLeroth and Coffin's report of the action at Halfway Swamp. "Coffin joined McLeroth . . . but no pursuit of the enemy was undertaken in consequence of this junction," Rawdon admitted to Cornwallis, his arrogant disbelief that these two trained British officers could manage so little against a band of Patriot rabble nearly dripping off the page. "McLeroth seems to think that there would have been no chance of getting up to them." Two days later, Rawdon was eager to approve McLeroth's return to Charleston. "I must immediately dislodge Marion, but as McLeroth has not quite enterprize enough, I shall let him go to Charleston (as he wishes)."[29]

Balfour didn't necessarily want him back, but McLeroth remained in command of the 64th in South Carolina until April or May 1781, when he received news of a promotion to lieutenant colonel of the 57th Regiment stationed in New York. A year later, he sold his commission and returned to England.[30]

Even in retreat, McLeroth continued to treat the people of the Pee Dee humanely, not only leaving behind his own surgeon to attend to those from both sides who had been wounded in the skirmishing with Marion, but also paying the tavern keeper with whom the wounded were lodged to ensure that subsisting the injured would not bring him financial hardship.[31] Ironically, McLeroth's compassionate approach to campaigning elevated his reputation in the South Carolina countryside, even as it was crumbling within the British army officer corps. "The character of Major McLeroth has been constantly represented by the inhabitants of this state, among whom he passed, as the most humane of all the officers of the British army. . . . It has been currently reported that he carried his dislike to house burning so far, that he neglected to carry into effect the orders of his commander in chief on that point to such an extent, as to gain his ill will and that of many other officers," writes James.[32]

Historian Stephen Conway suggests the humane approach of McLeroth and a few other British officers suggests that a policy of conciliation to the American countryside might have ultimately proven more successful in the American Revolution than the one of punishment adopted by Tarleton, Wemyss, and others. "Taking South Carolina as an illustration, the actions of Tarleton and Wemyss can be said to have overshadowed the efforts of McLeroth, who was made to appear as an admirable exception rather than an example of British moderation and leniency," Conway writes.[33]

Nevertheless, McLeroth's failure to pacify Marion, coupled with the abrupt resignation of Tynes and the ineffectual conduct of Coffin's newly raised dragoon regiment, left Marion once more in control of the Santee Road from Nelson's Ferry to Camden, forcing British supply trains and reinforcements to take the longer, more circuitous route from Monck's Ferry to Friday's Ferry on the Congaree River, just south of modern-day Columbia, South Carolina. From the British perspective, the timing was inauspicious, for Gen. Alexander Leslie had just arrived in Charleston with 2,500 troops, with 1,500 of those designated to travel upcountry to reinforce Cornwallis for his planned invasion of North Carolina, leaving Rawdon at

Camden to declare ruefully, "I must drive Marion out of that country but I cannot yet say what steps I shall take to effect it."[34]

In the meantime, Balfour suspended boat traffic on the Santee to Nelson's Ferry, but not before one British boat traveling downriver arrived there on December 14 and was promptly relieved of its cargo then burned by Marion's men. On the south side of the river, the British maintained an outpost manned by eighty Hessians, but Marion's men constantly harassed the work party of slaves the Hessians sent out to mend a nearby causeway. Finally, the British were able to chase Marion away from Nelson's with a combined force of 150 troops sent from Charleston and the British 64th, now under the command of Maj. John Campbell, forcing the uber cautious Marion to retreat to Black River. To Nathanael Greene, however, who had now relieved Gates of command in the American South, he promised to keep these reinforcements "close to their post and prevent them from forage and provisions," though as always, he longed for Continental reinforcement and supply. "If I had a few Continental troops I should be able to do much more than I am at present by our militia, who act with Diffidence. One hundred woud be Sufficient for our purpose."[35]

Unlike Gates, Greene would heed Marion's call, sending him not only reinforcements, but also Henry Lee, one of his most capable officers, forming perhaps the most talented and successful tag team of partisan officers in American history. But these reinforcements were still weeks away, and for the time being, Marion would have to plot and scheme from his swampy hideouts while the British once more regained control of the Santee and continued preparations for their second attempt at a North Carolina invasion.

TWENTY-ONE

BRIGADIER MARION

W HILE MARION CONTINUED TO DISRUPT British plans for the Pee Dee, and Sumter convalesced from the serious wound he received at Blackstocks, the Continental army's Southern Department was undergoing a transformational change in the command transition from Horatio Gates to Gen. Nathanael Greene.

Greene had been George Washington's choice for the job since the fall of Charleston. But Greene had ruffled feathers in Congress during the more tumultuous moments of his stint as quartermaster general, and the available Gates, still recognized by many in Congress as the "Hero of Saratoga," if not a viable alternative to Washington as commander in chief to those that Washington had also irked, was deemed the more prudent choice. It would be unfair to Gates to claim his failures at Camden had proven the backing of his congressional allies wrong. Fate surely also played a role. Nevertheless, his defeat at Camden, and perhaps more devastatingly, his flight to Hillsborough afterward, had left his reputation in ruins.

Of course, the American forces in the Carolinas had rebounded quite nicely despite Gates's humiliation, with a resounding victory at Kings Mountain that forced Cornwallis to flee Charlotte, along with the more equivocal victory of Sumter over Tarleton at Blackstocks. Marion was raising havoc in the Pee Dee, with considerable propaganda effects. And Gates was not completely without influence or effect in these matters, for he continued to oversee the Southern Department's operations throughout the fall, focusing primarily on administrative matters while allowing his junior officers, men such as Daniel Morgan and William Smallwood, along with Marion and Sumter, to successfully manage operations in the field.

But perhaps it is fair to say the Camden debacle deprived Gates of his gumption, especially after Congress passed a resolution on October 6 suspending Gates from command until a court of inquiry could be held concerning his conduct at Camden, and in the same motion, delegating the choice of Gates's successor to Washington, who instantly chose his protégé, Greene. In essence, this made Gates not only a lame duck commander until Greene could make his way south, which would take another few weeks, but also placed the looming indignity of a military court of inquiry over his head.[1]

Which isn't to say Gate's Continental army had completely lost its mojo. On October 21, Smallwood, Morgan, and William Washington's cavalry, along with North Carolina militia, established their camp on Edwards Branch south of Charlotte called Camp New Providence. This forward position threatened Rawdon at Camden and held control of the Great Wagon Road, should the British contemplate another incursion up it into central North Carolina, as Cornwallis was most certainly doing.

On November 2, Col. Otho Holland Williams marched south from Hillsboro under the command of about seven hundred Maryland, Delaware, and Virginia Continentals to join Smallwood and Morgan at Charlotte. A few days later Gates followed with 130 Continental Cavalry, soon to be joined by three hundred Virginia militia under the command of Gen. Edward Stevens. On November 20, this entire entourage—Gates, Williams, and about 1,100 men total—arrived at Charlotte, bringing the combined American forces there to 2,600.[2]

This was more than enough to threaten British operations in South Carolina, if not take another crack at Camden, but right around this time tragedy struck Gates again, when he learned of the death of his only son,

Robert, age twenty-two. The young man had actually died on October 4, but Gates's army colleagues kept the news as long as they could, worried about the effect it would have on him. Gates's biographer, Paul David Nelson, suggests the news acted as a final blow. "Gates was now more than willing to give up the command and retire to the comforts of his wife and farm," he writes.[3] But in the meantime, his correspondence slackened, leaving field officers like Marion desperate for news and reinforcement from Continental army command.

Even among critics such as Otho Holland Williams, there was regret, even sadness, regarding Gates's fate, perhaps borne from the knowledge such calamity is so often the product of fate in war, a fate that could befall them just as easily as it had Gates. So, when Gates called a council of officers on November 25, condemning "The want of Provisions and Forage in this camp—the advanced Season of the Year . . . the increasing Sickness and unwholesome Situation of the Camp" the body agreed to suspend further operations until the arrival of Greene and set up winter camp around Charlotte. "Light troops were to keep the field," wrote Otho Holland Williams of this decision, "and act as an advanced guard." The meeting's notes suggest the decision was unanimous, save for Smallwood, "who was for the Army's moving to the Waxhaws," though both William R. Davie and North Carolina militia general William L. Davidson were also disappointed in the decision. Davidson proposed a strategy remarkably similar to the one Greene would later adopt, leading to Daniel Morgan's victory at Cowpens. Davidson's plan was to send Morgan with his light troops westward to threaten Ninety Six, while the remainder of the army moved down to the Waxhaws, "which will oblige the Enemy to divide (which will put them in our power) or vacate their present Posts & collect to one point in which case we can command the Country and cut off their supplies." Although Greene's correspondence suggests he was already contemplating a similar scheme, much of Davidson's plan was so similar to the one Greene ultimately adopted that some historical sources suggest it was Greene's sole inspiration. At this time Davie was back in Salisbury, attempting another enlistment for his company of mounted rangers, as the previous enlistment had recently expired, and also wanted to keep up the fight.[4]

Sympathy for the grieving Gates, however, did not supplant a natural curiosity among those who witnessed the transfer of power between Gates and Greene on December 3, 1780. The antagonism between Gates and Washington was well-known in the American camp, as was Greene's devout allegiance to the commander in chief. Officers and enlisted in camp could hardly be criticized for idle speculation about some hint of conflict between the two men, when Greene finally arrived to relieve Gates of his command. The occasion, however, was addressed with dignity and respect from both sides, as memorably recounted by Otho Holland Williams:

A manly resignation marked the conduct of General Gates on the arrival of his successor, whom he received at head quarters with that liberal and gentlemanly air which was habitual to him. General Greene observed a plain, candid, respectful manner, neither betraying compassion or the want of it. . . . In short, the officers who were present had an elegant lesson of propriety exhibited on a most delicate and intervening occasion.[5]

Nevertheless, with Gates ignominiously riding off into the sunset, those same officers soon found their lot much improved under the command of their new general. After spending the first night with Greene assessing all conditions of the theater, Thomas Polk remarked, "By the following morning Greene better understood the resources of the country than Gates had during the whole period of his command."[6]

Even more powerful than understanding was prophecy. On December 1, Daniel Morgan and his light troops, patrolling near Camden, had taken a Loyalist outpost under the command of Loyalist officer Henry Rugeley in a ruse de guerre known as the "Quaker guns." Located about twelve miles north of Camden, guarding the wagon road, the outpost was a fortified mill on Rugeley's property. Finding the position too well defended to attack, Continental cavalry officer William Washington ordered his troops to disguise the trunk of an old pine tree as a field piece to falsely threaten Rugeley and his men. That the ruse worked to perfection had the British suspecting Rugeley of betrayal. But to the American camp at Charlotte, who learned of Morgan's "victory" at Rugeley's Mill on December 2, the same day Greene arrived in camp, the incident had the appearance of omen.

"Soldiers, like sailors, have always a little superstition about them," wrote Otho Holland Williams. "Although neither General Gates nor General Greene could be considered as having any agency in this little successful affair, it was regarded by some, and even mentioned, as a presage of the future good fortune which the army would derive from the genius of the latter."[7]

Count Francis Marion among the Continental officers who felt his lot improved under Greene's command. By December 4, Greene had met with John Melton, Marion's courier to the Continental army headquarters, learning about Marion's operations, including his need for supplies and ammu-

nition. That day Greene wrote to Marion, assuring him of his importance
to American strategy. "I have not had the Honor of your Acquaintance but
am no Stranger to your character and merit," wrote Greene. "Your Services
in the lower Part of South Carolina in aiding the Forces and preventing
the Enemy from extending their limits have been very important and it is
my earnest Desire that you continue where you are until further Advice
from me."[8]

For a soldier who had spent the fall pleading for guidance and support
from Gates, Greene's blatant flattery no doubt soothed Marion's bruised
ego, though he responded in curmudgeonly fashion: "I . . . shall endeavor
to procure intelligence as you desire, but shall meet with great Difficulty,
as nothing but gold or Silver passes here, and I am Destitute of Either."
He pleaded with Greene for Continental troops, "one hundred would be
sufficient," for what was probably another planned attempt to capture
Georgetown, though Marion's biographer Rankin writes Marion "knew
this was but a daydream."[9]

Nevertheless, Greene's strategic eye was forever trained up and down
rivers and roads, and clearly, he contemplated a strategic value for Marion
that Gates either couldn't see or ignored due to his damaged reputation.
Just over a month later, Greene would send Marion the mounted legion of
Henry Lee, one of the finest light regiments of the Continental army, led
by the legendary "Light Horse Harry," an extraordinary American officer
whose exploits during the American Revolution are well documented in
other sources, including Lee's own memoir of the war.

Despite some quarrels along the way, Greene and Marion would go on
to form a strong strategic alliance based on a trust and mutual respect Marion never seemed to have fully enjoyed with Gates.

However, the relationship between Greene and Sumter would not be as
successful, despite a relatively positive beginning.

When Greene arrived in Charlotte in December, Sumter was only thirteen days removed from the serious wound he had received at Blackstock's
on November 20. Though recently proclaimed dead, and still in convalescence, the ever-active Sumter still directed operations from his recovery
bed, supervising his spies, organizing supply, and directing his troops. He
even found time to propose to Gates an attack on Cornwallis at Winnsboro,
which he deemed vulnerable to attack. "I have this moment received from
undoubted authority, that Earl Cornwallis still lies at Winnsborough with
less than five hundred much exposed," reads his December 1 letter to
Gates.[10]

Sumter was also receiving visitors at his headquarters in York County, including on November 29 a delegation from South Carolina governor-in-exile John Rutledge, who had accompanied Gates to nearby Charlotte, as well as Continental army doctor William Read, who recalled being chased from Sumter's hideout by a Loyalist patrol as he returned to the Continental army hospital in Salisbury.

On December 8, Greene himself traveled to convey his respects to Sumter, in the company of Rutledge, this time to the home of John Price near Tuckaseegee Ford, a location deemed more secure than the threatened York County location. This was the same Tuckaseegee Ford where Sumter had assumed command of the Refugees a mere five months before, though it must've seemed a millennium to Sumter. Greene was again in politician mode, receiving Sumter's repeated recommendations for an attack on Cornwallis at Winnsboro with diplomacy. Following up in a letter of December 12, Greene regretted that Daniel Morgan and Robert Smallwood, his senior combat officers, were "pointedly" against the scheme. "I am not altogether of their opinion," Greene soothed, "and therefore wish you keep up a communication of intelligence, and of any changes of their disposition that may take place."[11]

Though benign in his correspondence, Greene's negative assessments of the South's militia forces undoubtedly influenced his response. "As I expected, so I find the great bodies of militia that have been in the field and the manner in which they came out, being all on horse back, has laid waste all the Country in such a manner that I am really afraid it will be impossible to subsist the few troops we have," he complained in a letter to George Washington on December 7. "The inhabitants of this country are too remote from one another to be animated into great exertions; and the people appear notwithstanding their danger, very intent upon their own private affairs."[12]

But Greene possessed a great leader's ability to find value in the opinions of others, even if he didn't properly acknowledge their contribution, and surely Sumter's schemes influenced his decision to split his army into two forces in mid-December. In this strategy, Daniel Morgan and his "flying army" were to move to the west, threatening the British garrison at Ninety Six, while Greene would take the remainder of the army to Cheraw, where his scouts reported provisions were more abundant than in Charlotte. Morgan's mission was to "spirit up the people, to annoy the enemy in that quarter," and "collect the provisions and forage out of the way of the enemy." Morgan was not prohibited from engaging the enemy but was to act "with caution" and avoid "surprises by every possible precaution." Once west of the Catawba, Morgan was to take command of "a body of Volunteer Militia under the command of Brig'r Genl [William L.] Davidson of this State, and by Militia lately under the command of Brig'r Genl [Thomas] Sumter," and "For the present I give you entire command in that quarter, and do hereby require all Officers and Soldiers engaged in the American cause to be subject to your orders and command."[13]

Never mind Greene was adopting a strategy close to the one recommended by Sumter, to threaten Cornwallis on his western flank (and also of Davidson, as described above). The real danger in these orders was the affront to the prickly ego of the South Carolina Gamecock, a brigadier general of the state of South Carolina. But if Greene was oblivious to the Gamecock's easily ruffled ego, John Rutledge immediately recognized their potential to provoke Sumter. No doubt, Sumter's quarrel over rank with James Williams from the first of October was still a fresh memory for South Carolina's governor-in-exile. Attempting to mitigate the issue, Rutledge wrote Sumter on December 20, 1780, advising him that Morgan would call on his way to the Catawba, cautioning his prickly general, "I wish he may have what Aid he wants, from the South Carolina Militia, westward of the Catawba."[14]

Rutledge soon wrote Sumter again, apparently in response to Sumter's complaints over the matter: "General Greene and you understand the matter with respect to you not having any command at present in a very different way—as I perceived on speaking to him a few days ago on that point."[15]

That Rutledge's entreaties failed to placate the prickly Gamecock would be revealed in weeks to come. For the time being, the matter seemed to pass, as Morgan made his way west, establishing a camp at Grindal Shoals on the Pacolet River south of modern-day Spartanburg, positioned strategically on one of the main roads leading south to Ninety Six. There he began to gather the militia of western South Carolina and eastern Georgia, including James Williams's old comrade Thomas Brandon and the Fair Forest Regiment, along with the Long Canes militia of Andrew Pickens.

Today considered one-third of the renowned South Carolina triumvirate of militia commanders, including Marion and Sumter, Pickens had spent the majority of the 1780 Backcountry War inactive, after accepting British parole earlier in the summer following the surrender of Charleston. Considered a man of great integrity, despite a historic legacy that includes brutal treatment of Native Americans, Pickens had resisted numerous calls to break his parole while Sumter and Marion spearheaded Patriot resistance as summer turned to fall, but after his plantation was plundered by a Tory raid in late fall 1780, Pickens considered the terms of his parole violated, and the appearance of Morgan's Continentals on the western frontier proved the perfect opportunity for him to resume his fight for the American cause.[16]

Notably absent from Morgan's camp, however, were the New Acquisition District regiments considered the heart of Sumter's brigade—the regiments of William Hill, Edward Lacey, and Richard Winn. And Morgan soon discovered that the reason for this absence stemmed from Greene's disposition of command. Writing to Greene on January 15, Morgan complained,

I dispatched Captain [C. K.] Chitty, (whom I have appointed as commissary of purchases for my command,) with orders to collect and store all the provisions that could be obtained between the Catawba and Broad rivers. I gave him directions to call on Colonel [William] Hill, who commands a regiment of militia in that quarter, to furnish him with a proper number of men to assist him in the execution of this commission, but he, to my great surprise, has just returned without effecting any thing. He tells me that his failure proceeded from the want of countenance and assistance of Colonel Hill, who assured him that General Sumter directed him to obey no orders from me, unless they came through him.[17]

Greene seemed surprised in his response: "I am surprised General Sumter should give such an order as you mention to Col. [William] Hill; nor can I persuade myself that there must be some mistake in the matter." Greene promised to write Sumter on the matter, assuring Morgan, "it is better to conciliate than aggravate matters, where every thing depends so much upon voluntary principles."[18]

If only he had taken his own advice. In his promised response to Sumter, Greene starts out in a conciliatory mood: "I have just received letters from General Morgan informing me of his situation, and representing the difficulty he meets with collecting provisions, and among other things he mentions some embarrassment which has arisen from an order of yours to Colonel [William] Hill, not to obey an order from him, unless it came through you. I imagine there must be some misapprehension about the matter; for I cannot suppose you could give an improper order, or that you have the most distant wish to embarrass the public affairs."[19]

All well and good, but in the following paragraphs he succumbed to a pretentiousness that often revealed itself in his letters, lecturing Sumter on the hierarchies of military power:

It is certainly right that all orders should go through the principal to the dependants. . . . This is a general rule and should never be deviated from but in cases of necessity. . . . In that case the order should be directed to the branches and not the principal; and as the head is subject to the order the branches are of course: for it would be very extraordinary if a Captain should presume to dispute an order from his General because it was not communicated through his Colonel.[20]

No doubt, Sumter found Greene's pedantry insulting, although circumstances appeared to put the matter to rest, at least for the time being. For even as Morgan was writing to complain of Hill's insubordination, he was being chased from the Pacolet River by Banastre Tarleton in the days leading up to the Battle of Cowpens.

Following Blackstocks, Cornwallis had ordered Tarleton to remain in the Ninety Six District, though these orders afforded Tarleton unusual latitude. "In short, I leave all to your discretion; you know the importance of putting the district of Ninety Six into a set of security, and will act accordingly." Tarleton was not completely idle during this interim. Following Blackstocks, he had chased the injured Sumter for several days, until convinced erroneously of his death, then visited with Robert Cunningham, recently appointed brigadier general of the Loyalist militia in the Ninety-Six District, finding him a "man of spirit and conduct."

But by November 28, Tarleton optimistically reported that "All affairs in this district are settled," and by the beginning of December he had settled into a bivouac at a place called Woodward's Plantation, in the vicinity of Brierley's Ferry on the Broad River, from which he could patrol the region in between the British garrisons at Winnsboro and Ninety Six and also lend support to that strategic river crossing if necessary.[21]

Tarleton's biographer Robert D. Bass reports that in this hiatus Tarleton caught up on correspondence. Not only had he failed to win support for his candidacy in November's parliamentary election, but his efforts also to collect some inheritance from a deceased aunt had failed. This followed news he had been passed over for a regular army commission to lieutenant colonel, with Secretary of War Lord Amherst reporting to Cornwallis, "His Majesty was pleased to express his sense of Major Tarleton's service in very flattering Terms, but did not think proper to give him any additional rank, he having very lately only been appointed to the Rank of a Major."[22]

No doubt disappointed by this news, Tarleton responded cheerfully to his brother John: "I have had many heir [sic] breadth Escapes since my last—my good Genius still smiles—I hope will hover around me till I once more see my native Country."[23] Still just twenty-six-years old, these set-backs must've seemed only temporary to a man who had enjoyed so much success and good fortune over the last five years.

But like all luck, Tarleton's was bound to run out. Indeed, he was fortunate to escape Blackstock's with his reputation intact, Sumter's wounds and the mistaken reports of the Gamecock's death for the most part masking what had been Tarleton's first tactical defeat. On December 18, Cornwallis sent Tarleton intelligence "that Morgan's Corps and the Cavalry had passed the Catawba,"[24] and by December 27, when Tarleton was summoned to Winnsboro to meet with Cornwallis, several intelligence reports about the movement of Morgan had passed back and forth between Cornwallis and Tarleton's camp.

Although we have no record of precisely what was discussed at Cornwallis and Tarleton's meeting the following day, December 28, the topic of Daniel Morgan was surely in the mix. Still, as of that date, there appeared to be no urgency to the matter of Morgan, as Leslie was not yet in position to reinforce Cornwallis for the winter campaign and Cornwallis did not believe the garrison at Ninety-Six threatened. Undoubtedly, they discussed strategy for the weeks ahead, including the recommencement of the long-delayed invasion of North Carolina. By this time, Tarleton was in command of his 450-man Legion, along with a battalion of the British 71st infantry, the 71st light infantry, and an artillery company with two field pieces that included the 16th Regiment's light infantry, in all a little over eight hundred men. This embodied almost all of Cornwallis's light troops, whose mobility would be crucial for the winter invasion to come. That Cornwallis had entrusted this vital strategic asset to a twenty-six-year-old major suggests the unfettered confidence the commander in chief placed in Tarleton.[25]

But nonchalance turned to worry on January 1, when Cornwallis received reports that a detachment of Morgan's army under cavalry commander William Washington had routed a party of Georgia Loyalists on December 29 at a place called Hammond's Store and chased Cunningham and his Loyalist militia from Williams' Fort (the redoubt on the property of James Williams they had occupied since early that summer). A Tory spy named David George reported to Cornwallis he was "well inform'd" that Morgan and Washington intended to "march as fast as they can for Ninety Six" with artillery and up to three thousand men.[26] The report was wildly inaccurate. Morgan was still at Grindal Shoals, had no cannon, and had ordered Washington's detachment to return there.[27] Yet the action at Hammond's Store was yielding a disruptive effect, leading to panic and wild rumor among the Loyalists of the region, upon whom Cornwallis relied for intelligence. And with the (false) reports that Morgan was headed to Ninety-Six with cannon, Cornwallis decided he must move against Morgan.

Again, he turned to Tarleton, sending a message to Tarleton's camp on January 1 with orders for him to cross the Broad River and defend Ninety Six against Morgan's reported attack.[28] The next day, Cornwallis wrote to Tarleton: "If Morgan . . . is anywhere within your reach, I should wish you to push him to the utmost. . . . Ninety-Six is of so much consequence that no time is to be lost."[29]

Now on the move, Tarleton soon determined Morgan was still on the Pacolet, posing no immediate threat to Ninety Six. Yet his blood was up. Tarleton halted at Brooke's River Plantation, just twenty miles north of Brierly's, to provision his men and forage his horses. Here he proposed a scheme to Cornwallis: "When I advance, I must either destroy Morgan's corps, or push it before me over Broad River, toward Kings Mountain." Meanwhile, Tarleton suggested Cornwallis move north with the main army, putting Morgan in a trap between the two British divisions. "The advance of the army should commence (when his lordship orders his corps to move) onward's for Kings Mountain," Tarleton wrote.[30] Cornwallis replied the next day, January 5: "You have exactly done what I wished you to do and understand my intentions perfectly." At Tarleton's request, he reinforced Tarleton with cavalry from the 17th Light Dragoons and 167 infantry of the 7th Royal Fusiliers, so named because it was originally formed as a fusilier regiment, or ordnance regiment, to escort artillery, bringing Tarleton's total combined force to 1,100 within the following days, including all of the British mounted regiments in the South and most of its light infantry.[31]

If the plan had been executed in the mindset with which Cornwallis and Tarleton shared at that moment, history might tell a different tale of the British "Southern Strategy." But again, Cornwallis's innate conservatism failed him. His communications with Tarleton hindered by bad weather and bad reconnaissance, Cornwallis delayed his planned joint operation against Morgan waiting for Leslie's reinforcements to finally complete their long march from Charleston by way of Camden.

In the interim, the impetuous Tarleton pushed on against Morgan, learning of Morgan's encampment at Grindal Shoals on the Pacolet on January 12. The same day, Cornwallis wrote to Rawdon from his headquarters at McAlister's Plantation, from where he had pushed up from Winnsboro but had stopped, still awaiting his junction with Leslie's reinforcements. There, Cornwallis's communication system faltered. On January 12, still at McAlister's, he wrote to Leslie, "The Broad River exceedingly high, I have not heard from Tarleton. . . . I believe he is as much embarrassed by the waters as you are." On the same day, he informed Rawdon, "the rains have impeded operations on all sides."[32]

But impediment was not a word in Tarleton's vocabulary. Either ignoring his plan to coordinate with Cornwallis, or falsely believing Cornwallis was still moving up the other side of the Broad for a coordinated attack, Tarleton pushed Morgan from his camp on the Pacolet on January 15 and pursued him north by northeast to a well-known crossroads called Hannah's Cowpens, or simply "The Cowpens," where he found Morgan and his Flying Army waiting for him in battle formation on the cold, clear morning of January 17. In one short morning, the ascendant military career of Banastre Tarleton would forever be diminished by the complete defeat he suffered there at Morgan's hands. Tarleton, the still-young "Green Dragoon," had enjoyed some of the most spectacular campaigns of any British officer in the American Revolution. But at Cowpens, Tarleton's ascendent career began to fall, ending his role in the Backcountry War.

WHILE SUMTER CONVALESCED, Cornwallis schemed, and Tarleton pursued Morgan across western South Carolina, Marion kept an eye on British troop movements along the Santee, reporting on the progress of Leslie and his 1,500 reinforcements on their slow march toward Cornwallis at Winnsboro, but for the moment, not strong enough to disrupt them.

Momentarily pacified, the Swamp Fox remained a distraction for Cornwallis. "On considering your situation," Cornwallis wrote to Rawdon on December 21, clearly referring to Marion, "I have determined to leave the 64th Regiment as well as Watson's crops under your command," their mission to guard the Santee supply routes.[33]

The Watson referred to in this letter was John Watson Tadwell-Watson, who held a dual commission of captain in the 3rd Regiment of Foot Guards (the Scottish Guards) and also lieutenant colonel in a Provincial regiment of light infantry that had arrived in Charleston with Leslie. Previously serving as an aide-de-camp to Clinton, Watson's reputation as a difficult officer proceeded his appointment to Cornwallis's command. "Seemingly puffed up with self-importance and reluctant to obey or cooperate with ranking officers whom he considered his professional inferiors . . . he presented a problem for Cornwallis, who decided not to take him and his light troops on the winter campaign," writes Ian Saberton, the editor of Cornwallis's letters.

Tarleton, apparently, enjoyed a special enmity with the new arrival, a rivalry much on Cornwallis's mind. "Lord Rawdon has very readily agreed to undertake Watson," Cornwallis informed Tarleton, "so that we shall be relieved from that plague." Rawdon also had a personality conflict with Watson earlier in the war, with Watson apparently attempting to assert some authority over the young lord. In an apparent reference to this incident, Cornwallis observed to Rawdon, "Now your Lordship can make him obey you."[34]

Despite his disagreeable personality, however, Watson was blessed as a builder of forts. Immediately deeming the current British outpost at Sumter's house at the Great Savannah on the Santee an inferior position, he began constructing a new fort at Wright's Bluff, at an impoundment on the Santee River known as Scott's Lake (the current site of Lake Marion), ten miles above Nelson's Ferry. The site he chose was on top of an old Native American burial mound, already thirty to forty feet high, the position rising from an open plain that commanded control of both the road from Nelson's Ferry to Camden and the Santee River. There, Watson constructed a strong redoubt, complete with two rows of abatis and two rows of artillery, that he with characteristic arrogance named for himself.

Fort Watson would go on to play an important role in the spring campaign. Both Sumter and Marion would try to capture the fort in the months to come, with Sumter's attempt on February 28, 1781, unsuccessful. Marion's attempt later that April, however, resulted in the fort's surrender thanks to the assistance of Henry Lee and his Legion, who had by this time rejoined Marion after the winter campaign in North Carolina. Playing a crucial role in the success of Marion and Lee's attack was an ingenious siege-works designed by South Carolina officer Hezekiah Maham, who was serving with Marion. Maham designed a thirty-foot tower with a platform that was constructed offsite and then erected within firing range of Fort Watson on the night of April 22, allowing American forces to pour fire down into the British outpost the following day. Thanks to this "Maham Tower," Marion and Lee's combined force was able to force Fort Watson's surrender the following day, April 23, 1781, making it the first British outpost in the South Carolina interior to fall to the American forces.[35]

For the time being, however, Marion could do little except order his scouts to observe the construction of Watson's fort and keep track of movements on the Santee. Instead, he retired again to Snow Island, his plans once more turning to Georgetown, although his prospects there were little improved. Writing to Nathanael Greene in early January, Marion reported the post at Georgetown numbered two hundred men, including "fifteen "regular horse & twenty mounted Infantry," the entire force remaining "close in their redoubt," so that Marion could not attack them.[36]

Nevertheless, Marion did receive some welcome news at his Snow Island bivouac. On New Year's Day, 1781, a courier arrived from South Carolina governor-in-exile John Rutledge with a brigadier general's commission for Francis Marion. The commission made Marion Sumter's equal in terms of authority from South Carolina, with the added distinction that Marion's Continental army commission was still active, while Sumter's was not. Indeed, the commission placed under Marion's command of all South Carolina regiments eastward of the Santee, Wateree, and Catawba Rivers, while "those to the Westward" would remain under command of Thomas Sumter.[37]

Although we have little else from Rutledge regarding the timing of this commission, we can construct a rationale from other known facts. Rutledge had accompanied Greene to Cheraw, South Carolina, at this time, and presumably had heard from his constituents there about the success of Marion's campaigns. Recall that Gates had placed Marion subordinate to North Carolina militia brigadier general William H. Harrington earlier in the fall, displeasing Marion, who deemed Harrington apathetic. However, Harrington had resigned his commission on December 2 in a dispute over rank with the North Carolina legislature.[38]

No doubt the influence of Nathanael Greene, and Greene's plans for Marion in the South Carolina interior, had a strong influence on Rutledge's decision, as did the severity of Sumter's recent wound. In the same letter in which he announces Marion's commission to South Carolina's Continental Congress delegation, Rutledge reports Sumter's "wound (the doctors say), will disable him from taking the field for several months—This is a very unfortunate circumstance, & we shall feel the Loss of his Services very much."[39]

Whatever the reason, the normally taciturn Marion was temporarily humbled by the news. With it had also come a colonel's commission for Peter Horry, who recalled the moment in his memoir: "Scarcely had I perused my commission, before Marion reached me HIS; and with a smile, desired me to read it. Soon as I came to his new title, 'brigadier general,' I snatched his hand and exclaimed, 'Huzza! God save my friend! My noble

General Marion . . . Aye that will do! That sounds somewhat in unison with your deserts."[40]

For Horry, the reasons for Marion's promotion were clear: "Notwithstanding the many follies and failures of northern generals and armies; notwithstanding the victories, and proclamation, and threats of Cornwallis and Tarleton, Marion still stood his ground, and fought and conquered for Carolina." Still, Horry noted that of the domain to which Marion had been granted military control "the excellent governor had no more power to grant military jurisdiction, than to give kingdoms to the moon; for the whole of it was in the hands of the British, and their friends the tories."[41]

Indeed, the year 1780 closed with Cornwallis and his forces still firmly in control of South Carolina and Georgia, along with their own province of Florida. In the course of their southern campaigns, they had handed the American forces two of their worst defeats of the war—Charleston and Camden—and set the Southern Department of the Continental army reeling on its heels, its commanding general Horatio Gates disgraced, and its soldiers near destitute for want of discipline and provision.

However, American resilience had not crumbled in the face of these disasters but rather had adapted and transformed. The genius of Thomas Sumter was that he understood the psychology of the southern Whig. It was a psychology driven by prejudice, jealousy, and aspiration. Even principle. And when those forces were marshalled and embodied through the enterprise and spirit of a motivated leader, they could be applied to pressure points in the British defenses, spreading much damage and disruption. Marion's genius was a more supple one, the tactics of surprise, ambush, and strategic retreat that confounded British propriety and destabilized the vast, inhospitable terrain of eastern South Carolina.

And if their genius was not quite enough to reclaim their state during the 1780 Backcountry War, it was more than enough to sow the seeds of victory, for in Nathanael Greene they had a new partner, capable not only of recognizing their genius but of applying his own. Thanks to these three, the year to come would have a much different outcome than the year just passed.

THUNDER, LIGHTNING, or in RAIN

When shall we three meet again?
In thunder, lightning, or in rain?
When the hurleyburly's done,
When the battle's lost and won.
—Macbeth, Act 1, Scene 1

F OLLOWING THEIR SURRENDER at Yorktown on October 19, 1781, the British officers were invited to dinner. Washington invited Cornwallis, who declined in the grips of the kind of fugue that frequently visited him in moments of crisis, as in the retreat from Charlotte. Similarly, junior American and French officers invited their British counterparts. Yet Banastre Tarleton, perhaps alone, received no invitation.

Tarleton asked American lieutenant colonel John Laurens, serving as Washington's aide-de-camp, if the slight was accidental. The son of Henry Laurens, a wealthy South Carolina planter and former president of the

Continental Congress, Laurens is said to have assured Tarleton there was no accident at all: "Intentional, I assure you, and meant as a reproof for certain cruelties practiced by the troops under your command in campaigns in the Carolinas."

Tarleton disagreed: "Is it, sir, for a faithful discharge of my duty to my king and my country, that I am thus humiliated in the eyes of three armies?"

"There are modes, sir, of discharging a soldier's duties," Laurens purportedly replied. "And where mercy has a share in the mode, it renders the duty more acceptable to both friends and foes."[1]

Tarleton would end his service in America with more damage than just a bruised ego. At the Battle of Guilford Courthouse on March 15, 1781, he suffered his worst injury of the war, when his hand was shot in a prebattle skirmish. Though the British Legion stayed mostly in reserve during the main battle, Tarleton still fought courageously with a squadron of dragoons ordered to support the British right flank under Gen. Alexander Leslie, despite his wound. According to Bass, Tarleton led his men with "his right hand in a sling and his bridle reins held in his left." A tactical victory for the British, with the combined American forces under the command of Nathanael Greene ceding the field, the British victory at Guilford Courthouse came at a high cost, with Cornwallis losing approximately 25 percent of his troops killed or wounded. Tarleton lost a portion of his right hand after a field surgeon amputated his middle and index fingers.[2]

For Cornwallis, the pyrrhic victory at Guilford Courthouse was the final affront in the failed effort to "conquer" North Carolina. Despite the battle's favorable outcome, the response to it of North Carolina's Loyalist community was moribund, and whatever last hopes Cornwallis held that a Loyalist uprising could be ignited by only a small expeditionary force of just over two thousand men died along with ninety-three British soldiers killed on the field that day.

He would try his luck in Virginia, after refitting in Wilmington, leaving the vast majority of North Carolina to the Whigs, though his outposts in South Carolina still held nominal control there, at least until Greene turned his attentions toward that state later in 1781, refusing to follow Cornwallis.

In Virginia, Tarleton was back to his old ways, leading raids and skirmishes, looting, burning, and pillaging Patriot homes, even while he learned to write and handle his sword with his left hand. In a famous raid on Charlottesville, where the British learned some members of the Virginia Assembly had taken refuge, Tarleton missed capturing Thomas Jefferson at his home in Monticello by only a few minutes. In consolation, Tarleton and his thirsty troops razed Jefferson's plantation and liberated his wine cellar but, thankfully, spared Monticello from the torch, preserving what has become an American treasure.

Tarleton hardly needed another feather in his cap, nor perhaps, after the debacle at Cowpens, deserved one, but still they came. On June 15, he was promoted to lieutenant colonel in the regular army, matching his provisional rank. Made by "order of the King," the official recommendation praised Tarleton as "indefatigably laborious and active" and "cool and intrepid in battle," among other accolades.[3] He was still just twenty-six-years old.

During the Virginia campaign, Cornwallis continued to show confidence in Tarleton, giving him command of several important detachments, yet perhaps after the disastrous outcome at Yorktown, and the armchair quarterbacking that followed, it was inevitable their relationship would sour in the years to come. Returned to England on parole in January 1782, Tarleton for a time became a star of the London social set, resuming his taste for gambling and wanton women. He soon befriended the Prince of Wales, the future King George IV, whose licentious tastes mirrored Tarleton's for a time. Meanwhile, he was celebrated as a British hero. And painted as one.

On January 28, just ten days after his return to London, Tarleton first sat for Sir Joshua Reynolds, president of the Royal Academy and one of the most famous artists of his age. Described by the art critic Daniel O'Quinn as a "vigorous, heavily eroticized painting,"[4] the portrait created a sensation when displayed at the Royal Academy exhibition of 1782. In the same room where Tarleton's portrait was displayed was displayed another Reynolds's portrait of the famous actress Mary Robinson, with whom Tarleton had shared at least three sitting appointments in Reynolds's studio. Likely it was here that their famous romance was sparked.

Despite a shared reputation for philandering, Tarleton and Robinson eventually settled into a stable, if not quite respectable, relationship. Often referred to by her nickname "Perdita," from her most famous role in Shakespeare's *The Winter's Tale*, Robinson and Tarleton lived extravagantly, reportedly spending £2,500 per year, financed partially by Tarleton's gambling. The pair were together for fifteen years, though separated in 1797 allegedly over Tarleton's designs on Robinson's daughter, who was only twenty-one. A year later, on December 17, 1798, Tarleton married twenty-three-year-old Susan Bertie, the wealthy daughter of the Duke of Ancaster, and would eventually settle down at an estate inherited by Susan in Shropshire.[5]

Tarleton remained in the army, eventually achieving the rank of full general in 1812. He briefly held an independent command in Portugal but was mostly relegated to domestic postings for the rest of his military career and never again saw combat. In the meantime, he took to politics, allying himself with the Whig Party and its leader Charles James Fox, an ardent critic of King George and the American conflict. This surprising alliance with George III's political opponents no doubt hindered his military career. Nevertheless, Tarleton proved a durable if unexceptional politician. With the exception of one year, he represented his hometown of Liverpool in the House of Commons from 1790 to 1812, speaking most frequently on military matters and in defense of the slave trade, with which his family had a long and profitable history. At political rallies, he was famous for crying out "For King and Country!" while raising his mangled right hand.[6]

In 1787, with his gambling debts mounting, Tarleton published his memoirs, *A History of the Campaigns of 1780 and 1781, in the Southern Provinces of North America*. With the debacle of Cowpens still haunting his reputation, Tarleton shifted blame for many of his mistakes to Cornwallis, earning the dismay of his former benefactor. "Tarleton's is a most malicious and false attack; he knew and approved the reasons for the measures which he now blames," Cornwallis wrote to his brother. "I know it is very foolish to be vexed about these things, but yet it touches me in a tender point."

Of particular chagrin to Cornwallis was Tarleton's account of Kings Mountain. In it, Tarleton claims that Cornwallis dispatched him to support Patrick Ferguson only after the battle had already occurred, on October 10, 1781 (the battle occurred on October 7), an order Tarleton claimed he dutifully attempted to execute. In response, Cornwallis complained, "My not sending relief to Colonel Ferguson, although he was positively ordered to retire, was entirely owing to Tarleton himself; he pleaded weakness from the remains of a fever, and refused to make the attempt, although I used the most earnest entreaties. I mention this as proof, amongst many others, of his candour."[7]

By then, however, Cornwallis had been named governor-general of Bengal and commander in chief of British forces in India. Well on his way to a successful resurrection of his own tarnished career, Cornwallis kept his complaints of Tarleton private. Roderick McKenzie, a former officer of the 71st Regiment, would have no such qualms. As noted earlier, McKenzie had been wounded at Cowpens while serving under Tarleton's command. Enraged by Tarleton's memoir, McKenzie published a rebuttal titled *Strictures on Lt. Col. Tarleton's History*, primarily blasting Tarleton for his conduct at Cowpens though reserving some of his ire for the Green Dragoon's dubious claims of victory at Blackstock's. While the British army in the Carolinas were "led to celebrate" at Tarleton's "victory" at Blackstock's, McKenzie complains it was "amidst the contempt and derision of the inhabitants, who had much better information."[8]

Though clearly self-serving, Tarleton's *Campaigns* remains a significant reference of the American Revolution, in particular British operations in the South. In part this significance is due to the valuable collection of letters and documents it contains, in part because it serves as the sole primary account from a British perspective of many of the events it describes, and in part because Tarleton the writer is capable of weaving a damned good tale. Certainly, this work references it extensively, as any biographical account of Tarleton must.

In January 1816, Tarleton was awarded a baronetcy by the Duke of York, making him *Sir* Banastre Tarleton, and in 1820, after his old friend the Prince of Wales finally became King George IV, he became a Knight Grand Cross of the Order of Bath, marching with the other knights in the coronation procession. He died on January 15, 1833, having long before retired to the quiet life of a country squire. Though barely known in England today, his legacy in America lives on, thanks primarily to the numerous iterations of the British dragoon portrayed in American popular media. Though none of them are quite accurate, and most are quite cartoonish, there was an arrogance and savagery in the true Tarleton most capture, but also a bravery and courage in battle they inevitably neglect to portray.

OF OUR THREE PROTAGONISTS, only Francis Marion's wartime status was still rising as the story of the 1780 Backcountry War comes to a close. Bolstered by his promotion to brigadier general of the South Carolina militia, Marion's tactical capacities also increased dramatically by the arrival of Continental officer Henry Lee and his Legion of dragoons and light infantry.

When last we saw Henry Lee, he was a twenty-one-year-old cavalry commander, fending off Tarleton's surprise attack at Spread Eagle Tavern on the outskirts of Philadelphia on January 20, 1778. In August 1779, Lee's successful surprise attack on the British garrison at Paulus Hook, New Jersey, earned him one of only eight gold medals awarded during the war. Though a relatively minor action, the attack showcased Lee's bravery and valor, and boosted Patriot morale during a moribund period of the war.

Lee was promoted to lieutenant colonel on November 30, 1780, and specially requested by Nathanael Greene to join his southern command.

Once arrived, Lee was promptly dispatched by Greene to Marion's camp, where he arrived on January 22, 1781. Immediately, the two partisan commanders planned yet another attempt to take the British redoubt in Georgetown.

Attempted on January 25, that attack failed, and Lee was soon recalled to Greene's command for the campaign that would end at Guilford Courthouse on March 15, 1781. However, when Greene turned his sights on South Carolina following Cornwallis's move into Virginia, Marion and Lee would reunite, successfully capturing British outposts at Fort Watson on April 15 and Fort Motte on May 15. And finally, on May 28, Marion would take Georgetown, after it was abandoned by the British.

With Lee, Marion had completed one of the most successful and renowned partisan campaigns of the American Revolution, but the scale of war in South Carolina had changed with the arrival of Greene, who expected militia commanders like Marion, Sumter, and Pickens to act in support of his own strategies and objectives. Both Marion and Sumter struggled under this enhanced supervision, though Marion's allegiance to the Continental army kept him mostly obedient to Greene's orders, even when they rankled.[9]

By the summer of 1781, Marion's militia regiment numbered in the hundreds, not the dozens or scores he had started out with in the fall of 1780. At the Battle of Shubrick's Plantation on July 17, 1781, Marion's forces numbered approximately 180 men; at the Battle of Eutaw Springs on September 8, 1781, they numbered seven hundred.

Clearly the scale of the Backcountry War was changing and also its temperament. At Shubrick's Plantation, Sumter had served in overall command of a combined force including Henry Lee's Legion and Marion's brigade. After the British had formed into a defensive position, supported by field artillery, Sumter ordered one of his trademark straight-ahead attacks. After the battle, Marion and Lee became so frustrated with the butchery of Sumter's tactics they left in the night, without informing Sumter of their departure. Meanwhile, once-loyal subordinates like Peter Horry and Hezekiah Maham now commanded their own regiments and began to assert an independence, if not disobedience, that rankled Marion anew.[10]

Following the Battle of Eutaw Springs, the British retreated into their defenses at Charleston. The Backcountry War was drawing to a close but not yet over, for bands of Loyalists still roamed the Pee Dee region, and the British continued to conduct raids on the outskirts of Charleston. Marion remained in command of his militia regiment, supporting Greene on the perimeter of Charleston and providing security in the Pee Dee, but clearly his priorities were shifting. In December 1781, Marion was elected to the South Carolina General Assembly even as his attention shifted back to the operation of his plantation at Pond Bluff and other family properties. In December 1782, after a year of guard duty on the outskirts of Charleston, and efforts to keep the remaining Loyalists of the Pee Dee region in check, Marion finally dismissed his militia when the British evacuated Charleston on December 14.

Even as Marion struggled to revive Pond Bluff, which had been confiscated during the Backcountry War and left to deteriorate, he resumed his political and military duties. In 1783, he served in the South Carolina Senate. In September 1783, he was promoted by Congress from a lieutenant colonel to full colonel in the Continental line, and in March 1784, he was named commandant at Fort Johnson in Charleston Harbor, serving essentially in the role of a port collector. In this role Marion was compensated a generous five hundred British pounds sterling a year but required to live within the fort's dreary walls.

A lifelong bachelor, Marion married spinster Mary Esther Videau on April 20, 1786. He was fifty-four and she was forty-nine. Though the union would not yield children, it did yield considerable assets, for over the years Mary Esther had inherited money and land from deceased parents and siblings. The windfall allowed Marion to settle into the life of a country farmer, which included the ownership of slaves, raising cattle and hogs, and cultivating rice. On February 27, 1795, Marion died at Pond Bluff and was later buried at Belle Isle, his brother Gabriel's plantation. According to his gravestone, he was sixty-three years old. At his death, his estate was valued at 6,453 pounds sterling, more than half of that value in the seventy-four slaves he owned.[11]

In an age obsessed with newspaper accounts, Marion's partisan campaigns were reported up and down the American states during the war, although South Carolina historian Steven D. Smith observes that Marion played a respectable though not central role in the first published history of the American Revolution in South Carolina, David Ramsay's *History of the Revolution in South Carolina*, published in 1785. Smith counts six mentions of Marion in Ramsay's work, and none of them mentioned the rebel hideout at Snow's Island or the name "The Swamp Fox."[12]

It was only with the 1809 publication of Peter Horry's account of the Marion campaigns, authored with considerable embellishment by Rev. Mason Lock Weems, that Marion's status as a folkloric icon began to grow.

A Virginia bookseller, publisher of religious tracts, and author, Weems had gained some measure of fame as the first popular biographer of George Washington. Chapter 6 describes how Horry turned over to Weems a vast collection of Marion-related documents and letters, along with a simply written memorial, expecting Weems to turn this material into a factual account. This Weems did not do, and instead used Horry's account as a romantic framework for an allegorical tale of American virtue and ethics. "With anti-British sentiment growing in the young nation, Weems fed the national mood by turning the British into 'fiends devoid of human compassion' in his Marion biography," Smith observes.[13]

William Dobein James published his own account of Marion's wartime exploits in 1821. As noted previously, James was the son of Marion's officer John James, and also personally participated in some of Marion's campaigns. Quoted heavily here, James's is considered a more factual account than that of Horry and Weems, though its chronology is often jumbled. Nevertheless, it was the Horry/Weems version that captured the public's imagination and influenced the next popular biography of Marion by William Gilmore Simms, first published in 1844.

Like Weems, Simms was one of the most popular biographers and writers of his day. And though Simms attempted to mitigate the excesses of the Horry/Weems version of Marion's biography, his version contains its own fair share of flowery speeches and exaggerated accounts. Nevertheless, it was Simms who introduced the name "Swamp Fox" into the national vocabulary, turning a pair of anecdotes in Horry/Weems and James (the latter probably influenced by the former) into the popular nickname. In the Horry/Weems account, Tarleton refers to Marion as a "swamp fox"; in the James account it is a "vile fox." Simms translated these anecdotes into the following account: "He turned the head of his column at the very moment when his object was attainable . . . exclaiming, 'Come, my boys! Let us go back. We will soon find the *Game Cock* (meaning Sumter), but as for this d——d *Swamp Fox*, the devil himself could not catch him."[14]

Whether anyone who knew Marion called him "Swamp Fox" is highly doubtable. Smith scanned 8,431 pension applications of former South Carolina militia soldiers without finding a single mention. Still, popularized decades later, the name stuck. "It seems reasonable to infer that during the Revolution a swamp fox was a term of derision, and it was only by the time of Simms that it became a popular sobriquet," writes Smith. Simms went on to feature Marion as a character in at least two historical novels and a popular poem. "Consideration of these works helps illuminate how Simms, and many of his readers, thought about military leadership and conflict as the Civil War approached," writes Smith.[15]

And the legacy lives on. Writing in 2013, Smith counted twenty-four biographies of Marion in a "selected" bibliography and at least fourteen books of fiction with Marion as the protagonist or inspiration, and there have been several written since. That's not to mention the numerous depictions of Marion on television and film, including the aforementioned *The Patriot*, starring Mel Gibson, and the eight-episode series called "The Swamp Fox," featuring a young Leslie Nielsen in the title role, which ran on *Walt Disney Presents* from 1959 to 1961. Similarly, Smith counted twenty-nine towns and seventeen counties in the United States named in Marion's honor. Marion's home state of South Carolina not only features both a Marion County and a town named Marion, but also Francis Marion University, part of the state's university system, with an annual enrollment of approximately 4,100, along with Francis Marion National Forest.[16]

Why this enduring popularity? Smith suggests that "The Swamp Fox" has assumed a place in our national consciousness as our own "Robin Hood," his secret lair on Snow's Island (also romanticized in the works of Simms and Horry/Weems) an American version of Sherwood Forest. The analogy is not incorrect, even if the real-life narrative bore little resemblance to either the fictional Robin Hood or Marion's own fictional portrayals in popular biographies, novels, and television. What is undisputable is the incredible and unlikely role Marion played in the American Revolution and the enduring appeal of the guerilla tactics he employed expertly during the 1780 Backcountry War. If Marion the myth still serves some fundamental role in our American psychology, then the wartime service of Marion the man still deserves our consideration, even if, from the perspective of 250 years, the two sometimes blur into one.

THE HISTORIAN JOHN S. PANCAKE SUGGESTS Sumter's serious wound at Blackstock's led to a psychological schism, altering his character and demeanor for the remainder of the war. "Did this experience sap some of the bold courage of the Gamecock? Did he not press his attack with the same hard courage he had once displayed?" asks Pancake. "Probably Thomas Sumter himself could not have answered such questions, but the terrible wound and its painful aftermath may have affected his fighting spirit in ways of which he himself was not aware."[17]

Pancake's analysis refers to the erratic behavior the Gamecock sometimes exhibited during the campaigns of 1781 and the personality conflicts with American leaders, including both Francis Marion and Nathanael Greene, in which he frequently engaged.

As to the erratic behavior, glimpses of it have already been displayed in this account, as in his curious decision not to post advance guards at either Fishing Creek or Fishdam Ford, and his solitary escapes from both of those engagements. Never a gifted battlefield tactician, Sumter's straight-ahead attacks against superior defensives positions, as at Rocky Mount, might also serve as examples.

In February 1781, with Greene's Continental army on the run from Cornwallis during the Race to the Dan, and the subsequent Battle of Guilford Courthouse that March, Sumter again embodied his brigade for a campaign against the British supply line from Charleston to Camden, long an object of his strategic attention. The planning of a militia campaign in the South Carolina backcountry often depended on the crop cycle, and Sumter understood he needed to muster his militia in February if he hoped to campaign before the spring planting season.

Yet this campaign lacked the focus and momentum of those of 1780. Answering Sumter's call to assemble at his old campground in the Waxhaws were only 280 men, a far cry from the thousand-plus he had fought with at Blackstocks, despite the promise of both British and Loyalist plunder with which he enticed them. Known as "Sumter's Rounds," the campaign was, not surprisingly, something of a disorganized mess, with little to show for it other than many slaves captured from Loyalist farms and plantations.[18]

Sumter was clearly not in his old "Gamecock" form during the "Rounds," his forty-six-year-old body still recovering from his Blackstocks wounds. Yet he also seemed to lack the charisma and magnetism of his previous campaigns. His letters from this period display little of the enthusiasm and spirit of industry they displayed in much of his 1780 correspondence. At the end of the "Sumter's Rounds," many of his men accused him of deliberate deception or keeping an unfair share of the Loyalist plunder for himself, with some abandoning his brigade.

As Greene and his Continental army returned to South Carolina in April 1780, following their stalemate with Cornwallis's British army at Guilford Courthouse, the scale of the war in South Carolina grew, revealing personality conflicts between the Gamecock and both Sumter and Marion. Already during the Sumter's Rounds campaign, Marion had ignored Sumter's request for reinforcements. In turn, at the Battle of Hobkirk's Hill on April 25, Greene's own failed attempt to capture the British garrison at

Camden, Sumter repeatedly ignored Greene's request for reinforcements, prompting Greene to despair over Sumter's loyalties in a famous lament recorded by William R. Davie, now serving as Greene's commissary general. "Sumter refuses to obey my orders, and carries off with him all the active forces of this unhappy state on rambling predatory expeditions unconnected with the operations of the army," Greene said according to Davie's account. "These are his very words, they make a deep and melancholy expression."[19]

The Battle of Shubrick's Plantation on July 17, 1781, where Sumter was abandoned in the night following the fighting by both Marion and Henry Lee, proved to be Sumter's last battlefield command of the war. As Greene coalesced Patriot forces for the campaign that would result in the Battle of Eutaw Springs that September, Sumter disappeared on another of his mysterious trips to North Carolina, this one allegedly for gathering supplies for his troops, though its timing was more than inauspicious.

It would be easy to attribute this behavior to a psychological schism created by Sumter's Blackstocks wound. Pure ego, no doubt, also played a role. In my previous work on Sumter, I have theorized that he may have suffered from more significant psychological illness. "From a modern perspective, these incidents of reckless behavior, general irritability, and conflicts with colleagues suggest some evidence of bipolar disorder. Of course, the 1780s were a long time before the era of modern psychoanalysis, and bipolar disorder requires a medical diagnosis, making any such conclusion pure speculation, even if this evidence persists as our narrative progresses, his manic and depressive episodes becoming more pronounced after Blackstocks," I wrote in my account of the Sumter/Greene feud.[20]

This is conjecture, of course. But what fun is writing a military history if you can't occasionally play armchair psychiatrist for its generals? Whatever the case, Sumter's status as the great or primary general of South Carolina militia inevitably diminished after 1780, and by the end of 1781, Greene had successfully relegated him to guard duty in the South Carolina interior, before Sumter, too, left his command to join the South Carolina General Assembly in January 1782.

If the Backcountry War of 1780 was the Gamecock's sparkling first act, and the campaigns of 1781 the dour second one, Sumter enjoyed a prolonged third act as a successful politician. In 1789, Sumter became a representative to the first Congress of the United States, at a time when the state general assembly elected both congressmen and senators to the national body. Though never one of the most vocal members of Congress, he became known as a fierce defender of states' rights and went on to become a stalwart of the South Carolina congressional delegation, losing an election in 1793 but regaining his seat in the election of 1795.

And in 1801, Thomas Sumter became a United States senator, winning an election in the South Carolina General Assembly over his old benefactor and sometimes adversary John Rutledge. He served in the United States Senate until 1810, when he resigned at the age of seventy-six. Yet he continued to live an active life until dying at the age of ninety-seven on June 1, 1832, allegedly the last surviving general of the American Revolutionary War.[21]

As a congressman and senator, Sumter leveraged his popular appeal to champion a new brand of democratic populism focused on states' incipient rights to control their own laws regarding a broad range of issues including finance, commerce, military power, and slavery. According to one of his biographers, his chief principles as a congressman were justice to claims of veterans and widows of veterans, economy in government, and the limitation of federal powers.[22]

Today, Sumter's legacy remains strongest in his home state of South Carolina, where he is revered for the crucial role he played in the American Revolution following the surrender of Charleston and remembered primarily for his successful leadership during the 1780 Backcountry War. Like Marion, he is the namesake for both a South Carolina county and town. Each year, millions visit historic Fort Sumter in Charleston Harbor, named in his honor, though he was long dead by the time it played its famous role in the Civil War. And perhaps most popularly, his famous nickname serves as the inspiration for the University of South Carolina's mascot, screamed and shouted by fans at sporting events, a bright crimson gamecock almost inevitably emblazoned on their chests or foreheads.

WHEN SHALL WE MEET THE LIKES OF Sumter, Marion, and Tarleton again? As I write this, brutal, nihilistic wars rage across the globe, in places like Gaza and the Ukraine, the outcomes of which can only lead to more violence, terror, and suffering. Certainly, no heroes are likely to emerge from their rubble. Perhaps Ukrainian president Volodymyr Zelenskyy might serve as a modern-day example of the type of defiant, underdog partisan embodied by Sumter and Marion, though Ukrainian corruption and the dehumanization of virtual war makes this comparison imperfect at best, if not uncomfortable.

So, it would be easy to suggest that Marion and Sumter's enduring legacy stems from our mythologizing of a simpler, more virtuous time. Certainly, the scale at which they fought, their numbers typically measured in the tens and hundreds, evokes myths of a more idealistic age, when men and boys left their farmsteads and families in pursuit of an ideal known as liberty and, perhaps miraculously, achieved it.

I hope, to some degree, this book dispels such myths. The violence and repression rendered by Patriot on Tory, Loyalist on Whig, during the American Revolution frequently had little to do with idealism, and much to do with greed, jealousy, and power. And whether Patriot or Tory, leaders and men from both sides acquired and owned slaves, a moral transgression our society no longer countenances.

It was never the aim of this book to present Sumter and Marion as idealized heroes, or Tarleton as a dastardly villain, although I do take time to explore the myths created around their lives. Nor did I intend to travel down the paths of sociocultural revisionism, destroying these myths for the sake of some version of political correctness whose ethics and values only seem to get murkier and more arbitrary over time.

I suppose the main reason I wrote this book was for myself, a storyteller spinning stories of a period and characters that still fascinate him, just as they did when he was a boy. Do I need a more complex or intellectual reason for keeping their stories alive than my own need to tell them?

For me, the appeal is geography and narrative. I moved to South Carolina in 2013 and returned to North Carolina after living in the Palmetto State for ten years. During that time, I became intimately acquainted with the landscape of the American Revolution in South Carolina, particularly places like Blackstocks and Musgroves Mill, which were just down the road from my Spartanburg home, not to mention Cowpens and Kings Mountain. To know a place, to drive its roads and ramble its forests and talk to its people, connects us more deeply to its history. And for me, once connected, I often want to tell that place's stories in my own voice. Maybe it is as simple as that.

Yet I must admit it is the narrative of men like Marion and Sumter, with Tarleton serving as their ideal foil, that draws me to them most deeply, just as it did when I was a child. As the Bard knew, we can't resist stories of thunder, lightning, and rain. Each age, of course, creates its own narratives, produces its own heroes. But the stories of Marion and Sumter draw me inevitably to my youth, a time when a young boy could thrill to Swamp Fox stories found on the shelf of an elementary school library without making amends to the thought police.

I read today seeking those same connections—call it mythology if you will—and hopefully you have found something in these pages also connecting you. For an even more idealistic motive, let me propose that I hope this story finds young readers as I was then, and inspires passion in them for American Revolution history, as the Swamp Fox's story inspired me. Myth or reality, or some combination of both, it is, after all, a story of remarkable lives in a remarkable time. Surely, there is something still indelible to we Americans about that.

NOTES

PROLOGUE: NO ORDINARY WAR

1. Franklin and Mary Wickwire, *Cornwallis and the War of Independence* (London: Faber and Faber, 1971), 15–16, 46.

2. Charles Cornwallis to Henry Clinton, July 15, 1780, in *The Cornwallis Papers: The Campaigns of 1780 and 1781 in the Southern Theatre of the American Revolutionary War*, Volume 1, ed. Ian Saberton (East Sussex, England: The Naval & Military Press Ltd., 2010), 170. Hereafter abbreviated as *CP* with volume and page number, as in *CP*, 1:170.

3. "Cornwallis to Germain," August 21, 1780, *CP*, 2:11.

4. Christopher Ward, *War of the Revolution* (New York: Skyhorse Publishing, 2011), 732.

5. Called the Catawba River as it traverses North Carolina and flows into South Carolina, the river changes name to the Wateree River at its confluence with Wateree Creek, about twenty miles northwest of Camden.

6. Cornwallis to Germain, August 21, 1780, *CP*, 2:11.

7. Ibid.

8. William R. Davie, *The Revolutionary War Sketches of William R. Davie*, Blackwell P. Robinson, ed. (Raleigh: North Carolina Department of Cultural Resources, 1976), 20.

9. "Cornwallis to Clinton," August 23, 1780, *CP*, 2:16.

10. "Cornwallis to Cruger," August 27, 1780, *CP*, 2:172.

CHAPTER ONE: SWIFT, VIGILANT, AND BOLD

1. C. Leon Harris, "American Soldiers at the Battle of Waxhaws, SC, 29 May 1780," *Southern Campaigns American Revolution Pension Statements and Rosters*, http://revwarapps.org/b221.pdf. Accessed on July 14, 2020. Also, Henry Bowyer, "Particular Account of Colonel Beaufort's Defeat," in Alexander Garden, *Anecdotes of the American Revolution, Illustrative of the Talents and Virtues of the Heroes and Patriots Who Acted the Most Conspicuous Parts Therein* (Charleston, SC: A. E. Miller, 1828), 135–38.

2. Mark M. Boatner, *Encyclopedia of the American Revolution* (New York: David McKay Co., 1974), 616. For casualties at Lenud's Ferry, Banastre Tarleton, *A History of the Campaigns of*

1780 and 1781, in the Southern Provinces of North America (London: T. Cadell, 1787), 20.

3. Charles Stedman, *The History of the Origin, Progress, and Termination of the American War* (London: printed for the author, 1794), 2:183.

4. "Abraham Buford to Virginia General Assembly," June 2, 1780, Thomas Addis Emmet Collection, New York Public Library. From James Piecuch, "Massacre or Myth? Banastre Tarleton at the Waxhaws, May 29, 1780," *The Southern Campaigns of the American Revolution*, edited by Charles B. Baxley, 1:2 (October 2004), http://southerncampaign.org/newsletter/v1n2.pdf., accessed May 25, 2020. Hereafter *Piecuch: SCAR*, with original reference where available.

5. "Dr. Robert Brownfield to William Dobein James," from William Dobein James, *A Sketch of the Life of Brigadier General Francis Marion and a History of the Brigade* (Marietta, GA: Continental Book Company, 1948), Appendix 1-7.

6. Ibid.

7. Tarleton, *Campaigns*, 28.

8. "Abraham Buford to Virginia General Assembly," June 2, 1780, *Piecuch: SCAR.*

9. Edward McCrady, *The History of South Carolina in the Revolution*, 1775–1780 (New York: The Macmillan Company, 1901), 520.

10. John Buchanan, *The Road to Guilford Courthouse: The American Revolution in the Carolinas* (New York: John Wiley & Sons, 1997), 58.

11. Anthony J. Scotti, *Brutal Virtue: The Myth and Reality of Banastre Tarleton* (Bowie, MD: Heritage Books, 2002), 22–23, n1.

12. Robert D. Bass, *The Green Dragoon: The Lives of Banastre Tarleton and Mary Robinson* (Orangeburg, SC: Sandlapper Publishing Co., 1973), 12.

13. Ibid., 13–14.

14. Scotti, *Brutal Virtue*, 15. While Bass provides a florid and entertaining account of Tarleton's life, Scotti's portrait is, thankfully, footnoted.

15. Ibid., 16.

16. John W. Shy, "Charles Lee: The Soldier as Radical," in *George Washington's Generals and Opponents: Their Exploits and Leadership*, ed. George Athan Billias (New York: Da Capo Press edition, 1994), 1:22–48.

17. "Banastre Tarleton to unnamed correspondent," December 17, 1776, in "New War Letters of Banastre Tarleton," ed. Richard M. Ketchum, *New York Historical Society Quarterly Report*, vol. 51, no. 1, 69–70. Also, "Banastre Tarleton to Jane Parker Tarleton," December 18, 1776, in Bass, *The Green Dragoon*, 20–21.

18. Scotti, *Brutal Virtue*, 18. Tarleton quote from "Banastre Tarleton to Jane Parker Tarleton," December 18, 1776, referenced directly above.

19. Ketchum, "New War Letters of Banastre Tarleton," 79. Also Bass, *Green Dragoon*, 37, for the *Political Magazine* quote.

20. Bass, *Green Dragoon*, 38.

21. Boatner, *Encyclopedia*, 608.

22. Scotti, *Brutal Virtue*, 18, 26, n11.

23. Christopher Ward, *War of the Revolution* (New York: Skyhorse Publishing, 2011), 576–86.

24. Henry Clinton, *The American Rebellion: Sir Henry Clinton's Narrative of His Campaigns, 1775–1782*, ed. William B. Willcox (New Haven, CT: Yale University Press, 1954), 110–11.

25. Bass, *Green Dragoon*, 48.

26. Scotti, *Brutal Virtue*, 19.

27. John Graves Simcoe, *Simcoe's Military Journal: A History of the Operations of a Partisan Corps Called the Queen's Rangers* (New York: Bartlett & Welford, 1844), 84–88.

28. Bass, *Green Dragoon*, 51.

29. Boatner, *Encyclopedia*, 189.

30. Washington Irving, *Wolfert's Roost and Other Papers, Now First Collected* (New York: G.P. Putnam & Co., 1855), 17.

31. John Milton Hutchins, "Cavalry Action at Poundridge, New York: Bloody Ban's Early Education, in *Cavalry of the American Revolution*, ed. Jim Piecuch (Yardley, PA: Westholme Publishing, 2012), 66.

32. This reference and all of the account of the action at Pound Ridge is from John Milton Hutchins, "Cavalry Action at Poundridge," 56–75. Hutchins reports that Tarleton probably underreported his troop strength to bolster his report.

CHAPTER TWO: A SHY BITCH'S REVENGE

1. Boatner, *Encyclopedia*, 206.

2. Ward, *War of the Revolution*, 209.

3. Edward E. Curtis, *The British Army in the American Revolution* (New Haven, CT: Yale University Press, 1926), 2–3. Also, Holger Hoock, *Scars of Independence: America's Violent Birth* (New York: Crown, 2017), 101.

4. Quotes from Martin, Dunmore, and Campbell from David K. Wilson, *The Southern Strategy: Britain's Conquest of South Carolina and Georgia, 1775–1780* (Columbia: University of South Carolina Press, 2005), 2.

5. Fortescue quote extracted from Wilson, *The Southern Strategy*, 4.

6. William B. Willcox, *Portrait of a General: Sir Henry Clinton in the War of Independence* (New York: Knopf, 1964), 77.

7. Wilson, *The Southern Strategy*, 22, 32-35. Approximately 6,000 Loyalists embodied prior to the Moore's Creek Bridge, but by the time of the battle, only 1,400 participated, according to Wilson.

8. Willcox, *Portrait of a General*, 75–77 and Ward, *War of the Revolution*, 669–70.

9. William B. Willcox, *Portrait of a General*, 84–89.

10. "Henry Clinton Memorandum April 1776." Reprinted in Willcox, *Portrait of a General*, 83.

11. John Pancake, *This Destructive War: The British Campaign in the Carolinas, 1780–1782* (Tuscaloosa: University of Alabama Press, 2003), 5.

12. Willcox, *Portrait of a General*, 197, 208. Also, for background, Maldwyn A. Jones, "Sir William Howe: Conventional Strategist" and William B. Willcox, "Sir Henry Clinton: Paralysis of Command," from *George Washington's Generals and Opponents*, 2:39–72 and 2:79–80, respectively.

13. Willcox, *Portrait of a General*, 66.

14. William B. Willcox, "Sir Henry Clinton: Paralysis of Command," in *George Washington's Generals and Opponents: Their Exploits and Leadership*, 2:74.

15. Willcox, *Portrait of a General*, 506–11.

16. Pancake, *This Destructive War*, 14.

17. Ibid., 10. Also, for troop disposition, Willcox, *Portrait of a General*, 225.

18. "Lord Carlisle to his wife," June 14, 1778, quoted in Willcox, *Portrait of a General*, 230.

19. Pancake, *This Destructive War*, 26. Wilson, *Southern Strategy*, 61.

20. J. W. Fortescue, *A History of the British Army*, Vol. 3 (Edinburgh, Scotland: R & R Clark, no date), 252.

21. Don Higginbotham, *The War of American Independence*, 353.

22. Clinton quotes extracted from Willcox, *Portrait of a General*, 261.

23. Boatner, *Encyclopedia*, 981.

24. Clinton, *American Rebellion*, 116–17.

25. Ibid., 151.

26. "Charles Stuart to Lord Bute," August 1779, *A Prime Minister and His Son: From the Correspondence of the 3rd Earl of Bute and of Lt. General the Hon. Sir Charles Suart* (London: J. Murray, 1925), 149.

27. Johann Ewald, *Diary of the American War: A Hessian Journal*, ed. Joseph Tustin (New Haven, CT: Yale University Press, 1979), 159.

28. C. P. Borick, *A Gallant Defense: The Siege of Charleston, 1780* (Columbia: University of South Carolina Press), 23.

29. British troop strength taken from Bernard Uhlendorf, editor, *The Siege of Charleston with an Account of the Province of South Carolina: Diaries and Letters of Hessian Officers from the von Jungkenn Papers in the William L. Clements Library*, vol. 12 (Ann Arbor: University of Michigan Press, 1938), 108–9. The source is an embarkation list prepared by Major Carl Bauermeister. Taken from Carl P. Borick, *A Gallant Defense*, 23.

30. Ward, *War of the Revolution*, 698.

31. Curtis, *The British Army in the American Revolution*, 2–3. Also, Philip R. N. Katcher, *Encyclopedia of British, Provincial, and German Army Units, 1775–1783* (Harrisburg, PA: Stackpole Books, 1973), 21–24.

32. Ibid., 16.

33. Tarleton, *Campaigns*, 16. Casualty figures are from Stedman, *History*, 2:183.

34. Uzal Johnson, *Captured at King's Mountain: The Journal of Uzal Johnson, a Loyalist Surgeon*, eds. Wade S. Kolb III and Robert M. Weir (Columbia: University of South Carolina Press, 2011), 10.

35. Stedman, *The American War*, 2:183.

36. Tarleton, *Campaigns*, 19–20.

37. Boatner, *Encyclopedia*, 1169.

38. William Moultrie, *Memoirs of the American Revolution* (New York: David Longworth, 1802), 2:96–97.

39. Total Americans captured in Charleston is from Borick, *A Gallant Defense*, 222. The number of Continentals is from Buchanan, *Road to Guilford Courthouse*, 70. Quote from Boatner, *Encyclopedia*, 213.

40. "Germain to Clinton," November 4, 1779, from Clinton, *American Rebellion*, 434.

41. William B. Willcox, *Portrait of a General*, 316.

42. Ibid.

43. Armstrong Starkey, *War in the Age of Enlightenment, 1700–1789* (Westport, CT: Praeger Publishers, 2003), 21.

44. For an account of this ineffectual campaign, see Edward G. Lengel, *The Battles of Connecticut Farms and Springfield 1780* (Yardley, PA: Westholme Publishing, 2020).

45. Willcox, *Portrait of a General*, 60.

CHAPTER THREE: TARLETON'S QUARTERS

1. Clinton, *The American Rebellion*, 175. Cornwallis's troop strength and composition from Ward, *War of the Revolution*, 704.

2. Wickwire, *Cornwallis*, 18–20.

3. Ibid., 50.

4. Rankin, "Charles Lord Cornwallis: Study in Frustration," in *George Washington's Generals and Opponents*, 2:194.

5. Wickwire, *Cornwallis*, 45–46.

6. Quote about the vice treasurer of Ireland is from the Lords Hansard, https://api.parliament.uk/historic-hansard/commons/1823/feb/11/vice-treasurer-of-ireland. Accessed on March 19, 2021.

7. Armstrong Starkey, *War in the Age of Enlightenment*, 20–21. The de Tressan quote is taken from Starkey.

8. North quote excerpted from Rankin, "Charles Lord Cornwallis: Study in Frustration," *George Washington's Generals and Opponents*, 2:194.

9. Ibid., 2:198.

10. Ibid., 2:222.

11. McCrady, *The History of the Revolution in South Carolina, 1775–1780*, 517.

12. Boatner, *Encyclopedia*, 954–55.

13. Ward, *War of the Revolution*, 705.

14. Tarleton, *Campaigns*, 27.

15. Anne King Gregorie, *Thomas Sumter* (Columbia, SC: The R.L. Bryan Company, 1931), 75.

16. Robert Stansbury Lambert, *South Carolina Loyalists in the American Revolution* (Columbia: University of South Carolina Press, 1987), 117.

17. McCrady, *History of the Revolution in South Carolina, 1775–1780*, 517.

18. Tarleton, *Campaigns*, 28.

19. McCrady, *The History of the Revolution in South Carolina, 1775–1780*, 520; also, Piecuch, *SCAR*. Piecuch cites, "Report of Captain Cochrane, enclosed in Lord Geroge Germain to Sir Jeffrey Amherst, November 30, 1780," *Amherst Papers*, War Office Series 34/128. Cochrane reported he overheard an American officer remark the opposition "was only a few light Horse" just before the attack.

20. Piecuch, *SCAR*

21. Tarleton, *Campaigns*, 28-29.

22. Ibid., 29.

23. Ward, *War of the Revolution*, 705. Also, Buchanan, *Road to Guilford Courthouse*, 82. It is Ward who writes one hundred of Buford's infantry accompanied the wagons away from the battlefield.

24. Tarleton describes the battlefield as an "open wood" in *Campaigns*, 29. William Moultrie, *Memoirs of the American Revolution* (New York: David Longworth, 1802), 2:205, for the disposition of Buford's troops. It is I who presume Buford put his cavalry in the reserve, as I can't find this detail in other accounts. See also "Battle of Waxhaws, SC, May 29, 1780" map by the American Battlefield Trust at https://www.battlefields.org/learn/maps/battle-waxhaws. Accessed on June 3, 2020.

25. Tarleton, *Campaigns*, 28–30.

26. John Marshall, *The Life of George Washington, Special Edition for Schools*, Vol. 3, eds. Robert Faulkner and Paul Carrese (Indianapolis, IN: Liberty Fund, 2000), https://oll.libertyfund.org/titles/marshall-the-life-of-george-washington. Accessed November 10, 2019.

27. Bowyer, "Account of Colonel Beaufort's Defeat," 137.

28. Ibid.

29. Tarleton, *Campaigns*, 28. Also, "Dr. Robert Brownfield to William Dobein James," from William Dobein James, *Life of Marion*, Appendix 1-7.

30. Moultrie, *Memoirs*, 2:205–6; Scotti, *Brutal Virtue*, 175, for cavalry tactics.

31. Tarleton, *Campaigns*, 30.

32. Ibid. Also, "Brownfield to James."

33. Bowyer, "Account of Colonel Beaufort's Defeat,"138. Also, "Buford to Virginia Assembly," June 2, 1780, and "Brownfield to James."

34. Piecuch, *SCAR*. Also, "Buford to Virginia Assembly," June 2, 1780.

35. "Brownfield to James."

36. All quotes in previous two paragraphs from C. Leon Harris, "American Soldiers at the Battle of Waxhaws SC, 29 May 1780," revised March 28, 2018, on *Southern Campaigns*

Revolutionary War Pension Statements & Rosters website, http://revwarapps.org/b221.pdf, accessed on November 11, 2019.

37. "Brownfield to James."

38. Ibid.

39. Armstrong Starkey, "Paoli to Stony Point: Military Ethics and Weaponry During the American Revolution," *The Journal of American History*, Vol. 58, No. 1 (January 1994), 7–27.

40. Piecuch, *SCAR*.

41. Scotti, *Brutal Virtue*, 173.

42. C. Leon Harris, "Massacre at Waxhaws: The Evidence From Wounds," *Southern Campaigns of the American Revolution*, Vol. 11, Number 2.1 (June 2016), http://www.southern-campaign.org/wordpress/wp-content/uploads/2016/05/Harris-Massacre-at-Waxhaws.pdf. Accessed on July 16, 2020.

43. Tarleton, *Campaigns*, 31.

44. Stedman, *The American War*, 2:193.

45. Tarleton, *Campaigns*, 31.

46. Ward, *War of the Revolution*, 706.

47. David Ramsay, *History of the Revolution of South Carolina* (Trenton, NJ: Isaac Collins, 1785), 2:110.

48. Boatner, *Encyclopedia*, 912.

49. "Otho Holland Williams to his Brother, Elie Williams," June 20, 1780, *Otho Holland Williams Papers*, Maryland Historical Society. Excerpted from Piecuch, *SCAR*.

50. J. Tracy Power, "The Virtue of Humanity was Totally Forgot: Buford's Massacre, May 29, 1780," *The South Carolina Historical Magazine*, Vol. 93, No. 1 (January 1992), 10.

51. Jim Piecuch, *The Blood Be Upon Your Head: Tarleton and the Myth of Buford's Massacre* (Lugoff, SC: Southern Campaigns of the American Revolution Press, 2010), 71.

52. "Brownfield to James." Also, Piecuch, *SCAR*, for the accounts of Winn, Davie, and Gaston.

53. Joseph Graham, *General Joseph Graham and His Papers on North Carolina Revolutionary History*, ed. William A. Graham (Raleigh, NC: Edwards & Broughton, 1904), 234.

54. Hoock, *Scars of Independence*, 267.

CHAPTER FOUR: OLD SCORES

1. Walter Edgar, *South Carolina: A History* (Columbia: University of South Carolina Press, 1998), 1–78.

2. Robert D. Bass, *Ninety Six: The Struggle for the South Carolina Back Country* (Orangeburg, SC: Sandlapper Publishing, 1978), 17–18.

3. This broad introduction to the Great Wagon Road is amalgamated from Parke Rouse Jr., *The Great Wagon Road: How Scotch-Irish and Germanics Settled the Upland* (Richmond, VA: Dietz Press, 2008).

4. Buchanan, *Road to Guilford Courthouse*, 86–88.

5. Walter Edgar, *Partisans & Redcoats: The Southern Conflict that Turned the Tide of the American Revolution* (New York: William Morrow, 2001), 1–2.

6. Blackwell P. Robinson, *William R. Davie* (Chapel Hill: University of North Carolina Press, 1957), 11. Also, Rhett A. Adams, "Waxhaws (Region)," *South Carolina Encyclopedia*, http://www.scencyclopedia.org/sce/entries/waxhaws-region/. Accessed June 10, 2020.

7. Michael C. Scoggins, *The Day It Rained Militia: Huck's Defeat and the Revolution in the South Carolina Backcountry May–July 1780* (Charleston, SC: The History Press, 2005), 22.

8. Edgar, *Partisans & Redcoats*, 2, 10–11.

9. Bass, *Ninety Six*, 40–45.

10. The South Carolina Militia Act of 1747 is described in footnotes 96 and 97 of William T. Graves, *Backcountry Revolutionary: James Williams (1740–1780)* (Lugoff, SC: Southern Campaigns of the American Revolution Press, 2012), 47.

11. Oscar E. and Catherine R. Gilbert, *True for the Cause of Liberty: The Second Spartan Regiment in the American Revolution* (Philadelphia, PA: Casemate Publishers, 2015), 33–34.

12. Edgar, *South Carolina*, 214.

13. Bass, *Ninety Six*, 64–67; Edgar, *Paristans and Redcoats*, 19–20.

14. Bass, *Ninety Six*, 67; Lambert, *South Carolina Loyalists*, 19.

15. Andrew Waters, *Quaker and the Gamecock: Nathanael Greene, Thomas Sumter, and the Revolutionary War for the Soul of the South* (Philadelphia, PA: Casemate Publishers, 2019), 62.

16. Peter Moore, "The Local Origins of Allegiance in Revolutionary South Carolina," *South Carolina Historical Magazine*, 107(1), 30, 36.

17. Saberton, "Biographical Note on Robert Cunningham," *CP*, 1:117, n13.

18. Lambert, *South Carolina Loyalists*, 23–24. Also, Bass, *Ninety Six*, 95.

19. Edgar, *Partisans & Redcoats*, 27.

20. Ibid., 28–29.

21. Andrew Pickens quote excerpted from Bass, *Ninety Six*, 81–82.

22. Robert M. Weir, "Campbell, Lord William," *South Carolina Encyclopedia*, https://www.scencyclopedia.org/sce/entries/campbell-lord-william/, accessed on June 15, 2020.

23. Hoock, *Scars of Independence*, 29.

24. Bass, *Ninety Six*, 87.

25. Buchanan, *Road to Guilford Courthouse*, 96—97. Also, Boatner, *Encyclopedia*, 117.

26. Buchanan, *Road to Guilford Courthouse*, 87–112.

27. John W. Gordon, *South Carolina and the American Revolution: A Battlefield History* (Columbia: University of South Carolina Press, 2003), 30–31.

28. Ibid., 31–32.

29. Bass, *Ninety Six*, 121.

30. Lambert, *South Carolina Loyalists*, 42.

31. Bass, *Ninety Six*, 43–45.

32. Lambert, *South Carolina Loyalists*, 50.

33. Boatner, *Encyclopedia*, 117–18, 360–61; Ian Saberton, *CP*, 1:271–72, n50. Also, David Fanning, *The Narrative of Colonel David Fanning* (New York: Joseph Sabin, 1865), 3–11.

34. Lambert, *South Carolina Loyalists*, 52.

35. Joseph Johnson, *Traditions and Reminiscences, Chiefly of the American Revolution in the South* (Charleston, SC: Walker & James, 1851), 484.

CHAPTER FIVE: A LION ROUSED

1. Anne King Gregorie, *Thomas Sumter* (Columbia, SC: The R.L. Bryan Company, 1931), 73–74.

2. Stephen Conway, "To Subdue America: British Army Officers and the Conduct of the Revolutionary War," *The William and Mary Quarterly* 43, no. 3 (July 1986), 386–87.

3. James, *Marion*, 40. Also, Robert D. Bass, *Gamecock: The Life and Campaigns of General Thomas Sumter* (Orangeburg, SC: Sandlapper Publishing Co., 1961), 54.

4. Gregorie, *Thomas Sumter*, 4.

5. Bass, *Gamecock*, 6–7.

6. Ibid., 12.

7. Ibid., 15.

8. Ibid., 21.

9. Gregorie, *Thomas Sumter*, 31.

10. Ibid., 32.

11. Ibid., 40.

12. Moultrie, *Memoirs*, 1:1.

13. Gregorie, *Thomas Sumter*, 47.

14. Bass, *Gamecock*, 37.

15. Robert L. Ganyard, "Threat from the West: North Carolina and the Cherokee, 1776–1778," *The North Carolina Historical Review*, January, 1968, 45:1, 51–57.

16. Gregorie, *Thomas Sumter*, 49–54. Also, Bass, *Ninety Six*, 143–44.

17. Bass, *Ninety Six*, 145.

18. With exceptions noted, this biographical sketch of Thomas Sumter was derived primarily from Gregorie and Bass, the only two writers who have published full-length biographies of him. Also referenced was my own work on Sumter, *The Quaker and the Gamecock*, for some of the material.

CHAPTER SIX: IN THE RIGHT

1. "National Register Properties in South Carolina: Colonel John Stuart House, Charleston County (104-106 Tradd Street)," South Carolina Department of Archives and History, accessed November 22, 2023, http://www.nationalregister.sc.gov/charleston/S108177 10027/index.htm.

2. Lambert, *South Carolina Loyalists*, 17.

3. *Encyclopedia Britannica*, online edition, entry for "Whig and Tory," https://www.britannica.com/topic/Whig-Party-England, accessed August 15, 2020. Also, Arthur Herman, *How the Scots Invented the Modern World: The True Story of How Western Europe's Poorest Nation Created Our World and Everything in It* (New York: Crown Publishers, 2001), 135.

4. Francis Marion, "Orderly Book," collected in *Unwaried Patience & Fortitude: Francis Marion's Orderly Book*, ed. Patrick O'Kelly (West Conshohocken, PA: Infinity Publishing Co., 2006), 500.

5. James, *Life of Marion*, 46.

6. Peter Horry and M. L. Weems, *The Life of General Francis Marion* (Winston-Salem, NC: John F. Blair, Publisher edition, 200), 64–65.

7. Hugh F. Rankin, *Francis Marion: The Swamp Fox* (New York: Thomas Y. Crowell Company, 1973); also, Moultrie, *Memoirs of the American Revolution*, 2:222.

8. Borick, *A Gallant Defense*, 223. Figures for the number of Continental prisoners taken in the surrender at Charleston are from Boatner, *Encyclopedia*, 213. Citing the August 21, 1780, report of the Board of War, he reports 245 Continental and 2,326 enlisted and noncommissioned officers captured in the surrender.

9. Rankin, *The Swamp Fox*, 45.

10. Edgar, *South Carolina*, 50–51. Also, "Hugueots, French Protesants," *Encyclopedia Britannica*, accessed August 15, 2020, https://www.britannica.com/topic/Huguenot.

11. John Lawson, *A New Voyage to Carolina*, ed. Hugh Talmage Lefler (Chapel Hill: University of North Carolina Press edition, 1967), 19.

12. Ibid., 20.

13. Horry and Weems, *General Francis Marion*, 15. Also, Robert D. Bass, *Swamp Fox: The Life and Campaigns of General Francis Marion* (Orangeburg, SC: Sandlapper Publishing Co., 1974), 5–6.

14. Horry and Weems, *General Francis Marion*, 15.

15. James, *Life of Marion*, 23.

16. Rankin, *The Swamp Fox*, 4–5.

17. Edgar, *South Carolina*, 207.

18. Hoock, *Scars of Independence*, 281.

19. Moultrie, *Memoirs*, 2:223n; also, Rankin, *The Swamp Fox*, 6.

20. Moutrie, *Memoirs*, 1:65.

21. Roy Talbert Jr. "Horry, Peter," *South Carolina Encyclopedia*, accessed June 29, 2020, http://www.scencyclopedia.org/sce/entries/horry-peter/.

22. This quote from Horry is extracted from the "Publisher's Introduction" to *General Francis Marion* by Horry and Weems.

23. Moultrie, *Memoirs*, 1:90–91. Also, Richard W. Hatcher, "Moultrie Flag," *South Carolina Encyclopedia*, accessed July 1, 2020, http://www.scencyclopedia.org/sce/entries/moultrie-flag/.

24. Rankin, *The Swamp Fox*, 18–20.

25. Buchanan, *Road to Guilford Courthouse*, 13–16.

26. Marion, "Orderly Book," 82.

27. Bass, *Swamp Fox*, 21.

28. Horry and Weems, *General Francis Marion*, 27, 29–30.

29. Rankin, *The Swamp Fox*, 27–28.

30. Ibid., 28. Also, Boatner, *Encyclopedia*, 636.

31. Boatner, *Encylopedia*, 984.

32. Ibid.

33. Horry and Weems, *General Francis Marion*, 58–60.

34. Boatner, *Encyclopedia*, 989.

35. Rankin, *The Swamp Fox*, 39.

36. Except otherwise noted, this biographical sketch of Francis Marion was comprised primarily from Hugh Rankin, *The Swamp Fox*, and John D. Bass, *Swamp Fox*. Rankin has the good grace to document his sources, while Bass does not, and so it is upon Rankin I primarily relied, although I generally find Bass to be in concert with Rankin on most matters, with a greater prose flair. Horry, of course, provides colorful insight and is used primarily in that capacity.

CHAPTER SEVEN: TURNED TO FLOOD

1. Katcher, *Encyclopedia of British, Provincial, and German Army Units*, 82.

2. "Balfour to Cornwallis," May 30, 1780, *CP*, 1:74.

3. Rankin, *The Swamp Fox*, 50.

4. See "Turnbull to Cornwallis," June 14, 1780, *CP*, 1:138.

5. Stedman, *History*, 2:194. Historian Walter Edgar estimates the British occupation force at 3,700 men in *Partisan and Redcoats*, 88.

6. Scoggins, *Day It Rained Militia*, 52–62.

7. "Turnbull to Cornwallis," *CP*, 1:140.

8. Moore, "The Local Origins of Allegiance in Revolutionary South Carolina: The Waxhaws as a Case Study," 39.

9. Saberton, "Note on Henry Rugeley" and also "Rawdon to Cornwallis," June 15, 1780, *CP*, 1:128–29. A more detailed account of Henry Rugeley appears in my book *To The End of the World* (Yardley, PA: Westholme Publishing, 2020). See chapter 3, "That Rascal Rugeley."

10. James P. Collins quote excerpted from Scoggins, *Day It Rained Militia*, 50.

11. Lyman Draper, *King's Mountain and Its Heroes: History of the Battle of King's Mountain* (Cincinnati, OH: Peter O. Thomson, 1881), 240.

12. Scoggins, *Day It Rained Militia*, 54. Also Boatner, *Encyclopedia*, 574.

13. Draper, *King's Mountain*, 240.

14. Ramsay, *History of the Revolution of South Carolina*, 2:110.

15. Lambert, *South Carolina Loyalists*, 85–86; Robert Gray, "Robert Gray's Observations on the War in Carolina," *South Carolina Historical and Genealogical Magazine*, vol. 11, no.3, June 1910, 140.

16. Draper, *King's Mountain*, 242.

17. William S. Powell and Michael Hill, *The North Carolina Gazetteer: A Dictionary of Tar Heel Places and Their History* (Chapel Hill: University of North Carolina Press, 2010), 401.

18. Edgar, *South Carolina*, 57–58.

19. William W. Boddie, *History of Williamsburg: Something About the People of Williamsburg County, South Carolina, from the First Settlement by Europeans about 1705 until 1923* (Columbia, SC: The State Company, 1923), 22.

20. Edgar, *South Carolina*, 52–62, 78. Also, Boddie, *Williamsburg*, 41.

21. Boddie, *Williamsburg*, 59.

22. Boddie, *Williamsburg*, 90. "Cryptomnesic" is a derivation of the medical term "cryptomnesia," meaning "the appearance in consciousness of memory images which are not recognized as such, but which appear as original creations," according to the *Merriam Webster Dictionary*.

23. Ibid., 96.

24. Ibid., 93.

25. Lambert, *South Carolina Loyalists*, 83–84; Saberton, CP, 1:132n, 135n, 161n; Robert Gray, "Robert Gray's Observations on the War in Carolina," *South Carolina Historical and Genealogical Magazine*, vol. 11, no.3, June 1910, 139–40.

26. Alexander Gregg, *History of the Old Cheraws* (New York: Richardson & Company, 1867), 250, 287.

27. "McArthur to Cornwallis," June 18, 1780, *CP*, 1:135.

28. Stedman, *The American War*, 2:191.

29. "Clinton Proclamation of May 22, 1780" reprinted in Tarleton, *Campaigns*, 71–72.

30. "Clinton to Eden," May 30, 1780. Excerpted from William B. Willcox, *Portrait of a General*, 320.

31. John Shy, "British Strategy for Pacifying the Southern Colonies, 1778–1781," *The Southern Experience in the American Revolution*, eds. Jeffrey Crow and Larry Tise (Chapel Hill: University of North Carolina Press, 1978), 167.

32. Lambert, *South Carolina Loyalists*, 67.

33. "Henry Clinton Proclamation of June 3, 1780," reprinted in Tarleton, *Campaigns*, 73–74.

34. Draper, *King's Mountain and Its Heroes*, 46.

35. Clinton, *American Rebellion*, 181.

36. Willcox, *Portrait of a General*, 321.

37. "Cornwallis to Clinton," June 30, 1780, CP, 1:159–61.

38. Stedman, *The American War*, 2:199.

39. James, *Life of Marion*, 43.

40. Ibid.

CHAPTER EIGHT: WHAT WE CALL REFUGEES

1. "Corwnallis to Clinton," June 30, 1780, *CP*, 1:163.

2. "Clinton to Cornwallis," June 1, 1780, and "Observations on Some Parts of the Answer of Earl Cornwallis to Sir Henry Clinton's Narrative," both appearing in *The Campaign in Virginia, Part 1*, ed. Benjamin Franklin Stevens (London: 1887), 214 and 106–7, respectively.

3. Scoggins, *Day It Rained Militia*, 74.

4. Richard Winn, "General Richard Winn's Notes: 1780," ed. Samuel C. Winn; *The South Carolina Historical Review* 43, no. 4 (1942), 202.

5. Draper, *King's Mountain and Its Heroes*, 45.

6. Scoggins, *Day It Rained Militia*, 53.

7. Stedman, *The American War*, 198.

8. Ibid., 193-194.

9. Scoggins, *Day It Rained Militia*, 52.

10. Winn, "Winn's Notes," 1:202.

11. Graves, *Backcountry Revolutionary*, 77–78.

12. Thomas Young, *The Memoir of Major Thomas Young* (1764–1848), *Orion Magazine*, November 1843.

13. Walter Edgar, *Partisans and Redcoats*, 63–64.

14. Scoggins, *Day It Rained Militia*, 29.

15. Ibid., 58.

16. Winn, "Winn's Notes," 1:202.

17. Ibid., 204 (n8).

18. Saberton, "Biographical Footnote on George Turnbull," *CP*, 1:138(n).

19. Ibid., 205 (n9).

20. Joseph McJunkin, "Memoirs of Major Joseph McJunkin," excerpted in Scoggins, *Day it Rained Militia*, 73.

21. William Hill, *Col. William Hill's Memoir of the Revolution*, ed. A. S. Salley (Columbia, SC: The Historical Commission of South Carolina, 1921), 6–7.

22. Graham, *Papers*, 214–15.

23. "Cornwallis to Clinton," June 30, 1780, *CP*, 1:162.

24. Gregorie, *Thomas Sumter*, 78.

25. "Turnbull to Cornwallis," June 16, 1780, *CP*, 1:142.

26. Hill, "William Hill's Memoir," 8.

27. "Turnbull to Cornwallis," June 19, 1780, *CP*, 1:143.

28. Hill, *William Hill's Memoir*, 8.

29. Benson J. Lossing, *The Pictorial Field-Book of the Revolution, Vol. II* (New York: Harper Brothers, 1852), 627.

30. Scoggins, *Day It Rained Militia*, 83–84. Anne King Gregorie lists the date as June 15, 1780, but I am more confident in Scoggins's scholarship in this instance. Also, Emily D. Ramsey, "A Brief Historical Sketch of Tuckaseegee Ford" (Mecklenburg County Landmarks Commission Report, n.d.), accessed August 28, 2020, http://landmarkscommission.org/wp-content/uploads/2017/07/Tuckaseegee-Ford-Trail.pdf.

31. Gilbert, *True for the Cause of Liberty*, 98–100. Also, Scoggins, *Day It Rained Militia*, 82–83.

32. Gregorie, *Thomas Sumter*, 79. Also, Scoggins, *Day It Rained Militia*, 27, 61.

33. Joseph McJunkin, "Pension Application of Joseph McJunkin," transcribed and annotated by Will Graves, accessed May 21, 2020, http://revwarapps.org/s18118.pdf.

34. Gregorie, *Thomas Sumter*, 79.

35. Ramsay, *History of the Revolution of South Carolina*, 2:130.

36. Gregorie, *Thomas Sumter*, 79–80. Also, Bass, *Gamecock*, 50–53.

37. Winn, "Winn's Notes," 1:203.

38. Ibid., 1:203.

39. Joseph McJunkin, "Memoirs of Major Joseph McJunkin, Revolutionary Patriot," ed. Rev. James Hodge Saye. Originally printed in the *Watchman and Observer* (Richmond, VA:

1848). Transcribed online by Phil Norfleet at http://sc_tories.tripod.com/thomas_sumter_assumes_command.htm, accessed May 22, 2020.

40. Gregorie, *Thomas Sumter*, 80.

41. John Adair, "Pension application of John Adair," transcribed and annotated by Will Graves, http://revwarapps.org/w2895.pdf, accessed May 22, 2020.

42. Gregorie, *Thomas Sumter*, 80. Gregorie references the source of Wilson's recollection to the "Transcript of Logan MS," in Lyman Draper's *Sumter Papers*, 16VV319.

CHAPTER NINE: HUCK'S WAR

1. Scotti, *Brutal Virtue*, 234–35.

2. Conway, "To Subdue America."

3. "Tarleton to Cornwallis," November 8, 1780. Extracted from Conway, "To Subdue America."

4. Rawdon quote excerpted from Starkey, *War in the Age of Enlightenment*, 165.

5. "Patrick Ferguson to Henry Clinton," August 1, 1778, from "An Officer Out of His Time: Major Patrick Ferguson, 1779–1780," ed. Hugh F. Rankin, appearing in *Sources of American Independence*, ed. Howard H. Peckham (Chicago, IL: University of Chicago Press, 1778), 2:308.

6. Scoggins, *Day It Rained Militia*, 51–52.

7. Tarleton, *Campaigns*, 87.

8. Bass, *Green Dragoon*, 84–85. Also, Saberton, "Introduction to the Rest of Part Two," *CP*, 1:38, for the date of Tarleton's departure from Camden.

9. Edgar, *Partisans & Redcoats*, 59.

10. For the account of the Battle of Ramsour's Mill I have relied on Graham, *General Joseph Graham and His Papers on North Carolina Revolutionary History*, 219–26. Also referenced is Davie, *Revolutionary War Sketches*, 5–7.

11. "Rawdon to Cornwallis," June 22, 1780, *CP*, 1:182.

12. "Cornwallis to Rawdon," June 29, 1780, *CP*, 1:185; also, "Cornwallis to Clinton," June 30, 1780, *CP*, 1:162–63.

13. "Cornwallis to Clinton," June 30, 1780, *CP*, 1:163.

14. Ward, *War of the Revolution*, 715.

15. Quotes are from Otho Holland Williams, "A Narrative of the Campaign of 1780," appearing as Appendix B in *Sketches of the Life and Correspondence of Nathanael Greene: Major General of the Armies of the United States* by William Johnson, Vol. 1 (Charleston, SC: A.E. Miller, 1822), 48. Hereafter Williams, "Narrative," with page number. Also, Ward, *War of the Revolution*, 712–14 and Boatner, *Encyclopedia of the American Revolution*, 570–71.

16. Joseph McJunkin, "Ms. Statement," in the *Lyman C. Draper Thomas Sumter Collection*, MSS, 23VV208. Excerpted from Scoggins, *Day It Rained Militia*, 87.

17. Hill, *William Hill's Memoir*, 9.

18. Scoggins, *Day It Rained Militia*, 93–95.

19. "James Williams to Mary Williams," July 4, 1780, *Documentary History of the American Revolution*, ed. Robert W. Gibbes (New York: D. Appleton & Co., 1857), 2:135–36.

20. Scoggins, *Day It Rained Militia*, 97–98.

21. "Rawdon to Cornwallis," July 2, 1780, *CP*, 1:190.

22. Hill, *William Hill's Memoir*, 8–9.

23. Gregorie, *Thomas Sumter*, 103–4.

24. Johnson, *Traditions and Reminiscences*, 336.

25. Elizabeth E. Ellett, *The Women of the American Revolution* (New York: Charles Scribner, 1853–1854), 3, 180–83.

26. Scoggins, *Day It Rained Militia*, 114.

27. James Collins, *Autobiography of a Revolutionary Soldier*, ed. John M. Roberts (Clinton, LA: Feliciana Democrat, 1859), 26.

28. Scoggins, *Day It Rained Militia*, 109–26.

29. Tarleton, *Campaigns*, 93.

30. Winn, "Winn's Notes," 1:207.

31. "General Thomas Sumter to Baron De Kalb," July 17, 1780, *The State Records of North Carolina*, ed. Walter Clark, Vol. 14 (Winston, NC: M. L. and J. C. Stewart, 1896), 505–7. Hereafter, *SRNC*.

32. "Tarleton to John André," July 16, 1780, reprinted in Bass, *The Green Dragoon*, 90.

33. "Cornwallis to Rawdon," July 15, 1780, *CP*, 1:205–6; Bass, *The Green Dragoon*, 89–90.

34. Tarleton, *Campaigns*, 93. Also, Bass, *The Green Dragoon*, 89–90.

35. "Cornwallis to Rawdon," July 15, 1780, *CP*, 1:205. Also, "Cornwallis to Clinton," July 15, 1780, *CP*, 1:170.

CHAPTER 10: PROVIDENCE AND MOTION

1. Max M. Mintz, *The Generals of Saratoga: John Burgoyne & Horatio Gates* (New Haven, CT: Yale University Press, 1990), 17.

2. George A. Billias, "Horatio Gates: Professional Soldier," in *George Washington's General and Opponents*, ed. George A. Billias (New York: Da Capo Press edition, 1994), 89.

3. Ibid., 92.

4. This sketch of Gates is primarily derived from Billias and Mintz, as referenced above. Also helpful were Boatner, *Encyclopedia of the American Revolution*, and Paul David Nelson, *General Horatio Gates: A Biography* (Baton Rouge: Louisiana State University Press, 1976).

5. Charles Royster, *A Revolutionary People at War: The Continental Army & American Character, 1775–1783* (Chapel Hill: University of North Carolina Press, 1979), 314–15.

6. McCrady, *History of South Carolina in the Revolution, 1775–1780*, 620–21.

7. David Shenck, *North Carolina, 1780–'81: Being a History of the Invasion of the Carolinas by the British Army Under Lord Cornwallis* (Raleigh, NC: Edwards & Broughton, 1889), 64–65.

8. The following online sources were used in this biographical sketch of William R. Davie: Jeff Broadwater, "William Richardson Davie," (2016), North Carolina History Project, https://northcarolinahistory.org/encyclopedia/william-richardson-davie-1756-1820/; Jennifer L. Larson, "William R. Davie: UNC's Founding Father" (no date), Documenting the American South, https://docsouth.unc.edu/highlights/davie.html; and Blackwell P. Robinson, "Davie, William Richardson" (1986), NCPedia website, https://www.ncpedia.org/biography/davie-william-richardson; all were accessed on December 20, 2019. Also, Boatner, *Encyclopedia*, 318, and David Shenck, *North Carolina, 1780–'81: Being a History of the Invasion of the Carolinas by the British Army Under Lord Cornwallis* (Raleigh, NC: Edwards & Broughton, 1889), 64–65,

9. McCrady, *The History of South Carolina in the Revolution, 1775–1780*, 620–21.

10. Davie, *Revolutionary War Sketches*, 8–9.

11. Ibid., 9–11.

12. Graham, *Papers*, 235–36.

13. Both Graham, 236, and Davie, 11, left detailed descriptions of the fortifications at Rocky Mount.

14. Davie, *Revolutionary War Sketches*, 11–12.

15. Graham, *Papers*, 236–37.

16. Hill, *William Hill's Memoir*, 12–13.

17. Boatner, *Encyclopedia*, 1208–09. Also, John Beakes, *Otho Holland Williams in the American Revolution* (Charleston, SC: Nautical & Aviation Publishing Co., 2015), 59–60.
18. Henry Lee, *The Revolutionary War Memoir of General Henry Lee* (New York: Da Capo Press edition, 1998), 593.
19. Williams, "Narrative," 486.
20. "Baron De Kalb to Major Genl. Gates," July 16, 1780; "Millett & Estis to Major General Gates," July 22, 1780; "General Griffith Rutherford to General Gates," July 30, 1780; "Richard Caswell to General Horatio Gates," July 30, 1780, all in *SRNC*, 14:503, 508, 514, 515–16, respectively.
21. Williams, "Narrative," 486–87.
22. Thomas Pinckney, "Thomas Pinckney and the Last Campaign of Horatio Gates," ed. Robert Scott Davis, *The South Carolina Historical Magazine*, 86:2 (April 1985), 94–96.
23. Nelson, *General Horatio Gates*, 222; also, Pinckney, "Last Campaign of Horatio Gates," 94.
24. Williams, "Narrative," 488.
25. Ibid.
26. Rankin, *Francis Marion*, 57–58.
27. William Seymour, *A Journal of the Southern Expedition, 1780–1783* (Wilmington: The Historical Society of Delaware, 1896), 4. Also, Williams, "Narrative," 487.
28. Tarleton, *Campaigns*, 99.
29. "Cornwallis to Lord George Germain," August 20, 1780, from Jim Piecuch, ed., *The Battle of Camden: A Documentary History* (Charleston, SC: The History Press, 2006), 52. Also, "Rawdon to Cornwallis," July 31, 1780, *CP*, 1:223.
30. "Proclamation Issued by Horatio Gates at Pedee, the 4th of August 1780," from Banastre Tarleton, *Campaigns*, 140–41.
31. Charles Stedman, *The American War*, 2:200 and 205.
32. McCrady, *The History of South Carolina in the Revolution, 1775–1780*, 648–51.
33. "Cornwallis to Rawdon," July 30, 178, *CP*, 1:217.
34. Bass, *Green Dragoon*, 93. Quote is from Tarleton, *Campaigns*, 100.
35. McCrady, *The History of South Carolina in the Revolution, 1775–1780*, 709.
36. Draper, *King's Mountain and Its Heroes*, 74–83.
37. "Banastre Tarleton to Cornwallis," August 5, 1780, *CP*, 1:365.

CHAPTER ELEVEN: ENTERPRISE AND EMPLOYMENT

1. Joseph Graham, *Papers*, 237.
2. Tarleton, *Campaigns*, 94.
3. Davie, *Revolutionary War Memoirs*, 13.
4. Rawdon, Earl of Moira, "Account of the Battle of Camden," January 19, 1801, in *The Battle of Camden*, ed. Jim Piecuch, 58.
5. Philip R. Katcher, *Encyclopedia of British, Provincial, and German Army Units, 1775–1783*, 95; Patrick O'Kelley, *Nothing But Blood and Slaughter* (Harnett, NC: Blue House Tavern Press, 2004), 2:221–23.
6. "Rawdon to Cornwallis," July 31, 1780, *CP*, 1:222–23. Also, "Balfour to Cornwallis," June 12, 1780, and "Note 1 on John Carden," *CP*, 1:84, 183, respectively.
7. "Rawdon to Cornwallis," July 31, 1780 and "Return of the troops etc. at Camden, 13th August, 1780," *CP*, 1:229, 233–34, respectively.
8. "Rawdon to Cornwallis," August 2, 1780, *CP*, 1:228.
9. Gregorie, *Thomas Sumter*, 91.
10. Davie, *Revolutionary War Memoirs*, 13.
11. Lossing, *The Pictorial Field-Book of the Revolution*, 661.

12. Davie, *Revolutionary War Memoirs*, 13. Sources about British troop disposition and numbers at Hanging Rock vary widely. Here I have relied primarily on Davie, with assistance from historian Patrick O'Kelley, *Nothing But Blood and Slaughter*, 2:223. Also referenced here is Bass, *Gamecock*, 68, and Bass's map on 69, and Gregorie, *Thomas Sumter*, 91–912.

13. Buchanan, *Road to Guilford Courthouse*, 134.

14. Davie, *Revolutionary War Memoir*, 14.

15. Bass, *The Gamecock*, 70.

16. Gregorie, *Thomas Sumter*, 93.

17. "Thomas Sumter to Thomas Pinckney," August 9, 1780, *SRNC*, 14:540–41. Bass, *The Gamecock*, 70.

18. Graham, *Papers*, 240.

19. Buchanan, *The Road to Guilford Courthouse*, 136.

20. This account of the Battle of Hanging Rock, including quoted material, is taken from Davie, *Revolutionary War Sketches*, 13–14, unless otherwise noted. Buchanan, *The Road to Guilford Courthouse*, 133–37, was also an important reference.

21. "Thomas Sumter to Thomas Pinckney," August 9, 1780, *SRNC*, 14:540–41.

22. "Cornwallis to Germain," August 20, 1780, *CP*, 2:10.

23. "Cornwallis to Clinton," August 10, 1780, *CP*, 1:180.

24. Rawdon, "Account of the Battle of Camden," 58.

25. Ibid., 59.

26. Bass, *The Gamecock*, 71–72.

27. "Thomas Sumter to Thomas Pinckney," August 9, 1780, *SRNC*, 14:540–41.

28. Draper, *King's Mountain and Its Heroes*, 78.

29. Alexander Chesney, *The Journal of Alexander Chesney*, ed. E. Alfred Jones (Columbus: Ohio State University, 1905), 11, n76.

30. Draper, *King's Mountain and Its Heroes*, 90–95; O'Kelley, *Nothing But Blood and Slaughter*, 2:234–36.

31. McJunkin, "Joseph McJunkin's Memoir."

32. Lyman Draper, "McJunkin's Narrative," Draper MSS, Sumter Papers 23VV153-203, excerpted from William T. Graves, *Backcountry Revolutionary*, Appendix 17, 299. Graves notes Draper transcribed this account from a hand believed to be McJunkin's.

33. Hill, "William Hill's Memoir," 16.

34. Graves, *Backcountry Revolutionary*, 94.

35. Hill, "William Hill's Memoir," 16; Draper, *King's Mountain and Its Heroes*, 166–67.

36. Williams, "Narrative," 490.

37. Stedman, *The American War*, 2:204.

38. Graham, *Papers*, 241.

39. "Thomas Sumter to Major Pinckney," August 12, 1780, *SRNC*, 14:553–54. Also, Williams, "Narrative," 492.

40. Ward, *War of the Revolution*, 721.

41. McCrady, *The History of South Carolina in the Revolution, 1775–1780*, 648–51.

42. Ibid., 653. For the date of Marion's first meeting with the militia of the Pee Dee, I am relying on Hugh Rankin, *Francis Marion*, 59.

43. James, *Life of Marion*, 23.

44. Rankin, *The Swamp Fox*, 58. Quote is from "Peter Horry to Nathanael Greene," April 20, 1781, extracted in Rankin.

45. Pinckney, "The Last Campaign of Horatio Gates," 91.

46. "Banastre Tarleton to Cornwallis," August 5, 1780, *CP*, 1:365.

47. Tarleton, *Campaigns*, 100–101.

48. Ibid.

49. Tarleton, *Campaigns*, 101.

50. See reference to Mouzon's friendship with Tarleton in Parker, *Parker's Guide to the Revolutionary War in South Carolina*, 440.

51. Bass, *Green Dragoon*, 93.

52. Tarleton, *Campaigns*, 101.

53. Stedman, *The American War*, 2:204.

CHAPTER TWELVE: COOL INTREPIDITY

1. "Cornwallis to Germain," August 21, 1780, *CP*, 2:11.

2. Pinckney, *Gen. Gates's Southern Campaign*, 91.

3. Ibid., 85–86.

4. "General Horatio Gates to Samuel Huntington," August 20, 1780, appearing in Piecuch, *The Battle of Camden*, 19.

5. Ward, *War of the Revolution*, 722.

6. Buchanan, *Road to Guilford Courthouse*, 155.

7. "Sumter to Gates," August 15, 1780, *SRNC*, 14:550. N.b., this letter is misdated August 10, 1780. With slight alterations, this letter also appears in Tarleton, *Campaigns*, 147–48.

8. Senf, "Extract of a Journal, in Piecuch, *The Battle of Camden*, 22.

9. "Sumter to Gates," August 15, 1780, *SRNC*, 14:550.

10. Senf, "Extract of a Journal," in Piecuch, *The Battle of Camden*, 22.

11. Williams, "Narrative," 492.

12. Ibid., 493.

13. Robert Middlekauff, *The Glorious Cause: The American Revolution, 1763–1789* (New York: Oxford University Press, 1982), 455; John Ferling, *Almost a Miracle: The American Victory in the War of Independence* (New York: Oxford University Press, 2007), 441.

14. Reported as Sanders Creek in Piecuch but Granny's Creek elsewhere.

15. Colonel John Christian Senf, "Extract of a Journal concerning the Action of the 16th of August," *Magazine of American History*, Vol. 5, No. 4, appearing in Piecuch, *The Battle of Camden*, 22–23.

16. "Major Charles Magill to his father," n.d., appearing in Piecuch, *The Battle of Camden*, 43.

17. Pinckney, "Last Campaign of Horatio Gates," 86–87.

18. Senf, "Extract of a Journal," 23.

19. "Cornwallis to Germain," August 21, 1780, *CP*, 2:11–12.

20. Tarleton, *Campaigns*, 103.

21. "Cornwallis to Germain," August 21, 1780, *CP*, 2:11–12.

22. Tarleton, *Campaigns*, 104. Quote is from Williams, "Narrative," 494.

23. "Cornwallis to Germain," August 21, 1780, *CP*, 2:12.

24. Williams, "Narrative," 494–95.

25. Quote is from Tarleton, *Campaigns*, 106. American and British troop disposition is derived from Ward, *War of the Revolution*, 725–26, and Buchanan, *Road to Guilford Courthouse*, 162–65.

26. "Cornwallis to Germain," August 21, 1780, *CP*, 2:13.

27. Williams, "Narrative," 495.

28. Ibid., 493.

29. "Gates to Huntington," August 20, 1780, appearing in Piecuch, *The Battle of Camden*, 20.

30. Ibid.

31. "Cornwallis to Germain," August 21, 1780, *CP*, 2:13.

32. Williams, "Narrative," 495.

33. "Cornwallis to Germain," August 21, 1780, *CP*, 2:13.

34. "Gates to Huntington," August 20, 1780, in Piecuch, *The Battle of Camden*, 20.

35. Williams, "Narrative," 495–96.

36. "Gates to Huntington," August 20, 1780, appearing in Piecuch, *Battle of Camden*, 20; Williams, "Narrative," 497.

37. "Cornwallis to Germain," August 21, 1780, *CP*, 2:13.

38. Williams, "Narrative," 496.

39. Wickwire, *Cornwallis and the War of Independence*, 162.

40. Tarleton, *Campaigns*, 108.

41. Williams, "Narrative," 497.

42. Tarleton, *Campaigns*, 108; Robert D. Bass, *Green Dragoon*, 100.

43. Excerpted from Ward, *War of the Revolution*, 731.

44. "Cornwallis to Cruger," August 18, 1780, *CP*, 2:19.

45. Ward, *War of the Revolution*, 732.

46. Williams, "Narrative," 502.

47. For further analysis of the consequences of Camden, see my *To the End of the World* (Yardley, PA: Westholme Publishing, 2023).

48. "Gates to Huntington," August 20, 1780, in Piecuch, *Battle of Camden*, 20.

49. Nelson, *General Horatio Gates*, 237.

50. Schenck, *North Carolina, 1780–'81*, 74.

51. Ibid.

52. Williams, "Narrative," 499.

53. "Gates to Huntington," August 20, 1780, in Piecuch, *Battle of Camden*, 20.

54. Alexander Hamilton quote extracted from Boatner, *Encyclopedia*, 415.

55. Lyman Draper, *King's Mountain and Its Heroes*, 106.

56. Ibid., 107.

57. Draper, *King's Mountain and Its Heroes*, 108.

58. This account of the Battle of Musgrove's Mill is derived primarily from Draper, *King's Mountain and Its Heroes*, and also John Buchanan, *Road to Guilford Courthouse*, 176–80.

CHAPTER THIRTEEN: CONSPICUOUS MANEUVERS

1. Davie, *Revolutionary War Sketches*, 18.

2. Bass, *Gamecock*, 82.

3. Tarleton, *Campaigns*, 111.

4. See Davie, *Revolutionary War Sketches*, 20, and Lee, *Revolutionary War Memoirs*, 188, for these diverging accounts. The credibility of Davie's account in this matter is hard to dispute, as he was the one with the most direct knowledge of the events, although Sumter's behavior indicates he was unaware of Tarleton's pursuit.

5. Davie, *Revolutionary War Sketches*, 20.

6. Bass, *Gamecock*, 82.

7. Davie, *Revolutionary War Sketches*, 20.

8. Tarleton, *Campaigns*, 113.

9. Ibid., 113–14.

10. Ibid.

11. Gregorie, *Thomas Sumter*, 101.

12. Ibid., 115. Also, Boatner, *Encyclopedia*, 369, for a count of Tarleton's prisoners.

13. "Germain to Cornwallis," November 9, 1780, extracted from Bass, *Green Dragoon*, 103.

14. "Francis Marion to Peter Horry," August 17, 1780, from *Gibbes Documentary History, 1781–1782*, 11.

15. Rankin, *Swamp Fox*, 64.
16. Marion reports the date as August 20 in "Francis Marion to Peter Horry, August 27, 1780," but British accounts date the action to August 25.
17. "Francis Marion to Peter Horry," August 27, 1780, *Gibbes Documentary History, 1781–1782*, 11–12.
18. "Horatio Gates to Continental Congress," September 5, 1780, Papers of the Continental Congress, M247, 279–80. Accessed at https://www.fold3.com/image/252304 on October 12, 2020.
19. Bass, *Swamp Fox*, 47. For this account of Great Savannah, I have relied on Bass, Rankin, and also John Oller, *The Swamp Fox: How Francis Marion Saved the American Revolution* (New York: Hachette Books, 2020), 54–57.
20. "Cornwallis to Cruger," August 27, 1780, *CP*, 2:172.
21. "Cornwallis to Germain," September 19, 1780, *CP*, 2:38.
22. Randy A. Purvis, "Major James Wemyss: Second Most Hated British Officer in the South," *Journal of the American Revolution*, accessed October 14, 2020, https://allthingsliberty.com/2018/11/major-james-wemyss-second-most-hated-british-officer-in-the-south/.
23. "Wemyss to Cornwallis," July 11, 1780, *CP*, 1:304.
24. "Cornwallis to Wemyss," July 30 and 31, *CP*, 1:320–21.
25. McCrady, *The History of South Carolina in the Revolution, 1775–1780*, 641.
26. "Cornwallis to Wemyss," August 28, 1780, *CP*, 2:208–9.
27. "Cornwallis to De Peyster," August 31, 1780, *CP*, 2:212.
28. "Wemyss to Cornwallis," August 28, 1780, *CP*, 2:209.
29. "Marion to Peter Horry," August 27, 1780, *Gibbes Documentary History, 1781–1782*, 11–12.
30. Bass, *Swamp Fox*, 56.
31. Ibid., 50.
32. "Marion to Gates," September 15, 1780, *SRNC*, 14:627.
33. James, *Life of Marion*, 47.
34. Oller, *The Swamp Fox*, 60–61; and Bass, *Swamp Fox*, 49–51.
35. "Marion to Gates," September 15, 1780, *SRNC*, 14:627.
36. James, *Life of Marion*, 47.
37. Saberton, "Introduction to the Rest of Part Five," *CP*, 2:26. Also, Rankin, *The Swamp Fox*, 73–74.
38. James, *Life of Marion*, 57.
39. "Marion to Gates," September 15, 1780, *SRNC*, 14:616–17.
40. Ibid.
41. "Wemyss to Cornwallis," September 20, 1780, *CP*, 2:214–15.
42. James, *Life of Marion*, 57.
43. Ibid., 58.
44. James, *Life of Marion*, v, 78.
45. "Cornwallis to Wemyss," August 28, 1780, *CP*, 2:209.
46. "Wemyss to Cornwallis," September 20, 1780, *CP*, 2:214–15.
47. Ibid.
48. "Cornwallis to Wemyss," September 26, 1780, *CP*, 2:216.

CHAPTER FOURTEEN: THE HORNET'S NEST

1. "Cornwallis to Cruger," August 24, 1780, *CP*, 2:169.
2. Williams, "Narrative," 500.
3. Ibid., 500–501.
4. Ibid., 501.

5. Ibid., 505.

6. Davie, *Revolutionary War Sketches*, 20; "Governor Nash to the Delegates of North Carolina," August 23, 1780, extracted in Tarleton, *Campaigns*, 149–50.

7. Schenck, *North Carolina, 1780–'81*, 99–100.

8. James, *Life of Marion*, n73.

9. "Cornwallis to Germain," September 19, 1780, *CP*, 2:38.

10. "Cornwallis to Clinton," September 3, 1780, *CP*, 2:43.

11. Tarleton, *Campaigns*, 155.

12. Stedman, *The American War*, 2:215. The number of Cornwallis's men on his march is from Franklin and Mary Wickwire, *Cornwallis and the War of Independence*, 195.

13. "Cornwallis to Clinton," August 29, 1780, also "Ferguson to Cornwallis," August 29, 1780, and "Ferguson to Cornwallis," September 14, 1780, *CP*, 2:42, 145–49. Ferguson makes reference to these orders in these letters. Also, Tarleton, *Campaigns*, 156.

14. "Balfour to Cornwallis," May 30, 1780, *CP*, 1:74; "Cornwallis to Balfour," June 11, 1780, *CP*, 1:83.

15. "Cornwallis to Ferguson," September 20, 1780, *CP*, 2:153.

16. Tarleton, *Campaigns*, 158.

17. Charles Stedman, *The American War*, 2:215–16.

18. "Cornwallis to Balfour," September 20, 1780, extracted in Bass, *Green Dragoon*, 106.

19. John Money, "The Journal of Lt. John Money," *CP*, 2:363–64.

20. "Cornwallis to Balfour," September 21, 1780, *CP*, 2:88.

21. Graham, *Papers*, 249.

22. "Gen. Wm. Davidson to General Gates," September 14, 1780, and "Gen. Jethro Sumner to Maj. Gen. Gates," September 24, 1780, *SRNC*, 14: 614–15, 646–47.

23. Davie, *Revolutionary War Sketches*, 23.

24. "Balfour to Cornwallis," September 20 and 22, 1780, *CP*, 2:94. Also, McCrady, *History of the Revolution, 1775–1780*, 733–38.

25. Tarleton, *Campaigns*, 161.

26. Gregorie, *Thomas Sumter*, 105.

27. Hill, "William Hill's Memoirs," 17.

28. Graves, *Backcountry Revolutionary*, 89.

29. "Abner Nash to James Williams," September 8, 1780, *Gibbes Documentary History*, 3:138.

30. "Gov. John Rutledge to the Delegates of South Carolina in Congress, September 20, 1780," Letter of John Rutledge, *The South Carolina Historical and Genealogical Magazine*, ed. John W. Barnwell, Vol. 17, No. 4 (October 1916), 138.

31. Hill, "William Hill's Memoir," 17.

32. Graves, *Backcountry Revolutionary*, 89.

33. Hill, "William Hill's Memoir," 17.

34. "Gov. John Rutledge to the Delegates of South Carolina in Congress, September 20, 1780," Letter of John Rutledge, 138. Also, "Cornwallis to Ferguson, October 1, 1780," *CP*, 2:158.

35. Hill, "William Hill's Memoir," 18.

36. Richard Winn, "Winn's Notes (Continued)," *South Carolina Historical and Genealogical Magazine*, ed. Samuel C. Williams, 44, 1 (January 1943), 1–2.

37. Bass, *Gamecock*, 87; King, *Thomas Sumter*, 107. For Draper's account, see *King's Mountain and Its Heroes*, 168.

38. King, *Thomas Sumter*, 109.

39. Graham, *Papers*, 251–52.

40. Stedman, *The American War*, 2:216.

41. Money, "The Journal of Lt. John Money," *CP*, 2:365.

42. "Cornwallis to Clinton," September 22 and 23, 1780, *CP*, 2:46.

43. Ibid. for the quote "Charlottetown will be a great security." The rest from Stedman, *The American War*, 2:216.

44. Joseph Graham, *Papers*, 257–61.

45. Tarleton, *Campaigns*, 159–60.

46. Ibid., 160.

CHAPTER FIFTEEN: A STEP TOO FAR

1. "Marion to Gates," September 15, 1780, *SRNC*, 14:617–18.

2. Rankin, *The Swamp Fox*, 82.

3. James, *Life of Marion*, 57–58.

4. Ibid.

5. Ibid., 149.

6. Horry and Weems, *General Francis Marion*, 119.

7. Oller, *The Swamp Fox*, 73; "Marion to Gates," October 4, 1780, *SRNC*, 14:666.

8. Rankin, *The Swamp Fox*, 84–85.

9. "Marion to Gates," October 4, 1780, *SRNC*, 14:666.

10. Ibid.

11. "Robert Gray to Cornwallis," September 30, 1780, *CP*, 2:217–18.

12. "Balfour to Cornwallis," October 1, 1780, *CP*, 2:113–14.

13. "Cornwallis to Clinton," September 22 & 23, *CP*, 2:46.

14. "Wemyss to Cornwallis," September 30, 1780, *CP*, 2:216.

15. "Marion to Gates," October 4, 1780, *SRNC*, 14, 666; "Wemyss to Cornwallis," September 30, 1780, *CP*, 2:216; Rankin, *The Swamp Fox*, 88–89.

16 "Marion to Gates," October 4, 1780, *SRNC*, 14:666.

17. John C. Parker, *Parker's Guide to Revolutionary War in S.C.*, 479–80.

18. "Cornwallis to Wemyss," October 7, 1780, *CP*, 2:222.

19. Clinton, "Instructions to Major Ferguson, Inspector of Militia," *CP*, 1:103–5.

20. "Ferguson to Clinton," August 1, 1778. From Ferguson, "An Officer Out of His Time," 2:308.

21. M. M. Gilchrist, *Patrick Ferguson: A Man of Some Genius* (Edinburgh: NMS Publishing, 2003), 47–49.

22. "Balfour to Cornwallis," May 30, 1780, *CP*, 1:74.

23. "Balfour to Cornwallis," June 9, 1780, *CP*, 1:81.

24. Draper, *King's Mountain and Its Heroes*, 169.

25. "Ferguson to Cornwallis," September 19, 1780, *CP*, 2:154–55.

26. Hill, "William Hill's Memoir," 19–21. Also, Draper, *King's Mountain and Its Heroes*, 194–95, 216–17.

27. "Cornwallis to Ferguson," October 5, 1780, *CP*, 2:161; also, *CP*, 2:28, for the location of Armour's Ford, which now appears to be under Lake Wylie.

28. "Ferguson to Cornwallis," October 6, 1780, *CP*, 2:165.

29. Hill, "William Hill's Memoir," 22.

30. Mark M. Boatner, *Encyclopedia*, 581.

31. Hill, "William Hill's Memoir," 23.

32. Boatner, *Encyclopedia*, 581–82.

33. Ferguson correspondence from *CP*, 2:159–65.

34. "Charles Cornwallis to Rev. Dr. James Cornwallis," December 12, 1787, excerpted from Bass, *The Green Dragon*, 258.

CHAPTER SIXTEEN: A GENERAL RETREATS, A GENERAL RETURNS

1. For a complete description of the Williams/Sumter/Hill controversy, see William T. Graves, *Backcountry Revolutionary: James Williams (1740-1780)* (Lugoff, SC: Southern Campaigns of the American Revolution Press, 2012), the definitive contemporary source on the subject.

2. William B. Heseltine, "Lyman Draper and the South," *The Journal of Southern History*, Vol. 19, No. 1 (Feb. 1953), 27.

3. Gregorie, *Thomas Sumter*, 109.

4. Indeed, elements of Hill's memoir, referenced through Draper, even show up in *The Road to Guilford Courthouse* by John Buchanan. Published in 1997, the book is considered canon of the American Revolution in the South.

5. "Rawdon to Clinton," October 28, 1780, *CP*, 2:58.

6. "Cornwallis to Turnbull," October 2, 1780, CP, 2:244.

7. Anderson, "Camp New Providence," (2011), http://elehistory.com/amrev/CampNew-Providence.pdf, accessed on October 31, 2020. Also, Graham, *Papers*, 270.

8. Anderson, "Camp New Providence."

9. Tarleton, *Campaigns*, 165.

10. Stedman, *The American War*, 2:224.

11. Tarleton, *Campaigns*, 169.

12. Ibid., 77–78.

13. Richard M. Ketchum, *The Winter Soldiers* (New York: Doubleday, 1973), 230–31.

14. Tarleton, *Campaigns*, 167. James Graham reports the sunset departure in *Papers on North Carolina Revolutionary History*, 270.

15. Graham, *Papers*, 270–71.

16. Ibid.

17. Stedman, *The American War*, 2:224.

18. George Hanger, *The Life, Adventures, and Opinions of Col. George Hanger, Written by Himself*, Vol. II (London: J. Debrett, 1801), 408–11.

19 Ibid.

20. Stedman, *The American War*, 225.

21. Ibid

22. "Rawdon to Turnbull," October 19, 1780," *CP*, 2:255.

23. McCrady, *The History of South Carolina in the Revolution, 1775–1780*, 813. Also, Gregorie, *Thomas Sumter*, 110. Quoted portions from Rutledge's commission and letter are excerpted from these sources. Gregorie references original documents to "Rutledge to Sumter," October 6, 1780, Nos. 1231 & 1232, in the "Sumter Papers," located in the manuscript division of the Library of Congress.

24. "Genl. Smallwood to Maj. Genl. Gates," October 20, 1780, *SRNC*, 14: 703–5.

25. James Graham, *The Life of General Daniel Morgan of the Virginia Line of the Army of the United States* (New York: Derby & Jackson, 1859), 237.

26. "Smallwood to Gates," October 20, 1780, *SRNC*, 14:703–5.

27. King, *Thomas Sumter*, 110.

28. Waters, *To the End of the World*, 34–37.

29. Gregorie, *Thomas Sumter*, 110.

30. "Gen. Smallwood to Maj. Genl. Gates," October 31, 1780, *SRNC*, 14:721.

CHAPTER SEVENTEEN: THE SWAMP FOX

1. "Gen. H.W. Harrington to Gates," October 10, 1780, *SRNC*, 14:683.

2. Henry A. Robertson Jr., "Harrington, William Henry," NCPedia (1988), https://www.nc-pedia.org/biography/harrington-henry-william, accessed on October 31, 2020.

3. "Gen. H.W. Harrington to Gates," September 25, 1780, *SRNC*, 14:652; also, Rankin, *Francis Marion*, 106.

4. "Marion to Gates," October 4, 1780, *SRNC*, 14:666.

5. "Marion to Gates," October 15, 1780, *SRNC*, 14:621–22.

6. "Gates to Marion," October 11, 1780, extracted from Bass, *Swamp Fox*, 74.

7. Rankin, *The Swamp Fox*, 92.

8. McCrady, *The History of S.C. in the Revolution, 1775–1780*, 751.

9. Saberton, "Note on Samuel Tynes," *CP*, 2:92.

10. Bass, *Swamp Fox*, 75–76.

11. James, *Life of Marion*, 71.

12. Ibid., 60–61.

13. Rankin, *The Swamp Fox*, 103–05.

14. Rankin, *The Swamp Fox*, 110–11, for press reports; "Balfour to Rawdon," November 1, 1780, *CP*, 3:61–62; and Tarleton, *Campaigns*, 171.

15. "Turnbull to Rawdon," October 29, 1780, *CP*, 2:263.

16. "Clinton to Cornwallis," November 6, 1780, *CP*, 3:22.

17. Tarleton, *Campaigns*, 171; "Cornwallis to Tarleton," November 2, 1780 and "Tarleton to Cornwallis," November 1, 1780, *CP*, 3:332.

18. "Tarleton to Cornwallis," November 11, 1780, *CP*, 3:337; also, Tarleton, *Campaigns*, 172.

19. "Tarleton to Cornwallis," November 5, 1780, *CP*, 3:334.

20. "Marion to Harrington" (undated), November 9, *Papers Relating Chiefly to the Maryland Line During the Revolution*, ed. Thomas Balch (Philadelphia: T.K. & P.G. Collins, 1857), 127.

21. "Tarleton to Cornwallis," November 11, 1780, *CP*, 3:337.

22. Ibid.

23. Tarleton, *Campaigns*, 171–72; Rankin, *The Swamp Fox*, 111–12. For the location of Richardson's plantation, see Parker, *Parker's Guide to the Revolutionary War in South Carolina*, 170–71.

24. Alexander Garden, *Anecdotes of the Revolutionary War in America* (Charleston, SC: A.E. Miller, 1822), 287.

25. Bass, *Swamp Fox*, 82–83.

26. Karl G. Heider, "The Gamecock, the Swamp Fox, and the Wizard Owl: The Development of Good Form in an American Totemic Set," *The Journal of American Folklore*, 93:67 (January–March 1980), 1–22.

27. James, *Life of Marion*, 62.

28. Tarleton, *Campaigns*, 172.

29. "Tarleton to Cornwallis," November 11, 1780, *CP*, 3:337.

30. "Cornwallis to Clinton," December 3, 1780, *CP*, 3:24–25.

31. James, *Life of Marion*, 65.

32. Rankin, *The Swamp Fox*, 117. Also, Horry and Weems, *General Francis Marion*, 131.

33. Rankin, *The Swamp Fox*, 117–18.

34. Horry and Weems, *General Francis Marion*, 127–28.

35. "Marion to Gates," November 4, 1780, *SRNC*, 14:7146.

36. James, *Life of Marion*, 66; Horry and Weems, *General Francis Marion*, 133.

37. "Marion to Gates," November 4, 1780, *SRNC*, 14:7146.

38. Rankin, *The Swamp Fox*, 120.

39. Horry and Weems, *Life of Marion*, 133–34.

40. "Marion to Gates," November 4, 1780, *SRNC*, 14:726.

41. "Marion to Gates," November 21, 1780, *SRNC*, 14:746–47.

42. "Cornwallis to Balfour," November 12, 1780, *CP*, 3:71 and "Cornwallis to Balfour," November 16, 1781, *CP*, 3:73.

43. "Cornwallis to Balfour," November 17, 1780, *CP*, 3:75. Also, Rankin, *The Swamp Fox*, 122, for McLeroth's troop strength and composition.

CHAPTER EIGHTEEN: FISHDAM FORD

1. "Rawdon to Clinton," October 28, 1780, *CP*, 2:58.

2. "Rawdon to Cruger," October 31, 1780, *CP*, 2:204.

3. "Rawdon to Turnbull," October 21, 1780, *CP*, 2:258.

4. "Col. William R. Davie to Gen. Jethro Sumner," October 16, 1780 and "Proceedings of the North Carolina Board of War, October 25, 1780," *SRNC*, 14:789 and 434, respectively.

5. "Gen. W. Smallwood to Maj. Genl. Gates," October 31, 1780, *SRNC*, 14:720–21.

6. Nelson, *General Horatio Gates*, 241.

7. Gregorie, *Thomas Sumter*, 112–13.

8. "Genl. Smallwood to Maj. Genl. Gates," October 20, 1780, *SRNC*, 14:704–5.

9. "Turnbull to Cornwallis," November 3, 1780, *CP*, 3:135.

10. William Lee Anderson, "Camp New Providence," accessed August 20, 2021., http://ele-history.com/amrev/CampNewProvidence.pdf. The author was lucky enough to find this excellent and thoroughly researched article on Anderson's website in 2017, only to discover Anderson had died a few years before.

11. Robert Kirkwood, "The Journal of Captain Robert Kirkwood," from *Papers of the Historical Society of Delaware, LVI: The Journal and Order Book of Captain Robert Kirkwood of the Delaware Regiment of the Continental Line* (Wilmington: The Historical Society of Delaware, 1910), 12. Also, Graham, *The Life of General Daniel Morgan*, 243.

12. "Gen. W. Smallwood to Major General Gates," October 27, 1780, *SRNC*, 14:712.

13. Anderson, "Camp New Providence." Also, Davie, *Revolutionary War Sketches*, 28.

14. American Revolution militia pensions of Christopher Strong, Samuel Otterson, and William Barnet are available at https://revwarapps.org/, a remarkable online resource of over twenty-four thousand pension applications, land claims, and related public records. Christopher Strong pension application edited by C. Leon Harris. Otterson and Barnett applications edited by Will Graves, accessed on May 6, 2020.

15. Winn, "Richard Winn's Notes: 1780 (Continued)," 1.

16. For more on this topic, please see Andrew Waters, *The Quaker and the Gamecock: Nathanael Greene, Thomas Sumter, and the Revolutionary War for the Soul of the South* (Philadelphia, PA: Casemater, 2019).

17. Parker, *Parker's Guide to the Revolutionary War*, 154, 221.

18. Gregorie, *Thomas Sumter*, 115.

19. "Gen. B. Few to Major General Gates," November 8, 1780, *SRNC*, 14:763–64.

20. "Cornwallis to Clinton," December 3, 1780, *CP*, 3:25.

21. Ibid.

22. Winn, "Richard Winn's Notes: 1780 (Continued)," 2–3. Winn recalls Sumter arrived at Fishdam Ford on November 9, though this date does not correspond with other accounts.

23. Hugh McCall, *The History of Georgia* (Atlanta, GA: A.B. Caldwell, 1909), 2:339. McCall does not provide a reference for such a detailed description though his father was there. He died the following year of the war, 1781, from smallpox.

24. Ibid., 339–40. Also, Winn, "Richard Winn's Notes: 1780 (Continued)," 3. McCall's account is clearly influenced by Winn's.

25. Buchanan, *Road to Guilford Courthouse*, 248–51.

26. Winn, "Richard Winn's Notes: 1780 (Continued)," 3.

27. In this account of the Tory guide, Sealy is amalgamated from several sources. He is mentioned briefly in the accounts of Winn and McCall in *History of Georgia*, though not in a prominent role. Sumter biographer Anne King Gregorie describes him more prominently in her *Thomas Sumter*, 115–16, listing as her reference an account of Dr. Alex Q. Bradley to Lyman Draper in Draper's *Sumter Papers*, 14VV92.

28. "Cornwallis to Turnbull," November 9, 1780, *CP*, 3:139. Also, Winn, "Richard Winn's Notes: 1780 (Continued)," 3.

29. "Cornwallis to Clinton," December 3, 1780, *CP*, 3:25.

30. Winn, "Richard Winn's Notes: 1780 (Continued)," 3.

31. "Cornwallis to Balfour," November 10, 1780, *CP*, 3:68, for the description of Wemyss's injury; 3; Buchanan, *Road to Guilford Courthouse*, 250, for the name of John Stark, Wemyss's second-in-command.

32. McCall, *The History of Georgia*, 2:340–41; "Sumter to Smallwood," November 9, 1780, is excerpted from Bass, *Gamecock*, 99.

33. McCall and Winn as cited in n625 and 626; Buchanan, *Road to Guilford Courthouse*, 250–51.

34. Winn, "Richard Winn's Notes: 1780 (Continued)," 3.

35. Hill, *William Hill's Memoirs*, 13.

36. Winn, "Richard Winn's Notes: 1780 (Continued)," 4.

37. "Cornwallis to Turnbull," November 9, 1780, *CP*, 3:139.

38. Winn, "Richard Winn's Notes: 1780 (Continued)," 4.

39. King, *Thomas Sumter*, 117; Bass, *Gamecock*, 98.

40. Winn, "Richard Winn's Notes: 1780 (Continued)," 4.

41. "Sumter to Smallwood," November 9, 1780, from Robert D. Bass, *Gamecock*, 99.

CHAPTER NINETEEN: BLACKSTOCKS

1. "Cornwallis to Cruger," November 11, 1780, *CP*, 3:268; also, "Cornwallis to Balfour," November 10, 1780, *CP*, 3:68.

2. Hill, "William Hill's Memoir," 14; Gregorie, *Thomas Sumter*, 117, for the account of Sumter throwing the list into the fire.

3. "Harrington to Turnbull," November 12, 1780, *CP*, 3:162–63.

4. "Cornwallis to Clinton," December 3, 1780, *CP*, 3:25; also, Ian Saberton, "Note on James Wemyss," *CP*, 1:305.

5. "Cornwallis to Clinton," December 3, 1780, *CP*.

6. "Cornwallis to Tarleton," November 10, 1780, *CP*, 3:335–36.

7. Draper, *King's Mountain and Its Heroes*, 467.

8. Bass, *Gamecock*, 102.

9. Gregorie, *Thomas Sumter*, 118.

10. "Cornwallis to Balfour," November 10, 1780, CP, 3:68.

11. Cornwallis to Tarleton, November 10, 1780, *CP*, 3:335–36.

12. "Cornwallis to Rawdon," November 13, 1780, *CP*, 3:144; "Cornwallis to Tarleton," November 13, 1780, *CP*, 3:339; "Cornwallis to McArthur," November 14, 1780, *CP*, 3:311; and "Rawdon to Cornwallis," November 14, 1780, *CP*, 3:147.

13. "Cornwallis to Balfour," November 10, 1780, *CP*, 3:68 and "Cornwallis to Balfour," November 16, 1780, *CP*, 3:74; "Cornwallis to Sumter," November 15, 1780, *CP*, 3:402.

14. Samuel Hammond, "The Battle of Blackstocks, November 20th, 1780," in *Traditions and Reminscences, Chiefly of the American Revolution in the South*, ed. Joseph Johnson (Charleston, SC: Walker & James, 1851), 523.

15. Winn, "General Richard Winn's Notes: 1780 (Continued)," 4.

16. "McArthur to Cornwallis," November 18, 1780, *CP*, 3:316.

17. Bass, *Green Dragoon*, 117. Also, "Cornwallis to Tarleton," November 13, 1780, in Bass, *Green Dragoon*, 117.

18. Tarleton, *Campaigns*, 175.

19. Ibid.

20. Ibid., 175–76. For Tarleton's troop strength, Buchanan, *Road to Guilford Courthouse*, 251.

21. Graham, *Papers*, 235.

22. Bass, *Gamecock*, 103; see Buchanan, *Road to Guilford Courthouse*, 253, for evidence of this influence.

23. Buchanan, *Road to Guilford Courthouse*, 253.

24 Hammond, "The Battle of Blackstocks, November 20, 1781," 523–24.

25. For more on the colonial-era prominence of the Blackstock Road, see John Belton O'Neall, *Colonial and Revolutionary History of Upper South Carolina* (Greenville, SC: Shannon & Co., 1897), 31–33 and elsewhere.

26. Oscar E. and Catherine R. Gilbert, *True for the Cause of Liberty*, 183.

27. Hammond, "The Battle of Blackstocks, November 20th, 1781," 524.

28. Tarleton, *Campaigns*, 176.

29. Ibid., 177.

30. Hammond, "The Battle of Blackstocks, November 20th, 1781," 524.

31. McCall, *The History of Georgia*, 343–45.

32. Roderick McKenzie, *Strictures on Lt. Tarleton's History of the Campaigns of 1780 and 1781* (London, 1787), 74.

33. Gilbert, *True for the Cause of Liberty*, 185–87, for Lacey quote and elevations.

34. Hill, "William Hill's Memoirs," 14.

35. McCall, *The History of Georgia*, 343–45.

36. Draper accounts and pension record of John Calhoun are taken from Gilbert, *True for the Cause of Liberty*, 188–90.

37. Winn, "General Richard Winn's Notes: 1780 (Continued)," 5. Also, Hammond, "The Battle of Blackstocks, November 20th, 1781," 524.

38. Tarleton, *Campaigns*, 177–78.

39. "Tarleton to Cornwallis," November 22, 1780, *CP*, 3:341.

40. Ibid.

41. Hammond, "The Battle of Blackstocks, November 20th, 1781," 525.

42. Ibid.

43. McCall, *The History of Georgia*, 345. Also, Hammond, "The Battle of Blackstocks, November 20th, 1781," 525.

44. Gregorie, *Thomas Sumter*, 123. This account appears in several secondary sources and is attributed to a letter from William Cain to Lyman Draper dated May 27, 1875, in Draper's *Sumter Papers* 5VV57. Also, Buchanan, *Road to Guilford Courthouse*, 257, for additional details about the nature of Sumter's wound.

45. Bass, *Gamecock*, 108.

46. Winn, "General Richard Winn's Notes: 1780 (Continued)," 5.

47. "Tarleton to Cornwallis," November 21, 1780, *CP*, 3:340.

48. Gregorie, *Thomas Sumter*, 123.

49. Roderick McKenzie, *Strictures on Lt. Tarleton's History of the Campaigns of 1780 and 1781* (London, 1787), 74. Also, Winn, "General Richard Winn's Notes: 1780 (Continued)," 6, for the distance of Tarleton's camp from the battlefield.

50. McCall, *The History of Georgia*, 347.

51. Ibid.
52. "Tarleton to Cornwallis," November 21, 1780, *CP*, 3:340.
53. Tarleton, *Campaigns*, 180.
54. "Cornwallis to Tarleton," November 23, 1780, *CP*, 3:342.
55. "Cornwallis to Clinton," December 3, 1780, CP, 3:24.
56. Mackenzie, *Strictures*, 71.
57. "Tarleton to Cornwallis," November 22, 1780, *CP*, 3:341.
58. "Tarleton to Cornwallis," November 21, 1780, *CP*, 3:340.
59. Stedman, *The American War*, 2:231.
60. Mackenzie, *Strictures*, 75–78.
61. "Tarleton to Cornwallis," November 21, 1780, *CP*, 3:340; Gregorie, *Thomas Sumter*, 124.
62. Tarleton, *Campaigns*, 180–81.
63. "Tarleton to Cornwallis," November 24, 1780, *CP*, 3:343; Winn, "General Richard Winn's Notes: 1780 (Continued)," 6.
64. "Tarleton to Cornwallis," November 25, 1780, *CP*, 3:345; "Cornwallis to Balfour," November 25, 1780; *Correspondence of Charles, First Marquis Cornwallis*, ed. Charles Ross (London: John Murray, 1859), 1:70; and "Cornwallis to Tarleton," November 23, 1780, *CP*, 3:342.
65. "Sumter to Gates," November 25, 1780, excerpted from Bass, *Gamecock*, 112.

CHAPTER TWENTY: THE DUEL

1. Saberton, "Footnote on Robert McLeroth," *CP*, 3:77, n31.
2. Thomas J. McGuire, *The Philadelphia Campaign: Brandywine and the Fall of Philadelphia* (Harrisburg, PA: Stackpole Books, 2006), 259.
3. "Balfour to Cornwallis," November 24 & 25, 1780, CP, 3:92.
4. "Cornwallis to Rawdon," December 3, 1780, *CP*, 3:191.
5. "Balfour to Cornwallis," November 24 and 25, 1780, *CP*, 392; also, "Rawdon to Cornwallis," November 28, 1780, *CP*, 3:182.
6. "Rawdon to Cornwallis," November 20, 1780, *CP*, 3:161. Also, O'Kelly, *Nothing But Blood and Slaughter*, 2:384.
7. "Marion to Gates," November 21, 1780, *SRNC*, 14:746.
8. "Rawdon to Cornwallis," November 20, 1780, *CP*, 3:161.
9. "Marion to Gates," November 21, 1780, *SRNC*, 14:746–47.
10. Rankin, *The Swamp Fox*, 125.
11. Saberton, "Note on James Cassells," *CP*, 1:307, n4.
12. James, *Life of Marion*, 67.
13. Rankin, *The Swamp Fox*, 126–27.
14. James, *Life of Marion*, 67–69.
15. "Rawdon to Cornwallis," December 5, 1780, *CP*, 3:196.
16. "Rawdon to Cornwallis," December 8, 1780, *CP*, 3:200. Also, Rankin, *The Swamp Fox*, 67.
17. Horry and Weems, *General Francis Marion*, 213.
18. "Rawdon to Cornwallis," December 8, 1780, *CP*, 3:200.
19. Balfour to Cornwallis," December 11, 1780, *CP*, 3:111. Also, Rankin, *The Swamp Fox*, 130.
20. James, *Life of Marion*, 70–71.
21. "Francis Marion to Nathanael Greene," December 22, 1780, *Papers of General Nathanael Greene*, Volume VI, 605 (Hereafter *NG* with volume:page number, as in *NG*, 6:605).
22. Ibid.
23. Rankin, *The Swamp Fox*, 131.

24. James, *Life of Marion*, 95.

25. Ibid., 95–97.

26. "Note 3," *NG*, 6:606.

27. "Rawdon to Cornwallis," December 15, 1780, *CP*, 3:213.

28. See "Note 3," *NG*, 6:606.

29. "Rawdon to Cornwallis," December 14, 1780, *CP*, 3:213–14; and "Rawdon to Cornwallis," December 16, 1780, CP, 3:215.

30. Saberton, "Biographical Note on Robert McLeroth," CP, 3:77, n31. Also, Katcher, *Encyclopedia of British, Provincial, and German Army Units, 1775–1783*, 61.

31. Rankin, *The Swamp Fox*, 134.

32. James, *Life of Marion*, 97–98.

33. Conway, "To Subdue America," 407.

34. "Rawdon to Cornwallis," December 15, 1780, *CP*, 3:212.

35. "Marion to Greene," December 22, 1780, *NG*, 6:605.

CHAPTER TWENTY-ONE: BRIGADIER MARION

1. Showman and Conrad, "Introduction," *NG*, 6:xvi.

2. Anderson, "Camp New Providence," http://elehistory.com/amrev/CampNewProvidence.pdf.

3. Nelson, *General Horatio Gates*, 251.

4. Anderson, "Camp New Providence."

5. Williams, "Narrative," 510.

6. Thomas Polk as quoted in Anderson, "Camp New Providence."

7. Williams, "Narrative," 509–10.

8. "Nathanael Greene to Francis Marion," December 4, 1780, *NG*, 6:519–20.

9. "Francis Marion to Nathanael Greene," December 22, 1780, *NG*, 6:605. Also, Rankin, *The Swamp Fox*, 138.

10. Bass, *Gamecock*, 113.

11. "Nathanael Greene to Thomas Sumter," December 12, 1780, *NG*, 6:563–64.

12. "NG to George Washington," December 7, 1781, *NG*, 6:543–44.

13. "NG to Daniel Morgan," December 16, 1781, *NG*, 6:589.

14. Gregorie, *Thomas Sumter*, 128–29; Bass, *Gamecock*, 117. The meeting between Morgan and Sumter never took place.

15. Edward McCrady, *The History of South Carolina in the Revolution 1780–1783* (New York: The Macmillan Company, 1902), 69. This letter is dated only "Sunday night, nine o'clock," but evidence suggests it was written on Sunday, December 21, 1780.

16. Boatner, *Encyclopedia of the American Revolution*, 291–96, 866; biographical information about Pickens also comprised from Buchanan, *The Road to Guilford Courthouse*, 299–301; and *NG*, 8:33 (n3).

17. "Daniel Morgan to NG," January 15, 1781, *NG*, 7:127.

18. "NG to Daniel Morgan," January 19, 1781, *NG*, 7:146.

19. "NG to TS," January 19, 1781, *NG*, 7:149.

20. Ibid.

21. "Tarleton to Cornwallis," November 28, 1780, *CP*, 3:346.

22. "Lord Amherst to Cornwallis," November 6, 1780; excerpted in Bass, *Green Dragoon*, 139.

23. "Banastre Tarleton to John Tarleton," December 16, 1780; reprinted in Bass, *Green Dragoon*, 125–26.

24. "Cornwallis to Tarleton," December 18, 1780, *CP*, 3:352.

25. Ian Saberton, *CP*, 3:11.

26. "George to Cornwallis," December 30, 1781, Letter One and Two, *CP*, 3:417–18.

27. "Cornwallis to Rawdon," January 3, 1781, *CP*, 3:239.

28. Tarleton, *Campaigns*, 210.

29. "Cornwallis to Tarleton," January 2, 1781, from Tarleton's *Campaigns*, 244.

30. "Tarleton to Cornwallis," January 4, 1781, from Tarleton's *Campaigns*, 245–46.

31. "Cornwallis to Tarleton," January 5, 1781, from Tarleton's *Campaigns*, 246–47.

32. "Cornwallis to Leslie," January 12, 1781, *CP*, 3:371; also, "Cornwallis to Rawdon," January 12, 1781, *CP*, 3:249.

33. "Cornwallis to Rawdon," December 21, 1780, *CP*, 3:220.

34. Saberton, "Note on John Watson Tadwell-Watson," *CP*, ,39, 2:199–200.

35. Rankin, *The Swamp Fox*, 141. Also, Parker, *Parker's Guide*, 173.

36. "Francis Marion to Nathanael Greene," January 9, 1781, *NG*, 7:86.

37. "John Rutledge to the South Carolina Delegates of the Continental Congress," December 30, 1780. Reprinted in "Letters of John Rutledge, Part II," ed. Joseph W. Barnwell, *The South Carolina Historical and Genealogical Magazine*, 13, 2 (April 1917), 63.

38. Showman et al., eds., "Note 1 on William Harrington," *NG*, 6:519.

39. "John Rutledge to the South Carolina Delegates of the Continental Congress."

40. Horry and Weems, *General Francis Marion*, 115.

41. Ibid., 115–16.

EPILOGUE: THUNDER, LIGHTNING, OR IN RAIN

1. Bass, *Green Dragoon*, 4–5. Attributed to Custis, *Recollections and Private Memories of Washington* (1861) and Sallie DuPuy Harper, "Colonial Men of Times, Containing the Journals of Colonel Daniel Trabue," *William and Mary College Quarterly* (1948). Though I find Bass takes liberties with his quotes, this account is widely repeated.

2. Bass, *Green Dragoon*, 169–70; John Knight, *War at Saber Point: Banastre Tarleton and the British Legion* (Yardley, PA: Westholme Publishing, 2020), 188–90.

3. Knight, *War at Saber Point*, 191.

4. Daniel O'Quinn, "Sir Joshua Reynolds, Decolonization, and the Pictorial Dialectics of Crisis," *SEL Studies in English Literature 1500–1900*, vol. 58, no. 3 (2018).

5. Bass, *Green Dragoon*, 387–89, 442.

6. Conway, "Tarleton, Sir Banastre, baronet (1754–1833)." *Oxford Dictionary of National Biography* (online edition), article first published September 23, 2004, revised January 5, 2012. Also, Buchanan, *Road to Guilford Courthouse*, 387–88.

7. Bass, *Green Dragoon*, 259. Bass quotes a letter dated December 12, 1787, from Cornwallis to his brother, the Rev. Doctor James Cornwallis.

8. MacKenzie, *Strictures*, 75–78.

9. For a discussion of these personality conflicts and an overview of Marion's campaign with Henry Lee, please refer to my book *The Quaker and the Gamecock: Nathanael Greene, Thomas Sumter, and the Revolutionary War for the Soul of the South* (Havertown, PA: Casemate, 2019).

10. Oller, *The Swamp Fox*, 193, 203.

11. Ibid., 241–44.

12. Steven D. Smith, "Imagining the Swamp Fox: William Gilmore Simms and the National Memory of Francis Marion," in *William Gilmore Simms's Unfinished Civil War: Consequences for a Southern Man of Letters*, ed. David Moltke-Hansen (Columbia: University of South Carolina Press, 2013), 32–47.

13. Ibid.

14. William Gilmore Simms, *The Life of Francis Marion* (New York: Henry G. Langley, 1845), 152.

15. Ibid.

16. Ibid.

17. Pancake, *This Destructive War*, 207.

18. Andrew Waters, "Sumter's Rounds," *Journal of the American Revolution*, https://allthingsliberty.com/2018/05/sumters-rounds-the-ill-fated-campaign-of-thomas-sumter-february-march-1781/. See also my chapter on Sumter's Rounds in *The Quaker and the Gamecock*.

19. Davie, *Revolutionary War Sketches*, 44–45.

20. Waters, *Quaker and the Gamecock*, 52.

21. Gregorie, *Thomas Sumter*, 282.

22. Bass, *Gamecock*, 235.

BIBLIOGRAPHY

Primary and Contemporary Sources

Adair, John. "Pension application of John Adair," transcribed and annotated by Will Graves. Southern Campaigns American Revolution Pension Statements & Rosters. Revised January 2006, 2009, and August 12, 2014. http://revwarapps.org/w2895.pdf.

Balch, Thomas, ed. *Papers Relating Chiefly to the Maryland Line During the Revolution*. Philadelphia: T.K. & P.G. Collins, 1857.

Chesney, Alexander. *The Journal of Alexander Chesney*, edited by E. Alfred Jones. Columbus, OH: University of Columbus, 1905.

Clark, Walter, ed. *The State Records of North Carolina*, Walter Clark, Vol. 14. Winston, NC: M. L. and J. C. Stewart, 1896.

Clinton, Henry. *The American Rebellion: Sir Henry Clinton's Narrative of His Campaigns, 1775–1782*, ed. William B. Willcox. New Haven, CT: Yale University Press edition, 1954.

Collins, James. *Autobiography of a Revolutionary Soldier*, ed. John W. Roberts. Clinton, LA: Feliciana Democrat Printing, 1859.

Cornwallis, Charles. *Correspondence of Charles, First Marquis Cornwallis*, ed. Charles Ross. London: John Murray, 1859. In three volumes, although only Volume One pertains to the American Revolution.

———. *The Cornwallis Papers: The Campaigns of 1780 and 1781 in the Southern Theatre of the American Revolutionary War*, ed. Ian Saberton. East Sussex, England: The Naval and Military Press Ltd., 2010. In six volumes.

Davie, William R. *The Revolutionary War Sketches of William R. Davie*. Raleigh: N.C. Department of Cultural Resources, 1976.

Ewald, Johann. *Diary of the American War: A Hessian Journal*, ed. Joseph Tustin. New Haven, CT: Yale University Press, 1979.

Fanning, David. *The Narrative of Colonel David Fanning.* New York: Joseph Sabin, 1865.

Ferguson, Patrick. "An Officer Out of His Time: Major Patrick Ferguson, 1779–1780," ed. Hugh F. Rankin. Appearing in *Sources of American Independence*, ed. Howard H. Peckham. Chicago, IL: University of Chicago Press, 1978.

Garden, Alexander, ed. *Anecdotes of the American Revolution, Illustrative of the Talents and Virtues of the Heroes and Patriots Who Acted the Most Conspicuous Parts Therein.* Charleston, SC: A.E. Miller, 1828.

Gibbes, Robert W., ed. *Documentary History of the American Revolution.* New York: D. Appleton & Co., 1857.

Graham, James. *The Life of General Daniel Morgan of the Virginia Line of the Army of the United States.* New York: Derby & Jackson, 1859.

Graham, Joseph. *General Joseph Graham and His Papers on North Carolina Revolutionary History*, ed. William A. Graham. Raleigh, NC: Edwards & Broughton, 1904.

Gray, Robert. "Robert Gray's Observations on the War in Carolina." *South Carolina Historical and Genealogical Magazine*, Vol. 11, No. 3 (June 1910).

Greene, Nathanael. *The Papers of Nathanael Greene*, eds. Richard K. Showman, Margaret Cobb, and Robert E. McCarthy. Chapel Hill: University of North Carolina Press for Rhode Island Historical Society, 1976–2005.

Hammond, Samuel. "Notes on the Battle of Camden," in *Traditions and Reminiscences, Chiefly of the American Revolution in the South*, ed. Joseph Johnson. Charleston, SC: Walker & James, 1851.

Hanger, George. *The Life, Adventures, and Opinions of Col. George Hanger, Written by Himself*, Vol. II. London: J. Debrett, 1801.

Hill, William. *Col. William Hill's Memoir of the Revolution*, ed. A. S. Salley. Columbia: The Historical Commission of South Carolina, 1921.

Horry, Peter, and M. L. Weems. *The Life of General Francis Marion.* Winston-Salem, NC: John F. Blair, Publisher edition, 2000.

James, William Dobein. *A Sketch of the Life of Brigadier General Francis Marion and a History of the Brigade.* Marietta, GA: Continental Book Company, 1948.

Johnson, Uzal. *Captured at King's Mountain: The Journal of Uzal Johnson, a Loyalist Surgeon*, eds. Wade S. Kolb III and Robert M. Weir. Columbia: University of South Carolina Press, 2011.

Ketchum, Richard M., ed. "New War Letters of Banastre Tarleton." *New York Historical Society Quarterly Report*, Vol. 51, No. 1, 69–70.

Kirkwood, Robert. *The Journal and Order Book of Captain Robert Kirkwood of the Delaware Regiment of the Continental Line in Two Parts*, ed. Joseph Brown Turner. Wilmington: The Historical Society of Delaware.

Lawson, John. *A New Voyage to Carolina*, ed. Hugh Talmage Lefler. Chapel Hill: University of North Carolina Press edition, 1967.

Lee, Henry. *The Revolutionary War Memoirs of General Henry Lee*, ed. Robert E. Lee with introduction by Charles Royster. New York: Da Capo Press edition, 1998; originally published in 1812.

MacKenzie, Roderick. *Strictures on Lt. Col. Tarleton's History of "Campaigns of 1780 and 1781, In the Southern Provinces of North America" in a Series of Letters to a Friend*. London, 1787.

Marion, Francis. "Orderly Book." In *Unwaried Patience & Fortitude: Francis Marion's Orderly Book*, ed. Patrick O'Kelly. West Conshohocken, PA: Infinity Publishing Co., 2006.

McJunkin, Joseph. "Memoirs of Major Joseph McJunkin, Revolutionary Patriot," ed. Rev. James Hodge Saye. Originally printed in the *Watchman and Observer*. Richmond, VA: 1848. Transcribed online by Phil Norfleet at http://sc_tories.tripod.com/thomas_sumter_assumes_command.htm.

———. "Pension Application of Joseph McJunkin," transcribed and annotated by Will Graves. Southern Campaigns American Revolution Pension Statements & Rosters. http://revwarapps.org/s18118.pdf.

Moultrie, William. *Memoirs of the American Revolution: So Far as It Relates to the States of North and South Carolina, and Georgia*, in 2 volumes. New York: David Longworth, 1802.

Piecuch, Jim, ed. *The Battle of Camden: A Documentary History*. Charleston, SC: The History Press, 2006.

———. *The Blood Be Upon Your Head: Tarleton and the Myth of Buford's Massacre*. Lugoff, SC: Southern Campaigns of the American Revolution Press, 2010.

Pinckney, Thomas. "Thomas Pinckney and the Last Campaign of Horatio Gates," ed. Robert Scott Davis Jr. *The South Carolina Historical Magazine*, Vol. 86, No. 2 (April 1985).

Power, J. Tracy. "The Virtue of Humanity was Totally Forgot: Buford's Massacre, May 29, 1780." *The South Carolina Historical Magazine*, Vol. 93, No. 1 (January 1992).

Ramsay, David. *History of the Revolution of South Carolina*. Trenton, NJ: Isaac Collins, 1785.

Read, William. "Reminiscences of Dr. William Read, Arranged from His Notes and Papers." In *Documentary History of the American Revolution, 1776–1782*, ed. R. W. Gibbes, 248–93. New York: D. Appleton & Co., 1857.

Rutledge, John. "Gov. John Rutledge to the Delegates of South Carolina in Congress, September 20, 1780," ed. John W. Barnwell. *The South Carolina Historical and Genealogical Magazine*, Vol. 17, No. 4.

Seymour, William. *A Journal of the Southern Expedition, 1780-1783*. Wilmington: The Historical Society of Delaware, 1896.

Simcoe, John Graves. *Simcoe's Military Journal: A History of the Operations of a Partisan Corps Called the Queen's Rangers*. New York: Bartlett & Welford, 1844.

Stedman, Charles. *The History of the Origin, Progress, and Termination of the American War*, in two volumes. London: published for the author, 1794.

Stuart, Charles. *A Prime Minister and His Son: From the Correspondence of the 3rd Earl of Bute and of Lt. General the Hon. Sir Charles Suart*. London: J. Murray, 1925.

Tarleton, Banastre. *A History of the Campaigns of 1780 and 1781, in the Southern Provinces of North America*. London: 1787.

Turner, Rev. Joseph Brown, ed. *Papers of the Historical Society of Delaware. LVI. The Journal and Order Book of Captain Robert Kirkwood of the Delaware Regiment of the Continental Line*. Wilmington: The Historical Society of Delaware, 1910.

Uhlendorf, Bernard, ed. *The Siege of Charleston with an Account of the Province of South Carolina: Diaries and Letters of Hessian Officers from the von Jungkenn Papers in the William L. Clements Library*, Vol. 12. Ann Arbor: University of Michigan Press, 1938.

Watson, Elkanah. *Men and the Times of the Revolution: or, Memoirs of Elkanah Watson, Including His Journals of Travel in Europe and America from the Year 1772 to 1842*, ed. Winslow C. Watson. New York: Dana and Company, 1857, 2nd edition. The reminiscences of Gates's commissariat officer, Colonel Thomas Polk, are found here.

Williams, Otho Holland. "A Narrative of the Campaign of 1780." In Appendix B of *Sketches of the Life and Correspondence of Nathanael Greene* by William Johnson. Charleston, SC: A.E. Miller, 1822.

Winn, Richard, "General Richard Winn's Notes: 1780," ed. Samuel C. Williams. *The South Carolina Historical Review*, Vol. 43, No. 4 (1942).

———. "General Richard Winn's Notes: 1780 (Continued)," ed. Samuel C. Williams. *The South Carolina Historical Review*, Vol. 44, No. 1 (January 1943).

Young, Thomas. "Memoir of Major Thomas Young," *Orion Magazine*, November 1843. http://www.carolinamilitia.com/memoir-of-major-thomas-young/.

Secondary Sources

Adams, Rhett A. "Waxhaws (Region)." South Carolina Encyclopedia, http://www.scencyclopedia.org/sce/entries/waxhaws-region/.

Anderson, William Lee. "Camp New Providence: Large Encampment of Southern Continental Army and militia on Providence Road at Six Mile Creek, October-December 1780" (2008–2011). http://elehistory.com/amrev/CampNewProvidence.pdf.

Babits, Lawrence E., and Joshua B. Howard. "Continentals in Tarleton's British Legion: May 1780 to October 1781." In *Cavalry of the American Revolution*, edited by Jim Piecuch, 182–202. Yardley, PA: Westholme Publishing, 2012.

Bass, Robert D. *Gamecock: The Life and Campaigns of General Thomas Sumter.* Orangeburg, SC: Sandlapper Publishing Co., 1961.

———. *The Green Dragoon: The Lives of Banastre Tarleton and Mary Robinson.* Orangeburg, SC: Sandlapper Publishing Company, 1973.

———. *Ninety Six: The Struggle for the South Carolina Back Country.* Orangeburg, SC: Sandlapper Publishing, 1978.

———. *Swamp Fox: The Life and Campaigns of General Francis Marion.* Orangeburg, SC: Sandlapper Publishing Co., 1974.

Bayly, C. A., and Katherine Prior. "Cornwallis, Charles, first Marquess Cornwallis," article first published September 23, 2004, revised September 22, 2011. Oxford Dictionary of National Biography (online edition).

Beakes, John. *Otho Holland Williams in the American Revolution.* Mount Pleasant, SC: The Nautical and Aviation Publishing Company, 2015.

Bew, John. "The Case for Cornwallis." *National Interest*, Nov/Dec 2014, Issue 134.

Billias, George A. "Horatio Gates: Professional Soldier." In *George Washington's General and Opponents*, edited by George A. Billias, 79–108X. New York: Da Capo Press edition, 1994.

Boatner, Mark M., III. *Encyclopedia of the American Revolution.* Mechanicsburg, PA: Stackpole Books edition, 1994. (Originally published in 1966 by David McKay Company.)

Boddi, William W. *History of Williamsburg: Something About the People of Williamsburg County, South Carolina, from the First Settlement by Europeans about 1705 until 1923.* Columbia, SC: The State Company, 1923.

Borick, C. P. *A Gallant Defense: The Siege of Charleston, 1780.* Columbia: University of South Carolina Press, 2003.

Broadwater, Jeff. "William Richardson Davie." North Carolina History Project, 2016. https://northcarolinahistory.org/encyclopedia/william-richardson-davie-1756-1820/.

Buchanan, John. *The Road to Guilford Courthouse: The American Revolution in the Carolinas.* New York: John Wiley & Sons, 1997.

Clark, Murtie June. *Loyalists in the Southern Campaign of the Revolutionary War.* Baltimore, MD: Genealogical Publishing Co., Inc., 1981.

Conway, Stephen. "To Subdue America: British Army Officers and the Conduct of the Revolutionary War." *The William and Mary Quarterly,* 43(3), July 1986.

Curtis, Edward E. *The British Army in the American Revolution.* New Haven, CT: Yale University Press, 1926.

Draper, Lyman. *King's Mountain and Its Heroes: History of the Battle of King's Mountain.* Cincinnati, OH: Peter O. Thomson, 1881.

Edgar, Walter. *Partisans & Redcoats: The Southern Conflict That Turned the Tide of the American Revolution.* New York: William Morrow, 2001.

———. *South Carolina: A History.* Columbia: University of South Carolina Press, 1998.

Ellet, Elizabeth E. *The Women of the American Revolution.* New York: Charles Scribner, 1853-1854.

Ferling, John. *Almost a Miracle: The American Victory in the War of Independence.* New York: Oxford University Press, 2007.

Fiske, John. *The American Revolution,* 2 vols. Boston: Houghton Mifflin, 1902.

Fortescue, J. W. *A History of the British Army,* Vol. 3. Edinburgh, Scotland: R & R Clark, no date.

Ganyard, Robert L. "Threat from the West: North Carolina and the Cherokee, 1776–1778." *The North Carolina Historical Review,* 45:1, January 1968.

Gilbert, Oscar E. and Catherine R. *True for the Cause of Liberty: The Second Spartan Regiment in the American Revolution.* Philadelphia, PA: Casemate Publishers, 2015.

Gilchrist, M. M. *Patrick Ferguson: A Man of Some Genius.* Edinburgh, Scotland: NMS Publishing, 2003.

Gordon, John W. *South Carolina and the American Revolution: A Battlefield History.* Columbia: University of South Carolina Press, 2003.

Graham, James. *The Life of General Daniel Morgan: Of the Virginia Line of the Army of the United States, With Portions of His Correspondence.* New York: Derby & Jackson, 1859.

Graves, William T. *Backcountry Revolutionary: James Williams (1740–1780) with Source Documents.* Lugoff, SC: Southern Campaigns of the American Revolution Press, 2012.

Gregg, Alexander. *History of the Old Cheraws.* New York: Richardson & Company, 1867.

Gregorie, Anne King. *Thomas Sumter.* Columbia, SC: R.L. Bryan Company, 1931.

Harris, C. Leon. "American Soldiers at the Battle of Waxhaws, SC, 29 May 1780." Southern Campaigns American Revolution Pension Statements and Rosters, last modified August 11, 2021, http://revwarapps.org/b221.pdf.

———. "Massacre at Waxhaws: The Evidence From Wounds." *Southern Campaigns of the American Revolution*, Vol. 11, Number 2.1 (June 2016), http://www.southerncampaign.org/wordpress/wp-content/uploads/2016/05/Harris-Massacre-at-Waxhaws.pdf. Accessed on July 16, 2020.

Hatcher, Richard W. "Moultrie Flag." South Carolina Encyclopedia, http://www.scencyclopedia.org/sce/entries/moultrie-flag/.

Heider, Karl G. "The Gamecock, the Swamp Fox, and the Wizard Owl: The Development of Good Form in an American Totemic Set." *The Journal of American Folklore*, 93:67 (Jan.–Mar. 1980).

Herman, Arthur. *How the Scots Invented the Modern World: The True Story of How Western Europe's Poorest Nation Created Our World and Everything in It.* New York: Crown Publishers, 2001.

Heseltine, William B. "Lyman Draper and the South." *The Journal of Southern History*, Vol. 19, No. 1 (February 1953).

Higginbotham, Don. *The War of the American Independence: Military Attitudes, Policies, and Practice, 1763-1789.* Bloomington: Indiana University Press paperback edition, 1978.

Hoock, Holger. *Scars of Independence: America's Violent Birth.* New York: Crown, 2017.

Hutchins, John Milton. "Cavalry Action at Poundridge, New York: Bloody Ban's Early Education." In *Cavalry of the American Revolution*, edited by Jim Piecuch, 56–75. Yardley, PA: Westholme Publishing, 2012.

Irving, Washington. *Wolfert's Roost and Other Papers, Now First Collected.* New York: G.P. Putnam & Co., 1855.

Johnson, Joseph. *Traditions and Reminiscences Chiefly of the American Revolution in the South: Including Biographical Sketches, Incidents and Anecdotes.* Charleston, SC: Walker & James, 1851.

Johnson, William. *Sketches of the Life and Correspondence of Nathanael Greene*, 2 vols. Charleston, SC: A.E. Miller, 1822.

Katcher, Philip R.N. *Encyclopedia of British, Provincial, and German Army Units, 1775–1783.* Harrisburg, PA: Stackpole Books, 1973.

Ketchum, Richard M. *The Winter Soldiers.* New York: Doubleday, 1973.

Knight, John. *War at Saber Point: Banastre Tarleton and the British Legion.* Yardley, PA: Westholme Publishing, 2020.

Lambert, Robert Stansbury. *South Carolina Loyalists in the American Revolution.* Columbia: University of South Carolina Press, 1987.

Larson, Jennifer L. "William R. Davie: UNC's Founding Father." Documenting the American South (no date). https://docsouth.unc.edu/highlights/davie.html.

Lengel, Edward G. *The Battles of Connecticut Farms and Springfield 1780.* Yardley, PA: Westholme Publishing, 2020.

Lossing, Benson J. *The Pictorial Field-Book of The Revolution,* 2 volumes. New York: Harper & Brothers, Publishers, 1860.

Marshall, John. *The Life of George Washington, Special Edition for Schools,* Vol. 3, eds. Robert Faulkner and Paul Carrese. Indianapolis, IN: Liberty Fund, 2000. https://oll.libertyfund.org/titles/marshall-the-life-of-george-washington.

McCall, Hugh. *The History of Georgia,* 2 volumes. Atlanta, GA: A.B. Caldwell, reprint edition, 1909.

McCrady, Edward. *The History of South Carolina in the Revolution, 1775–1780.* New York: The Macmillan Company, 1901.

———. *The History of South Carolina in the Revolution: 1780–1783.* New York: The Macmillan and Company, 1902.

Middlekauff, Robert. *The Glorious Cause: The American Revolution, 1763–1789.* New York: Oxford University Press, 1982.

Mintz, Max M. *The Generals of Saratoga: John Burgoyne & Horatio Gates.* New Haven, CT: Yale University Press, 1990.

Moore, Peter. "The Local Origins of Allegiance in Revolutionary South Carolina." *South Carolina Historical Magazine,* 107(1).

Nelson, Paul David. *General Horatio Gates: A Biography.* Baton Rouge: Louisiana State University Press, 1976.

O'Kelley, Patrick. *Nothing But Blood and Slaughter: The Revolutionary War in the Carolinas.* Blue House Tavern Press, 2004. In four volumes, one for each year beginning in 1779–1782.

O'Neall, John Belton. *Colonial and Revolutionary History of Upper South Carolina.* Greenville, SC: Shannon & Co., 1897.

O'Quinn, Daniel. "Sir Joshua Reynolds, Decolonization, and the Pictorial Dialectics of Crisis." *SEL Studies in English Literature 1500–1900,* Vol. 58, No. 3 (2018).

Oller, John. *The Swamp Fox: How Francis Marion Saved the American Revolution.* New York: Hachette Books, 2020.

Pancake, John S. *This Destructive War: The British Campaign in the Carolinas, 1780–1782.* Tuscaloosa: University of Alabama Press, 2003 (originally published 1985).

Parker, John C. *Parker's Guide to the Revolutionary War in South Carolina.* West Conshohocken, PA: Infinity Publishing, 2015.

Piecuch, James. "Massacre or Myth? Banastre Tarleton at the Waxhaws, May 29, 1780." *The Southern Campaigns of the American Revolution*, ed. Charles B. Baxley, Vol. 1, No. 2 (October 2004), accessed May 25, 2020, http://southerncampaign.org/newsletter/v1n2.pdf.

Peicuch, Jim, and Gregory D. Massey, eds. *General Nathanael Greene and the American Revolution in the South.* Columbia: University of South Carolina Press, 2012. A fine collection of essays about the life, legacy, and influence of Nathanael Greene.

Powell, William S., and Michael Hill. *The North Carolina Gazetteer: A Dictionary of Tar Heel Places and Their History*, 2nd Edition. Chapel Hill: University of North Carolina Press, 2010.

Power, J. Tracy. "The Virtue of Humanity was Totally Forgot: Buford's Massacre, May 29, 1780." *The South Carolina Historical Magazine*, Vol. 93, No. 1 (Jan. 1992).

Purvis, Randy A. "Major James Wemyss: Second Most Hated British Officer in the South." *Journal of American Revolution*, https://allthingsliberty.com/2018/11/major-james-wemyss-second-most-hated-british-officer-in-the-south/.

Ramsey, Emily. "A Brief Historical Sketch of Tuckaseegee Ford." Mecklenburg County Landmarks Commission Report (n.d.). http://landmarkscommission.org/wp-content/uploads/2017/07/Tuckaseegee-Ford-Trail.pdf.

Rankin, Hugh F. "Charles Lord Cornwallis: Study in Frustration," in *George Washington's Generals and Opponents*, edited by George Athan Billias, 193–232. New York: Da Capo Press edition, 1994.

———. *Francis Marion: The Swamp Fox.* New York: Thomas Y. Crowell Company, 1973.

Robertson, Henry A. Jr. "Harrington, William Henry" (1988). NCPedia, https://www.ncpedia.org/biography/harrington-henry-william.

Robinson, Blackwell P. "Davie, William Richardson" (1986). NCPedia Website, https://www.ncpedia.org/biography/davie-william-richardson.

———. *William R. Davie.* Chapel Hill: University of North Carolina Press, 1957.

Rouse, Parke Jr. *The Great Wagon Road: How Scotch-Irish and Germanics Settled the Uplands.* Richmond, VA: The Dietz Press, 1995.

Royster, Charles. *A Revolutionary People at War: The Continental Army & American Character, 1775–1783.* Chapel Hill: University of North Carolina Press, 1979.

Scheer, George F., and Hugh Rankin. *Rebels & Redcoats: The American Revolution Through the Eyes of Those Who Fought and Lived It.* New York: Da Capo Press, 1957.

Schenck, David. *North Carolina, 1780–'81: Being a History of the Invasion of the Carolinas by the British Army Under Lord Cornwallis in 1780–'81.* Raleigh, NC: Edwards & Broughton, Publishers, 1889.

Scoggins, Michael C. *The Day It Rained Militia: Huck's Defeat and the Revolution in the South Carolina Backcountry May-July 1780.* Charleston, SC: The History Press, 2005.

Scotti, Anthony J. *Brutal Virtue: The Myth and Reality of Banastre Tarleton.* Bowie, MD: Heritage Books, 2002.

Shy, John. "British Strategy for Pacifying the Southern Colonies, 1778–1781." In *The Southern Experience in the American Revolution*, edited by Jeffrey J. Crow and Larry E. Tise, 155–73. Chapel Hill: University of North Carolina Press, 1978.

———. "Charles Lee: The Soldier as Radical." In *George Washington's Generals and Opponents: Their Exploits and Leadership*, edited by George Athan Billias, 22–53. New York: Da Capo Press edition, 1994.

Smith, Steven D. "Imagining the Swamp Fox: William Gilmore Simms and the National Memory of Francis Marion." In *William Gilmore Simms's Unfinished Civil War: Consequences for a Southern Man of Letters*, edited by David Moltke-Hansen. Columbia: University of South Carolina Press, 2013.

Starkey, Armstrong. "Paoli to Stony Point: Military Ethics and Weaponry During the American Revolution." *The Journal of American History*, Vol. 58, No. 1 (January 1994).

———. *War in the Age of Enlightenment, 1700–1789.* Westport, CT: Praeger Publishing, 2003.

Stevens, Benjamin Franklin, ed. *The Campaign in Virginia, Part One.* London: 1887.

Talbert, Roy Jr. "Horry, Peter." South Carolina Encyclopedia, http://www.scencyclopedia.org/sce/entries/horry-peter/.

Ward, Christopher. *The War of the Revolution.* New York: Skyhorse Publishing edition, 2011.

Waters, Andrew. "Sumter's Rounds." *Journal of the American Revolution*, https://allthingsliberty.com/2018/05/sumters-rounds-the-ill-fated-campaign-of-thomas-sumter-february-march-1781/.

———. *To the End of the World: Nathanael Greene, Charles Cornwallis, and the Race to the Dan.* Yardley, PA: Westholme Publishing, 2020.

———. *The Quaker and the Gamecock: Nathanael Greene, Thomas Sumter, and the Revolutionary War for the Soul of the South.* Philadelphia, PA: Casemate Publishers, 2019.

Weir, Robert M. "Campbell, Lord William." South Carolina Encyclopedia, https://www.scencyclopedia.org/sce/entries/campbell-lord-william/.

Wickwire, Franklin and Mary. *Cornwallis and the War of Independence.* London: Faber and Faber, 1971.

———. *Cornwallis: The American Adventure.* Boston: Houghton Mifflin Company, 1970.

Willcox, William B. *Portrait of a General: Sir Henry Clinton in the War of Independence.* New York: Alfred A. Knopf, 1964.

———. "Sir Henry Clinton: Paralysis of Command." In *George Washington's Generals and Opponents: Their Exploits and Leadership*, edited by George Athan Billias, 73–102.. New York: Da Capo Press edition, 1994.

Wilson, David K. *The Southern Strategy: Britain's Conquest of South Carolina and Georgia, 1775–1780.* Columbia: University of South Carolina Press, 2005.

WEBSITES, MAPS, ETC.

American Battlefield Trust. "Battle of Waxhaws, SC, May 29, 1780" map. https://www.battlefields.org/learn/maps/battle-waxhaws, accessed on June 3, 2020.

Cook, James. "A map of the province of South Carolina with all the rivers, bays, inlets, islands, inland navigation, soundings, time of high water on the sea coast, roads, marshes, ferrys, bridges, swamps, parishes, churches, towns, townships, county, parish, district, and provincial lines," 1773. Library of Congress website, https://www.loc.gov/item/74692124/.

Documenting the American South web page, University Library, University of North Carolina at Chapel Hill, https://docsouth.unc.edu.

South Carolina Department of Archives and History. "National Register Properties in South Carolina: Colonel John Stuart House, Charleston County (104-106 Tradd Street)." http://www.nationalregister.sc.gov/charleston/S10817710027/index.htm.

ACKNOWLEDGMENTS

FIRST AND FOREMOST, I would like to thank the many hundreds of people who have come out to hear my author talks and presentations over the years, along with the programming personnel who have invited me to present at these events. Especially I would like to thank the National Park Service staff at the Cowpens National Battlefield, who have embraced my books and given me so many opportunities to promote them over the years. Truly, interacting with audiences at these events has been the highlight of my career as an author of American Revolution histories. Their passion for this history inspires my own.

I could not be prouder to have this book published by Westholme Publishing, who I consider to be the United States' premiere publisher of American Revolution history (and other histories as well). Thank you, Bruce Franklin, for your support of my writing and for your commitment to such beautifully published books. Thanks also to my copyeditor on this project, Christine Florie, for your careful attention and thoughtful recommendations. And a very special thank you to my "mapmaker," Tracy Dungan, who patiently cultivated our vision for the maps in this book and played such an important role in telling the story of the Backcountry War.

My wife, Anne Waters, is my rock and inspiration. If a mutual love for books was part of our initial attraction, her enduring support of my writing has sustained me over the years. And I do not know a more astute student of history than our son, Eli Waters. As he has grown into a talented and intelligent young man, his insightful observations on the American Revolution increasingly inspire my own, a trend that I hope will continue in the years to come.

Speaking of inspirations, my father, Charles Waters, passed away over the course of writing this book. A history major at Duke University, Dad influenced me deeply in so many ways, but certainly his love of history was a major influence on my own. Thank you, Dad, for everything. A consolation for his loss is the fact that I got to spend time with him regularly over the last decade of his life.

And thanks to you, for reading (and hopefully buying) this book. I have a theory that, to remain relevant, history needs to be rewritten every twenty to twenty-five years. But that theory is contingent on their being an audience to read it. That makes you a mutual participant in this effort to keep the history of the American Revolution vibrant and alive. Keep reading! We can't do it without you.

INDEX